WARRIOR SOUL

THE MEMOIR OF A NAVY SEAL

CHUCK PFARRER

PRESIDIO PRESS

BALLANTINE BOOKS • NEW YORK

A Presidio Press Book
Published by The Random House Publishing Group
Copyright © 2004 by Chuck Pfarrer

Published in the United States by Presidio Press, an imprint of The Random House Publishing Group, a division of Random House, Inc., New York, and simultaneously in Canada by Random House of Canada Limited, Toronto.

Originally published in hardcover by Random House in 2004.

Presidio Press and colophon are trademarks of Random House, Inc.

www.presidiopress.com

ISBN 0-89141-863-6

Manufactured in the United States of America

First Edition: January 2004
First Mass Market Edition: January 2005

OPM 9 8 7 6 5 4

Praise for
Warrior Soul

"Chuck Pfarrer has been to hell and back as a soldier, and he writes about it like an angel on fire. *Warrior Soul* is beautifully written, crisp, spare, lushly honest, and poignant beyond belief. If you wonder about the men who roam the world's shadows, hunting those who hunt us, Pfarrer's story is yours, first-rate reading, hard to put down. His flair as a storyteller is matched only by the wildness of his tale."

—DOUG STANTON,
New York Times bestselling author of
In Harm's Way

"Chuck Pfarrer's *Warrior Soul* reads like a thriller. He describes training, deployments on the run, puts you on the ground in Beirut for the bombing of the marine barracks, and makes you grateful that these warrior souls are protecting us. Pfarrer shows what they pay for doing it."

—ROBERT MASON, author of *Chickenhawk*

"You get caught up in his riveting transformation from 'pooka-shell-wearing surf dude' to Navy SEAL commando."

—*Entertainment Weekly*

"*Warrior Soul* is a convincing portrait of the SEAL's dedication to duty and gives an insight into what it takes to be among the best of the best. Contemporary readers will get a hint of what the U.S. peacekeepers in Iraq are most likely confronting."

—*USA Today*

For my wife,
who is teaching me how to love,
and for Paddy,
who is teaching me how to live

People sleep peaceably in their beds at night only because rough men stand ready to do violence on their behalf.

—GEORGE ORWELL

AUTHOR'S NOTE

AS A NAVY SEAL, I was trained to notice little things: a blade of grass bent by the side of a trail, the small shadow cast by a trip wire. I was taught to plan methodically, to attack where I was not expected, and to vanish when the enemy attempted to strike back. These skills kept me alive through seven months of combat on the streets of Beirut, and during more than two hundred classified operations in every climate and ocean around the world.

The "SEAL" in SEAL Team stands for the elements in which we are trained to operate: sea, air, and land. Naval special warfare is the smallest and most elite special operations force in the United States military. Although the exact number of SEALs operational at any one time is classified, I can say that our organization is considerably smaller than Hells Angels.

Team members refer to themselves not as SEALs but as Frogs, Team guys, or shooters. Within this society, a man's reputation is earned solely by his standing as an operator. A SEAL is judged not only by the missions he has undertaken but by the manner in which he conducts himself, his courage, operational skill, physical ability, and character.

Since the first navy frogmen crawled onto the beaches of Normandy, no SEAL has ever surrendered. No SEAL has ever been captured, and not one teammate or body has ever been left in the field. This legacy of valor is unmatched in modern warfare. In Korea, Vietnam, Lebanon, Grenada, Somalia, Panama, Iraq, and Afghanistan, SEALs appeared where no enemy thought possible and struck with a ferocity far out of proportion to their number.

My proper share of this glory is a small one. Because of a few twists of fate, some luck—good and bad—and the courage and honor of my teammates, I am on hand to tell this story.

The exceptional among our number we count as heroes. My service, though varied and geographically diverse, was workmanlike. I was in combat. More than some, and less than others. I served as a military adviser in Central America. I conducted reconnaissance and denied area operations in places the United States and Americans were not thought to be. I served as an assault element commander in a top-secret "black" counterterrorism outfit. I was in the game, and I was an operator.

It is the failing of a first-person narrative that the spotlight will fall disproportionately on the writer. This is unfair both to the whole story and to my teammates. Sometimes I was a leader, and sometimes I was led; my point of view was never impartial, and many times it did not extend beyond my own small operational circle. What you will read is what I remember, what I saw, and what I felt.

There are many operations that I am not presently at liberty to write about. I will leave those stories for another time, or for some other SEAL to describe. I have omitted the specific details of some operations, leaving out tricks and techniques that would contribute to the tactical education of our enemies. Likewise, I have obscured the location of some of the adventures I describe, as it might be necessary for some other SEAL, on some future moonless night, to revisit the scene of the crime.

Since the time of my service, a few of the men who worked with me have become public figures: I have made use of their real names. I have kept the secrecy of others, and in all cases I have changed the names of my operational teammates. I have tried to draw the characters as accurately as possible, flattering or not. To teammates who see themselves portrayed badly (not unflatteringly but *badly*), I apologize. And to friends who do not find themselves in these pages, again I ask forgiveness. They will know that in writing this book some accommodations were made, not only with certain facts, but with dates and participants. The operators I left in shadow have my complete respect and profound gratitude.

I have also changed the names of the women in my story. That might be just as well; I cannot say that I have always been fondly remembered, and what I am able to write would not paint an adequate picture of their beauty, kindness, or patience. I have tried to be honest about my faults, which are many. It is not my intention to drag up old hurts or to surprise with unknown offenses. I did not always love well, and that was the greatest failing of all.

You know you've made it in the SEAL community when you attend a reunion and someone comes up, shakes your hand, and says, "I thought you were dead." It's time to retire when you answer, "I thought I was too."

I left when I felt I had used up all of my luck. I flatter myself to think that I got out before I had lost my courage. If you stay in the Teams long enough, complacency, accident, or the enemy will eventually take you. I've seen it happen to operators braver and more accomplished than I am; sooner or later, it would have happened to me.

SEALs are not often mentioned in dispatches, nor are their operations frequently revealed in the press. It is more common that our missions, highly classified, are not disclosed for years. Even within the community, there are operations only whispered about. The actors in them are sworn to secrecy by duty, honor, and an oath.

In the SEALs, the reward is simply knowing that the job was done. The prize is the quiet pride felt for an operation that remains unknown to the American public and continues to be a distressing nightmare to the enemy.

If operators who were there read this book and then say, "That's the way it was"—that is enough.

CONTENTS

BOOK ONE

JOINING
THE
CIRCUS

GOODBYE TO ALL THAT

IT WAS A FRIDAY NIGHT, and Gate 14 at Norfolk International was not crowded. American Airlines Flight 405 was a scheduled hop from Norfolk, Virginia, to Miami, with continuing service to San Juan, Puerto Rico. The maybe two dozen people in the departure lounge were hardly sufficient to fill even a third of the seats of the 727 now completing fueling at the end of the Jetway. The bulk of American 405's passengers were said to be boarding in Miami for a weekend junket to the casinos and nightlife of San Juan.

When my row was called, I lifted my carry-on, showed my boarding pass, and walked down the Jetway. Through the windows, I could see thunderclouds pressing low on the horizon. It was 8:25 P.M., only ten minutes before our scheduled departure, and the last red light of day was showing in the west. As the flight attendants closed the doors and made ready for departure, I found my seat and managed to push my duffel into the overhead rack. I had definitely exceeded the recommended dimensions for carry-on luggage. Concealed in my bag was an MT-1-X military parachute.

I wasn't going to Miami.

Like a dozen of my fellow passengers, I was going to jump from the airplane.

A closer look at the people in the departure lounge might have been instructive. Most of the passengers were under thirty-five, and the men all hard-eyed and fit. Some might have noticed that the passengers had a predilection for Rolex watches and expensive running shoes. Beyond that, they hardly seemed remarkable. The passengers were no mixed bag of civilians; they included a twelve-man Navy SEAL assault team. The balance of the people on American 405 included members of the Defense Intelligence Agency, air force combat controllers, navy parachute riggers, and a handful of officers from the Special Operations Command, based in Tampa, Florida. All were in civilian clothes; all exhibited what the military calls "relaxed grooming standards." In short, they blended in.

I was as unassuming as my fellow passengers. My reddish hair was collar-length, and my face was swathed by a luxuriant Wyatt Earp mustache, something I'd grown to add some authority to my perennially freckled face. My father used to tell me that I looked like a shaggy tennis pro, or some kind of overmuscled yachtsman. I certainly didn't look like what I was—an active-duty lieutenant in the United States Navy. Not just any lieutenant. As far as I was concerned, next to being a space-shuttle pilot, I had the best job in God's navy. I was an assault element commander at the navy's premier counterterrorist unit, SEAL Team Six. The other men hefting duffel bags were my shooters, my "boat crew," as the parlance went. I was in charge of tonight's festivities, a low-profile exfiltration and insertion exercise.

Two hours before flight time, we packed gear and weapons in the SEAL Team Six compound and individually proceeded to the airport. We checked unmarked suitcases containing our weapons and assault gear, and were issued tickets on a flight that was never intended to reach its scheduled destination. With the complicity of the airline, we were conducting a practice run for a covert mission.

There are a hundred ways that SEALs can insert into a target area. We can scuba dive from a submerged nuclear submarine. Boats can be dropped from airplanes in an event we call a "rubber duck." We can patrol across glacier, jungle, or desert. We can parachute or fast-rope from helicopters. Jumping out of commercial airliners is an operation, or op, we call a "D. B. Cooper." Using scheduled air traffic to insert into a hostile country, or a denied area, is a SEAL specialty.

Most people do not parachute on purpose from jet aircraft.

The planes are too fast, and the turbulent air dragging in their wake can snap your spine and pop your hips from your pelvis. We were trained to jump from commercial airliners because they are ubiquitous and nonattributable. It is one thing to prohibit American military aircraft from flying over your country. It is quite another to close down your airspace to all commercial traffic. Libya, Syria, Cuba, and a host of other thug nations allow commercial flights to fly through their airspace. This is all the opening a SEAL Team needs. Unknown and unseen, a SEAL element can parachute into any place on earth. One might insert: that is, provided one survives the jump. The trick is to exit in correct body position and deploy your parachute after the appropriate delay. There are two principal types of SEAL parachute operations: HALO, or high altitude, low opening; and HAHO, high altitude, high opening.

In a HALO drop, you exit the aircraft at 35,000 feet on oxygen and open your parachute low, at 2,000 feet, to avoid detection. A jumper falling at terminal velocity, roughly 120 miles an hour, would scream in for a full three minutes before opening his parachute.

In a HAHO drop, jumpers exit the aircraft above 35,000 feet, but their parachutes are deployed after a brief delay, maybe three seconds, opening high instead of low—sometimes literally in the jet stream. The team floats under canopy at 33,000 feet, then groups together and glides in formation toward the target.

At six and a half miles up, the MT-1-X parachute has a thirty-knot forward airspeed, and you can cover a lot of miles before you ever see any dirt. Depending on the winds aloft, a jumper can touch down twenty or thirty miles from where he exited the aircraft. It's a good way to drop into a place where you are neither expected nor welcome.

We had all done both types of parachute missions, hundreds of them, and tonight's jump was supposed to be routine. This was a practice mission. In fact, it would be my last operational act as a Navy SEAL. I settled into my row, nodding hello to a woman seated across the aisle. I had been introduced to her at a briefing earlier. She said she was a State Department employee: the usual handle, we both knew, for a CIA officer. Like the brass from the Special Operations Command, she was aboard to observe our jump.

The plane was pushed back from the ramp, and the flight attendants pantomimed their safety briefings. Not surprisingly, nobody paid attention. American 405 was directed onto the active runway and cleared for takeoff. On the flight deck, in addition to an American Airlines captain, was a Navy SEAL, one of our operators rated as captain and pilot in command of more than a dozen types of commercial aircraft, everything from puddle jumpers to 747s and wide-bodied DC-10s. The SEAL pilot would fly the mission's insert and jump legs.

American 405 started her roll. As the plane climbed into the night, the pilot was advised by Norfolk ground to contact departure control on frequency 234.32. Switching to this frequency, the pilot now used the call sign Assailant 26, that of a navy aircraft. American Flight 405 had ceased to exist.

The blip on the radar screens of departure control did not turn south for the Blue Hair State, but headed north and east over the Virginia capes. Using the navy call sign, the pilot requested and was granted a direct route to SEAL DZ, a block of restricted airspace twenty-five miles off Virginia Beach.

As I looked out the window, Assailant 26 banked over the Cape Henry light tower. The plane shook as we flew into thickening rain clouds. I unbuckled my seat belt, stood, and turned to my leading petty officer, Alex Remero, a short, muscular Costa Rican, a demolition expert and decorated veteran of Grenada.

"Time to get dressed," I said.

My assault element was composed of three Cuban-Americans, a Costa Rican, a dreadlocked Puerto Rican, and a couple of white surfer dudes like me. We were famous for blaring reggae music in the Team room, and other assault elements called us the Rastamen. It was a moniker we were proud of. The Rastas had served together for three years, in all parts of the globe, in all elements—earth, wind, ocean, and fire—and we were a band of brothers.

As Assailant 26 rotated over SEAL DZ, we pulled our parachutes from the overhead racks. A hatch was opened on the deck of the rear galley, and Phil Fenko dropped into the luggage compartment. Like Alex, Phil was not a large man, but he was powerfully built; he had what we called a high thrust-to-weight ratio. You can forget the movies—most SEALs are not large men. I am six-three and weigh 220 pounds, considered large and slow for a Team guy. Most SEALs are around five-ten and 160 pounds. Not body-builders but triathletes. As Phil handed our suitcases up through the galley hatch, the parachute riggers went to work. They hooked carabiners to the deck track securing the seats and laid cables, pulleys, and come-alongs down the aisle of the aircraft to assist in opening and closing the tail ramp when jump time came.

Military parachuting differs from civilian jumping in two ways. First, in military parachuting, an adoring girlfriend isn't waiting for you on the drop zone—the enemy is. Second, we haul cargo. If there is a piece of equipment you think you might want on the ground, you jump with it. Although tonight's op was a training mission, we were jumping with full combat loads: weapons, ammunition, body armor, and assault gear, sixty-five pounds per jumper. During a "full mission profile," or real-world operation, it would not be un-usual for a SEAL jumper to leave the airplane with 100 or even 150 pounds of gear. Satellite radios, night-vision equip-ment, antitank rockets, breaching demolitions, and diving gear are a few such pieces of "optional" equipment. Tonight we wore and carried only our shooting gear. This drop was considered a "Hollywood jump," the stuff of sissies.

We donned our baggy, light-gray jumpsuits. Over them we strapped on inflatable UDT life jackets, pistol belts, and low-draw holsters. This gear was considered our safety equip-ment. It included a .40-caliber Glock model 17 pistol, four magazines, a K-bar knife, a Mark-13 flare, and an infrared strobe light. Heckler & Koch MP-5 machine pistols were strapped to our thighs. This first line of gear would be our last line of defense—if it came down to life jackets, pistols, and smoke flares, we would be in a world of hurt.

The second line, our assault gear, was loaded into back-packs and cinched down tight. It consisted of Zainer water-proof body armor, a first-aid kit, a CamelBak water canteen, an encrypted radio, a Madonna-style headset, a ballistic hel-met, an assault vest, and sixteen magazines for our MP-5s. Even on this practice mission, each man carried 480 rounds of .40-caliber Teflon-coated hollowpoint ammunition. These rounds were specially designed to pass through all known types of body armor, including our own.

Why carry live ammunition on a peacetime jump? In the SEALs, we train like we fight. It is essential that each jumper practices with the same equipment he would use on a com-bat jump. Learning how to exit the airplane, deploy your parachute, and land your rig with a combat load is not some-thing you want to practice over downtown Baghdad.

We strapped on our parachutes, then connected the heavy backpacks to D rings on the front of each harness. All of our gear was secured with quick-release fittings. Within seconds of landing, we would be fully equipped and ready to rock.

As the riggers laid their cables, the air force combat con-trollers established radio communications with Landing Zone Green, a soccer field in Virginia Beach that would be our jump target. On LZ Green were parked three unmarked Chevy Suburbans from the Team. The drop zone crew was our reception committee, playing the role of friendly agents who would meet us as we touched down. In a real-world op, they would drive us to the target area or a safe house. Tonight all they had to do was hang out, make radio communications with the airplane, and wait for us to float to earth. Our exer-cise would end when my twelve-man assault element got to the ground.

As we completed equipment checks, one of the air force combat controllers came up to me. He didn't look happy. "The DZ reports winds northeast, twenty knots and gusting to thirty. Visibility is less than half a mile in heavy rain. Do you want to abort?"

"No," I said, "we can handle it."

As I said those words, lightning lit the sky around us, and the plane buffeted sharply. The air force guy grabbed a seat back to steady himself. He smirked. "Very studly."

The conditions were marginal, actually outside of parameters, but the parameters were guidelines. We had all jumped in worse. Besides, if we got this over with, we could make it to the Raven and grab a few beers before closing time. This would be my last op, and I was buying when we got to the bar. Although I wasn't looking forward to the tab, I was anxious to get on the ground before the weather got worse.

Nearly twenty months before, I had submitted a letter to the secretary of the navy, asking to resign my commission and leave the Teams. It had taken the navy almost two years to answer my request. When you hold a commission in the armed forces, you serve at the pleasure of the president. It had apparently not pleased the White House to let me go any sooner. The navy took its time in processing my letter, and I had been operational every day since putting in my papers. That was fine with me; there was nothing else I wanted to do in the navy. I just wanted out—eventually. Three days before, I'd gotten an answer to my request. My commission was to expire in three hours, at midnight.

So what was I doing standing in the back of a 727, waiting to jump into a soccer field in the middle of a Virginia suburb? As the plane shook and banked, I began to ask myself the same thing. As weird as it might sound, I was making the jump because I didn't want to.

I hated to jump. Unfortunately for me, my aversion to gravity was well known. I was teased for it, but I still made every jump, more than three hundred of them, three of them combat insertions, and I had to be a competent operator in the air. When you are trying to group twelve parachutes together in a stack at thirty-three thousand feet on night-vision goggles, there is no room for substandard performance. Besides, as they say in SEAL basic training, I didn't have to like it, I just had to do it. I was the boat-crew leader, and my boat crew drew this operation. If the Rastas were going to jump, then I would, too.

I turned to the combat controller and said, "Go for depressurization."

The riggers and observers scrambled for their seats and buckled in. The combat controllers each pulled on a jet pilot's helmet, their oxygen masks connected to carry bottles strapped to their belts. They could continue to communicate with the drop zone through radio microphones in their oxygen masks. There was a loud rushing sound as the cabin filled with fog. The aircraft depressurized, and I looked at the altimeter on my wrist. It read twelve thousand feet, the same as the altitude outside the aircraft.

Alex pulled back the latch on the aft hatch and secured it to the galley with a piece of bungee cord. The cabin was filled with the earsplitting roar of the engines. The sound was deafening, agonizingly loud. It actually made your chest hurt. The combat controller touched me on the shoulder. Talking was now out of the question; from now on we would communicate with hand signals. He held up five fingers and a thumb. We were six minutes from showtime.

The jumpers shuffled into the aft galley of the plane. José "Hoser" Lopez stepped onto the folded stairs and clambered to the end of the aft ramp. As D. B. Cooper discovered, much to his peril, the tail ramp of a 727 will not completely deploy when the aircraft is in flight. The force of the air streaming under the fuselage prevents the hydraulics from pushing the stairs into a full down-and-locked position. As the stick of jumpers packed into the galley and watched, Hoser climbed to the end of the folded stairs and did the bounce: Hanging on to the handrails, he jumped up and down, forcing the stairs down until the tail ramp clicked into a full down-and-locked position.

This was not as easy as it sounds. While you are playing jumpy-jumpy, the aircraft is doing over 140 miles an hour. Until the hydraulics overcome the wind resistance, the thousand-pound tail ramp bucks like a depraved mule. People have been killed and crippled attempting the bounce, but tonight, Hoser got it down and locked after just a few wild gyrations.

Once the ramp was down, a cable was affixed to the metal steps. This line would winch the ramp closed after we bailed out. Hoser took a position on the lowest step and turned to face the other jumpers, hands gripping the rails. He would be the first man off, exiting backward, and he needed to see my signal to go. We all packed onto the stairs tightly, nuts to butts. I was the last man in the stick, standing on the top stair in the galley next to the combat controller, who looked like a giant insect in his helmet. He turned to me and held up three fingers. I passed the signal to Hoser, who lifted one hand off the rail and gave a three-fingered "hang loose" to the Rastas.

I checked my altimeter. It read five thousand feet and was descending rapidly. Past the open tail ramp, through sheets of driving rain, I could see car headlights on the Chesapeake Bay Bridge-Tunnel a mile below. It was raining hard, and lightning zigzagged through the cloud deck. The bay was rough, the clouds were descending, and the storm was on us fully. I could see raindrops frozen in the strobing of the airliner's anticollision lights. The 727 pulled a broad, lazy turn over the Chesapeake and entered the landing pattern for Norfolk International.

The purpose of tonight's exercise was to see if a stick of jumpers would show up on airport approach radar. After orbiting over SEAL DZ, Assailant 26 had requested a touch-and-go at Norfolk International. The plan was for Assailant to put flaps and landing gear down and enter the pattern. Our landing zone was maybe two and half miles from the airport's tower, between the Chesapeake shore and the runways. As the airliner swooped for a landing, my element would jump when the soccer field came into sight.

We would be leaving the airplane at seven hundred feet, pretty low for a free-fall drop. After we exited the aircraft, the tail ramp would be winched shut. Assailant 26 would then execute a touch-and-go, divert, and land at the nearby naval air station at Oceana, Virginia. That was the plan, anyway. Moments from now, for me, that plan would completely go to hell.

The combat controller held up his right hand, index finger and thumb half an inch apart. I passed the signal to Hoser: thirty seconds to drop. I checked my altimeter: We were passing through a thousand feet. The combat controller slapped me on the leg. I yelled, "GO! GO! GO!" into my radio headset. At the bottom of the ramp, Hoser let go of the railing and was instantly sucked off the stairs. I watched as he disappeared into the wall of blinking raindrops. The rest of the jumpers clattered down the stairs and dived into black. I was the last man to leave the airplane. Plunging off, I could feel the hot blast of the engines and smell the acrid scent of burning jet fuel.

As my body slammed into the slipstream, I arched my back. The exit from an airliner is not unlike bodysurfing a gigantic wave. The drop feels the same, and you have to arch your back hard so you don't somersault. I waited three seconds, my fingers hooked the rip cord, and I pulled. I felt the cable whip through its channels and open the parachute container on my back. The spring-loaded pilot chute fired, and my main parachute and deployment bag shot skyward. I braced for opening shock, preparing my body for deceleration from 120 miles an hour to almost zero. I took a deep breath and held it.

But my parachute did not open. Virginia was still coming at me fast. I had maybe ten seconds to live.

I've heard it said that in times of peril, victims flash back on their entire lives. I have been in bad places many times, in mortal, violent moments when I did not really know if I would live or die, but a flashback has never happened to me. Maybe I'm not sufficiently contemplative. Maybe I've never considered myself a victim. All I knew was that I was hurtling toward earth, and I was going to die if I didn't solve a mystery. The mystery involving my main canopy. Why hadn't it opened?

Actually, "why" didn't matter. What mattered now was getting a reserve chute deployed. I did not flash back over my life, but I did go to adrenaline world. This has happened to me almost every time I have faced imminent destruction. The planet seems to stop. Everything slows and is silent. I no longer heard the roar of the jet. I did not hear the rush of the wind past my helmet. I no longer felt the raindrops slamming like BBs into my face. The world was in slow mo. The only problem was, in about five seconds I would auger into the planet at 176 feet per second.

On the stairs of the airplane, my altimeter had read 750 feet. That was almost four seconds ago. I estimated I was falling through 500 feet now, without a working parachute.

You will read these words in about the same relative time that my accident seemed to unfold. My mind was racing with clear, fluid thought: relative velocities; probabilities; actions and outcomes. I seemed to be falling in perfect silence, but my mind was rapidly processing. Everything I am about to describe unfolded in fewer than fifteen seconds. That amount of time would decide if I lived or died.

I knew whatever I tried might well be futile, but I was going to stay with this problem and fight it until I opened a parachute or I bounced. I had been trained to deal with a variety of nonoptimal parachute functions, and my mind did a pull-down menu of malfunctions and their remedies. Live or die, I would carry out my malfunction drill. The problem was, I didn't know what sort of malfunction I had.

I lifted my knees to my chest, which pulled me into a sitting position. I was now falling as though strapped to a chair. I looked up; my pilot chute had fired, but the parachute, which is held in the nylon deployment container, was stuck. Instead of having hundreds of square feet of canopy, I had a lump of nylon the size of a large loaf of bread. And it wasn't slowing me down. My eyes racked focus; hundreds of feet above me, in an even line, I could see the square canopies of the other jumpers. Disappearing into the low cloud deck, the Rastas' parachutes were getting smaller. I was dropping like an anvil.

Stay with the procedure, I told myself, stay with the drill. I threw away my rip cord and moved my hand to the "twinkie" on my harness. This was a padded nylon strap on my right shoulder, connected to the cutaway cables of my main parachute. Before I tried to put up my reserve, I would have to detach my main parachute, or my second chute would tangle uselessly in the mess that was already up there.

Releasing the twinkie was a two-step process. First, it had to be ripped away from the double-sewn Velcro that held it in place. Then, the twinkie and approximately two feet of cable had to be pulled clear so my main parachute would cut away from the riser straps connecting it to my harness. My eyes fell on the glowing dial of my altimeter. I was now at four hundred feet, the lowest recommended altitude at which a reserve parachute can be deployed. Stay with the emergency procedure, I told myself. Improvisation is for desperate people.

I had the twinkie in my hand. I'd pulled it free of the Velcro, and I was about to cut away. In that instant, my main parachute opened. Sort of. Three of the eight cells of my main canopy worked free of the deployment bag. My head jerked skyward as my body decelerated. This was definitely luck of the Irish: I had half a parachute.

I looked again at the altimeter: three hundred feet. One hundred feet below the minimum altitude to deploy my reserve. I was desperate. It was time to improvise.

I made a command decision. I was too low to cut away my main, fall clear, and deploy my reserve. My one chance was to stay with what little parachute I had and try to ride it in. My altimeter was basically useless below 500 feet. The device worked by measuring atmospheric pressure, and I was falling through a thunderstorm. I might be at 300 feet, I might be lower. My altimeter might still be reading 300 feet when I smashed through somebody's skylight.

My eyes flicked down for the first time since I left the airplane. I was over water, an L-shaped inlet I knew to be Desert Cove in the Little Creek neighborhood of Virginia Beach. The cove was maybe half a mile from the soccer field where I was supposed to land.

My mind raced. I was doing the math faster than a science

nerd's solar-powered calculator. I was still falling ninety miles an hour, at least; I had a marginal opportunity to get my rig fully deployed. If I hit the water, it was possible the impact would not kill me. Theoretically possible but unlikely. If I was not killed outright by the sudden stop, I would almost certainly be knocked unconscious. With sixty-five pounds of gear strapped to my body, I would sink and drown. I had to get my rig open.

The MT-1-X parachute is not a round chute, it is shaped like a wing. And like a wing, it can be steered precisely and flown in any direction the jumper wishes to go. It's an excellent rig; with this equipment I'd made pinpoint landings from six miles up. But I had only half a wing. Worse, I was no longer falling vertically: The three inflated cells of my canopy were spinning me in a wild spiral. I was in a flat spin, making two full 360-degree revolutions a second. Below me, Desert Cove was spinning like a Frisbee. Like a fighter pilot pulling too many G's, the centrifugal force was pushing the blood away from my brain and into my legs. I was getting tunnel vision and was close to blacking out. I had to get the rest of the canopy open before I lost consciousness.

I reached up and grabbed the parachute's risers with both hands and pulled at them with all my might. It was a last, desperate move—and it worked. With a loud *pop,* the remaining five cells on my canopy opened. One cell was tattered and deflated, but I had an almost full parachute. I was now at approximately 250 feet.

I was still over water, and although I was prepared to ditch, I thought it better to try flying toward land instead of attempting a swim with sixty-five pounds of assorted metal objects. Lightning flashed; through the rain, I could see a boat ramp and an empty parking lot a hundred yards to my right. I turned in to the wind and headed for a perfect landing.

I was congratulating myself on my brilliant airmanship when something salty splashed my face. Blood dripped down my wrists and spattered my goggles. I had ripped two fingernails off my right hand, clawing at the twinkie. I didn't feel any pain, but I knew the nails had been ripped clear of their beds. I pulled the blood-spattered goggles from my face.

Looming out of the rain, a trio of high-tension wires draped over the parking lot. I hadn't just cheated death in order to be hung up and electrocuted. I made a hard right 180. As I pulled the turn, my parachute fluttered violently. The damaged center of my rig sucked in the remaining cells, the canopy collapsed and dropped me a heart-stopping fifty feet before it again caught the wind. No more turns were possible. I was now headed straight downwind. And that was not a good thing. My parachute was in full flight, and I was riding a twenty-knot gust. I was doing maybe forty miles an hour over ground. Landing was inevitable. Landing at this speed, with no steering, would not be pleasant.

A hundred and fifty yards away was a strip of sand, Demonstration Beach, a place where we sometimes launched practice diving missions. I had just enough altitude to make it, but I was still going too fast. Even if I completely braked my canopy, I'd still be traveling at the speed of the wind, maybe thirty miles an hour. I dared not try to put the canopy into a stall; the rig would fold up and drop me. Full speed was my only speed. I reached up and nursed my steering paddles, gingerly making a series of corrections right and left. I glided for the beach, puckered my ass, and braced for impact.

A galaxy of stars exploded in my head. My knees slammed into my backpack, my MP-5 machine pistol jammed into my ribs, and I heard a sickening snap. Half conscious, I bounced and was dragged by my still-inflated canopy across the beach. Digging a trench with my heels, I was pulled across the sand through a strip of grass and out onto the road that circled the cove. Caught by a gust, the parachute that had saved my life was going to drag me until I was hamburger. I clutched the twinkie with my bloody fingers and jerked it clear. The main canopy cut away and drifted off. I came to a stop in a ditch on the other side of the road.

Finally, the ride was over.

Sand and blood covered my face and hands. My ribs crackled as I sucked in air. I lay in the weeds, and the rain beat into my face. I started to laugh; it was 2356 hours in the eastern time zone, 11:56 P.M. In three minutes and twenty seconds, I would be a civilian.

CHARM SCHOOL

IT WAS PROBABLY INEVITABLE that I joined the navy, though I resisted it. I am the son of a career navy officer and a navy nurse. My father, Pat, was an Annapolis graduate, a destroyer captain, and ended his navy career as a professor of tactics at the Naval War College. He'd met my mom, Joni, when she was a navy nurse stationed at the Oak Knoll Naval Hospital outside San Francisco. I am the oldest of four kids, two boys and two girls. In my family, the apple doesn't fall very far from the tree. My brother, Sean, is a chief engineer in the merchant marine, and my sisters, Colleen and Katie, are registered nurses.

We moved around quite a bit as a navy family, and we were close. We weren't rich, but we lacked nothing, and I count my childhood, essentially, as a happy one.

I was raised a Catholic. I went to catechism, collected holy cards, and had my first communion in full regalia. Though my family was not overly religious, we ate fish sticks with ketchup on Fridays. I was a typical Catholic kid, felt vaguely guilty about something (though at age twelve, I didn't know what yet), but I accepted my faith, the sacraments, the saints, and the whole enchilada without question. That wasn't to last.

About a month after Neil Armstrong walked on the moon, in August 1969, a single towering thunderstorm drifted off the coast of West Africa. Borne offshore on the trade winds, the clutch of thunderstorms meandered west across the Atlantic. Soon this evolving low-pressure system had a name: Camille.

Hurricane Camille would turn into the most devastating weather system ever to strike North America. Swirling, gathering power from the warm waters of the tropical Atlantic, Camille stalked the Florida straits, made a brief feint at Tampa, and roared into the Gulf of Mexico. The 85-degree waters of the Gulf turned Camille into a monster.

And my hometown was directly in her sights.

On the seventeenth of August, 1969, Biloxi, Mississippi, was laid waste by Hurricane Camille. At the time, my father was assigned to MACV, the Military Assistance Command, Vietnam. Unlike Dad's previous tours as a destroyer captain, this tour was on the ground. The war in Vietnam was at its bloody height, and he'd deposited us in Biloxi to await his return.

At twelve years old I was the man of the house. As the eldest son and a navy brat, I'd grown used to the job. We'd lived in every navy town from Newport to Pearl Harbor, and by the sixth grade, I'd attended five different elementary schools. Beyond having a very real stake in the war, my siblings and I were children without a care in the world. It was high summer, a time of bicycles and snow cones with a new set of friends.

Storm-track prediction in 1969 was not what it is now, and no one, forecasters included, could conceive of Camille's power. My family had no clue. As the hurricane turned north, we didn't have the sense to evacuate. Only hours before the storm hit, we moved from our waterfront home to a multi-story hotel on the beach. In hindsight our move was idiotic, but it saved our lives. My brother and sisters, our mother, and I rode out the storm in one of the few buildings in the city to survive intact, a 1920s-era hotel on Biloxi's main beach.

In the morning we rose to find the city wiped from the face of the map.

Around the hotel, oceangoing freighters had been tossed up hundreds of yards from the sea. Bodies hung in trees. Debris, dead animals, shrimp boats, wrecked cars, and the mud-soaked possessions of the dead were scattered for miles. Biloxi was no more.

I found our station wagon half a mile from the hotel, upside down in what was left of a Dairy Queen. Of our home we had only hopes. We were ferried back across the bay by the National Guard to find our house and the neighborhood around it reduced to kindling. Mud covered everything. It looked like a war zone. No. It looked worse.

There was no food or water to be found. Bewildered survivors wandered the rubble, sobbing. There were no police, no emergency services, and no government. Camille had been a great equalizer; every survivor was a destitute, mud-spattered refugee. Class and possession no longer mattered. The veneer of civilization had been ripped away. Martial law was declared, and gunfire crackled in the night as survivors battled looters.

We had no way to communicate with my father, no way to tell him or anyone else where we were, or even that we were alive. My mother was nearly catatonic, overcome by shock and grief. There was nothing to do but sit in the wreckage and wait.

We lived in the ruins of our house for three days, scrounging intact cans of food and soft drinks from the mud. Finally, my father was able to receive emergency leave. Dad traveled ten thousand miles from Saigon by plane, train, and truck to find us huddled in what was left of the house. We had lost everything but one another. Now Dad was home, and we slowly started to rebuild our lives.

It was in the mud of Biloxi where my separation from God occurred. I was not even thirteen years old, and I had seen a city destroyed—plowed flat as though it had been carpet-bombed. Had this been the work of men, an act of war, I could have comprehended it. I could have excused it. But this was not an act of man. This was an act of God.

In the wreckage of my home, I cursed God. I cursed him for what he had done, and dared him to do worse. These people, my family, and this sleepy Mississippi town had done nothing to deserve annihilation.

I did not rage long, but I put God, or any concept of a benign, enlightened deity, completely out of mind. The good little Catholic boy was no more. I didn't need flag-burning war protesters to tell me God was dead. I knew it. For a long time God and I would get along without each other just fine.

In 1973 we were again stationed in Newport, Rhode Island, and I was totally into surfing. I'd picked up the sport a couple of tours before, when we were stationed in Hawaii, and catching waves became the driving passion of my young life. Not much mattered to me except getting in the water. Some kids skipped English. I ditched classes a week at a time and stayed away as long as the swell lasted.

I had hooky down to a fine art. I'd stash my surfboard and wet suit in the bushes behind our quarters and bum a ride to the beach. After I'd surfed my brains out, I'd change back into my school clothes, return the board and wet suit to their hiding places, and arrive home at the same time my classmates were stepping off the school bus. My parents had no idea. If they ever asked why my hair was wet, I'd tell them I took a shower after gym class. I was loving life.

It didn't last. My parents were called into a conference with the dean of boys, who informed them I was an incorrigible class skipper pulling straight D-minuses. My father acted swiftly. One afternoon I came home to find the catalogs of five military schools lined up on the dining room table. My dad told me to read through them and pick one out. I was fifteen years old, a pooka-shell-wearing surf dude, and I was damned if I was gonna read about a bunch of idiots in Nazi uniforms. I jabbed my finger at the closest catalog and said, "How about this one?"

My finger was pressed against a gray catalog embossed with the letters "SMA." I didn't know it, but I'd randomly selected the prospectus of the oldest and toughest military prep school in the nation: Staunton Military Academy.

My dad just smiled.

Two weeks later, I was standing atop a pair of footprints painted on an asphalt parade deck tucked deep in the bosom of the Shenandoah Valley. I was one of a hundred new cadets, called "rats," being welcomed to my new high school. An upper-class cadet was screaming in my face. I could see his tonsils as he shrieked at me. His breath was bad, and he seemed incapable of speaking without ejecting a vast quantity of saliva. I was dressed in a baggy aloha shirt, and my hair was to my shoulders. I'd left the pooka shells at home, luckily. I remember being called a communist, morphodite, hippie-surfer bitch as I was marched with my fellow "new boys" to the academy's barbershop.

I was to spend two long years at SMA. Like every cadet who ever went there, I remember it as the kind of place you could hate every day and miss for the rest of your life. The academics were tough and the military rules unbending. Rats had little free time. We were formed into a battalion three times a day and marched to the mess hall. Companies were served on the basis of their performance at parade, with the honor company eating first and the slackers last. Eating last sometimes meant going hungry. When the mess hall ran out of food, they served powdered eggs for breakfast, lunch, and dinner.

At meals and every other time, we were harried by upperclassmen—the usual *Lords of Discipline* stuff. Our rooms were subject to surprise inspections three times a week. To discourage desertion, we were forbidden to possess luggage or civilian clothing. Our persons, uniforms, and weapons were inspected regularly. We drilled every afternoon and had a dress parade every Sunday, rain or shine. Breaches of discipline garnered demerits and assignment to the Beat Squad, which generally meant running around the school's track with rifle and rucksack, or shoveling snow or raking leaves.

SMA was an old school, steeped in tradition. The Academy was founded in 1860 by William Hartman Kable. Not long after the school admitted its first students, hostilities opened in the American Civil War. Like many a good Virginian, Billy Kable joined up. He served with distinction as a captain in the 10th Virginia Cavalry, in the Confederate States Army. Like Captain Kable, Staunton cadets wore gray.

Staunton alumni have served in almost every conflict fought by the United States since the Civil War—in America's army, chiefly, but also in the navy, air force, and Marine Corps. One of Staunton's professors, Major Thomas Dry

Howie, led the Allied breakout from Saint-Lô after the landings at Normandy. In so doing, he won the Congressional Medal of Honor—the hard way. Among the academy's alumni are senators, admirals, generals, fighter aces, congressmen, and the CEOs of Fortune 500 companies, people like John Dean and Barry Goldwater. It was the kind of school that did not bend its ways to suit the student body. You adapted or you perished.

It is interesting that at my high school, everyone carried a gun, and we didn't have a problem with school violence. There was, however, the occasional suicide. Although no one did himself in while I was a cadet, a couple of kids had nervous breakdowns. The phenomenon was called, in cadet argot, "snapping out," and it happened a few times a year. Someone would be taken, blubbering, from his room and led by the officer of the day to the infirmary and the school nurse. The next day the unfortunate cadet's room would be cleaned out. No one talked much about it. Like I said, SMA was a tough place.

The school rewarded compliance. If a cadet was on the dean's list, pulling A's and B's, he didn't have to attend daily study halls. An hour or two of free time a day was precious. Idle hours could be spent in the cadet canteen, smoking and hanging out. Cadets were supposed to have a permit signed by their parents in order to buy cigarettes, but I never heard of anyone asking to see one. Consequently, everybody smoked. Another way out of the military hassles was to go out for a varsity sport. Athletes were allowed the afternoons to practice, and there was no military bullshit on the playing fields. Away games off the academy grounds were a welcome break from marching and polishing brass.

At SMA I learned a lot more than how to clean a rifle, drill a company, and shine my shoes. As you might imagine, young men are not sent to military schools because they have comported themselves like model citizens. My brother cadets were a multitalented lot. Some might question the wisdom of grouping together twelve hundred world-class juvenile delinquents. In our battalions were the scions of the first families of Virginia, the sons of Watergate conspirators, the offspring of Latin American dictators, and the bastard kids of movie stars. We also had our share of vandals, felons, and drug dealers.

It was at SMA that I acquired many of the skills that would serve me later in the SEAL Teams. At SMA I learned to pick a lock, hot-wire a car, and perfectly forge the laminated New Jersey driver's license that would permit me to buy beer until I turned twenty-one.

In many ways, SMA was like Stalag 17, the escape-proof camp where the Nazis locked up Allied officers prone to breaking out. By concentrating the experts, our jailers had created Escape Central. Like intrepid POWs, we cut holes in the fence, ditched our uniforms, and sneaked into town wearing civvies stashed in secret hiding places. To go AWOL for beer was to risk expulsion. Unlike the prisoners in the German camps, we made our escapes round-trips, and we'd always be back in our bunks by reveille.

Staunton taught me another vital skill: how to put up a front. I learned to shine my shoes, keep my uniform pressed, and say "Yes sir." At SMA cadets learned to toe the line during the day and howl at night.

I can't say I enjoyed Staunton, but I needed it. My grades went from D-minuses to A's and B's. I earned letters in track and soccer. On the day I graduated, I had been offered an appointment to the U.S. Naval Academy and three full-ride ROTC scholarships. The hippie surfer had been made into a patriot.

What did I do? I picked a college in California that would be close to the surf. I turned down the Annapolis appointment and the ROTC rides. I'd had enough of the military. Or so I thought. My father, naturally, was disappointed, but I was never hassled about turning down Annapolis. He never brought it up, and I thank him for his indulgence.

After military school, college was a breeze. Staunton had taught me how to budget my time and how to study. At California State University at Northridge, I was a varsity athlete, an officer in my fraternity, and held a full-time job while I pulled down mostly A's. I majored in clinical psychology and looked forward to graduate school and a practice in the suburbs.

It wasn't to happen.

I was in love. Heart-attack-serious, all-consuming, major hound-dog love with a woman I'd met back in Newport. Lisa Wheaton was the daughter of another Naval War College professor. About the time I was shipped off to Staunton, Lisa's dad, a colonel in the engineers, was transferred to Germany. She and I wrote to each other incessantly, and when she came back to the U.S. to attend Mount Holyoke College in Massachusetts, I became a frequent flier. We spent our junior year in Great Britain together—well, almost together. Lisa attended the University of London, and I went to the University of Bath. We saw each other every weekend and spent our "vacays" traveling together through England, Scotland, and Ireland.

When we returned to the U.S. in our senior year, things started to cool off for her. By the time I'd started grad school, it was over. Our breakup had unfolded in excruciating slow motion and was marked by extreme civility on both sides. I can tell you in all honesty that I was let down in the kindest manner possible.

In the tragic fashion of the self-absorbed, I was devastated. Nothing mattered to me anymore. Not getting a Ph.D., not becoming a psychologist, nothing. I'd lost the most important thing in my life, and I was adrift and alone.

Then one day I was walking across campus, and it hit me. I was going to spend my twenties wearing out a path to the library. Three more years of school, a dissertation, an internship . . . then I would spend the rest of my life trying to convince rich white ladies not to be afraid of spiders.

There has to be more to living, I thought. My father has seven stars on his Vietnam service ribbon . . . that's right, I said seven. When I was a boy, I would stand on the pier waiting for his destroyer to come in. It was like a carnival. Bands played, and hundreds of wives and kids crowded the pier, waving signs, holding balloons. All waiting for fathers and loved ones to return from halfway around the world.

When the gangplank was put over, we'd all rush aboard, all four kids and our mom grabbing Dad in a massive hug. He'd always return with exotic presents: silk scarves from Thailand for the girls, opals for our mother, teak-handled pocketknives for the boys. Although he never talked much of Vietnam, Dad would pile the kids on his knees and show us on the globe the places he had been. He told us of seeing polar bears swimming in arctic seas. Of sunsets off the coast of Africa. Of sea snakes covering the surface of the ocean as far as he could see in the Gulf of Siam. The names of the places he'd been were magical to me: Zamboanga. Cam Rahn Bay. The Ionian Sea. The Straits of Magellan.

I said it was almost inevitable that I joined the navy. It's probably more serious than that. My father's side of the family had been in the United States for three generations. With the exception of my great-grandfather, who emigrated from Switzerland in 1900, every man in my family has served as an officer in the navy or the Marine Corps. My grandfather was a navy intelligence officer in the Pacific during World War II. My father was career navy, my uncle Don was a navy gunfire officer in Vietnam, and my uncle Steve waded through rice paddies as a marine platoon leader. My mother's older brother Bob was a navy fighter ace in the Pacific; her brother Mickey was at Normandy and Remagen.

I wanted to see the world, too. Now I wanted my life to be an adventure.

I walked into the psychology offices and said, "I quit." I got into my 1969 Kingswood Estate station wagon and drove to the navy recruiter's office on Wilshire Boulevard in L.A. I told them, "I want to be a Navy SEAL."

This was a long time before SEALs became a staple in movies, TV, and popular culture. For many years the navy denied the very existence of the SEAL Teams. The lieutenant commander behind the desk looked me over. "What do you know about the SEALs?" he asked.

What I knew, I had been told by my father, who worked

with the SEALs during his ground tour in Vietnam. I told the recruiter I was a navy brat and an SMA graduate. I told him I wanted a challenge. I seemed sincere, because I was.

The recruiter told me the SEAL program was full, but they needed helicopter pilots. I was born into a navy family, and I knew that where there was a will, there was a waiver. I agreed to take the flight aptitude test, along with the test for SEAL training. I passed both. The recruiter said they still needed helicopter pilots, so I played a trump card. I said that if I couldn't become a SEAL, maybe I'd wander down the hall to his army colleague's office and become a Green Beret.

Two days later there was an opening in the SEAL program. I wound up with a "contract": I would attend navy officer candidate school in Newport, Rhode Island. After that, the navy guaranteed that I would receive orders to Basic Underwater Demolition/SEAL training in Coronado, California. But they didn't guarantee that I would pass, or that I would get a second chance if I was injured and forced to drop out. If I failed, I'd be sent to the fleet: haze gray and under way, just like the regular navy. I had no intention of joining the regular navy; I wanted to be a SEAL, I said. The recruiter reminded me patiently that I *was* joining the regular navy—and if I flunked out of OCS, I'd be sent directly to the fleet, as an enlisted man.

I signed on the dotted line.

In the span of three days, I'd gone from budding psychologist to wanna-be naval commando. I'd turned my back on everything I thought I would be. Gone were five years of study and my plan for a life. I'd jumped off the end of the world. I have been told that breaking up with my girlfriend was a very B-movie reason to join the SEALs. Maybe it was. It all seems very beau geste now, but it didn't then. I wanted to change the direction of my life.

I called home and told my parents I'd just joined the SEALs. There was a long pause. This from the kid who turned down an appointment and said he'd had enough of the military. This from the hippie psych major who'd picked a school that was close to the surf. Again Dad passed up a great chance to razz me. He said, "Well, be careful."

I cleaned out my apartment, sold my books, and drove back to my parents' home, now back in Biloxi, Mississippi. My dad had since retired from the navy and was the southern manager for a company that manufactured bow thrusters for oil-field support ships. Dad got me a job installing and repairing bow thrusters, and I spent the summer waiting for my OCS class to start and pining over Lisa.

Three weeks before I was to report to Newport, I flew to New England. After graduation from Mount Holyoke, Lisa was working as the news director of a country-music station in Brunswick, Maine. I don't know what I was thinking, that we would suddenly patch things up, or what. I wasn't even really invited; I just called her up and said I was coming.

Our reunion was strained. Lisa's job at the radio station required her to get up at four A.M., in time to have the morning news cobbled together from the Associated Press wire. Sitting in her apartment, I'd listen to her read the news between songs about broken hearts and wrecked pickup trucks. I hung around for a few days like a Christmas puppy no one wanted. One night at dinner I said quietly, "I think I should go." She didn't try to talk me out of it.

On our last night together, we made love in a bitter and selfish way. Then I lay awake in the dark and watched her sleep, and when her alarm clock rattled, I stared at the ceiling as she dressed, brushed her hair, and pushed through the front door. "Lock it when you go," she said.

I remember that moment as the last of my boyhood. I had loved her in a desperate, complete, and frightening way. I think now that I loved her with a heart that had never been broken, and that is why I have loved badly since.

Carrying my seabag, I walked to the bus station and paid $33.50 for a one-way ticket to Newport. When the bus pulled up, rain was falling in a terrific sheet, and I was drenched in the few moments it took the driver to punch my ticket and toss the seabag into the luggage compartment. I found a seat in the back of the empty bus, placed my head against the glass, and wept silently.

I remember officer candidate school only as a jostle of shouting instructors and the sharp smell of floor wax. It was, I thought, considerably less difficult than Staunton. I commanded a company, studied very little, and nearly flunked celestial navigation. In sixteen weeks I spent every dime I earned on bourbon and hotel rooms in Newport, which was still something of a hometown to me, and when I was on liberty, I ripped a new hole in it. I dated nurses, dental technicians, and the daughter of a commodore. Counting time until graduation, I sat in my OCS room and listened to Vivaldi, Pure Prairie League, and pop music I'd taped from British radio stations. At night the wind would blow down Narragansett Bay and rattle the frost from my windows. Alone in the dark, I told myself I was over Lisa.

A week before I was to ship out, Lisa surprised me by driving down from Maine. She met me on the OCS quarterdeck, and we got a room in town. The night before my commissioning, she put on a blue nightgown and slept next to me. She kissed me, called me pet names, but would not make love to me. In the morning I got up early, put on my uniform, and she drove me back to the base.

When she dropped me off, she said, "Now, just walk away like Marlon Brando."

The following morning my father administered the oath and swore me in as an ensign in the United States Navy.

It would be ten years before I saw or spoke to Lisa again. By then I would be a completely different person. A man who had passed through fire.

MARCH 1981. SAN DIEGO, CALIFORNIA. It was a good hour and a half before sunrise, and a cold fog scudded across the moon and rolled over the ten-mile stretch of beach called the Silver Strand. It was 0435 hours Pacific standard time, that somniferous span of the twenty-four-hour clock referred to in the navy as "oh-dark-thirty." One hundred and forty-five SEAL trainees were assembled before a podium on the asphalt "grinder" of the special warfare training compound on the Naval Amphibious Base, Coronado. Thin wisps of fog blew between the ranks. Standing silently, the men looked like a formation of ghosts.

I was one of ten officers—nine ensigns and a lieutenant—standing at parade rest before evenly spaced columns of sailors and petty officers. We all wore the uniform of SEAL trainees: starched green fatigues and jungle boots, with our names stenciled on white tape across our right pec and the right ass cheek of our trousers. The only thing distinguishing an officer from an enlisted man was a stripe painted fore and aft on the officer's helmet.

These men were all who remained of the perhaps three hundred who had requested to attend SEAL training. Before this group had undergone a single day of instruction, the number of volunteers had been culled by two thirds. During pretraining, prospective students had been investigated, inspected, jabbed with needles, placed in hyperbaric chambers, and quizzed by shrinks. The tests washed out claustrophobics and those afraid of heights, the overly aggressive and the passive, people without perfect vision or hearing, those with trick knees, flat feet, color blindness, or heart murmurs, people with allergies, and those with criminal or juvenile records. One hundred and forty-five men had been judged by the navy to have the physical, academic, and psychological qualifications necessary to undergo SEAL training. They would start Basic Underwater Demolition/SEAL Class 114, the hundred and fourteenth class of naval commandos to be trained by the United States. The course we were about to undertake was declared by the Department of Defense to be "physically and mentally demanding."

That's a no-shitter.

Basic Underwater Demolition/SEAL training, BUD/S to its initiates, is the most brutal training meted out by the U.S. military. Attrition rates of 60 to 90 percent are the norm. There have been classes, in fact, from which no one graduated. No one graduated because everybody quit.

Every man standing on the asphalt this morning knew the

odds, and the navy did, too. These volunteers had been literally X-rayed to make sure any impediment was identified. Only those deemed most likely to succeed would be allowed into a class. The navy needed SEALs and did everything in their power to make sure the men assigned to BUD/S would make it through training. The navy would do everything, that is, except make training easier.

What lay ahead of Class 114 was a course much evolved since the navy first trained frogmen at Force Pierce, Florida. A punishing regime of twelve- to twenty-hour days would be devoted to physical conditioning, small-unit and guerrilla tactics, ambushes, demolition, and booby traps, as well as familiarization with a plethora of U.S., allied, and enemy weapons. In addition to discovering the more visceral aspects of being a commando, trainees would learn hyperbaric medicine, cartography, land and maritime navigation, open- and closed-circuit scuba diving, hand-to-hand combat, communications, and intelligence-gathering operations.

We'd learn all this stuff, that is, if we made it through the first day.

It is axiomatic in the military that training is tough because war is tougher. But what lay ahead of Class 114 was more than a training regimen; it was a rite of passage, an experience that would forever separate the men who had been there from the men who had not.

These were the sorts of lofty thoughts I had as I stood in the fog. You could almost hear "God Bless America" playing in my shaved little head. I had no goddamn idea what I was in for. The truth was, I was a tadpole, a wanna-be frogman, and I didn't know shit about what it would take to become a Navy SEAL. And, it turns out, neither did the navy.

The Defense Department's best physicians, physiologists, and psychiatrists had assembled profiles of SEAL graduates in an attempt to fill classes with men who would survive BUD/S. Despite their best efforts, farm boys, surfers, professional athletes, deep-sea divers, and Olympic hopefuls numbered among the dropouts, and regular 140-pound Joes were among the people who would succeed. The truth was, nobody knew what kind of man would make it through SEAL training. There is no way to quantify motivation.

I don't remember much about the group that started Class 114. I will never forget the handful of men who were to graduate with me. The dropouts left my memory. The men who were to graduate were a slice of America. There were kids from Nebraska who had never seen the ocean before. There were beach bums. Cubans from Miami. Tough guys and quiet types. The bony and the buff. Those who would make it through Class 114 were the most unlikely set of bastards you ever laid eyes on. Standing in the fog that morning, no one could know that only thirty-two men would still be around on graduation day six long months from now.

Our class's student leader was Lieutenant Mike Heyward, a Citadel graduate and surface warfare officer. He was older than the ensigns by a couple of years and had volunteered for BUD/S after serving for four years in the fleet, mostly on destroyers. Mike was the oldest of the officers save one, Ensign Rick James, who, at the ripe old age of thirty, had gotten a waiver to attempt training. Like Mike, Rick had previous service, having been an artilleryman in the 82d Airborne before attending naval officer candidate school. The remainder of the officers in my class were also OCS graduates.

Prior to Class 114, it had been difficult for OCS types, ninety-day wonders, to receive orders to SEAL training. The slots were reserved for men the navy felt would be better motivated and more thoroughly prepared: that is, four-year ROTC graduates. Times change. As I write this, nearly every officer assigned to BUD/S now comes directly from the Naval Academy. When I went through, NROTC types got most of the slots, with an occasional OCS guy tossed in as food for the lions. Special preference seemed to be granted to the navy's premier ROTC units: Duke, Notre Dame, and Boston College, some of the schools I'd blown off to surf in California.

In 114 all of the officers except Mike were liberal-arts majors from state schools. Why the switch? In the several classes previous, NROTC officers had attrited at an alarming rate. They succumbed to a variety of medical calamities. They fractured their skulls and had near-drownings, they gave in to hypothermia and stress fractures, but mostly, they just quit. Not enough officers were graduating. It was decided, as a test case, to put a load of OCS guys through. That's why there was a sudden opening for me when I threatened to join the army: We were going to be guinea pigs.

When the navy switched from NROTC grads, they seemed to go in heavy for college jocks. The officers in my class included a member of the U.S. water-polo team, a four-time all-American decathlete, a college football player, a former paratrooper, one wild-ass redneck, a couple of California Beach Boy types, and me. I was taller than most and not as muscled as many. In college I had rowed NCAA crew and was a varsity fencer, two sports not noted for plebeian appeal.

A national-caliber athlete I was not, but I had been an ocean lifeguard and scuba diver since I was sixteen. I was a strong swimmer; I could handle sail- and powerboats and felt I knew my way around the surf zone. I knew that the odds were against me. I had no idea if I would make it to graduation; I knew only that I would not quit. I had turned my back on my previous life. I'd told myself and anyone who would listen that I would leave BUD/S on graduation day or in a bag. From a twenty-one-year-old ex-fencer, it was tough talk.

The door to the first-phase instructor's office opened, and a long shadow fell on the formation. Master Chief Dick Roy, the naval special warfare training group's command master chief, stepped onto the asphalt. A Vietnam veteran of both UDT and SEAL Teams, Dick Roy at forty years of age was athlete enough for any ten of us. The master chief sprang to the podium, six-five and 220 pounds of muscle. Want a visual? Imagine Arnold Schwarzenegger's body and Clark Gable's head, pencil-thin mustache, jug ears, and all.

Mike Heyward called the class to attention: "Class 114 all present and accounted for, Master Chief."

The master chief spit a wad of Red Man chewing tobacco

off the dais. His voice was clipped. "On behalf of the director, gentlemen, it is my privilege to welcome you to Basic Underwater Demolition, SEAL training. No one invited you here. No one requested that you attend this course. You volunteered. And you may volunteer to leave us anytime you wish. Seven days a week, twenty-four hours a day." The master chief pointed to a brass bell hanging in front of the first-phase office. "Just ring that bell over there three times, and you're free to go. No questions asked. No prejudicial comments will be placed in your records. You will be free to go back to doing whatever fucked-up shit you were into before you came here. It's that easy."

The class stood at attention; the only sound was the booming of the surf behind the compound. The master chief continued, hands on his hips. "In the next twenty-six weeks, we're not going to try to train you. We're going to try to kill you. You will be asked to do things you'll think are beyond the limits of your endurance. You will run faster, swim farther, and dig deeper than you thought humanly possible. When you are tired, you will be pushed. When you are hungry, you will go without food. When you are cold, the wind will be your blanket. You will suffer, you will sweat, and you will bleed.

"One hundred and forty-five men comprise this class. In the next six months, approximately seventy-five of you will ring that bell, ring out—simply quit. Fifteen to twenty of you will receive significant injuries during the course of training and will request to be medically dropped."

The master chief worked the Red Man, shifting the lump in his cheek from right to left. I would never see Dick Roy without a plug of tobacco in his mouth, not during exercises, not on ocean swims, not on ten-mile runs. He was probably born with a chaw tucked into his cheek.

"If you came here to prove something to your daddy or your girlfriend, if you came here to find yourself, if you came here because you love America and you wanna be a coe-man-doe, do yourself a favor, do my instructors a favor: Ring out now."

The master chief looked us over. "Maybe ten or fifteen of you clowns will make it. The rest of you will quit, flunk out academically, or be injured seriously. The men who remain at graduation will receive additional specialized training and go on to become members of the smallest and most elite spec-ops unit of the United States military: the operational SEAL Teams. This is the first and only pep talk you will receive at this command. Whether or not you graduate is entirely up to you." He spit another glob of Red Man. This one landed within six inches of my left boot.

"Good luck," he said.

By eight o'clock that morning we had done maybe seven hundred push-ups, run four miles in the sand, and performed an hour of calisthenics. Stragglers had been made to hit the surf, then roll in wet beach sand to make themselves into "sugar cookies." Sugar cookies went on exercising in wet, sandy uniforms. But the day was still young.

BUD/S students do not march; they run, everywhere. After our predawn PT session, the formation double-timed across the amphibious base, where we reperformed the physical screening test, doing push-ups, sit-ups, pull-ups, a four-hundred-yard swim, and another run in long pants and combat boots. After lunch we were introduced to the obstacle course and got to carry telephone poles around for a while. Six guys had fallen out of formation by the time the class ran the mile to the chow hall for dinner. The three round-trips to the mess hall for meals amounted to six additional miles a day, every day. Vomit spattered the pavement as the formation returned to the barracks long after dark.

If the instructors were trying to get my attention, they'd succeeded. Looking back, that first day of training would be the easiest day we'd ever have. On the wall of the BUD/S compound is painted one of the SEALs' favorite mottoes: "The only easy day was yesterday." As I collapsed into my bunk that night, even my ears hurt. That night I made up my own motto: All I had to fear was hope itself.

I'd survived my first day of BUD/S, but hundreds of thousands of push-ups, hundreds of miles of sand runs, and countless hours in the cruel sea remained between me and graduation. The following morning eight helmets were lined up under the bell in front of the first-phase office. Overnight eight of our classmates had taken the master chief's advice and quit. The helmets were how the instructors counted coup; each day the row would get longer as more students were injured, flunked out, or came to the realization that they wanted to be SEALs, but not this bad.

BUD/S training is broken into three phases, each of eight weeks' duration. First phase is devoted almost exclusively to physical conditioning—and weeding out students. For twelve to twenty hours a day, trainees run, swim, paddle inflatable boats, navigate the obstacle course, then run some more. As often as the students are kept wet, they are just as often kept sandy. Chafing and blisters can quickly become ulcerous, infected sores. Other common first-phase injuries include joint inflammation and stress fractures of the lower legs. Twisted knees, ankles, and injuries from falls are also routine.

A major enemy is hypothermia. When most people think of San Diego, they think of sun-drenched beaches and palm trees. A BUD/S student will remember the cold. The water in San Diego is seldom above 60 degrees and is often much colder. A human being's core temperature is about 98 degrees—well, you can do the math. BUD/S students are kept constantly wet, in the water and in the wind. Hours of exposure can result in mind-numbing, teeth-chattering hypothermia. There is not a BUD/S student who can't tell you about muscle cramps and hallucinations. Instructor Ocean was one bad dude, and he was always available to provide negative reinforcement. In an event called a "surf torture," instructors have the class link arms and sit down in the pounding shore break behind the compound. Plunging waves beat on the formation. Smashed and rolled by the breakers, the class struggles to keep hold of one another in the icy water. The megaphone would blare: "We're going to stay here until someone quits."

Sooner or later, somebody always would.

Nor is there much rest for the wicked. The running is all done in combat boots—a sore ankle will not get better banging six miles to and from the mess hall each day. Longer runs, called "conditioning hikes," are pounded out on miles of soft beach sand. The most a BUD/S student will run in a day is approximately twenty miles, with most days averaging between eight and fifteen. Gangs of instructors lead and follow each run, harrying the class formation like wolves after a herd of migrating caribou.

On a long run, the faster runners move toward the front as the lame, tired, and out of condition fall back. The formation is not allowed to straggle. On each outing, instructors separate the last 20 percent from the main body. This group is called the "goon squad," and they are singled out for special attention. That means at least an extra half hour out on the sand, running in circles, doing push-ups, rope climbs, or carrying telephone poles out into the surf zone. The weakest and slowest are the ones who get screwed the hardest. During first phase, the goon squad contributes the majority of the helmets under the bell.

For every student, the push-ups are uncountable. Any breach of decorum, military etiquette, or operational procedure earns the transgressor fifty push-ups. Any time a class member superior in rank to you is "dropped," everyone in the unit does push-ups as well. When a boat-crew leader is made to do push-ups, his boat crew does them with him. When the class leader is dropped, the entire class does push-ups. It's an effective way to teach accountability.

It isn't just the instructors who are sons of bitches. Another nemesis is the obstacle course. Scattered across a couple hundred yards of sand are two dozen contraptions made from telephone poles, hawser, cargo net, and barbed wire. Obstacles with names like the Belly Robber, the Dirty Name, and the Slide for Life teach balance, physical technique, and confidence to students who will later scale embassy walls, climb offshore oil rigs, and pull themselves down lines attached to submerged submarines. Each time a student runs the O-course, his completion time is expected to improve. If it does not, the student can enjoy a refreshing dip in the Pacific, a bracing roll in beach sand, and the opportunity to run the O-course one more time. Wet.

Another first-phase pastime is boat work. The class is broken into seven-man boat crews and each is assigned to an IBS, or inflatable boat, small. Dressed in kapok life jackets, the boat crews paddle through the surf zone for hours in a series of races and long-distance paddles. Although boats are frequently swamped and run ashore by gigantic surf, and hands are rubbed raw from miles and miles of paddling, the surf zone offers some relief: It's the only place in first phase where the instructors can't scream in your face.

At an Olympic-sized pool reserved for SEALs, students learn Red Cross lifesaving and drown-proofing, a technique that allows individuals to stay afloat and swim without the use of their arms and legs. In the drown-proofing practical, students are thrown in the pool, hands and feet tied together with parachute cord. They have to swim four hundred yards, retrieve a face mask from the bottom of the deep end with their teeth, then "tread water" for forty minutes—all of this while trussed up like Esther Williams in bondage.

Between runs, swims, and surf work, first-phase students take academic classes in advanced first aid, the history of naval special warfare, communications, beach reconnaissance, and cartography. Any grade below 3.0 is considered failing. Exhausted students who fall asleep during lectures are splashed awake with a wastebasket full of seawater and have a tear-gas grenade placed in their hands. The instructor then pulls the pin, requiring the sleepy student to keep his hand tightly on the grenade, holding the safety handle down to prevent the tear gas from going off.

The fourth week of first phase is Hell Week, which begins around midnight on Sunday and ends sometime the following Saturday. The first event is "Break Out," a daunting affair in which students are rousted from the barracks by instructors armed with concussion grenades, artillery simulators, and M-60 machine guns. Students rush about while smoke grenades billow, machine guns are fired, and a fire hose sprays water. Explosions rip the night as a contradictory series of orders and uniforms are announced. The net result is that students begin their weeklong ordeal with every piece of equipment and every scrap of uniform wet, sandy, and scattered in heaps. The event is designed to disorient, and it does. While explosions rock the formation, the bell clangs as shell-shocked students begin to quit.

During Hell Week, students are allowed from zero to three hours of sleep—the entire week. Events continue twenty-four hours a day for six days. Students run, swim, paddle, and generally get fucked about by three shifts of instructors who rotate in around the clock.

The class is again broken up into boat crews, and every event, called an "evolution," is a race. Students drag three-hundred-pound IBSs with them everywhere they go. It pays to be a winner: Boat crews who win an evolution such as the paddle around Coronado Island might be allowed a cup of coffee, chow earlier, or a twenty-minute nap on their boat. Those who finish last must do the evolution over again. Like the denizens of the goon squad, losing boat crews are hammered by the instructors.

The boats must constantly be ready for sea, that is, be in perfect operational order. Likewise the students. The task is nearly impossible; the instructors can always find a twisted life-jacket strap or an unbuttoned pocket. Then it's hammer time.

The constant running, paddling, and cold-water immersions require huge amounts of energy. Students burn upward of five thousand calories a day and are fed four meals: breakfast, lunch, dinner, and a midnight meal called "mid-rats." Students are not allowed to talk or doze off during meals. It is not unusual to watch students pass out facedown in their oatmeal. Those who face-plant are tossed out of the chow hall and into the surf zone.

With lack of sleep come hallucinations, and tempers and judgment fray. This is part of the process. Instructors watch carefully, pressing officers to lead and boat crews to work together. Lack of organization is not tolerated.

Each time a boat-crew member quits, his mates are left to pull his load, humping the three-hundred-pound boat through the evolutions with one fewer person. Everyone works harder to make up for the lost man, but the boat is slower, and that makes the instructors very cross. It's easy to see how the loss of a single individual could lead to an entire crew washing out. Hell Week is an object lesson in teamwork.

It is not unheard of for a class to lose 60 percent of its members during Hell Week alone. Very few classes come through the entire week without losing a single individual. These classes are awarded a "No Bell Prize," and their class number is engraved on a plaque on the BUD/S quarterdeck. As I write this, that plaque has perhaps four class numbers carved into it—out of the 280 classes that have graduated.

Of all the experiences a student will have at BUD/S, Hell Week is probably the most crucial. Students emerge with the realization that the human body is capable of ten times the output previously thought possible. There are few limits and no limitations to what a determined individual can accomplish. After Hell Week, the class is allowed to commission a T-shirt emblazoned with the logo of the Naval Special Warfare Training Command and the class number. If you can survive Hell Week, you'll probably survive the remainder of training.

After Hell Week injuries are feared more than the instructors. Little provision is made for the wounded, and there is no convalescent leave. Nor is the medical attention particularly fawning. Advice from the corpsmen in sick bay is usually "Take an aspirin and run on it." More than once that advice has been given to a student with a broken leg.

Those who survive Hell Week embark on the second phase of training, land warfare. Stopwatches tick as blindfolded students strip and reassemble a dozen varieties of pistol, assault rifle, and machine gun. Instruction in marksmanship is intense, and students learn long-distance shooting as well as quick kill, fire and maneuver, and counterambush. Hand-to-hand combat, the use of a knife, of a garrote, and sentry stalking are taught by men who have done it for real. Students study land navigation, small-unit tactics, briefing techniques, and hydrographic and land reconnaissance.

The phase culminates with four weeks on San Clemente Island, where students learn basic and advanced demolitions and conduct a weeklong "war," reconnoitering and interdicting a variety of targets on the island. Naturally, students train with real explosives and live ammunition.

The final phase of training is diving. Open- and closed-circuit scuba, underwater navigation, the use of underwater mines, maritime reconnaissance, and sneak attacks are taught, as well as the operation of submarine escape trunks.

It's been said that becoming a SEAL is a calling rather than a vocation. That may be true. BUD/S is not so much a battle of wills but a struggle against oneself. No amount of physical training could be enough to prepare you. Whether you start training as an accomplished triathlete or a professional bowler, you will come to grips with misery. The instructors are always there to push each individual beyond maximum. The battle is always to make a cold, wet, tired, and hungry body take another step, run another mile, or climb another rung of the ladder. Quitting is easy. All you have to do is ring the bell, and the pain will stop. The test is against oneself.

But as difficult as BUD/S is, as many students quit, as almost impossibly difficult as training is made by instructors, it is more difficult in the Teams. BUD/S is practice. SEAL operations in the real world are combat. If a student screws up in BUD/S, he has to hit the surf. If a SEAL screws up on a real-world operation, he gets turned into a pink vapor.

BUD/S has to be difficult. It is imperative that the only men who come into the Teams are those who can be counted on: men who are superbly conditioned, adapted to adversity, and have rigorously demonstrated determination and teamwork. This does not mean BUD/S puts out a bunch of robots. Far from it. This persistence and determination BUD/S inculcates is not blind. SEALs don't charge machine-gun nests. That's what the Marine Corps is for. Throughout training, students are taught to fight smart; to attack the enemy where he is weakest, not where he is strongest.

Insertion into an enemy's backyard may involve a three-mile underwater swim, a parachute jump from an airliner, or a five-day walk across glacier and mountain. Just getting to the target can often be an adventure. Getting out of an operational area with an enraged enemy in pursuit can be a nightmare. It is vital that every operator knows he can count on the man next to him. There is no "I" in "SEAL Team."

BUD/S is one of the few schools in the United States military where officers and enlisted men train together; the course and curriculum are the same. In the Green Berets, there are separate officer and enlisted courses. At BUD/S, an officer is assigned to oversee each phase of training, but the principal instruction is given by enlisted men. It can reasonably be said that the enlisted men pick the officers who will eventually lead them. It's not just the weak officers who are culled from training. The imperious, the impulsive, and the reckless will also find it impossible to graduate.

The naval special warfare community is the smallest of all the special operations forces, and the bond between officers and enlisted is tight. Platoons and assault elements usually function on a first-name basis. At the apex of the military's special operations outfits, the "military" is kept to a minimum.

At the end of training, our graduation was low-key. On a warm September morning, a small group gathered on the grinder of the BUD/S compound. A band played "Anchors Away," and we sat in folding chairs before the same podium Dick Roy had addressed us from six months earlier. There were no friends or relatives in attendance. Our names were called one by one, and we were each handed a certificate from the naval amphibious school. The certificates were definitely not suitable for framing. They stated simply that "the following individual [typed name] has completed the following course [BUD/S]." My diploma looked like it cost $1.25, but to me, it was the most precious piece of paper in the world.

We were officially BUD/S graduates, but we were not SEALs. Not yet. Ahead of us were army airborne school at Fort Benning and months of advanced operator training in our respective SEAL Teams. We would receive hundreds of hours of additional training and serve a yearlong probationary period before earning the gold trident of a Navy SEAL.

Until then we were FNGs: fuckin' new guys. Good-for-nothing goldbrick class-2001 bananas. But that was fine with me. That afternoon I received orders to report to the commanding officer, SEAL Team Four, aboard the Naval Amphibious Base, Little Creek, Virginia.

I was in the Teams, and I was loving life.

OPERATOR 156

THE NIGHT WAS stupefyingly black. No stars, no moon, and a thin cold rain was pissing out of the sky, water dripping from darkness as I lay at the side of the road, my weapon on safe, listening to the night sounds, pupils cranked open to max, waiting. Above, a single canopy of trees rustled as wind stirred through it. Gusts passed now and again, fluttering leaves down on us and onto the road. I was lying maybe twenty meters back from where the two-track narrowed and turned sharply east. My squad, eight shooters, was arrayed close by, each man lying with legs spread, toes of boots touching the heels of the men to right and left, comfort and communication in the opaque night. From the west, low groans of thunder threatened a downpour. We had been in position for almost three hours. Not one man moving and none speaking, a lethal coil waiting to be sprung.

Our ambush had been diagrammed on a chalkboard like a football play. Circles and arrows marked fields of fire, lines of advance, plans of retreat, order for movement, procedures of fire and maneuver, and designated teams to count, search, and later booby-trap the bodies of the dead. Set about a 90-degree turn in the road, two SEAL squads lay pressed into cover, forming the arms of an L. One squad was set up on the portion of road before the curve, and the second squad covered the turn and its egress. Two shooting pairs concentrated on the apex, aimed down and waiting to pour a cross fire into the enemy as they entered what we called "the box," the kill zone. Lone men were tucked up against trees behind each squad, rear security covering the backs of the ambush parties. Two other men, trip wires, were stationed ten yards up and down the road. It would be their job to warn the others of the quarry's approach, and then to seal the trap, cutting down anyone who tried to flee from or through the kill zone.

All ambushes are custom jobs, and this one was planned for a jeep and a truck and the men in them. Our trap was set miles inside the enemy's zone of control, and the countryside surrounding us was theirs—a home game for the bad guys and an away game for the good guys. Tonight's mission was described as direct action, and its venue was what staff gumbies euphemistically call a "nonpermissive environment." Nothing had been left to chance; our actions were scripted and the enemy's moves anticipated. A low ditch circumscribed the outside of the turn, and this depression was likely to be the first cover the ambushed would seek once the trap was sprung. We had placed four claymore mines in the ditch. The detonator wires snaked back to electronic initiators, called "clackers," laid by my right elbow. Tonight, for our unfortunate guests, there would be a sudden torrent of bullets, there would be a place of cover, and then a cross fire. The end would come in a fiery swarm of shrapnel. The violence would be multiphased, three-dimensional, and as perfect as we could make it.

I lifted the night-vision goggles hung around my neck and switched them on. The NVGs rendered a pale, strangely visible darkness, an incandescent night based on green and light green instead of black. They worked by amplifying ambient light, but our place of ambush was so dark that the image was snowy and the turn in the road seemed flat. In moonlight or even starlight, the NVGs would have revealed the forest as clear as day. Tonight was darker than technology. Looking through the NVGs was like putting your nose to the tube of a 1950s vintage TV set. The images were half focused, without depth or real contrast. I looked up the road, scanning in the direction from which we expected company. I could see very little. The road to the north was uniformly green and silent.

Then from the darkness came a flutter of diesel exhaust and the sounds of gears shifting. The faintest glimmer of headlights swept the road, and the noise of a big truck came closer. Fifty meters from our ambush, the truck and jeep stopped. My heart pounded as I listened to a vehicle door open and slam. The headlights angled over the turn and reflected into the softly falling rain. Hidden in the glare of the truck lights, men were talking, their silhouettes casting huge shadows into the trees above the place we waited.

Shit. Shit. Get back into the fucking trucks.

I watched as one man walked down the road toward us. Next to me, our M-60 gunner gently snapped the safety off his weapon. I clearly heard the sound of the lever shifting from safe to fire, a small click no louder than the patter of a raindrop. The man in the road was carrying an AK-47 slung over his shoulder; in his hand a small flashlight switched on. I lowered my head and pressed my body as deeply into the leaf cover as I could. The flashlight scanned the road surface—sharp turns and steep hills are obvious places for ambushes, and the man with the flashlight was checking the muddy roadbed for boot prints. I could feel the squad around me draw a collective breath. The flashlight beam feebly searched the turn in the road, and as it swung toward me, I placed my face down against the stock of my M-16. Human eyes, like those of animals, will give back reflected light—the classic rat eyes glowing in the darkness—and I averted my face as the beam swept over us. The light switched off, and the man trudged back toward the headlights. We had not been discovered.

Doors slammed again. In the back of the truck was a sound like a chain rattling. We heard the big diesel and jeep grind into gear and come slowly toward us, the truck first and the jeep some ten or fifteen feet behind. Their headlights shoved light up the tunnel of trees, illuminating them brightly, and I felt the twinge of my pupils contracting, eyes wide open for hours in perfect darkness suddenly pinched by an overabundance of light.

I let the truck pass down to the tree I knew marked the end of my squad. The jeep came on, and when it was just even with me, I rocked the safety back on my M-16 to auto and squeezed a long burst into the passenger window. Instantly, my squad opened fire, and the truck and jeep were exposed in strobing muzzle blasts, overlit and blinking like the red carpet at a Hollywood premiere. The noise was astounding, a tearing convulsion of exploding rifles and machine guns. Immediately, the bullets tore sparks from the metal bodies of the vehicles, and I could see from the hits that fire was concentrated on the cab of the jeep and the high canvas-covered bed of the truck, the places where the people were. Torn by fire, the truck slowed slightly. The jeep remained on the road and collided into the high rear bumper of the slowing truck. Then bullets from the second squad jagged through the two vehicles, the noise of their fire redoubling the astounding din of the ambush.

I reached forward on my weapon, closing my hand over the tube of the M-203 grenade launcher under the barrel of my rifle. I aimed down over the carrying handle on the M-16, nearly point-blank at the hood of the jeep. I pulled the trigger, and a 40-millimeter grenade popped from the tube. The grenade tore the canvas roof from the vehicle, blasting it to rags, and the jeep bucked and jumped backward, spinning ass first and coming to rest on its side, one headlight blown out and the other pointing crazily into the sky. The fusillade continued, its volume a perfect roar, each man of the two squads conscious to slow or speed up shooting as others reloaded or resumed firing. From the bottom of the L, a second set of explosions ripped the killing ground. Two armor-piercing grenades slammed into the front of the truck. The first round smashed the radiator and sent the hood sailing up into the trees above our heads. The second grenade punched through the shattered windshield and detonated in the truck's cab, blowing open both doors and starting an orange fire inside. Now ablaze, the truck lurched to a stop, half on and half off the two-track.

Perhaps forty seconds had elapsed since we began firing, and the noise and the torrent of bullets had remained almost constant, a testament to fire discipline.

I rolled onto my side and lifted the claymore clackers. I

dropped the wire safety catches and squeezed them simultaneously. The night exploded into deafening red flashes as the antipersonnel mines blew up by the roadside. Hundreds of steel balls were sprayed from each claymore, riddling the vehicles, tearing through the ditches, and ripping the tires from the jeep. The mines reached every place bullets could not. There was no place in the kill box not torn by steel or touched by fire.

The detonation of the mines was the signal for the second squad to shift fire, and they now aimed off the road, behind the vehicles and toward the inside of the turn. I stood and pushed my foot down on the men to my right and left. To yell in the overwhelming din would be futile. In the light of the burning truck, I signaled my squad to advance on line. Shooting from the hip, the first squad moved toward the road. Anyone fleeing would cross the two-track and stumble into the barrage laid down by the second squad. I watched as tracers ripped through the woods across from us—waist-high, banging through trees, denying cover, refuge, or escape. We reached the burning vehicles and saw no movement from the truck or the jeep.

Standing in the road, I thumbed a flare into my grenade launcher, aimed the weapon straight up, and pulled the trigger. The illumination round sailed into the sky, dragging behind it a shower of sparks. A flare ignited under a silk parachute and drifted down, casting a stark light over the wreckage. I shouted, "Cease fire," and the command was repeated up and down the line. The shooting stopped as though someone had thrown a switch. My ears rang; the night was perfectly, eerily still. The crickets, night birds, and seemingly even the rain had been silenced by the horrific noise of the ambush. For a long moment there was only the hissing of the flare drifting down from the sky.

The second squad materialized from their hiding places, and in the lurching light of the flare, I could see the gas tubes of their rifles glowing red hot through the vent holes. In the crazily pointed headlights, the men emerged, faces painted green and black and their eyes wide, almost yellow, jacked up, adrenaline-hyped, and perfectly helter-skelter. Someone grunted, "Yeah, man, I got some," like a redneck at a Molly Hatchet concert.

I looked around as I shoved a fresh mag into my rifle. The attack had been flawless, and the ruin of the vehicles was complete. The jeep was now upside down, the truck was burning off the side of the road, and almost every square foot of both was shot through by bullets or perforated by the deadly shrapnel of claymores.

I said, "Set security. Search team in." Two pairs of men came forward to count and search the dead, while the rest of the squads arrayed themselves up and down the road, reloading weapons, taking cover, ready to meet any of the gallant enemy attracted by the sounds of our ambush.

Then headlights snapped on up and down the road. I could see men standing in their glow, one lighting a cigarette. Not enemy but friendlies. They were members of the training department of SEAL Team Four. Our ambush had been a final evolution in advanced operator training, or AOT—the highly realistic scenarios that SEAL platoons go through before deployment. The members of the cadre (and that's what they were called, "cadres") watched the ambushed vehicles as we searched them. They had watched everything, our setup, our attack, and now they were clocking what was called "time on target." I bent down on hands and knees and looked into the upside-down jeep. There was a mannequin behind the steering wheel, the dummy head of a woman shot through the face by a 5.56-millimeter bullet. On the ground under the passenger seat was a cheap plastic briefcase stuffed with papers and maps. I dragged this free as my radio operator pulled the mannequin out of the jeep and laid it on the road.

The truck and the jeep had both been "driven" by dummies: Rather, the jeep had been towed behind the truck by a twenty-foot shot of chain. The road on this specially designed ambush range was tracked a foot deep; the wheels of both the truck and jeep rolled in wood-sided tracks cut into the road. The truck had been placed in first gear and allowed to creep forward on idle. Both vehicles contained only mannequins and paper silhouettes. Until the grenades smashed into them, the vehicles could only roll down the middle of the road, stuck like slot cars.

I handed the briefcase off to a shooter as one of the cadre shined a light into the back of the truck, then under and into the upside-down seats of the jeep. He was making sure each mannequin or silhouette had at least one bullet hole in it. Clean targets and untouched dummies were expected to be shot again, point-blank. These were called "security rounds."

Within two minutes both vehicles had been searched, all items of intelligence value had been gathered up, unwounded targets had been shot, and several of the mannequins were planted with pressure-sensitive booby traps, rude surprises for anyone sent to recover the bodies. This trick, placing booby traps under the dead, had been learned from the Viet Cong.

The squads collapsed onto the ambush site, formed a column, and we departed as the rain fell and the burning truck gushed smoke into the black night. Forty minutes later, we were extracted by helicopter and landed in the SEAL compound at a U.S. Army reservation somewhere deep in the hills of central Virginia. There we were debriefed, cleaned our weapons, and drank beer as the sun came up on the last day of sixteen solid weeks of training. I remember on this cold spring morning, I was beginning to feel like a real SEAL.

I WOULD NOT ARRIVE at SEAL Team Four until early December 1981. After graduation from BUD/S, I was one of several officers from 114 held at the Naval Amphibious Base, Coronado—the navy term is "stashed"—and we were once again to be guinea pigs. This time we were to be put through a new academic program intended to make us better special warfare officers. I was in a hurry to get to my new command, but in plain truth, as BUD/S graduates, we were of little use to anyone. We weren't even SEALs yet; we were 1180s, probationary naval special warfare officers. Tadpoles. Six months of BUD/S had succeeded only in making us physically invincible morons, and we had only touched on the skills and knowledge we would require to operate as SEALs. We were soon to get a glimpse of exactly how much we didn't know.

Monday morning following graduation, I was assigned TAD, temporary additional duty, to the naval amphibious school across the road from BUD/S. For the next two months, eight hours a day, I would study special operations planning and political warfare. The political warfare curriculum had previously been entitled "counterinsurgency studies," and the name was changed, apparently, when a San Diego reporter got ahold of the amphibious school's catalog and wrote an article comparing the program to the army's infamous School of the Americas. Political warfare was going to be a BUD/S of the brain, our lecturers promised us. The course work came on fast and furious, and the assigned reading was voluminous. All of it was fascinating.

On the first morning of class, an instructor wrote two Japanese Kenji characters on the board, *"Bunbu Itchi."* It was a maxim of the Samurai, translating roughly to "pen and sword in accord." We were here to learn that fighting harder meant fighting smarter. Before we became pilgrims, we would be students.

We were assigned to read sociological works on peasant societies: Karl Marx's *Grundrisse,* and the impenetrable *Das Kapital*—the book and the Idea possibly the biggest shams ever perpetrated against mankind. If we were not made into good communists, we were at least made conversant in dialectical materialism. Our instructors were careful to make us understand the motivation of communist insurgencies and to see the armed struggle as progressively inspired. Whether or not we agreed with the process or the result, our enemies were trying to build a better life. Marxism we dismissed as an unworkable and oppressive mechanism of governance, but it was seen as a vital tool of sociological and historical analysis. The people we were fighting really *believed* this shit. In order to defeat them, we had to understand what made them fight.

We read books on guerrilla warfare by its master practitioners, Mao Tse-tung, Lin Biao, and Che Guevara. We wrote commentaries on articles by Ho Chi Minh and military treatises by General Vo Nguyen Giap, the commander of the North Vietnamese army. We studied the phased attacks of the Viet Cong during the Tet Offensive of 1968. Our instructors, several of whom had fought in Tet, observed that the Pyrrhic attacks of the Viet Cong were encouraged by the North Vietnamese. Tet was a military defeat for the North, but it was the Viet Cong who died, and that was the intended result: The cynical goal of the North was the reduction of the Viet Cong. Tet was intended to liquidate the VC, the North's subordinate and less ideologically reliable partners. Our instructors were frank about American failures in Vietnam. The American Phoenix Program, which effectively decapitated Viet Cong leadership, actually played in to North Vietnamese hands. The inability of American leadership to discern what was happening on the ground was also discussed bluntly. America didn't just lose the war in Southeast Asia; we actually helped the North Vietnamese win it. Any doubt that the Viet Cong were allies of the NVA was put to the lie after the fall of Saigon, when tens of thousands of Viet Cong fighters, cadres, and intellectuals were rounded up by the North and sent to reeducation camps.

Our studies eventually brought us closer to home. Latin America can probably be considered the world's testing lab for political warfare, and we devoted weeks to the causes and effects of *La Revolución.* We were introduced to Catholic revolution theology and the economic ramifications of oligarchy in Mexico, Panama, El Salvador, Colombia, and Nicaragua. We studied the operations of Pancho Villa in Mexico and Augusto Sandino in Nicaragua. We examined Peru's ongoing tragedy, a Maoist insurgency in a virulent modern guise, the *Sendero Luminoso,* or Shining Path. The revolution in Cuba made concrete the power of the Idea. Only eleven men survived Fidel Castro's initial landing on the west coast of the island. In four years Castro succeeded in taking down the best-armed military dictatorship in Latin

America: no mean feat. In his triumph we were made to see that revolution was what these guys did. And they did it well.

Central America was then heating up, and we were brought up to speed on the burgeoning rebellion in El Salvador. Later, one of our instructors, SEAL commander Al Shoffel-berger, would be assassinated on the streets of San Salvador. We read *The Minimanual of the Urban Guerrilla* by Brazil-ian revolutionary Carlos Marighella; we took him at his word that he was answering Che Guevara's call to lay many Vietnams at the feet of Uncle Sam. What is now called nar-coterrorism was then only an emerging trend. We studied the organization and methodology of the Medellín and Cali drug cartels. Examined in detail were several assassinations and bombings credited to the druggies and their emerging al-liance with FARC, *Fuezera Armas Revolucionario de Co-lombia,* the Revolutionary Armed Forces of Colombia.

Terrorism, we were taught, was a tactic, a facet of a greater purpose, not a strategy or an end in itself. Terrorism is war-fare waged by the powerless against the innocent. It is in the nature of asymmetrical conflict that terrorist acts are prov-ocations, whether the deed is a hand grenade in a market square or the destruction of the World Trade Center. The acts are outrageous, bloody, and violent because they are meant to shock. Terrorist acts are to be seen as armed propaganda, pinpricks intended to resonate far beyond their military sig-nificance. Every act of terror is intended to have political consequences. In every case, calculated atrocities extract a disproportionate response from the oppressor. The enemy has different names: Yankee Imperialist, Neocolonialist, Cap-italist Exploiter, Infidel, or Great Satan. We were reminded that the Perennial Foe was us. Terrorism, the instructors drilled into us, must always be examined in the context of politics; Trotsky said it best: "Terrorism is political theater."

Again we studied the masters. We absorbed selected passages by Marx, Lenin, and Mao on the dynamics and po-litical utility of terrorism. Middle Eastern terrorist organi-zations were investigated, including Black September and the Palestine Liberation Organization in all its aliases and guises. We examined several European terrorist organizations, all of them then thriving: Bader Meinhof, the Red Army Faction, the Basque ETA, and the Italian Red Brigades. Each, we were told, was either under the operational control of the Soviet KGB or had links for logistical support. Why would the KGB back such nihilistic and obviously criminal gangs? Orthodox Marxism taught that violence was the only legitimate mechanism of political change. And this dictum had permeated the world's struggles of liberation. In geographical areas of strategic interest, wars of liberation were proxy struggles between East and West, one puppet fighting another, and it was all about power. This was the Great Game. If we understood that, we would understand the process.

Having been made familiar with the causes and types of revolution, we were introduced to the triad of their remedy: tactical action, psychological warfare, and civil affairs. These ongoing and overlapping spheres translated roughly to: kick their asses; convince the world you're doing wonderful things; and quietly right the political and economic wrongs that sent the guerrillas into the hills in the first place. These processes would later coalesce into a term and methodology called "nation building."

Our final three weeks were spent in the special warfare operation planning course, a ball-buster of logistics, planning, and paperwork. Almost any operation you could think of had already been conducted, planned, or studied in detail, and we were introduced to the library of naval warfare publications for special operations. The NWPs were cookbooks for a variety of missions we had carried out in our "war" on San Clemente Island: sneaking and peeking, hijacking, kidnapping, bombing, and assassination. Of course, the military likes to euphemize, and these dirty tricks were individually called such prosaic terms as "reconnaissance and surveillance," "vessel board," "seizure and search," "personnel interdiction," "actions against command infrastructure," and "maritime sabotage." The missions were studied under the rubric "operations other than war."

We prepared detailed time-action-location studies, called "phase diagrams," of famous special operations. Chief among these was the Norwegian partisan raid on the Norsk Hydro heavy-water plant at Telemark during World War II. This op, a classic in the annals of unconventional warfare, is arguably the one operation that denied Nazi Germany the atomic bomb. We studied Allied defeats as well as successes, looking at Operation Eiche (Oak), the SS commando raid that liberated Mussolini; and the war history of the Italian 10th Light Flotilla in the Mediterranean—minisub and human-torpedo attacks that sank 86,000 tons of Allied warships and 130,000 tons of merchant shipping. We applied phased diagrams to the present and the past. Our class received a classified debrief on the American special operations debacle at Desert One. Code-named Operation Eagle Claw, the events at Desert One became a synonym for catastrophe. A top-secret attempt by the United States to free fifty-three American hostages held in Tehran, the rescue party was cobbled together from army, air force, and navy units. On the night of April 25, 1980, eight rescuers were killed and four seriously injured in a fiery collision at a desert refueling position. The wreckage of a C-130 and several helicopters were left in the Iranian desert as the operation was aborted and the hostage rescue teams hastily withdrawn. The embassy hostages were to remain in Iranian custody until January 21, 1981. The operation was a political and military disaster of the first order. The lessons of Desert One were these: First, everything that can go wrong will go wrong—plan for mistakes; second, it is not sufficient that the men survive the plan—the plan must also survive the blunders of men.

We were taught how to assemble a mission backward, starting at the successful completion of an operation and working in retrograde to identify critical nodes. We learned how to plan contingencies, to coordinate joint and combined operations, and to conduct a full mission profile: tasking, planning, rehearsal, insertion, infiltration, reconnaissance, actions at the objective, exfiltration, extraction, and debriefing.

Each of us departed the courses with fifty pounds of books.

Special warfare was not a vocation, we were told, it was a profession. The course work was intended only as an intro- duction. We were expected to keep up our study of the liter- ature, tactics, and science. It was fully expected of us to become scholars and specialists. I came away realizing that I didn't know my ass from a hole in the ground. We were in the big leagues now.

After the amphibious school came a less intellectual chal- lenge—learning to jump out of airplanes. Although the navy then had its own parachute school in Lakehurst, New Jersey, BUD/S graduates are sent to Fort Benning, Georgia, to the army's airborne school. There, the army trains its several va- rieties of paratroopers, and airborne school is the apogee of many a young soldier's career; for BUD/S graduates, jump school is a cakewalk and a time to get a little froggy. Mem- bers of all branches train at Fort Benning, and among the stu- dent battalions are recon marines, air force pararescuemen, cadets and midshipmen from West Point and Annapolis, and even a few coastguardsmen. But no one raises hell at jump school like the navy, and the army knew this. Like prisoners of war, officer and enlisted BUD/S graduates were segre- gated in the hope that the tadpoles would not get together and act in a coordinated fashion.

When I arrived at Benning, my orders were stamped, and I was told to report to the naval forces liaison officer, a no- bullshit marine major. I entered his office and saluted. He didn't take his feet off the desk. He said to me simply, "No fucking around while you're here, Mr. Pfarrer. No dicking with the instructors, no pranks, no sabotaging vehicles, no de- facement of government property. I will tolerate no behavior prejudicial to the conduct of good order." This was a very ma- rine term, and one we both knew came directly from Article 134 of the Uniform Code of Military Justice: the General Ar- ticle, the one they would charge you with if they needed to charge you with *something*.

The major went on to mention the shenanigans effected by the last several classes of BUD/S graduates. They'd hung BEAT ARMY banners from the 250-foot jump towers, plastered instructors' cars with bumper stickers that said GAY AND PROUD, swiped street signs, and painted HIRE THE HANDICAPPED on the parking lot of an officers' club. The major was due to transfer in four weeks, and he wanted a nice quiet tour. He told me that if he didn't finish in peace, he was going to refer to a very short list of suspects. We both knew that if I failed to graduate from airborne training, or if I was rolled back for any reason, I would be stripped of my precious designator, 1180. If I lost those four numbers, I would be sent, horror of frigging horrors, to the fleet. From the way the major wrinkled his low, receding forehead, I could tell he would like nothing better than to see me reassigned to a nice gray destroyer. I promised to be on my best behavior and saluted. He did not and told me to get a haircut as I left the office.

SEALs often describe jump school as two days of training intensely crammed into three weeks. There is a lot of bullshit, all of it mindless, and none of it could make a BUD/S graduate break a sweat. After six months on Coronado's Silver Strand, whatever the airborne instructors could throw at us was of little consequence. They gave out push-ups only ten at a time, there was no surf torture, and besides, in three weeks we would wake up back in the nav, not the dog-face army. For three weeks we just thought of ways to screw with the airborne instructors, a posse of hard-ass paratrooper noncoms collectively referred to as Black Hats.

We jogged, did PT, jumped off platforms, towers, and aircraft mock-ups. We practiced parachute landing falls, called PLFs, endlessly. We did front, back, right, and left PLFs. We got hassled and yelled at. The curriculum can be summed up thus: Stand up, hook up, shuffle to the door, jump right out, and count to four. Midway through the second week of training, it occurred to me that I was actually getting fat.

The Black Hats did their best to hammer us, and their humor was legendary. My favorite Black Hat expression was "Get on your face, Navy, and quit lookin' at me like I owe you money." Push-ups were the primary attention getter, unless we were wearing parachutes; then the preferred punishment was to "beat your boots." Beating your boots meant to bend at the knees and slap the leather of your jump boots; this exercise was done in sets of ten. It was supposed to be unpleasant when a student was geared up in forty pounds of parachute. The punishments were laughable, and the Black Hats knew it.

Mike Heyward was the only officer from 114 to be assigned to my battalion; about a dozen other characters from our class were scattered around in different companies. The Black Hats knew we were beyond whatever pain they thought they could dish out. While our fellow students moped around the barracks after hours putting moleskin on their ouchies, the members of 114 grouped up and went on fourteen-mile runs.

In the second week, airborne students jump from increasingly higher platforms and towers, culminating in actual parachute drops from 250-foot mock towers. Why they are called "mock towers," I never did figure out. They seemed pretty real to me. And goddamn high, too. During mock-tower drops, the apex of the student's parachute is hooked to a cable and drawn twenty-five stories up into the air. The parachute is stopped at the top of the tower in a round metal cage. The cable is popped, releasing the canopy, allowing the parachute to inflate, and dropping the student. The fledgling parachutist floats to earth, attempting to steer for a landing in the field below. All of this is made more interesting by a graphic demonstration of parachute malfunctions courtesy of the Black Hats. Before student battalions start their tower drops, they watch as a dozen life-sized dummies are dropped from the towers, each with malfunctioning parachutes. The malfunctions have spiffy nicknames—Line Overs, Mae Wests, Cigarette Rolls, and Totals—and all of them are lethal. The malfunctioned canopies delivered the dummies into the ground at about a hundred miles an hour while loudspeakers in the tower blared "Another One Bites the Dust." It was all very droll.

The last week of airborne school is jump week. Monday through Friday, five day jumps and a night jump are interspersed with six-mile runs to identify people with broken legs. Students jump by battalions. We donned our parachutes in cavernous warehouselike buildings. Black Hat jumpmasters checked our rigs, making sure we were buckled, tightened down, and fastened correctly, and then we were jogged out onto the airfield and shoved aboard a dozen C-141 jet transports.

The first jump is memorable. Students are hustled aboard the aircraft by shouting Black Hats and packed tightly into rows of nylon seats. Six minutes from the drop zone, students are commanded to stand and hook static lines to an overhead cable. Pressed close to the man (or woman) in front of you, the group of jumpers, called a "stick," approaches the door. The lead student assumes a semicrouching position, chin up, hands on the door frame, awaiting the tap from the Black Hat serving as jumpmaster. "Putting your knees in the breeze," this is called. When the plane arrives over the drop zone, the jumpmaster kicks out the lead jumper, and Black Hats at the back of the stick start shoving the line of jumpers toward the door. These initial jumps can hardly be called voluntary. Channeled down the aisles of the plane, pushed forward by the jumpers and Black Hats behind me, the first thing I knew, I was outside the aircraft and falling through hot jet wash. I counted to four, like I had been taught, and was jerked back to the real world by the tug of my parachute opening.

Outside the airplane was an astonishing sight, the sky filled as far as I could see with parachutes. The C-141s flew in echelons, dropping planeload after planeload of jumpers. Midair collisions were to be feared, and they were made more likely given that all of the several hundred parachutists in the sky that morning were on their first jump. I steered into the wind, executed a dynamite PLF, and made it to the ground without giving or receiving injury. The next day we did it again.

Friday of jump week is the graduation drop. Following a successful jump, we would form up by battalions on the drop zone and receive our silver wings. After the ceremony we'd be free to go, and I had leave coming. Sitting on the tarmac in my parachute, I was in a hurry to get it over with. From across the runway I saw two figures coming at me, wearing parachutes but carrying their helmets. Only instructors were allowed on the flight line without their helmets strapped down, so I paid little attention until the two men walked over to the head of my stick. It was Keller and Pearlman, both classmates from 114.

"Hey, Mr. Pfarrer, there you are." Keller grinned.

"We thought we'd come over and jump with you," Pearlman said. In a definite big-city move, they'd taken off their helmets and sauntered past maybe three hundred students to find me. Everyone thought they had to be instructors, including the Black Hats.

Keller stared at the student jumpers behind me. "Make a hole," he growled. They did.

We jogged aboard our airplane and took off for the graduation jump, the Black Hats none the wiser. Six minutes out we stood up, hooked up, and Keller stepped in front of me as he snapped his static line to the cable. "Watch this," he said.

When the light turned green, we began our mad rush for the door. The Black Hat standing by the hatch was tapping students as they jumped and dramatically yelling, "GO! GO! GO!" over the roar of the engines.

The stick of jumpers shuffled toward the door and dropped from sight. Pearlman was the first of our trio to reach the jumpmaster. Instead of pushing back his static line and assuming the correct airborne body position for exit, Pearlman thumbed his nose at the Black Hat. Before the disconcerted sergeant could react, Pearlman was out the door and gone. But Pearlman was the diversion. Keller was the hit. He came even with the door, reached out, and snatched the jumpmaster's hat off his head. In the blink of an eye, Keller had leaped from the plane, clutching his trophy. I was next to the hatch, and to the everlasting credit of the jumpmaster, I heard him yelling, "NAVY! COME BACK WITH MY DAMN HAT!"

I fell out of the door laughing my ass off.

On the drop zone it was the usual chaos, but the aircraft

had radioed the DZ crew and told them what happened. I did my best to blend with the crowd, but I was quickly located and submitted to the indignity of a stern questioning.

"Get over here, Navy!" one of the Black Hats snapped at me as I deposited my parachute in the back of a truck. I jogged over.

I smiled innocently. "Yes, Sergeant Airborne?" While at Fort Benning, we were supposed to yell "airborne" after we said anything. Not just "airborne" but "air-BORNE!" It was supposed to sound like "air-BONE." Since it was meant to show our enthusiasm, we complied in the blandest manner possible.

"Get on your face, Navy, and give me about one hundred thousand push-ups."

"Yes, Sergeant Airborne." I dropped down and started pumping them out.

"What do you know about a stolen hat?" The sergeant's eyes narrowed.

I continued to do push-ups. "What color hat, Sergeant Airborne?" I asked.

"Navy, my damn name is Sergeant. Airborne! Sergeant, period. Airborne! Not Sergeant Airborne."

"Airborne, Sergeant Airborne." I grinned.

I did push-ups for a while, and they eventually found Pearlman and Keller. By then Mike Heyward had the stolen ball cap stuffed into his pants. They questioned and searched us individually as we passed the hat off. The Black Hats always grabbed the wrong frog at the wrong time and were never any the wiser. Finally, we formed up by battalions on the drop zone and received the silver wings of an airborne paratrooper. The sergeant who'd questioned me about the hat pinned my wings on.

"This don't mean nothin', Navy," he said as he punched the prongs of the wings through my uniform and into my chest. "Now you ain't nothin' but a five-jump chump."

"If you ain't airborne, you ain't shit," I said.

"You're damn right," the sergeant growled as he walked

away. My meaning, I believe, was lost on my army colleague.

But the sergeant was right—we were rookies. The army called them "silver wings"; in the navy they were referred to as "lead wings." We would have to make ten jumps into water to earn our gold navy jump wings. It dulled the luster of our graduation somewhat. But we were finally on our way to our respective teams, and if you should happen to be reading this, Sergeant Airborne, we still have your goddamn hat.

I ARRIVED AT SEAL TEAM FOUR in my dress blue uniform, orders and personnel file under my left arm, fifteen minutes prior to officers' call, precisely as specified in my *Book of Service Etiquette, Third Edition*. I was ushered into the XO's office. Lieutenant Commander Jon Wallace was a red-haired, ass-chewing, no-bullshit officer, a decorated Vietnam platoon commander, and the men of SEAL Four looked up to him. He was an operator, and even though his job kept him behind a desk most of the time, he took every chance he could to get out into the field. I entered the office, and he closed the door behind me.

"Sit," he said. I found a chair, and he thumbed my file. "How do I pronounce your name?" he asked.

"Far-er," I said.

The XO looked me over. "Did you go to jump school?"

"Yes sir," I answered.

"Where are your jump wings?"

I was not wearing the detested lead wings. Adorning my uniform was all the fruit salad I rated—an expert pistol and an expert rifleman's ribbons. "I was waiting to earn my gold wings, sir," I said.

"Until then, wear your lead wings."

"Aye-aye, sir."

"What would you like to do at the command, Mr. Pfarrer?"

"I'd like to join a platoon, sir."

"So would I," the XO said. "So would I."

I was assigned to the Operations Department, and I would also occasionally work directly for Jon Wallace in a capacity that my fellow junior officers referred to as "the XO's out basket." I would start my SEAL career as the lowliest of the low, a headquarters puke. My disappointment was compounded when the Team mustered at quarters that morning. The uniform was PT gear, cool-guy blue sweat suits emblazoned with the individual's operator number and "ST-4." I was the only person in the formation wearing a uniform, and dress blues at that. After mustering the platoons, the XO introduced me as a freshly minted ensign, just checking aboard from BUD/S. He smirked and said that he hoped the Team would make me feel welcome. They did.

I was grabbed by about fifteen very athletic individuals and carried bodily to the dip tank, half of a jet-engine packing canister filled with water and used to check diving rigs for leaks. I struggled, but someone in the crowd reached out and calmly grabbed me by the scrotum. They twisted hard, and I calmed down pronto. I'd had my first lesson in SEAL Team hostage handling. They threw me in, and I broke through a quarter inch of ice as I splashed under. My hat had come off during the struggle, and as I surfaced, sputtering, the biggest dude I'd ever seen in my life tossed my cover in after me. Six-five, maybe 250 pounds of muscle, "Baby Zee" was the leading petty officer of the Training Department. He looked like a cross between Conan the Barbarian and the Creature from the Black Lagoon.

"Welcome aboard, sir," he said.

I dripped through the supply building and was issued uniforms and kit. The chief petty officer behind the cage hardly gave me a look as I signed for my equipment, web gear, ammo pouches, backpacks, wet suits, masks, swim fins, and all the other goodies that would eventually make me a frogman. Although I was not yet assigned to a platoon, I was issued PT gear with my operator number, 156. I marked it proudly on my gear, the numbers 156 used instead of my name to demark my equipment and the front of my locker. I felt an odd, simple delight to finally own a number.

As I stuffed gear into my locker, I was reunited with Rick James, my classmate from 114. Rick had missed out on the paper chase I'd gone through after graduation, and reported directly to the team. Having previously served as a para-trooper, he was spared the ignominy of reattending jump school. Also among the wardroom was Frank "Giff" Gif-fland, who was class leader of 113, the BUD/S class gradu-ating immediately before ours. Frank had been my neighbor in the BOQ back in Coronado, and we were friends. Rick and Frank looked at the puddle dripping from my best uni-form. I was relieved to hear that their welcomes had been identical to mine.

In the regular navy, sailors do not generally grab officers and shove them into dip tanks. It happens even less often with the executive officer watching and grinning. The Team's welcome was a message. We were officers, but we were FNGs, bananas, and we would be treated as nonentities until we proved that we deserved better. The community of naval special warfare was a meritocracy. We who were expected to lead would have to prove that we were worth following. We were all keenly aware that we were not yet SEALs; we were on probation, and if we failed to measure up, we would be gone.

I settled into my job, mostly paperwork, and I was soon able to carry out routine tasks with intense supervision. Working with me in the ops shop was Master Chief Mike Boynton, a gentle bear of a man, and he treated me with the patience of a saint. This particular saint had a stack of rib-bons that stretched from Little Creek all the way to the Mekong River: Bronze Stars, Purple Hearts, and a Silver Star, all piled on top of a couple of drawers of campaign medals and unit citations. The crowning glory of his decora-tions was a gold Special Warfare Badge—the true object of my lust.

One day the master chief caught me gawking at his rib-bons.

"Quit eye-fucking me, sir," he said.

I did my best to ride along on every training evolution leaving the compound, and Master Chief Boynton graciously covered my ass by doing my paperwork, often putting in extra time to allow me to get out and operate. I tagged along with platoons as they conducted sneak attack and swimmer operations in Little Creek Cove. I took diving supervisor training, became a rappel and fast-rope master, demolition supervisor, swam beach recons, and learned the art and craft of cartography. I did everything I could to get out from behind the desk, and it was the master chief who made that possible.

Many of the training cadre, like Master Chief Boynton, were high-time Vietnam operators, men who had fought in the Rug Sat Special Zone and the Mekong Delta, and from these men we learned skills and tricks small and large. There were new equations to master, not just the mathematics of demolition problems or the mixture of breathing gases in closed-circuit diving rigs. The cadre taught us that SEALs operate in a different polarity, in a different ethos, and in a different world. SEALs embrace what other people fear. Operators seek out bad terrain, shitty weather, and big-sea states. SEALs occupy the margins, ecological niches abandoned by humans: hard jungle, glacier, swamp, desert, blue water, and the surf zone.

In the course of my first months at the Team, night would become day and day would become night. Complex evolutions would first be practiced in daylight, but we operated almost exclusively at night. In darkness things were done by touch, by feel, and by instinct honed in hundreds of missions, operations, insertions, and extractions. The cadre taught how to "see" at night, looking around objects and not directly at them, maximizing our eyes' natural concentrations of rods, the structures in our eyes best able to process contrast. Moonlight became, for us, broad daylight. The darkness was not just a shield and cloak, the night became our sovereign territory.

"Fear the darkness," Baby Zee used to say, "for I am in it."

Word up, motherfucker.

Patrols were inserted into the middle of the Great Dismal Swamp, a very aptly named piece of real estate, and made to traverse kilometers of cypress bog, saw grass, and canal.

Sometimes we patrolled into the belly of the beast, one platoon against another in a big boys' game of hide-and-seek. The first team to locate the other would be extracted by helicopter. The losers had to walk out. In the Teams, like at BUD/S, it paid to be a winner. In other exercises, patrols laid up by the side of the intracoastal waterway and counted barge and push-boat traffic, photographing each tow and lighter that passed, noting boat names, registration numbers, type of cargo, visible crew, etc. This data was expected to be presentable immediately on extract, a nontrivial task when you have spent two days immersed in water up to your neck.

Bad weather became good weather; rain, sleet, and cold were our accomplices. Bad weather made the enemy pissy and miserable, and the enemy's vulnerability was always our strength. We learned to live, hide, and operate in places no one wanted to be. Sometimes when we were extracted by helicopter, I would look down as we flew off over miles of trackless swamp and couldn't believe that we had been *in* there . . . not just in there, Mom, but in there at *night*.

The cadre habituated us to the chaos of combat. In an event called a Monster Mash, operators would run five miles, swim two, emerge from the surf zone, and pair up with a shooting partner. After a brief sprint across beach sand, shooting pairs would run the gauntlet. Alternating hauling each other in a fireman's carry, the pair would traverse a section of dune laid with det cord (plastic explosive cast into "ropes"), smoke grenades, and half-pound blocks of TNT. As the pair struggled past, the explosives were cranked off within feet of the trail. The close detonations were mind-numbing. The gauntlet was followed by a quarter-mile dash to the rifle range, where individual operators would have to assemble an AK-47 rifle, then lock and load and shoot for score at a series of silhouette targets two hundred meters away. Pumped out from the run and swim, jacked up by the explosions and smoke, hitting the targets was at first almost impossible. In all of the training, there was method and purpose. We were being conditioned to overcome fatigue and the not always salutary effects of adrenaline. In my first months at the Team, the days passed like weeks and the weeks passed like days.

One Friday afternoon I pattered back to my desk, dripping in my wet suit, fresh from a water jump off Cape Henry. It was almost quitting time, and I'd left a pile of work on my desk. I got back to find that the master chief had done it all: drafted messages, written memos, forwarded reports. It was work that I had expected would take me all weekend.

"Jesus Christ. Soaking wet. Where have you been, sir?" he asked.

Obviously, I hadn't been out dancing. "Water drop," I said. "What happened to the stuff I left on my desk?"

"Fairies got it," he said. "Officer fairies, 'cause there ain't no such thing as chief petty officer fairies." I smiled. The master chief looked at me. "How many jumps is that?" he asked.

"Ten," I said.

Master Chief Boynton ambled toward me, unsnapping the gold navy wings he wore below his ribbons. "Here," he said, "you're gonna be needing some of these." He handed me his wings. "Before you go gettin' all misty-eyed, I probably own a hundred pairs of these. They don't cost very much, so don't go writing me a thank-you note. I was just gettin' tired of looking at your nasty-ass army lead wings." He walked out.

Navy jump wings cost five dollars at the uniform shop. But the gift meant a hell of a lot to me. Mike Boynton was a frogman's frogman, the corporate knowledge of the team, an *operator.*

Mike is gone now, but I still have those wings.

MOBILE, FLEXILE, AND HOSTILE

SENIOR CHIEF JOHN JAEGER did not have much use for new guys, and he did not care too much for officers, either. The one thing that annoyed him more than anything else was new-guy officers, and it was into his tender care that we were delivered when we formally started AOT in the spring. It seemed a very SEAL thing to do to assign a man who would not suffer fools as the leading chief of the Training Department. It cannot be said that the senior chief was a patient man. There was an incredible amount to teach us, and he was in a hurry to do so. Training with the senior chief, one always got the impression that this would all be going a lot faster if we weren't *so fucking stupid*.

Senior Chief was a red-faced, thickset man in his early forties. He'd done several tours in Vietnam as an M-60 gunner for SEAL Team One, and he was unapologetic about the fact that he loved war. The senior chief seemed to have a trace of a German accent, although this was not the most peculiar thing about his speech. He had a sort of verbal tic: He constantly used "or so" as an appositive. Any noun or verb was followed by "or so." He'd say things like "Get your ass over here before I shoot you, *or so*." Or "Youse guys are dumber than a bag of hammers, *or so*."

It was rumored that he was born in Germany during World War II, at a Lebensborn camp where SS men impregnated specially selected Aryan Uber-fräuleins. I heard the story that he was adopted after the war and later orphaned by U.S. Army parents. I knew for sure only that he grew up in a series of foster homes in the Midwest. Even after I came to know him well, I never asked about his German birth. I mean, really, what do you say to someone? "I heard you were born in a Nazi genetic experiment"?

Physically, the senior chief did not make much of an impression, but in the field he was tireless. He operated on about ten hours of sleep a week, and he made a point of winning the command's weekly two-mile swim. To the chagrin of many of our triathletes, John Jaeger usually crossed the finish line first, rolling onto his back, kicking his flippers, and smoking a cigarette he'd pull out of a plastic bag in his wet suit. If anyone dared to criticize his smoking, John would hold forth on nuclear war: "When the apocalypse comes, there's gonna be nothing but smoke and dust. All you granola-eating, nonsmoking motherfuckers are gonna be coughing, wheezing, and whining while I take over what's left, *or so.*"

I never doubted him for a second.

I first met the senior chief after a parachute drop into Fort A. P. Hill, a sprawling army preserve in central Virginia. The place was vast, hundreds of square miles of artillery ranges, woodland, marshland, lakes, streams, and hills. We'd parachuted in with full field gear, weapons, and ammo. On the drop zone we were met by Baby Zee and a few of the other training petty officers. We were not told where the SEAL camp was located; this being our first training deployment, we had no way of even guessing. We were each handed an eight-digit grid coordinate. The cadre told us that at our coordinates we would each find an ammunition can. In the can would be a second eight-digit grid coordinate. These coordinates would lead us to the SEAL camp. Some people were sent to road junctions, some to hilltops. Some were sent north and some south. I looked at my map and plotted my first coordinate. It was in the middle of a swamp. That swamp was six kilometers from where I now stood. Humping my pack and rifle, I took out over the hills.

Our navigation was to be conducted by handheld compass only, no GPS. The ammunition cans for which we searched were each about the size of a fat lady's pocketbook. They were painted green. The woods were green. Everything was green, and my can was hidden in a bog. When I got there, the swamp was green, too. Still, I had always prided myself on my navigational skills, and I was confident I'd find my cans. I counted my paces, followed contour lines, and walked a magnetic bearing straight through a waist-deep morass. I located can number one directly on my route of march, hanging from a cypress tree. I opened the lid and found the slip of paper with my next set of coordinates. They were at a road junction to the east—four clicks back the way I had just come.

It was obvious that we were getting screwed with. I had no idea how many cans I'd have to find before I found the camp. It was now almost noon, so I started to jog. I found my remaining eight cans and covered another twenty clicks, twelve miles, before I arrived at the SEAL camp, well after dark. Though I'd run most of the way across country, I was the third man in. I had been given the longest course.

As the other students tromped in, we settled into camp. It was not much to look at: a series of mobile-home bodies covered with camouflage netting. The trailers had electricity, but inside were plywood shells filled with bunk beds. There were windows but no screens or glass. I selected a bunk, hung my pack, and spread my sleeping bag out on the stained mattress. Baby Zee told me not to get too comfortable—we wouldn't be spending much time in the trailers.

I met Senior Chief Jaeger standing around the camp's fire. I thought I was pretty cool because I'd jumped in carrying an insulated cup and an empty coffee can in my pack to use for heating water and preparing MREs (meals, ready to eat). I noticed that the senior chief had a coffee can, too. He was sipping a beer and watching the can by the edge of the flames. Every now and then he used the cutting end of a pair of demolition cap crimpers to rotate the can in the flames.

"I see you got a coffee can, *or so,* Mr. Pfarrer," he said.

"Yes, Senior Chief."

"Whatcha gonna use it for?" he asked.

"Boiling water," I answered.

"Oh."

It was then that I noticed the top of the senior chief's coffee can was covered with aluminum foil. As I waited for my water to boil, I caught a whiff of something delicious. My can was boiling water, but the senior chief's rig was a Dutch oven. In John's coffee can was a pair of quail stuffed with wild onions and freshly picked morels. In a plastic bowl beside him was a salad made from wild watercress and cattail root. Senior Chief knew how to live off the land. He was a scrounge par excellence, and I would later watch him gather delicacies, munchies, and just plain weird stuff in every ocean and environment around the world. Seaweed, conch, tiny wild strawberries, sassafras roots, yucca plants, fish, birds, snakes, hickory nuts, and wild pineapples. All of it would end up in his pot and would emerge a marvel of camp cuisine. Before me was Euell Gibbons with a machine gun.

I poked at my beans and franks while the senior chief ate quail and drank beer. The fire crackled and snapped.

"How'd you like your walk, *or so*?" he asked.

"It was okay," I said.

"If you liked today, sir, you're gonna freakin' love tomorrow."

I watched him lick his fingers. He was right. I loved tomorrow, and the next day.

Senior Chief still didn't like FNGs, and it took him a while to tolerate me. In my AOT section was another officer, a guy we called Dwight Light. Dwight was an enthusiastic and personable ensign who graduated four classes behind me in 118. Dwight's blond hair was the color of snow, and that's not necessarily a good thing. While a bandana was sufficient to cover my reddish locks on operations, Dwight's hair made him stand out in darkness like a flashlight. Through night-vision goggles, Dwight glowed like a luminous object. And that's how he got his name.

Dwight Light and I slowly came to realize that only one thing pissed the senior chief off more than new-guy officers, and that was preppy college boys. If you were trying to find a preppy from central casting, it would probably be Dwight

Light. He'd grown up in Darien, Connecticut, spoke with a patrician lockjaw, and had been a varsity squash player at Penn. Dwight soon took any of the heat not directed at me, and eventually, he'd take all of it. We were very often the recipients of the longest compass courses, the hardest demolition problems, and the longest swims. Neither of us complained, pissed, or moaned. We just did it all. Dwight Light proved his mettle in AOT, and later, after he got out of the navy, he would set the human-powered crossing record for the Atlantic Ocean, cranking a pedal-powered boat nearly three thousand miles from Newfoundland to Plymouth, England.

The senior chief never did quite warm up to Dwight, but eventually I broke through. John Jaeger became my sea daddy. A sea daddy is a mentor, someone who shows you the ropes and teaches what the Team expects of you. He was an unlikely Yoda, and I was no Luke Skywalker. The lessons were hard, and the senior chief was a big fan of learning by doing. He'd let me make the mistake once, unless that mistake was going to kill him or someone on the cadre.

"If it freakin' kills you, *sir,* that's what we call Darwinism, *or so.*"

He was not above calling me a "donkey-dick motherfucker, *sir,*" when I screwed up, which was often. We soon came to realize that Fort A. P. Hill was the senior chief's world, and we were just living in it.

It was called advanced operator training for a reason. We had been exposed to the basics at BUD/S, only the basics, and now it was time to mold us into frogmen. We focused on the three tasks a commando must master to prevail in combat: how to shoot, how to move, and how to communicate.

We had been introduced to Russian weapons at BUD/S, but now we became virtuosos. The RPG-7 antitank rocket launcher was a good piece of kit, and we learned to use it against bunkers, vehicles, and aircraft. We crawled low while AK-47s and RPD machine guns were fired over our heads. We came to know the distinct sounds of Russian-made AKs and American M-16s, a vital skill in the furious whirl of combat. We worked with demolitions a lot. We learned how to rig charges that would drop trees across roads, and how to set up deadly claymore mines to sweep and decimate the scenes of ambushes. We learned how to put a hurtin' on bridges, how to crater runways and derail trains. We were shown how to use linear-shaped charges to do elegant little jobs, like blow the wheels off vehicles or cut through hardened steel such as a bank vault. We were taught where to strike a target with greatest economy, how to disable key pieces of equipment, and how to booby-trap almost everything. All of this we practiced with live ammunition and live explosives.

The training was structured to teach us component skills and subtasks; we would gradually assemble these skills into full mission profiles. We ran demolition raids against elaborate target mock-ups, underground command centers, bunker complexes, and communication facilities. We learned how to take down surface-to-air missile sites, and learned Russian tactics for guarding, securing, and reacting when these sites were attacked. We worked with the navy's Red Wolf helicopter squadrons to insert and extract from operations. We were taught how to attack and how to run away. We became masters of dirty tricks, like leaving booby-trapped backpacks along our line of retreat—claymore mines fused with time pencils to splatter anyone who attempted to follow. We learned how to fight guard dogs. We learned how to throw bloodhounds off our trails. We climbed fences, we climbed walls, we blew open safes and hangar doors. We made pizza-shaped platter charges and destroyed electrical substations. We had a blast, literally.

As our skills coalesced, we were instructed less and made to operate more. We planned, briefed, and executed under the watchful eyes of the cadre. We were accompanied in the field by Lane Graders, cadre members who geared up and patrolled with us. They gave no advice and offered no sympathy. They were there to keep eyes on, and to make sure we didn't lie our asses off in the debriefs. In the SEALs there is an expression, "Cheat if you must, but don't get caught." The

Lane Graders made cheating impossible. If the operation involved a six-mile hump, they went along to make sure you didn't steal a truck. (Bear in mind, we were encouraged to do things like steal trucks.) The Lane Graders made sure our out-of-the-box thinking remained on the planet.

The most important thing I learned from the senior chief was how to be a leader. He taught me that though my men carried machine guns, the platoon was my weapon. John Jaeger trained me how to take care of the men in my charge and to make sure the concept of Team remained foremost. The platoon required ammunition, radios, batteries, and antiarmor weapons; they also required food, sleep, praise, discipline, information, and responsibility. "Take care of the lads," John used to say, "and the lads will take care of you." Small, simple things were important: Eat last, and only after everyone has been served. Buy beer. Praise publicly, punish privately. Take the heat when things go wrong. Ask questions and solicit the opinions of the enlisted operators, and, most important, delegate subtasks within the mission. Fully 50 percent of the officers in SEAL Team are Mustangs, men who served first as enlisted troops and gained their commissions through merit and dedication. This percentage is higher than in any other part of the military. The reason is simple: The lads are motivated. Officers come and go, but enlisted men are the backbone and experience base of the Teams. They don't require micromanagement, they require guidance; it was often necessary only to wind 'em up and point them in the right direction. John taught me that if I trusted the men, the men would trust me.

Toward the end of AOT, our training ops were coordinated with a yearly army special forces exercise, a multiservice, multistate extravaganza code-named Robin Sage. The army uses Robin Sage to test its graduating classes of Green Beret candidates. The Green Berets are our counterpart units but not exactly our opposite numbers. Our roles are more complementary than reciprocal.

The Green Berets specialize in the organization and training of indigenous forces. They parachute into remote wadis and organize Afghani tribesmen into homegrown militia units. The army's special forces specialize in training—everything from basic marksmanship to advanced infantry tactics, sabotage, and assassination. This process is called "force multiplication." One Green Beret trains a dozen men. That dozen trains another twelve dozen. The special forces retain a considerable aptitude for direct action, and it goes without saying that to teach the black arts, you need to have mastered them.

The Green Berets inherited the mantle of the OSS, Office of Strategic Services, in World War II—they teach and organize resistance units and instruct partisans behind enemy lines. The SEALs also were an outgrowth of World War II combat. They trace their lineage to the navy's CDUs, or combat demolition units, the outfits that cleared the beaches of Normandy prior to D-Day, as well as the Underwater Demolition Teams and Scouts and Raiders who sneaked, peeked, and operated against the Japanese in the Pacific. The Green Berets and the SEALs were both created by President John F. Kennedy in 1962. The president had been a small-unit commander, a PT-boat skipper, and he understood that a well-trained David can kick Goliath in the balls. If the Green Berets' heritage is force multiplication, the SEALs' mandate is hurting the enemy.

The operational element of the Green Berets is an A-Team, a unit roughly analogous to a SEAL platoon, that is, two officers and twelve enlisted men. A-Teams tend to specialize: One team may be scuba-trained, another might be trained demolitionists, another, arctic-warfare specialists, and still another, HALO-trained. In the SEALs, we do it all, and every SEAL is proficient in all aspects of special ops: Each of us is trained to jump, dive, do demo, boat work, and operate in all environs: jungle, swamp, and glacier. There are presently twenty thousand people wearing green berets. Let's just say there are a lot fewer SEALs. A hell of a lot fewer. All of the SEALs who have ever served, since World War II, number fewer than ten thousand in total.

In Robin Sage, teams of Green Beret candidates are parachuted into remote locations, where they are expected to link up with partisan units operating against a conventional enemy force. The partisans are played by national guardsmen, reservists, and civilians specially recruited for the purpose. The exercise is as real as the army can make it. The student A-Teams have to find the partisans, convince them they are there to help, and train the locals to conduct a series of increasingly complicated special ops. The guardsmen selected as players tend to be clerks, cooks, and technicians with little skill in dirt soldiering. The civilians are, well, civilians. The partisan units are usually led by an experienced Green Beret or a SEAL who role-plays a local warlord. These partisan generalissimos prevaricate, make outrageous demands, and generally prove as difficult and mercurial as possible. Just like real warlords. For the student A-Team leader, it is an exercise in politics as much as tactics.

Our part in Robin Sage was to be OPFOR, opposing forces. We were to act in the capacity of the enemy's special operations units. It was our job to locate, frustrate, and terminate the partisans and their capitalist masters. Lest you think the aim was a huge game of Dungeons & Dragons, I'll point out that both sides were playing for keeps. The student A-Team had undergone months of training, and this was to be their final examination. If they failed, they'd be sent back to whatever evil world they came from, without the headgear of their dreams. For us it was the same, only worse.

Operations, even exercises, are taken with deadly seriousness in the Teams. SEALs are evaluated every time they operate. The job of the SEAL Teams is war fighting, not playing at war games; failure in a military exercise is unacceptable and inexcusable. SEAL officers have been relieved of command for screwing up on exercises. An operational SEAL platoon that cannot overcome a national guard unit and a mob of civilians has no business in the Teams. In this exercise, anything less than total success would be seen as a failure of leadership. *My* leadership. We were not expected to merely prevail, we were expected to dominate in this exercise and every time we geared up to operate. We were student

SEALs with something to prove. We were up against men who desperately wanted to earn a Green Beret. This was war, and failure was not an option.

We did not get off to an auspicious start. I was given a five-square-mile radius in which I was told the special forces camp was *probably* located. That's a great word, "probably." I held a council of war with my senior enlisted guys, and we selected several likely camp locations within the area. We figured they would want to be far from roads or habitations but close enough so that Green Beret Lane Graders and exercise referees could check up on them. The camp would need a water supply and to be situated on terrain that was defensible and offered multiple routes of escape. There were five or six places that fit this description. The operations planning course was coming in handy. I would find the Green Beanies by deconstructing their operation. I knew that Robin Sage teams are usually inserted by parachute, and I also knew that the teams are quite often ambushed by Green Beret instructors after insertion and then force-marched to their camp. There appeared to be only one place on the map where jumpers could be inserted. That location was twenty clicks from the center of our five-mile radius. The drop zone was to the north, and that eliminated two of the probable locations at the south end of the zone. We were guessing, but these were educated guesses.

The second problem was to determine where we would insert. We didn't want to land too close to the camp, and we didn't want to be too far away. The A-Team and their charges could be expected to put out patrols, and we had to be careful that we did not become the hunted. Ideally, we'd get into the game without attracting attention. Finally, we briefed, geared up, and climbed aboard a pair of Red Wolf helos. Baby Zee was in full field gear during the brief, and I was not surprised when he jumped aboard my helicopter.

The ride to the insert point took nearly an hour. As forest and swampland streaked by below us, I was careful to follow our position on my map. I knew it was not unusual for Lane Graders to throw some shit in the game and tell the aircrew to drop us deliberately in the wrong place. Baby Zee saw that I was paying attention, and he got a strange smile on his face.

The helos crested a stand of trees and dropped down close to a river. We flew ten feet from the surface, the helicopters one behind the other, banking through turns low and fast, the pilots flying by night-vision goggles. Six minutes from insert, the doors came back, and the gunners manned their weapons. The squad unbuckled seat belts as wind swirled through the cabin, hot and sweet with the smell of JP-5.

The crew chief's eyes found mine in the darkness. He held up two fingers. "Two minutes," I shouted. We stood. Pressed up next to Baby Zee, I crouched in the door and looked forward. The night was clear, and a quarter moon was low in the west. I could see a bend in the river and a steep wall of trees at the turn. We were coming at it fast. The helicopter lurched, the deck lifting against my feet, G forces pressing me down as the aircraft flared. The helicopter mushed up, slowing, rotors beating loudly while the ship descended. Now visible beyond the trees was a small meadow perpendicular to the river. Our insert point.

We set down and jumped from the bird. Both helos pedal-turned and roared back into the sky, flat gray shapes soon swallowed by night. We ran from the landing zone by squads. As the engine noise faded, the Red Wolves continued north, touching down empty at several other LZs, a standard tactic to mask our true insertion point.

We jogged to the tree line. Once into cover, we grouped together, taking a few moments to shake off the noise and smells of the aircraft, hunkering down and tuning in to the night. I had the radioman send our brevity code for successful insertion, the word "Otter." I was not entirely surprised when the headphones crackled back, "Lane Grader will make input." Baby Zee could see my face as I listened. He leaned close.

"What's up?" I whispered.

"*Chu Hoi*," he said. It was a Vietnamese expression that meant "surrender." The term was applied to defecting Viet Cong who agreed to work with the Americans. Defected

VC had been used occasionally to guide SEAL search-and-destroy missions. They were called Kit Carson scouts.

"Who's the scout?" I asked. "You?"

Baby Zee shook his head. He handed me a piece of paper. On it was an eight-digit grid. "You're supposed to pick him up here." The location was a road junction maybe six clicks away.

"When?"

"Dawn," Baby Zee said.

I wasn't digging this. Six clicks would be a long patrol, and I didn't want to be hanging around road junctions, especially at dawn.

"Why do I need to pick this guy up?" It was not necessarily a stupid question. My mission tasking was to locate and attack the SF camp. Nobody had said anything about a *Chu Hoi*. Just because Baby Zee told me to get the guy didn't mean this wasn't a setup. As we learned in AOT, "Situation dictates." This was my patrol, and I didn't want to get my ass into a situation that I could not handle.

"Who's going to be at the road junction?" I asked.

"People."

I was getting pissed. "Look, I'm not in the mood for a fucking discussion out here. Who's with this guy, and why do I need him?"

Baby Zee could see that I wasn't going to meet anyone without more information. "The Kit Carson is on the level," he said.

"Who's gonna be with him?"

"Third Platoon captured him last night. You meet up with them, and they'll hand him over. He can guide you to the SF camp."

Sure, I thought. Sure. But blessed are the flexible, for they shall not be broken. We mounted out and patrolled for the road junction.

We managed to link up with Third Platoon, and the *Chu Hoi,* a skinny young man in a cammie top, field jacket, and blue jeans, came into our hands. Third Platoon had been in the area for a week; they had searched the south end of the zone without finding the camp. The scout had been captured walking down a road three clicks south of our rendezvous. They'd reported the capture to exercise control, and an umpire had informed them that the kid had turned—that is, defected. Third Platoon was heading north to run a simulated attack on a Hawk missile battery to the west. They were supposed to make their hit the next night. The commander of Third Platoon was a guy we called Cowboy Bob, and he was considered a good operator. The scout had shown Bob the location of the SF camp on his map. It was nowhere near any of the sites we intended to search.

"What do you think?" I asked Cowboy.

"I think you're gonna step in some shit if you find that camp," he answered. I was sure he was right, and I wasn't very encouraged.

We spent the day laid up, the two platoons close by, waiting for darkness. During the day I questioned our scout. He didn't look like a Green Beret; he looked like a staff weenie.

"Let me see your ID card," I said.

"It's back at the camp."

"You were wandering around in civvies, on an exercise, without an ID card?"

He didn't say anything.

"What do you do in the army?" I asked.

"What's that got to do with the exercise?"

"It's got a lot to do with how I'm going to treat you." My face was green. My eyes were red. He thought about it.

"I'm a member of the 118th Military Police Company."

"Regular army?" I asked.

"North Carolina Guard."

I gave him a long, hard stare. "Are you gonna burn me?" I asked.

"I was told to lead you to the camp," he said.

"Who told you to do that?"

"My company commander."

"And you know where the camp is?"

"Yes." He pointed at my map. The location was a hilltop,

five, maybe six miles away. It was the same place he'd shown Bob.

"How many people?"

"Six SF, ten partisans."

"What kind of weapons?"

"M-16s. A couple of M-60s. The SF guys have AK-47s."

"You're sure?" I asked him.

"I was there."

The conversation went on very much as if he were a real *Chu Hoi*. It was a game, I knew, but it could easily become one I might lose. I talked to him for a while and gradually came to the conclusion that he really was going to show me the camp; he didn't seem smart enough not to. Though his intentions might have been honorable, that didn't mean he wasn't being used. Just because he was following orders didn't mean we weren't being led into a nice airtight ambush. That's why they call this stuff "special operations." It was wheels within wheels, games within games, and I could see the hand of Senior Chief Jaeger in it. The bastard.

When night fell, we separated from Third Platoon and headed southeast. The going was slow, hard, and noisy; the underbrush was thick, and little light made it to the forest floor. We navigated by dead reckoning, walking a compass bearing when we could, following easier terrain when possible. We patrolled tight, dialed in and aware that somewhere out there was an A-Team with our name on it. The scout was kept behind me in the patrol order, with a specially tasked guy behind him. I doubt our guide had even half a clue that in the real world, the *Chu Hoi* would be shot in the head at the first sign of an ambush. Instant karma.

We made it to the vicinity of the hill, and the point man, the scout, and I went forward. We could see no sign of fires and could hear nothing. We skirted the base of the knoll, traveling almost completely around it, but found no tracks or obvious path leading to the top. The night was perfectly still, dark, and peaceful. We returned to the layup position and waited. There was no sound from the hilltop at dawn; no wood smoke, no sounds of men moving about, and no cooking smells. At midmorning I took one boat crew and the scout forward again, this time to search the hilltop. There was nothing there, no signs of habitation, no fire pits, no tracks, and no indication of sleeping places. The ground was undisturbed.

"You got the wrong hilltop," I said to the scout.

He looked at the map and blinked at me. "This isn't the place," he said. "But this is where they told me it was."

"You didn't get a fix yourself?" I asked.

"You mean plot the location?"

"You know how to read a map?" I asked. It was a question I should have asked days before.

"I'm an MP," the scout finally said. "Most of the time we follow roads."

No shit, I thought. Baby Zee looked at me and smirked.

There were four or five other hilltops around the area, most taller than the one we were on. The closest promontory was only two hundred meters away, much closer than I wanted to be in daylight. We spent the remainder of the day hiding in a creek bed to the south. As we dozed through the cool morning, I realized that we were in a world of hurt. We might be in the area of the SF camp and we might not. I was no longer worried that my scout might lead us into ambush. It was now obvious that he couldn't find his own ass with a ten-man search party. The hilltops would have to be checked one by one, at night, a dicey and time-consuming process. We waited, and by late that afternoon, our problem was solved for us.

It was a pig that would finally give the SF camp away. A real pig. While we were still in our creek-bed hide, an incredible series of screams echoed through the woods. Shrieks, squeals, and rooting, snorting noises, high-pitched and desperate. They never sounded human, but they didn't sound animal, either. The noise of murder had come from the north. It sounded like someone killing a pig. And that was exactly what had happened. The SF camp had been delivered "fresh food" in the form of a live hog. To feed the troops, the animal had to be butchered. We learned later that the hog was dispatched with a hatchet. There was only one hilltop in the direction of the squealing. We now had a target location, and we would find our quarry after nightfall. We spent the remaining hours planning the attack.

In fairness to the Green Berets, a camp makes a great target. They were required to have tents and shelters, cooking fires, and play host to a dozen gumbies selected primarily because they didn't know a goddamn thing about hiding in the woods. The SF guys were entrenched, we were mobile. They were at a training base, and we were on patrol. They dozed in hammocks at night, and we laid up. On patrol we cooked no food, made no fires, did not smoke, and seldom talked. We had shooting pairs constantly on guard, and layup positions were selected primarily for inaccessibility and ease of defense. The SF guys were constrained by the requirement that they train a dozen people, and we were compelled only by considerations of stealth, surprise, and offensive action.

We contacted Red Wolf and laid on a two-bird exfil package. We designated a time window for a primary extract, right on the target, and a secondary extract two hours later on the empty hill we had searched in the morning. Unlike our insertion, the extract would not require the helicopters to land. We arranged for Red Wolves to show up with SPIE rigs, or special insertion and extraction—a fancy term for hundred-foot sections of line dropped from the doors of helicopters. The line is rigged with loops into which we would hook carabiners. Connected to the line by climbing harnesses, the team would be lifted out, eight men per rope. We'd get back home dragged along under the helicopters. Dangling from the line is a wild ride and the fastest way to get the hell out of Dodge.

The plan depended mostly on timing. Tactically, the operation was simplicity itself. After nightfall, one boat crew would circle the hilltop and find a well-covered firing position to the south of the camp. The balance of the two squads would approach from the east. On signal, the four-man group would open fire. The second group would wait until the camp reacted and started shooting back at the four men to the south. Then the larger group would open fire and assault through the camp. Anyone retreating before the second attack would be driven back into a cross fire laid down by the first boat crew. Once in the compound, we would do a smash-and-grab job, destroying everything we could not carry away. The helicopters would then appear overhead, drop the SPIE rigs to us, we'd hook up, and be lifted out.

We were in position soon after full dark. The camp was outlined in the glow of two fires. There were two or three lean-tos, and a large tarp hung over a folding camp table. Sleeping arrangements seemed to be a few jungle hammocks positioned around the larger of the two fires. The camp looked pretty squared away. Around the fire farthest from where I lay pressed down behind a log was a group gathered in conference. Above the other fire, the unfortunate pig rotated on a spit. The smell of pork wafted down to us. I checked my watch—in fifteen minutes the extraction window would open, and the Red Wolves would be standing by. My stomach growled loudly. In almost three days I had eaten only a can of cling peaches and a handful of trail mix.

I was strangely calm and suddenly very aware that this was a game. Our weapons were loaded with blanks; in our assault no one would be killed or even hurt. The hard part of this operation was over. Our test was to find the camp and spring on it. Now would come the pretend ambush, the mock attack. All I needed to do to win was initiate the attack and make as big a demonstration as I could. We were here to send a message, make an impression.

Luck stayed with us. As we watched, the group around the fire gathered their weapons and mounted out in patrol order. Two pairs of men with AK-47s put the partisans into a column formation. I knew the men with the Russian rifles were SF students. Their motley charges bunched up and were led away into the darkness. They headed downhill, between the diversionary shooting pair and our main group. I considered ambushing this group as they passed but decided against it.

The squad passed close, rustling loudly in the leaf clutter. The first of the group walked within ten yards of me. I had no apprehension that they would find us. The patrol had been walked into the forest directly from the campfire. I knew they would have no night vision, I knew their faces would still be flushed, their ears still snapping with the crackle of firewood and their noses full of pig smoke. They had been led directly from camp into the clammy fist of the night, and that was exactly the kind of mistake a new patrol leader would make. As they shuffled past our ambush position, I knew they were deaf and blind.

I heard the SF patrol crunch away; now and then a canteen or magazine would rattle or someone would cough. They were louder than a troop of apes. Ten men had left the camp, which meant that two SF and four partisans remained in the compound. We were sixteen shooters total, enough of an advantage, but surprise also favored us. I waited an additional twenty minutes, until the SF patrol would be too far away to interfere with our attack. Although I knew that the Green Berets would be able to quickly return to the hilltop, running through the dark, thick forest, I expected the partisans could not. At any rate, it was probably not likely that the departed SF troopers would split off from their charges. If they left the partisans to respond to our attack, they'd spend the next week and a half looking for them.

I keyed the radio handset, breaking squelch twice. My signal was answered by three clicks: The boat crew to the south would fire at their discretion. Ten seconds later, they opened up. The first response of the camp was to stand there, puzzled. Then one of the AK-47s returned fire; then the other. Even though the AKs fired blanks, huge white tongues of fire belched from their muzzles. Two of the partisans hit the deck. Only one started to shoot back—and his M-16 jammed after a few rounds. All of them, SF and partisans alike, were now facing south. The SF guys put down a steady stream of fire, and in twenty seconds both AKs ran out of ammunition.

As they struggled to change magazines, the remaining boat crews opened fire. Even shooting blanks, the squads put down a withering barrage. We lobbed artillery simulators into the camp. They went off with crashing white explosions.

The booms echoed from the hills, and I could only imagine what the four SF troopers were thinking off in the woods. They'd know immediately that their base camp was under attack, and they'd almost certainly know that they had walked right past the attackers. We threw a dozen more artillery sims, then I fired a flare. The first boat crew shifted fire behind the camp, and the squad stood and charged, shooting as we came on. The SF guys did the right thing—they ran.

Two partisans followed the SF guys, skipping away into the night, ripping through branches, bouncing off trees, and stumbling down the hill. As we entered the camp, the remaining two partisans just stood there stupidly and put their hands in the air.

The point man ripped off a long burst at their feet. "Lay down, assholes," he said, "you're dead." The two partisans were shoved to the ground.

I looked around. We were in the camp and the proud owners of a barbecued pig. I yelled, "Time on target," and the lads set about kicking down lean-tos, flipping over tables, rifling through backpacks, and stuffing every piece of paper they could find down the front of their uniform blouses. I called in the Red Wolves, and within a few minutes a helicopter was overhead. The SPIE rigs were tossed out, and the first squad hooked up and were lifted straight up into the night.

Then it was our turn. The second helicopter hovered in over the camp. This bird came in lower, and its rotor blast scattered everything we had already flipped over. Pine needles swirled, tarps and poncho liners and sleeping hammocks lifted up and blew away. As the lads snapped into the SPIE rig, Baby Zee went down the rope, checking that carabiners were closed and locked. I snapped into the last loop, and Baby Zee clipped in next to me.

I flashed a thumbs-up to the helo, and the crew chief answered by pointing straight up. The head of the rope went up first, each of us moving slowly forward as the man ahead was lifted from the ground. I was next to the campfire, close to the pig. Its eyes were closed, and the spit went through its mouth and out its backside. In front of me, Baby Zee was lifted from the ground, and I felt my climbing harness take the strain as the rope tightened. From out of the darkness, Baby Zee yelled down, "Hey, I would've given you extra points if you'd taken the pig."

As my feet sang over the fire, I reached down and gave the pig a kick. The spit broke, and the big hog dropped into the coals. Sparks from the fire swarmed around us as we were lifted up and through the trees, and then the helicopter gathered speed and we were dragged away into the night.

Connected to the helicopter by the SPIE rig, we were soaring through darkness, and I hooted like a banshee. Above me, the squad was strung out, arms spread, the wind howling around us. The forest ripped past below, an infinite carpet of black. I looked down between my legs as the campfires faded in the distance. The helicopters were headed for the second star from the right, and we were flying, spinning free and wild as Pan and his Lost Boys.

OPERATIONS OTHER THAN WAR

I DON'T KNOW how the Casino got its name. Glitzy it was not. The parking lot was dirt—sand, actually—the building was one story, with a low, slightly pitched roof; white vinyl siding was peeled back in several places, and in a few other spots the black tar paper under the siding was pulled back as well, exposing termite-gnawed plywood. Tucked under a span of the Chesapeake Bay Bridge-Tunnel in the Chick's Beach section of Norfolk, the Casino looked more like a shipwreck than a bar. It had a cultivated air of disrepute, like a permanent crime scene. Even the address was a goof: 169 Pleasure House Road. A neon sign was wired to the frame of the only window, advertising PBR ON TAP, and the letter "A" blinked on and off in a random, short-circuited kind of way. It was not the sort of joint that you just wandered into. It looked too dangerous to be entered casually. There was always some serious iron parked outside, Harleys, sidecar-packing BMWs and Triumphs, four-by-four pickup trucks with rifle racks and mud flaps. The transportation in the lot perfectly announced the Casino's demographic: Navy SEALs, bikers, and beer alcoholics of the lowest order.

The interior decoration could be described as "early demolition." The ceiling bowed low over an unevenly poured concrete floor. The bar was made of Formica and Sheetrock, and the several pool tables were angled haphazardly about the middle of the room, pulled away from serious leaks in the roof. Behind the bar were plaques from each of the East Coast SEAL Teams, Two and Four, as well as SDV (SEAL delivery vehicle) Team Two and Underwater Demolition Teams Twenty-one and Twenty-two.

The first time I stepped inside, two rednecks were in a hair-pulling, eye-gouging fight on and under one of the pool tables. Normally, a fight can be counted on to jack up a bar, and it isn't long until the other patrons discover or invent some reason to join in. Again, the Casino confounded. As the rednecks beat each other senseless, a bar full of SEALs ignored them completely. No one even swiveled a stool when one dude smashed the other through the door of the ladies' room. When the victor dragged the loser to the front door, the bartender calmly reached under the Formica, pulled out a big .357 Magnum, and pointed it at the panting, disconsolate redneck.

"Don't get no fuckin' ideas of comin' back in here with a gun, neither," he said evenly.

"You ain't gonna ban me, are ya?" the loser asked.

"You lost yer privileges for a week," the bartender answered. "Now git!"

And like that, it was over. Somebody dropped a quarter in the jukebox and played "Pressure Drop" by Toots & the Maytals. *Irie,* mon, cool running. It was just another night down at the Casino. I loved the place.

It was in this decorous atmosphere that I was wetted down after receiving my Navy SEAL designator, 1130, in the late spring of 1982. Rick James and I picked up our designations as naval special warfare officers on the same day, three months early, and we got our pins for different reasons. Rick got his because he was a squared-away operator and a great American. I may be the only SEAL in the history of naval special warfare to get his pin for turning down a mission.

Following my triumph over the Green Berets, I was returned to the Ops Department. My work was pretty much the same, messages and reports, except now I was deemed to be of some utility to the defense of the United States of America. In a word, I was deployable. Usable. Having survived the worst that John Jaeger could throw at me, I confidently expected to soon receive my badge and get assigned to an op-

erational platoon. SEAL platoons are commanded by one officer, and his assistant, the second officer, labors under the
much less august moniker of 2IC, or second in charge. It was
to this modest station that I hoped to be appointed, and I
was keen to get on with it. Once I was slotted for a platoon,
I was made available for detachments and odd jobs, mostly
tasks beneath the dignity of a platoon in the throes of predeployment training. Sometimes the jobs were shitty, like administrative beach surveys, pier and piling demolition, or
worse, harbor searches; and sometimes they were primo.

My first independent assignment was a piece of cake with
shit frosting. It would be the first and one of the few times I'd
decline to do my duty, or at least my duty as someone else
saw it. In late April I was tasked to lead a six-man detachment on temporary assignment to NASA. It was to be a
"space junk" operation, a mission SEALs inherited from
their Underwater Demolition Team forebearers. During the
Mercury, Gemini, and Apollo space programs, UDT frogmen recovered space capsules at sea after splashdown. When
the UDTs were phased out, the SEAL Teams inherited the
job. Although the space shuttle has replaced manned capsules, the Teams are still periodically called on to recover
odd items dropped into the ocean, deliberately or accidentally, by NASA.

No one in the operations office would tell us specifically
what the op would entail, and our orders said only to "report
to the National Aeronautic and Space Administration at the
Kennedy Space Center for temporary additional duty to include parachuting and the demolition of explosives." One of
the petty officers in the detachment, Gibby, had pulled the
operation before; or rather, he had trained for it.

"The mission was scrubbed when they aborted the launch,"
he said.

"The launch of what?" I asked.

"A Trident missile."

We drew equipment and flew a C-141 down to the air force
station at Cape Canaveral. During the flight down, Gibby
told me that his previous detachment had trained to conduct

the at-sea recovery of a Trident ballistic missile booster section. The Trident was then America's latest submarine-launched ICBM, a big honker of a missile that packed up to eight thermonuclear warheads, individually targeted H-bombs called MIRVs, or multiple independently targeted reentry vehicles. The Trident had a range in excess of four thousand nautical miles, and each missile was capable of dropping its MIRVs within a hundred meters of their assigned targets. I understand that's pretty much a direct hit when you're using H-bombs, and an amazing technical achievement considering the missile was fired underwater, exited the atmosphere, attained orbital velocities, reentered the atmosphere, and dropped straight down the chimney of its target. The ultimate bummer. A new Trident variant was undergoing testing, and we were to be a small part of the effort.

We arrived, checked in to a very down-market hotel in Cocoa Beach, and settled in for some Florida sunshine. The following day, Gibby and I attended a kickoff meeting at NASA. The conference table was filled with alpha geeks straight out of *Revenge of the Nerds*. Much of the meeting was as incomprehensible to us as rocket science, but the gist was that a Trident C-4 was to be launched from an Ohio-class ballistic missile submarine off Cape Canaveral. That missile, without its apocalyptic warhead, was to be targeted on an empty stretch of ocean in the North Atlantic. As the missile attained escape velocity, it would jettison a booster section, and our job would be to recover the first stage of the rocket motor after it was shed from the missile. The splashdown of the spent motor was computed to occur somewhere north of the Abacos Islands in the northern Bahamas. During the briefing, we were referred to as "the guys with the big necks."

We spent the next week training in a small cove near the space center. A crane would drop a large cylindrical mockup of the first stage into the water, and we'd jump in and practice attaching a flotation collar to the motor. Once the motor section was buoyant, it was to be recovered by a range support ship from the Military Sealift Command. We were to be deployed and recovered from a long-range MH-53 Pave Low special operations helicopter. The op could not have been more straightforward, and the only complication we faced in training came in the form of a ten-foot alligator that always showed up in the cove when the flotation collar was being inflated. Much to our consternation, the crane operator, a regular Florida Cracker, tossed marshmallows to the big reptile as we worked. I guessed this was by way of a diversion, and we could only hope the alligator wouldn't consider the treats as an appetizer. Thanks in part to the gator, we got the collar put on in record time.

We trained and then we waited. The launch was postponed several times, and we hung out on Cocoa Beach, went to bars, and picked up women, telling them we were astronauts in training. Finally, we loaded out and were flown from Patrick Air Force Base to Air Force Station Grand Bahama Island. We cooled our heels and rigged the helicopter to water-drop an F-470 Zodiac inflatable raiding boat, a package we called a "soft duck."

We launched at dawn the following morning to be in position at the south end of the impact zone in time for what was scheduled to be an 0700 launch. Our part of the operation was by far the simplest. Besides the submarine, which had the relatively uncomplicated task of firing the missile, there were NASA helicopters detailed to film the launch, land tracking stations to plot the missile's trajectory, and a pair of navy P-3 patrol planes that would sow the splashdown area with sonobuoys so the impact could be pinpointed for us to recover the motor.

The morning got off to a bad start when a Russian "fishing vessel" appeared four miles off Cape Canaveral and took up station within the submarine's launch area. This innocent trawler bristled with antennae and communications equipment; it was in fact a Vishnya-class AGI, a Russian intelligence ship equipped to monitor the launch. The launch was delayed half an hour, then another half an hour when one of the P-3s patrolling the first-stage impact area reported a second Russian trawler loitering in the vicinity of the splash-down point. Both of the trawlers were in international waters, and there was nothing to be done except marvel at the alacrity of the intrepid Russian fishermen. It was obvious that they had our number, and I wondered at the time why no one seemed to make a big deal of it. We flew around in circles north of the Bahamas as the submarine was shifted slightly closer to the cape, and the decision was made, somewhere, to just fire the missile and let the Russians watch.

We had been airborne for nearly two hours when the launch at last occurred. We saw nothing and heard little until it was reported that the booster section had impacted well north of the recovery zone—nearly a hundred miles from the place we were orbiting. The Pave Low was immediately directed north, and in the helicopter we readied for the water drop. We sprinted north at 150 knots, and the P-3s reported that the trawlers were converging on the drop point as well. The AGI off Cape Canaveral would not be a factor, but the second trawler was under twenty-five miles from the place the booster had splashed down. I did some quick math. The trawlers could not be expected to make any better than 15 knots, which would put the Canaveral boat six hours away from the motor section, but the closer trawler was an hour and forty minutes from the impact spot. At 150 knots, we could expect to be in the area of the splashdown in forty minutes, plus the time it would take to find the motor, not insignificant given that the sections had floated barely three feet above the surface during our practice recoveries. This was quickly turning into a race. The Military Sealift Command ship that would take aboard the motor section was a full fifty miles south of the point of impact. Clearly, we could expect no help from her.

Mr. Murphy had been active all morning, and as we closed in on the motor, he got busy with our end of the operation. The pilot was an air force bird colonel, and he called me up to the cockpit when we were about fifteen minutes out. "You guys ready to jump?" he asked.

I told him we were.

"We've got a little complication on this end," he said.

"How little?" I asked. I watched the copilot look away.

"We're getting a little low on fuel. We'll be able to insert you, but we won't have enough to hang around until the recovery ship gets there."

This wasn't what I wanted to hear. "Is there another helicopter?"

"Just us," he said breezily. "I figure we can put you in and head back to Grand Bahama to refuel."

"Then what?" I asked.

"We'll come back and pick you up."

That was the plan? This may have been my first rodeo, but I wasn't going to bite. Nonetheless, I had to be careful, or at least I thought I did; only later would I learn how to deal with air force colonels. For now I had to tread lightly but firmly. I was an ensign and he was a full colonel, but his big idea was a man killer.

"How are you going to find us?" I asked, genuinely curious.

"We'll mark the position on the GPS."

I was rapidly becoming aware of the difference between the air force and the navy. "Look, Colonel," I said, "I can't put my guys in the water unless you stay with us."

"Why not?"

"Because the impact point is in the Gulf Stream. There's a three-knot current running north. You might mark the position, but we'll be miles away from there by the time you get back."

"You have a boat, right?"

"That boat's small and black."

"We'll find you," he said with a bit of a sniff.

"Nothing personal, sir, but I don't think you can. I'm not going to put my guys in the big ocean, tethered to a damaged motor section that might sink, and hope that we'll be found after a brief search."

He was pissed. And so was I. I thought I was kissing my SEAL career good-bye, except I wasn't even a SEAL yet. Here I was calling bullshit on an operation, and not just any op—I was calling bullshit on my first independent assignment.

"You're aware that a Russian ship is closing in on the motor?" he asked.

"Yes sir. That's another reason I don't want to get left out there." He gave me a "What are you afraid of?" sort of sneer. I continued as evenly as I could. "Six guys in an inflatable boat won't be able to stop the Russians if they want to take the motor."

"You have weapons?" he asked, still looking at me like I was his daughter's prom date.

"Pistols."

"We're out here to recover the motor section," he said.

"I can't risk my team and hope you find us."

There was a long pause. The helicopter's engines droned and the rotors pounded.

"How long can you stay on target?" I asked.

"Thirty-five minutes, max," he said.

"Okay, I'll tell you what. You get us to the motor section, and I'll put a swim pair in. We'll sink it with a couple of socks of C-4."

He gulped. "You're going to destroy it?"

"You want the Russians to get it?" I asked.

Just like a movie, at that moment the trawler came into view, hull down on the horizon, heading north. It was another Russian AGI, beat up and rusty. We flew past it. Everybody on the flight deck knew that all the Russians had to do was track us on radar and we'd lead them right to the motor section.

The colonel continued to look pissed. "I don't know why you're refusing to deploy."

"It isn't safe," I said. "Call range control and tell them I'm offering to sink the motor."

"I'm going to tell them you're refusing to go in."

"Mention that I've got no water, no food, and six signal flares," I said. "I'm not jumping into the middle of the Atlantic Ocean and hoping someone can find me again."

I went back into the troop compartment and sat on the

boat. I felt like my party was over, but Gibby gave me a thumbs-up. He'd listened to our discussion on his headset. He bent close and yelled into my ear, "Fuck 'em. You did the right thing."

I hoped so, but I had a bad feeling about explaining this one back at the Team area. Five minutes later, the crew chief came up and yelled into my ear, "Range control wants to know if you can guarantee that this thing sinks."

"We'll blow the shit out of it," I said.

The crew chief spoke into his headset, listened, and then bent toward me again. "Okay, you guys are a go."

We readied the charges, three socks of C-4 plastic explosive. The socks were olive-drab canvas sleeves, a foot long and three inches wide, each containing a two-pound rectangular-shaped ribbon of C-4. Sewn onto the outside of each sock was a three-foot piece of cotton line, a bit thicker than clothesline. At the other end of the sock was a flat metal hook into which the line could be fitted and cinched tight. The arrangement permitted the line to be looped around the target and pulled snug, ensuring good contact and more bang for the buck. The bottom of each sock had a small hole punched through the canvas to permit the insertion of a det-cord booster or blasting cap into the explosive. Without a blasting cap or other high explosive to initiate, the C-4 would not go off. By itself, C-4 is an incredibly stable explosive, meaning that it is not likely to be accidentally detonated. Although I've never seen it myself, it is widely said that you can shoot a block of C-4 with a bullet and it won't go off. Definitely something I would not try at home.

The crew chief watched with some concern as I crimped blasting caps onto three sections of time fuse and screwed M-60 underwater fuse igniters onto each firing train.

"You guys know what you're doing, right?" he asked.

"Sure," Gibby answered. "We watched *Mission: Impossible.*"

We arrived at the splashdown coordinates and started a search pattern. It took an additional twenty-five minutes to find the motor section, floating sideways like a tree stump.

Gibby tucked the C-4 into his wet-suit top, and I stuffed the time fuse, blasting caps, and fuse igniters into mine. C-4 might be incredibly stable, but it was standard procedure to separate the explosives and the initiators during a jump, even a small jump like a swimmer cast. The trawler was closing in on us as we prepared to jump off the ramp. Spray kicked up from the rolling swells as the Pave Low sank into a twenty-foot hover.

"Pilot says you have seven minutes," the crew chief yelled as we stepped up to the ramp. Seven minutes was not much time to swim, set the charges, and get recovered by the helicopter. I wished we were taking the colonel with us.

Gibby jumped first, disappearing off the ramp and into the swirling spray blown up from the downdraft. I followed, stepping off the ramp and crossing my arms against my chest to further cushion the blasting caps. As I fell the two stories to the water, I straightened my legs and pointed my swim fins in preparation for impact. I splashed into the incline of a rolling swell, surfaced, turned, and flashed a thumbs-up to the helicopter. As Gibby and I swam for the first stage of the missile, the helicopter moved off slowly.

The motor section was a bit over six feet in diameter and maybe twelve feet long. Basically, its shape was that of a beer can with a short funnel stuck to its end. There were some void spaces and guidance equipment in the lower sections, just enough for it to have retained buoyancy, and the cylinder was slightly flattened from impact. Much of the first stage was made of carbon fiber, Kevlar, and in places where the motor's housing had fractured, carbon filaments spread out from the cylinder like a fine mat of dense blond hair. These Kevlar strands were extremely strong, and we had to avoid being snagged lest the motor section go down and drag us with it.

Waves surged over the first stage as we tried to find places to affix the charges. Gibby dove underwater and applied the socks to the lower sections of the motor housing, tying them tight against the base of the rocket nozzle and what was left of the steering actuators. As he cinched the explosives, I grabbed a lungful of air and dove down. I slipped blasting caps and fuses into the end of each sock, straightening the loops of time fuse and making sure the fuse igniters were screwed tightly.

As we were heaved to the top of a swell, we caught sight of the trawler. She was bow on and coming at us as fast as she could, her forepeak plowing down and through the rolling waves. The trawler was less than a thousand yards off when I bundled the three fuse igniters into my fist and simultaneously pulled the lanyards. The M-60s popped loudly, and I caught a whiff of cordite as the fuses started to burn within their waterproof plastic sheaths. There was maybe five minutes per fuse, but they'd burn at different rates, depending on water pressure and a host of variables that I no longer gave a shit about.

"Let's get the hell out of here!" I shouted to Gibby.

We put on the power and swam 150 meters from the booster section. It wasn't far enough to keep us clear of the blast, but it was as far as I thought we could go and still get aboard the helicopter. I raised my right hand over my head and clenched my fist, the SEAL hand signal for "I am ready to be extracted." Gibby put both his fists over his head and crossed them, the hand signal for "Extract me immediately."

The helicopter came on, and a wire caving ladder dropped from a hatch on its belly. The Pave Low settled to an altitude of about fifteen feet and flew at us, dragging the ladder in the water. I took a position fifty feet behind Gibby. The downblast from the rotors put out near-hurricane-force gusts; the tops were torn from the swells and slashed our faces and eyes. As the spray swept over me, I watched Gibby catch one of the rungs of the ladder in the crook of his elbow—classic frogman technique—and he started to climb up hand over hand.

Soon he was up and through the hatch, and the helicopter was directly over me. The downgusts diminished sharply as the fuselage blocked out the sun. I caught the ladder and climbed. As I came away from the surface of the water, the trawler was closer than ever, and I could see a pair of her crew standing on her port bridge wing, pointing binoculars.

As I pulled myself through the hatch, one of the air force crewmen fired a flare off the stern ramp of the Pave Low. Dragging a ribbon of smoke, a red star cluster snaked into the water a hundred yards in front of the trawler. They got the idea, I think; the Russian vessel turned sharply to starboard as the helicopter climbed. Half a minute later, two loud thumps were audible over the roar of the engines. I made it to a window in time to see a pair of white geysers falling back to the surface of the water. Five seconds later, the final charge went off, throwing pieces of motor housing into the sky. Ripped stem to stern, the first stage sank tail first and disappeared in a whirl of bubbles.

We flew back to the cape. Our presence was not required at the NASA debrief. We returned to our crummy hotel and spent the evening drinking lugubriously at a joint called Big Daddy's. The following afternoon we were cold-shouldered as we loaded out and flew another C-141 back to Norfolk. It was late evening when we arrived back at the Team area. I cut the guys loose, then sat down to write what I was certain would be my first and last operational summary. I then went to the Casino, arriving a little past midnight, and tied one on. As the jukebox played reggae, I watched a couple of lesbians shoot pool and drank like the soon-to-be unemployed.

Before officer's call the following morning, the XO called me into his office. I gave my report and told him the story. He listened, his face showing nothing. When he finished reading the report, he asked if I wanted to add anything. I first thought to say nothing—"No excuse, sir" was the stock answer—but dread got the better of me. I said that given the circumstances, I'd made the best call I could. I said that I had been respectful to the colonel, even if he was a moron, and that I was sorry if I had done the wrong thing. The XO shook his head and told me to get out of his office. Later that afternoon, Mike Boynton came into ops and told me to clean out my desk. My heart froze; then he said, "You just got reassigned, sir. You're the new assistant commander of Fifth Platoon."

"You're shitting me" was all I could think of to say.

"I wouldn't shit you, sir." The master chief grinned. "You're my favorite turd."

I was somebody's favorite turd. It was true: I'd been released from bondage in the operations shop and chopped to a newly forming line platoon. I'd apparently made the right call out there in mid-Atlantic. As far as the captain and the XO were concerned, tethering the Zodiac to a sinking missile motor and expecting the air force to return and find us was a bullshit idea. Although the mission was recovery, I had been prepared on short notice to destroy the missile section and had denied the Russians material intelligence. In short, I did okay.

As Master Chief Boynton put it, "You showed good judgment, sir. And it ain't like ensigns are necessarily known for that."

Not only was I made operational, but two days later, Rick and I were unceremoniously given our Budweisers. We spent a couple hundred bucks at the Casino, got every frogman on the East Coast a cold one, and I had a headache for days.

We were Navy SEALs at last.

FOR A WEEK OR TWO, Fifth Platoon was my temporary command. Rather, I acted as its commander. Operating out of a connex box in the back forty of SEAL Team Four, the Fifth was a provisional outfit, a skeleton of a platoon. Frank, my neighbor from San Diego, was slated to assume command after he finished Spanish-language school in Monterey, California. Before he arrived there was a lot to be done; we had yet to receive any equipment, any men, and in the first weeks we were a paper outfit—a name, basically—and that was about it.

Frank, an Annapolis graduate, had been commissioned a year before I joined the navy. Had I accepted my appointment out of high school, we would have been classmates. Frank had majored in naval architecture and graduated in the top ten of his class, considerably higher than I might have expected to place. I am hardly technically inclined, and I doubt

I would have acquitted myself in the rigors of an engineering education. While I dallied in graduate school, Frank chose to serve two years on a minesweeper in San Diego, waiting for a slot in BUD/S. It was thought at the time that naval special warfare was a career path unworthy of an Annapolis man. As a penance for even attempting to become a SEAL, Frank had to earn a surface warfare designator. Although a mine-sweeper was on the bottom of the warship totem pole, Frank knew the wardroom of an oceangoing mine hunter is small, and no officer is superfluous. In those two years Frank served as first lieutenant and damage control assistant. He earned his water wings in half the usual time and put in his chit to transfer across the bay to Coronado and BUD/S. A natural, he assumed the mantle of 113's class leader when the officer in charge broke his spine. It can't be said that the job was a picnic. Of the 105 students who started 113, thirteen graduated. These men later became famous as the 13 of 113. To the surprise of no one, Frank was the honor graduate.

Fifth Platoon was to be Frank's first command, and it had to be built from scratch—equipment and personnel assembled from the ground up, and the operators trained from square one. Our two seniormost operators were Stan and Tim, both ten-year veterans. In the weeks before Frank returned, these two proved their worth as scroungers, making the deals and steals that are frequently necessary in the military just to get the tools you need to do your job. At this, they excelled, and we were soon well and even abundantly equipped, if not fully manned.

The remainder of the platoon, ten operators, was to be taken in a single draft from BUD/S Class 117. This was unusual and not necessarily a good thing. All of them were fresh from Coronado and Fort Benning, and not one had been through Senior Chief Jaeger's AOT program. They were young, in superb shape, and extremely motivated. They knew one another well and worked together reliably; that was the upside. The downside was they didn't know their asses from their elbows.

Only four men out of the sixteen assigned to Fifth Platoon

were rated as fully qualified SEALs. I considered myself qualified but hardly knowledgeable. As the platoon assembled, I saw that we would be short on experience. As Frank settled into command, we were informed that the Fifth was immediately to begin predeployment training, or PDT. PDT is normally undertaken after all operators have gone through advanced operator training. We were not to have that luxury. We were expected to form our own cadre and undertake the AOT curriculum as we prepared for the ORE, or operational readiness exam. Any training shortfalls would soon become apparent to our superiors, and to other people as well. Fifth Platoon was slated to deploy to Honduras and serve in the capacity of a mobile training team, military advisers, on the Honduras-Nicaragua border.

We settled in and worked our asses off. PDT was a well-scripted series of evolutions, and the additional work of AOT had to be crammed around and on top of an already full schedule. The bulk of the extra training would fall to Stan and Tim and our newly arrived chief petty officer, Doc Jones. If Frank and I were expecting our chief, the seniormost enlisted man, to provide some adult leadership, we were to be disappointed. Well, if not disappointed, then disconcerted.

Our platoon chief actually wasn't even a chief yet. Hospitalman First Class Jack "Doc" Jones was a chief selectee, meaning he hadn't assumed the rank and title of a navy chief petty officer. Strangest of all, Doc was not even a BUD/S graduate. You might ask what a corpsman, a medic, was doing in an operational SEAL platoon in the first place. Doc might not have been to BUD/S, but he was a SEAL, a damn good one, and a Vietnam combat veteran.

In the throes of that late unpleasantness between the Vietnams, the navy found it impossible to get hospital corpsmen through BUD/S in sufficient numbers. So they asked for volunteers to attend an abbreviated special operations technicians' course. SOT was hardly eight weeks long, and all the corpsmen had time to do was learn one end of an M-16 from another, how to scuba dive, and how to spell "SEAL." The graduates were then sent to Vietnam to join operational

SEAL platoons and serve as medics. Well, not just medics. In the Teams, our corpsmen are armed, and patrol, jump, dive, and do demo just like everyone else. In short, they operate.

In Vietnam, SOT graduates were expected to fight Charlie and take care of wounded SEALs. Some lived and some died, and those corpsmen who survived a six-month combat deployment with an operational SEAL platoon received their Budweisers and earned the naval education code 5326, combat swimmer. Doc Jones was an SOT graduate and a freaking character even among a community of characters.

He would later prove to be one of the bravest men I have ever known. That could hardly be guessed at first look. Physically, he bore a striking resemblance to the actor Peter Falk, the guy who plays Columbo, and Doc had it down, rumpled clothes, wandering eye, and all. He was a short, compact man, and his reddish complexion and dark eyes sometimes made him look like a sturdy Portuguese fisherman. Doc was in fact a nearly full-blooded Cherokee Indian.

Initially, a few of the things Frank and I heard about Doc made us wonder about his sanity. As an SOT graduate, he had not attended jump school, but when he got back to his team stateside, he wanted to jump, so he followed a platoon out onto the drop zone and picked up a parachute. Using the ploy "Hey, could you help me buckle this," he was assisted by his platoon mates into the parachute. No one guessed that he had no idea how to put on a parachute, and no one could have guessed that he had zero idea how to operate one once he got out of the airplane. Doc sat calmly through the jumpmaster's briefing, then got in line and boarded the aircraft. Once inside the plane, he had his rig inspected by the jumpmaster just like everyone else. He hooked up his static line like everyone else, and then he jumped. Mercifully, the parachute gods smiled. Doc made ten water jumps and had legitimately earned his gold navy parachute wings before it was discovered that he never attended jump school. He was sent packing down to Fort Benning, and the story followed him throughout the navy.

Doc would soon have an opportunity to show off his aerial prowess. We jumped again into Fort A. P. Hill and ran live fire and demolition exercises against mobile and static targets. We jelled as an operational unit, and Doc became the growling, ass-kicking spark plug of the entire outfit. He addressed the men individually as "cock breath" and collectively as "you fucking idiots." To Frank, Doc was deferential, calling him mostly "Boss." As the 2IC, or second in charge, I was fair game. Doc called me *"Diawi,"* Vietnamese for "lieutenant," and a bit of a jab when applied to guys like me who were in grade school during much of Vietnam. There was nothing Doc wouldn't do, and few things he couldn't do better and faster than men half his age. He was one of the best I ever worked with; certainly he was the bravest, and the best platoon chief I ever had. We needed him. Our work-ups were everything AOT was, and more; there were specific missions we had to train for: recons, direct action, air ops, and boat work. Doc was the driving force through it all. He would repeatedly tell me, "You know, Mr. Pfarrer, it's not the little things that are going to kill you. It's the fucking BIG things."

Much of the training was out of the area, but there was the occasional weeknight and weekend at home. We worked hard and played harder. Friday nights, Frank and I would put on our working winter blue uniforms and make dramatic entrances into the Oceana officers' club at 2300 hours, fashionably late and resplendent in our tridents and gold navy jump wings. The place would be jumping, filled to the rafters with women invited for one purpose.

At the O club you picked your poison; new wave played in one room and disco in another. We partied hard, danced, and flirted, and were as charming as possible. Lisa was slowly evaporating from my heart, and in her place there was a poisonous void. What interest I had in women was strictly transactional, and though I did my best each night to find someone to come home with me, I rarely cared what happened afterward. Sex was solace and release.

In hindsight, I can say that our job—the Teams, the secrecy, the clannishness—was gradually separating us from society. We were a group apart, and that separation would become more severe as my career progressed. I would bed any woman who let me, and I took and gave back almost nothing. I was unknowable, unlovable, and on my way to becoming fully encapsulated. Not antisocial—feral. As a potential boyfriend, I was the worst possible type: self-absorbed, smugly self-confident, and nursing a life-changing wound.

There were a few women who I remember very well. One, I can say with some embarrassment, I remember specifically for my own cruelty. Another I remember for my own credulous foolishness. I dated a navy nurse, a lieutenant commander though she was only a year older than I was. I was an O-1, and she was an O-4, a dating arrangement not encouraged in today's action navy. Her name was Megan, and she was funny, smart, and blond, a delightful pixie of a woman. She had the most incredible freckles, and we had an absolutely torrid affair. We made love like bunnies with rabies, and over the course of a few wonderful months, Megan fell in love. I remained aloof. I deployed frequently. Sometimes I told her I was going away, and sometimes I did not. My inconsiderate behavior concerned and hurt her. She would have no idea where I'd gone or when I'd be back, and my teammates could give her no information. The end came when I got back from a three-week deployment and did not even call her. I ran into her in a parking lot on the base and said only "Hi." I was ashamed when she broke down and cried as we spoke.

I felt sick as I drove home. I wondered what was happening to me. Why had I hurt her? Why had I let her hurt herself? I took no joy in it. She was a fine, loving person, and I was being an asshole. What was it in me that made me treat a good person this way? Some innate cruelty? Was it because Lisa had hurt me? For a guy with a psychology degree, I had a remarkable lack of insight. Too ashamed to face myself and not enough of a man to face Megan, I just moved on. I was without scruple or compunction, and apparently, now I was even without mercy. An iceberg drifting, waiting to claim another ship.

I started to go out with an athletic Virginia-born chemist named Jenny. She played semipro tennis, and I think she saw in me at first something that was dangerous and attractive. In that she may have been right, but for the wrong reasons. I was not nearly as wild as she was. Jenny was a danger junkie, and it turned out I was only a nuisance.

Through a hot summer, Jenny and I slept together several nights a week, and there were uniforms in her closets and sundresses in mine. I loved her laugh, and the little-girl way she looked when she woke up. I loved the womanly way she kissed me. I cared a lot for Jenny. I enjoyed her when we were together and looked forward to seeing her when we were apart. I was naive enough to think that the things I revealed to her, the big plans, the boyish selfishness, and the burgeoning egomania, could ever really be attractive to anyone.

Falling in love with her made me less dangerous. On the night I was preparing to tell Jenny that I loved her, she told me that she thought it was time we started seeing other people. She held me while she said this. In her dismissal of me, she was calm and polite, and her reasons were well presented and avoided direct insults. As she let me down, I remember thinking two things. I was glad that she'd spoken first, since I'd have felt even more stupid had I just told her that I loved her. My second thought was even more selfish: I remember thinking that this was probably a really bad time for this to be happening to me.

In the coming week Jenny and I were to attend a formal dining-in at the special warfare group. For me, attendance was mandatory, and before the hammer fell, Jenny had agreed to be my date. Rather than leaving me to go alone, she graciously put on an evening gown and went with me. The night was strained. We smiled though the agonizing black-tie affair—I was nervous and awkward, and the evening was made infinitely worse when I got drunk off my ass, drove her home, and begged her to reconsider. I asked for another chance. I asked to spend the night. On all grounds, and now with even better reasons, she declined politely. She suggested I come back Monday so we could talk. I agreed and staggered back to my car.

But I didn't come back on Monday. I went to Panama instead.

Two days after I'd made an ass out of myself, Fifth Platoon was parachuted into the Gulf of Panama, and we established a forward operating base on an island in the Archipelago de las Perlas. Our mission was to again play OPFOR, opposing forces, this time in a joint American-Panamanian military exercise called Kindle Liberty. This was seven years before America would depose Manuel Noriega, and relations with the Panamanians were cordial, if a bit tense at the top. Also deployed to Las Perlas were the XO, a group from the operations office, and a scratch operational force from the cadre, including John Jaeger. We were to conduct a series of across-the-beach operations against the canal and its infrastructure. Our missions were intended to assess the response of U.S. Army and the PDF, the Panama defense forces. It would be their job to protect the canal and our job to try to break it.

Somewhere in Washington the decision was taken that our operations were to be conducted with units of the *Gardia Nacional,* Manuel Noriega's personal gang of thugs. A group of ten *comandos* joined us in Las Perlas and were integrated into our platoons. What they learned would serve them well and do us little good. In a macabre twist of fate, our same Team, SEAL Team Four, would suffer cruelly in the coming invasion of Panama, Operation Just Cause, in December 1989. A SEAL platoon sent to Patilla Airfield to disable Noriega's Learjet would be ambushed and sustain four killed and a number wounded. I am probably not the first person to wonder if the *Gardias* we trained at Las Perlas were the same men who waited for the SEALs on the runway at Patilla.

That disagreeable evening was far in the future, and to us unknowable, if not unimaginable. Not one of us on the island thought our collaboration was a good idea, but we followed orders, and the Panamanians keenly attended our planning and accompanied us as we ran successful ops against the Gatun Locks, the Summit electrical substation, key pumping facilities, and the liquid-oxygen storage tanks on Howard Air Force Base. The only operation from which they were excluded was the capture and simulated sinking of U.S.S. *Spiegel Grove* as she transited the canal. This operation, carried out by all SEAL Team Four elements, was the crowning evolution of the exercise. For obvious reasons, I won't go into the nuts and bolts of a warship takedown, but my assault element operated with John Jaeger's, and the action cemented our friendship.

A few days later, we were cooling our heels in the departure lounge at Howard Air Force Base, waiting for an airplane. Our flight was delayed twice, and finally, Senior Chief Jaeger wandered over and sat down next to me.

"Hey, Mr. Pfarrer." He had a sly look on his face, and I knew it meant he wanted something. Probably permission for something he'd already done or would soon do anyway.

"How's about I let the lads go across the street to the enlisted club and have a few beers, *or so,* before we get on the plane?"

I knew the guys would get as drunk as they could as fast as they could, and that might be a problem. The one thing guaranteeing their good behavior was the fact that no one, including me, had much money. I'd parachuted in with a fortune, fifty bucks, and I doubted all the lads together had even half that much.

"Sure, Senior Chief," I said. "Tell 'em to keep it within the pale of acceptable human conduct."

The guys clomped across the street. John Jaeger grinned, and for a while we sat together in an empty departure lounge.

"Hey, sir?"

"Yes, Senior Chief?"

"You got any money, *or so?*"

"I've got a little," I said.

"How's about you and me slide on over to the club and have a couple of cold pops? *Or so.*"

Now would come a major episode in my education as a

junior officer. The E club was for enlisted men. Officers had their own clubs, and chief petty officers had chiefs' clubs. Neither the senior chief nor I was supposed to drink at an enlisted club.

I sat there quietly and thought about this, and John looked at me like I was a moron. "Let's go," he said. He stood and removed the golden anchors from the collars of his cammies. Before I could think better of it, I stood and took off the gold bars that marked me as an ensign. I'd been in the jungle for the better part of two weeks, and I was thirsty. Without our rank devices, we were transformed instantly from an E-8 and an O-1 to a pair of E-1 no-count snuffies, slick-sleeves, military nonentities. I followed John across the street and into the dark, smoky confines of the club.

The joint was wound up. ZZ Top was playing. Pushed up against the bar was the most explosive mixture of men known to mankind. At one end were about twenty marines, recon dudes with high-and-tight haircuts; in the middle were the SEALs; and on the far end were about an equal number of Green Berets. All had played in the exercise, and the SEALs had operated against both groups. I sipped my beer like a Baptist. The insults were already flying, along with small items: rolled-up napkins, twist tops from beer bottles, and the occasional drink thrown whole. I knew it was only a matter of time until the place exploded. The senior chief and I would be doubly damned if it did. We would be dinged first for not stopping the riot from happening, and then we would be gigged for being here in the first place.

An empty shot glass bounced off the bar in front of John.

"Getting a little hairy in here, *or so,*" he said calmly.

I was just about to say "Let's get the hell out of here" when John picked up the glass from the bar. He stood on his bar stool and banged the glass off his beer mug. *Ding ding ding ding.*

"All right, you assholes," he bellowed, "pipe down!" The crowd quieted a little. The senior chief yelled again. "I'm telling you assholes to shut the fuck up! AT EASE!"

The bar quieted. It was a sullen, tense silence, and every

eye in the place was on John, balanced on his bar stool. I wanted the world to open up and swallow me, but the senior chief was in his glory. He stepped onto the bar and walked its entire length.

"All right," he growled. "Who's the roughest, toughest motherfucker in the bar?"

A gigantic Green Beret stood up. This guy was six-five and looked about 250. "I am," he said.

John looked him over. "You're the toughest motherfucker in this bar?"

"That's what I said, old man," the Green Beret answered.

"Good," John said. "You take over. I gotta take a piss."

The place exploded in laughter, the tension broken forever. John jumped down off the bar and gave me a wink. It was an epic stunt, and one I have never had the courage to repeat. I'd just watched a master in action.

FRIDAY WAS NEW YEAR'S EVE, and I'd been operational for a year and a half. Holiday leave had been granted in two sections: Half the command received a week off at Christmas, and the other half was allowed liberty the week of New Year's. I'd taken neither this year. I was a bachelor, and although I would have liked to see my parents back in Mississippi, I'd been able to get home for a weekend at Thanksgiving. I volunteered to take the watch on Christmas Eve and again during the New Year's leave section. The duty was easy, and apart from the two nights I spent in the Team area, it was like another week off. I was happy to let the guys who had families spend time at home.

I'd been invited to a New Year's party by a pilot friend who flew for the Red Wolves, an aviator with the redoubtable name of Wilbur. The bash was to be at Wilbur's house, on the north end of Virginia Beach, a neighborhood to which I am still partial. Wilbur's crowd was mostly airdales, and they called themselves the Fifty-eighth Street Beach Bullies. I was delighted to be invited, as I did not think a punch-up at the Casino would be the best way to start my year.

Wilbur's place was on the sand, a ramshackle three-story

1920s vintage beach palace. The wind was blowing hard and cold off the surf when I arrived. It was crowded and warm inside. I stashed my coat, thanked the host, and somebody mixed me a very large drink. A woman I didn't know came up, kissed me, and gave me a pointed hat that said BETTER LUCK NEXT YEAR.

Three minutes later, I ran into the woman I would later marry.

Margot Attman was blond, striking, six feet tall, and always had a wry smile crinkling the corner of her mouth. She looked vaguely like Faye Dunaway. Where the movie star seemed ephemeral, Margot was athletic and direct. She had a biting wit. When I first saw her, she was standing against a door leading out to the porch, one foot on the ground, the other tucked back, almost under her thigh. Her legs were extraordinarily long. She held a drink in one hand and had her other thumbed through a belt loop, like a cowboy. Her head was down, and her blue eyes were half closed; she was listening to, or ignoring, a small, balding man telling her a joke.

Our eyes met as I walked past. I am hardly a pickup artist, but as soon as the bald man walked off, I walked over.

"Thank God," she said. "They invited somebody tall."

I was smitten.

We talked and danced, and her friends watched us and asked one another who I was. Margot played them, and played me as well. She told her friend Wanda that I was her stepbrother. She told someone else I was her pool boy.

She was a teacher from upstate New York, in the country between Buffalo and Niagara. Her father was the postmaster of a small town called Hamlin. She asked what I did in the navy, and I said I was an astronaut. When pressed, I admitted that I was actually only a payload specialist.

"I just work the big arm," I said.

"Bullshit," she said. "Wilbur says you're a SEAL and I should keep away from you."

"Wilbur is a dangerous man," I said. "I've flown with him."

At midnight she said, "Come over here and kiss me."

I stood where I was. I said finally, "Come over here. I'm worth it."

She did, and I pulled her close, and I kissed her long and deeply, and when I let her up for air, I kissed the front of her throat twice. Lightly. And then I whispered into her ear, "When I kiss 'em, they *stay* kissed." It was the corniest line I knew, and it made her laugh brightly.

We left her car parked where it was and drove in mine to her place, a bungalow on the beach maybe a dozen blocks south. We were buzzed and happy and glad to be alone. I had come recently from the tropics; my skin was red, and I delighted in the cold wind that ripped into me. My heart was pounding as we climbed the wooden stairs to her apartment; inside, it was cool and drafty. I lit a fire, and she literally said she was going to slip into something more comfortable. I laughed and poured her a drink.

The wind blew in great gusts, and the little house occasionally shook as huge waves thundered down on the sand. In a few moments Margot came out of the bedroom nude, and the fire played on her skin.

"I forgot my pajamas," she said.

My eyes rolled over her hungrily. Her body was long, her breasts perfect and round. She had the light traces of a suntan marking out a bikini line. I took her into my arms. We went to bed and made love all night.

We were not apart much after that evening. I was deployed often, but Margot was always there when I got back, always droll, always unimpressed with the SEAL Team bullshit. And always her body was mine, and she would sleep in my arms, warm in my arms, and I started slowly and inexorably to need her in my life.

I am sorry to say that I wish I had been able to love her better.

SURFIN' SAFARI

IN THE EARLY 1980s, Puerto Lempira, Honduras, was a settlement of about five hundred people and half as many chickens. The lempira is the national currency of Honduras, and the name of the town was a bit of wishful thinking. Hard currency is in scarce supply in eastern Honduras.

The town is perched on a wisp of swampland jutting into Laguna de Caratasca, a broad, shallow bay on the Mosquito Coast. Puerto Lempira's citizens eked a precarious living from the fish of the Caribbean Sea and a handful of skinny cattle that wandered the dirt streets. The place was remarkable only for its small discotheque, the sole nightspot for a hundred kilometers. Plunked down in the maw of poverty was a joint that had frozen margaritas, a five-hundred-watt sound system, and a lighted *Saturday Night Fever* dance floor—all powered by a ten-horsepower portable generator.

La vida loca, writ large.

Puerto Lempira is the capital of the Honduran province, or *departmento,* of Gracias a Dios. Bordered to the south by the Coco River and Nicaragua, the *departmento* comprises the easternmost section of the country. It is the only Honduran provincial seat not connected to the rest of the nation by road. The sole land access is a rude dirt track meandering southwest to the town of Ausabila, on the border with El Salvador. No roads link Puerto Lempira, directly or indirectly, with the capital of Tegucigalpa over two hundred miles to the west.

Puerto Lempira's isolation from the rest of the nation is extreme. The Mosquito Coast is an almost wholly undeveloped stretch of mangrove spreading southeast to Cabo Gracias a Dios. Nearly everything, and everybody, comes and goes by boat. There was a dirt airstrip just outside of town, but back then the arrival of an airplane was an event of almost biblical proportion. Near the airfield stood a two-story cinder-block building painted in the national colors, powder blue and white. The building, without doors or windows, was the home of a company of Honduran infantry and the seat of government. Sorry as it may have been, in 1982, Puerto Lempira was about to become a very important place.

Two years before, the revolution had triumphed in Nicaragua. A handful of opposition groups, dominated by the Sandinista National Liberation Front, had toppled the U.S.-backed dictator, Anastasio Samosa. After Samosa's fall and exile, land was redistributed, the banks were nationalized, and education and health care were improved. But the people of Nicaragua had traded one despot for another.

The leader of the Sandinistas, Daniel Ortega, promptly consolidated his rule, jailed opponents and former allies, and established an orthodox communist state. Civil rights were curtailed and elections postponed. Cuban aid propped up the junta, as did Russian arms and advisers. The increasingly radical regime was accused of aiding the leftist insurgency in nearby El Salvador, a charge Commandante Ortega made no attempt to deny.

In Washington, it appeared that the dominoes were beginning to fall, and the perception was that a Cuban finger was doing the pushing. None of this sat very well with Ronald Reagan, who, I am told, never got used to Cuba in the first place. For Uncle Ronnie, one communist country in the hemisphere was enough.

As Sandinista repression intensified, dissidents began to take up arms. Some of the fighters were from the military of the old regime, some were from the oligarchy, but many were from liberal and democratic elements that felt betrayed by the Sandinistas' power grab. Harried by Sandinista patrols, most of these forces fled north across the Coco River and into Honduras. In 1981 their numbers were small and their equipment and arms almost nonexistent. They had no centralized command. They were not a viable military force in any sense of the word.

That would soon change.

These groups would come to be called *contrarevolucionarios,* or simply the Contras. With the backing of the CIA, these factions would be drawn together into a force dedicated to the overthrow of Daniel Ortega. The Contras were to become the pointy end of a continuing U.S. proxy war against the Evil Empire. The CIA needed a place where this surrogate army could be armed and trained, a place far from publicity or notice. That place was eastern Honduras: the *departmento de* Gracias a Dios.

ONE AFTERNOON IN LITTLE CREEK, Frank and I were on our way to the pistol range. Mike Boynton waved at us from inside the ops office. "XO wants to see you," he said.

As we started across the hall to the XO's office, Mike asked, "You guys up on your shots?"

He meant immunizations, and we both knew this meant traveling, usually to someplace where diarrhea was a national pastime.

We knocked on Jon Wallace's door. Rolled out on his desk were a nautical chart of the Mosquito Coast of Honduras and a few satellite photos of a crummy little village at the foot of an extraordinarily long pier. It was my first glimpse of Puerto Lempira.

The XO didn't say much. We were told that there would be a joint U.S.-Honduran amphibious operation, intended as a demonstration for the Nicaraguans. The operation was code-named Agas Tara. The U.S. intended to land marines and whatever forces the Honduran army could scrape together in the vicinity of Cabo Gracias a Dios, the cape that marked the border of Nicaragua and Honduras. Frank and I were to accompany the XO on a preliminary reconnaissance of the area and select a number of possible beach-landing sites.

"Hard data on this area is strictly guidebook stuff. The maps are a joke," the XO said.

I looked at the bottom of the nautical chart. It was based on an admiralty survey dated 1856. A small caution also stated: "Cabo Gracias a Dios is reported to lay 15 nautical miles east of the position indicated on this chart. Navigators should use extreme caution approaching the coast." The position of a major terrain feature was plotted with a fifteen-mile error!

If we were going to go there and make maps, our work was definitely cut out for us. I looked at the satellite photos. The vegetation around the Laguna was brutal. Swamp, jungle, mangrove, and various combinations of the above.

Fifth Platoon had just returned from a month of jungle training on Isla Peros and Vieques Island in Puerto Rico. I would have liked to think that we were selected for this operation because we were trained to razor sharpness. Actually, Frank and I had been picked because we were, well, available.

We would leave the next day, travel by commercial air to Panama, check in to a hotel, and wait for a go. We were to wear civilian clothes and carry nothing to identify ourselves as U.S. naval officers. Once the mission was green-lit, we'd report to Howard Air Force Base in the Canal Zone and insert by air force C-130. Once in-country, we would meet up with a Honduran naval vessel. We would be delivered into the area as discreetly as possible, scope the place out, and make a recommendation. The powers that be would select one of our suggested locations, and before the landings, a larger team would be dispatched to make a detailed reconnaissance, to include the creation of a beach-landing chart. It was a classic preinvasion operation, made a little spookier by the civvies.

We were to tell no one, in or out of the command, where we were going or what we were doing. In order to draw per diem and tickets, our orders would read that we were to travel to Fort Amador, Panama, for TAD, or temporary additional duty. Generic orders, until you read the fine print. We were authorized "to other locations as necessary and return," authorized to observe relaxed grooming standards, and authorized to carry concealed weapons. We were to travel under our civilian passports.

Frank and I returned to our platoon hut, packed our gear, and reported to sick bay to draw malaria pills. I took mine that night, and they made me violently ill. Malaria wouldn't have been any worse. Maybe I should have taken it as an omen.

The following morning we met at Norfolk International Airport for a flight to Miami. From Miami we would connect to another flight into Panama City. On the way to the airport, I stopped to buy a paper. *The New York Times*. It is axiomatic in the military that the more people there are who know about an operation, the more likely it is to go wrong. We were not off to a great start. Despite our civilian clothes and our circuitous, nonmilitary transportation arrangements, our mission was on the front page: U.S. TO STAGE AMPHIBIOUS OPERATION ON NICARAGUAN BORDER.

Even the code name was in the article. I handed the paper to Jon Wallace as we waited at the gate. He read it with a bemused look. Whoever leaked to the *Times* knew everything. It wouldn't be the first or the last time I would take part in an operation that was preannounced in the press. We got on the plane and hoped for the best.

We arrived in Panama and grabbed taxis to the hotel. At the time Panama was firmly under the rule of Manuel Noriega. Although it was nominally a U.S. ally and a "partner for peace," the isthmus was a haven for narcoterrorists, money launderers, drug dealers, and international refuse. We checked in to El Marriott in Panama City, the lobby of which was arguably the king-daddy nexus of shady operations in all of Latin America.

We cooled our heels at the hotel for a couple of days while people higher up the food chain tried to figure out what to do with a clandestine reconnaissance element that had been deployed the same day *The New York Times* blew Operation Agas Tara.

We hit the weight room and the pool and hung out. The bar at El Marriott was like something straight out of a Warren

Zevon song. Shoulder to shoulder were cocaine cowboys, thousand-dollar-a-night call girls, arms merchants, DEA agents, spies, squint-eyed bankers, and beribboned Panamanian military thugs. Swilling *ron y tonicas,* the crowd mixed it up until the wee hours. When asked what I was doing in Panama, I'd say I worked for a company that delivered sailing yachts. I said I was waiting for a ketch to transit the canal, and when the boat arrived in Panama City, I would sail it up the coast to San Diego. It was a cover I used frequently, and it always worked. It explained why I was just hanging around, why I was sunburned, why I owned decent rain gear; and chicks dug it. Sometimes people in hotel bars are not what they appear to be.

The decision was finally taken to let us do our thing. At 0400 we drove to Howard Air Force Base, boarded a C-130, and flew north to Honduras. The plan had changed, and "as discreetly as possible" now meant that we would fly directly to the airfield at Puerto Lempira. We'd still be in civvies, but since the amphibious landing was no longer a secret, we'd dispense with the midnight parachute drop.

We were met at the airfield by a CIA paramilitary officer. He was wearing an Izod shirt and tiger-striped camouflage pants. He had an Uzi slung around his neck, bolt back, ready to rock. Later, none of us remembered him mentioning his name. We were driven through "town" and out to Puerto Lempira's single pier. The Honduran naval vessel we boarded was a surplus World War II Mike boat. It was a landing craft right out of *The Longest Day.* Beat up and rusty, this one looked like it might have been used at Normandy.

We crossed the Laguna and dropped the ramp inside on the bar. The coxswain put Frank and the XO ashore on the southern side of the channel mouth. Mr. Uzi and I were landed on the north side. The beach was broad and the sand extremely soft. I doubted that wheeled vehicles, even six-wheel-drive trucks, could cross it. The day was rainy and gray, and although the surf was almost flat, I noticed debris and driftwood well up the beach. The surf had been big here recently. Big surf is a negative factor in amphibious landings.

As we walked back to the pickup point, I asked Mr. Uzi if there were any other Americans here.

"Three of us," he answered. He said he'd flown down from Tegucigalpa two days ago. There were some camps for "displaced persons" ten miles to the south of Puerto Lempira, and that's where they spent most of their time. He had been there when he was told to go to the airstrip and meet us. I guessed those displaced persons were Contras but said nothing.

We met back at the Mike boat. The XO and Frank had the same story to tell about the sand on the other side of the channel. I mentioned the debris on the beach. River mouths and bay entrances can get nasty when a swell is running. Though it was slack water at the time of our visit, the current out of the bay would also be a factor. Landing on the outer beaches was probably a nonstarter—there were beach exits, but they led only into mangrove and impassable swamp. If there was to be a landing here, it would have to be inside the lagoon.

We chugged back into the bay, the Mike boat doing maybe seven knots. As we crossed the bay, it started to rain, hard, and my malaria pills kicked in again. I spent most of the crossing puking over the front of the bow ramp.

Three miles east of Puerto Lempira, in a quiet mile-wide cove, we found a landing site. The exits led to a logging road, and the beach flanks were bordered by mangrove and several slow-moving streams. The terrain here would favor the landing force. Although it would not be within the line of sight of the landing ships, an amphibious squadron and attack helicopters could control access to the bay. It was a sweet piece of real estate.

"We're going to want to move trucks across the beach," Mr. Uzi said. The XO didn't think that was going to be a problem. This beach, unlike the others, was hard-packed sand.

Frank gave me a look. Those trucks, we guessed, would be

making deliveries to the displaced persons. This landing beach was out of Puerto Lempira's view and not visible to vessels offshore. Privacy was a plus. The beach exits connected to the road linking Puerto Lempira with the border. Besides being able to service the displaced persons, this landing site would be a perfect back door into El Salvador.

Our CIA friend was delighted, and we were happy for him.

We chugged back to Puerto Lempira, said good-bye to Mr. Uzi, and boarded the C-130. Five hours later, I was back in the bar at El Marriott, telling a Dutch stewardess how I got my job with the yacht delivery company. The following day we flew back to Virginia Beach.

Nothing happened for a couple of weeks. Then, as is usually the case in the navy, everything happened at once.

Fifth Platoon was preparing for another training deployment, this one to Fort A. P. Hill in central Virginia, where we would undergo three weeks of air-to-ground training, learning to call in air strikes and artillery. Our trucks were loading when Jon Wallace called Frank and me into his office.

"One of you is going back to Honduras," he said.

"When?" asked Frank.

"Agas Tara is on for next week," the XO said. "You'll need to select an element to conduct the prelanding recon and prepare a beach-landing chart. You're going to do an at-sea boat drop to rendezvous with the amphib ships after they leave Puerto Rico."

"We're scheduled to go to A. P. Hill tomorrow morning," said Frank. ANGLICO (Air/Naval Gunfire Liaison Company) was a critical part of our mission, and it was certain to figure in our operational readiness inspection, which was three weeks from now.

"Either Chuck takes the platoon to A. P. Hill or you do. But I want someone who's had eyes on the target to make the recon," said the XO.

"How many guys in the detachment?" I asked.

"No more than five," said the XO.

"Five guys to do a prelanding recon and survey?" I asked.

It was normally a job done by an entire platoon, sixteen men, or even two platoons.

"Not my problem," the XO said. "Now get out of here and make it happen."

Meeting over. Frank and I left.

Frank Giffland was one of the best officers I ever had the privilege to work with. "You're going," he said.

I couldn't believe my ears. This assignment was a plum, and there were few officers, me included, who would let it devolve on a subordinate. I said, "Frank, you're senior, you oughta go down there." Not that I didn't want the job—I did.

"This is going to involve a boat drop," I went on, "and briefing the commander of the landing forces, *and* the commodore of the amphibious squadron . . . Then there's the little problem of conducting a prelanding recon with only five guys. Not to mention the fact that I speak French—my Spanish is still limited to ordering beers and telling people to get fucked."

"I think you can handle it," Frank said. He said the recon would be fun, but his job was to prepare the platoon for deployment. The platoon was his command, and platoons were commanded by platoon commanders. Detachments were commanded by assistant platoon commanders. So that settled it. The entire time I worked for him, Frank Giffland applied this logic, and I was to be afforded opportunity after opportunity. It was not a lesson I would forget. Later, when I got my own command, I'd do things the Giffland way.

"You only get four guys, plus yourself," he said as we walked through the Team area. "You're going to need an air-ops guy, a cartographer, and an engineman."

"Dave, Tim, Stan, and Bubba," I said.

"Tell 'em to get their gear off the trucks," said Frank.

We worked all night preparing the rubber duck, an F-470 Zodiac raiding boat, rigged to be paradropped at sea. Actually, we prepared two of them. In the SEALs, we have a saying: "One is none, two is one." The inflatable boat would be mission-critical. If it burned in—that is, if its parachute failed to open—we'd have a spare.

I hit the Intel Department and loaded up on maps, charts, and satellite photos. I went to Operations, had everyone's orders cut, and sent coded messages to the amphibious squadron recommending a time and location for the boat drop. The location was two hundred miles south of Jamaica. The middle of tropical nowhere. We'd be able to make our parachute drop unobserved.

The guys selected for this operation were solid. Surfer Dave was the point man of my assault element and a fine cartographer. Stan was a second-class petty officer, a quartermaster, and could be expected to help Dave with the beach chart. Tim was the platoon's leading petty officer and had been around the block a time or two. He was our air-ops department head, a former member of the navy parachute team, and would be responsible for building up the rubber ducks. Bubba Nederlander was simply Bubba. A Tennessee hillbilly who was utterly without fear, he drank like a fish and fought like a tiger. He was an engineman, third class, and would probably stay that rank forever. He was a good guy, and later, like Dave, would prove unflappable in combat. I knew I could count on him to keep our outboards running, even with chewing gum and bailing wire.

After the rubber ducks were built, I gave the lads a warning order and told them we were going to Honduras. Nobody blinked. We went into isolation, meaning we were not allowed out of the Team area until we left for the airplane. It was standard operating procedure for a mission deployment. Frank and the rest of the Fifth had already left for A. P. Hill, and it was quiet. That night I watched *Breaker Morant* on video in the platoon hut and drank beer.

The plan for our first reconnaissance into Honduras had leaked—way above my pay grade—but this time we'd have airtight security. I hoped.

THE TAIL RAMP of the C-141 went down, and the back doors clamshelled open. After hours in the cold, dark tube of the aircraft, the tropical light was sudden and blinding. We'd left Norfolk on a sleety winter night, loaded our equipment and the two palleted ducks, and flown directly south to the at-sea rendezvous point. Now a hot blast of tropical air flooded into the airplane.

The plane was at fifteen hundred feet over the rendezvous point. The pilots had a visual on our ship, *Fairfax County,* a landing ship, tank, or LST. I bent down and looked off the ramp. Under the port wing, *Fairfax County* appeared as advertised. The C-141 pulled a wide circle and came into the wind.

We hooked static lines; the light turned green, and a drogue chute yanked the rubber duck off the tail ramp. We ran after it, plunging into the aircraft's jet blast as the huge cargo chute blossomed over the Zodiac. Static lines opened our parachutes, and we steered to the place the Zodiac would touch down.

As we floated toward the water, we pulled on swim fins. At a hundred feet, we released the chest straps of our parachute harnesses, turned in to the wind, and prepared for a water landing. Although the army-issue T-10 parachutes were not known for their steering capabilities, we all landed within fifty feet of the boat. The C-141 dropped our second boat, loaded with additional equipment. Forty minutes after we'd left the airplane, we were pulling the Zodiacs onto the stern ramp of *Fairfax County.*

We stowed our equipment, weapons, and ammunition and were shown to our quarters. I changed into a dry uniform and met the captain in the wardroom. I remember him as a tall, affable man; he said he had known my father at the Naval War College. It was always good when they said that, I thought. I was proud and happy to find in my travels that my father was universally liked and respected.

The captain introduced me to his officers, and to one who didn't need an introduction. Ralph Knight was also a JG, and he had been in my company at OCS. Ralph was a cryptological officer, an electronic spook, and, like me, was on detachment—not part of the ship's company.

As we'd motored up to *Fairfax County,* we'd noticed several large trailer vans parked on her decks. The trailers bristled with antennae. Ralph and a small crew of linguists and code breakers were here to keep an ear on the Nicaraguans as we played our little game. Ralph, of course, didn't say any of this. He never said much of anything. If you ever asked him what they did inside the vans, he'd tell you, "We repair flashlights." I wouldn't even have known he was a crypto officer if I hadn't seen his orders back in Newport.

The captain filled me in on his end of the operation, and I filled him in on ours. He said that another ship, *Boulder,* was en route from Puerto Rico. Aboard it were a company of marines, a Navy Seabee detachment, and three companies of infantry from the Puerto Rican national guard. The marines would secure the landing site; the Puerto Rican units would operate with the Honduran infantry; and the Seabees were to make road improvements and dig any defensive positions called for by the marines. They'd be ashore for a week, then be back-loaded. It was your basic amphib operation, *Fairfax County*'s stock-in-trade, and everyone seemed to have their shit together.

The captain told me that two days before, *Fairfax County* had been overflown by a Russian-made May-type maritime surveillance plane out of Cuba. Agas Tara had again been in the press, and *The New York Times* had published updates. Although the operation wouldn't be a surprise to the Nicaraguans, the timing and location of the landing were still to be kept as secret as possible. That meant the prelanding operations, principally our reconnaissance, were to be conducted with the greatest possible security. Although we would conduct the operation clandestinely, Honduras was a "permissive environment"; we were there at the request of an ostensible ally. I told the skipper that I expected no trouble.

The night before the operation, the captain, Ralph, and I were heloed to *Boulder* to brief the commodore and the commander of the landing force. At the briefing, there was an update from the intelligence officer. He indicated that there had been some activity in the Nicaraguan port of Puerto Cabezas. Troops had moved north on the highway toward the Honduran border, and at least two Russian-made patrol craft were in the harbor. Puerto Cabezas was less than fifty miles south of the border. This wasn't a surprise; nor did it particularly bother anyone at the briefing. The terrain of Gracias a Dios would strongly favor the defenders, meaning us, and two patrol boats were not an issue to amphibious ships armed with five-inch guns and attack helicopters.

Ralph gave a brief synopsis of the Nicaraguan electronic order of battle. They had coastal surveillance radars operational, he said, and there had been an increase in traffic on Sandinista army frequencies. "They know we're out here," he said.

I was one of the last to brief. My operation was extremely straightforward and had just four phases. I would conduct my reconnaissance at night and insert over the horizon. I would communicate using brevity codes to report our arrival into Laguna de Caratasca, the completion of the survey, and our exit back to sea. For code words, I had selected the names of three girlfriends who had dumped me: Susan, Katherine, and Avis.

Following the recon, our scheduled pickup would be in broad daylight, approximately twenty miles offshore, and radio communications for the final part of our operation would be in the clear—on open, rather than encrypted, radio circuits. I would have a hydrographic chart of the beach-landing site prepared two hours after my return to *Fairfax County.*

The commodore told us that *Boulder* was to remain far offshore, appearing with her troops and landing craft only on the morning of the actual landing. This might not be a big surprise to the Nicaraguans, the commodore said, but it would be a little one.

We were heloed back to *Fairfax County,* and I updated the guys. The following morning I inspected weapons and equipment and reviewed the charts. At 1400 I gave a patrol leader's order, briefing them in detail on our operation—a process that took the better part of two hours. SEALs tend to brief the hell out of everything. We plan thoroughly because operations very seldom go as you think they will.

This one would be no exception.

An hour after sundown, *Fairfax County* sailed to within thirty nautical miles of the coast, then turned southeast, remaining in conventional shipping lanes. To anyone watching on radar, *Fairfax County* would appear to be a slow-moving coastal trader and not a United States Navy warship inserting a reconnaissance element. So we hoped.

At 2030 hours we departed our briefing spaces and dragged our F-470 Zodiac raiding craft toward the gigantic door at the aft end of the well deck. When the door was completely down, water swept into the well deck, and the hollow door thudded as it was beaten on by a large, following sea. Timing our movement between waves, we dragged our boat down the ramp.

The Zodiac's bowline was attached to a cleat, and for a few moments we glided in *Fairfax County*'s wake, towed along as we secured equipment and weapons and tested the outboard engine. Night-vision goggles, marker buoys, radios, rucksacks, and personal weapons were secured with carabiners. As the bowline pulled tight, we worked without speaking. The only sound was water hissing down the huge ship's steel sides.

The night was blustery, and squalls swept in from the west. Above the blow, a bright first-quarter moon would occasionally burst through breaks in the cloud deck. The moon was not the way we wanted it—high and bright in the sky, it occasionally lit us and the ship—but we were happy for the storm and squalls. The weather was supposed to last all night, and there was some comfort in that. Visibility in the rain was often less than a hundred yards—perfect for gaining our objective undetected.

Finally, I nodded to the well-deck officer: We were good to go. We released the bowline, and our Zodiac dropped back into the silvery wake of the ship. I put the tiller over and we turned west, skittering over the top of a large, rolling swell. The stern of the ship disappeared as the wave rose between us. Within moments the LST was lost in rain and darkness. I knew *Fairfax County* would now turn north, again doing her best to seem like nothing more than a coast-wise merchant-man. I steadied up on course 170. Somewhere over the dark horizon lay the coast of Honduras, Laguna de Caratasca, and our area of operations.

Over twenty sea miles stood between the coast and us. We were a small black speck on an infinitely huge and dark ocean. We had eleven hours to infiltrate the target, conduct our recon, exfil, and move offshore to a prearranged rendezvous with *Fairfax County*. Until then we were on our own.

We plowed southeast, chugging up and down the faces of big swells. We were alternately thrust into bright patches of moonlight and swept over by cold, dark rainsqualls. I sat in the stern, working the outboard, as Dave, Bubba, Stan, and Tim pressed down on the boat's tubes, presenting as low a profile as possible. There was not a light or stars to be seen. Only the vaguest glimmer of bioluminescence stirred in our wake. I kept on course and strained my eyes against the night.

After about an hour and a half, the coastline rose into view. It wasn't much of a landfall. The low terrain was the merest smudge on the horizon; if not for dead reckoning, I'd have had no idea we were even getting close. To starboard, the coast seemed to be enveloped in a thin, low fog. There were no lights. The Mosquito Coast was, and is, a desolate, poor place, and there was not a single navigational light, nor the light from any dwelling, to mark the entry to the Laguna. After twenty miles on a compass heading, I hoped I was in the right place.

I slowed the engine to idle and listened. There was a steady sound from the shore—something like low, uninterrupted thunder. Occasionally, the noise was punctuated by a larger sound, a hollow boom merging into the general roar. I knew this was the noise of surf—big, big surf breaking in the channel's mouth. Even out here, three or four hundred yards from the beach, the swells were the size of houses. As we were thrust up on the crest of a roller, I glimpsed the shore in the middle distance, and on the crest of a second swell, I made out a break in the tree line: the mouth of the lagoon. A four-hundred-yard-long, three-hundred-yard-wide channel connected Laguna de Caratasca to the sea. Somewhere inside the surf zone were the channel bar and the entrance to the bay.

Another boom. This one sounded like not-so-distant artillery. The waves in the vicinity of the bar were piling up against the tide pouring down the throat of the channel. I wasn't overly concerned—yet. I had a visual on the channel mouth, and all I had to do was keep away from breaking waves and hit the slot.

The problem was that we were engulfed in another rainsquall. In a matter of seconds, visibility plunged to under a hundred yards. I told Bubba to keep an eye seaward, and we felt our way toward the channel. He was watching for the Big Kahuna, any rogue wave breaking far outside the rest. If we were caught from behind by a wave, we would broach. Although the Zodiac would not sink, it might capsize or pitchpole, scattering us and our equipment and flooding our radio. Not the way I wanted to arrive in Honduras.

The job now was to find the edge of the surf zone; we would then wait until we had timed several sets of waves. We had to pick the end of a smaller set and attempt to cross during a lull. It sounds easy. But poor visibility wasn't our sole problem. The tide was at full ebb, and a rush of current, maybe five knots' worth, was pouring down the channel. Laguna de Caratasca is over twenty-five miles long and five miles wide. The entire body of water emptied to sea through a three-hundred-yard opening. To maintain position off the bar against the ebbing tide would take some fancy boat handling.

Compounding matters, when swells met the rush of outgoing tide, they would occasionally lurch up, sucking out and pitching forward in what surfers call "closeouts." Most waves break in a predictable manner; closeouts break almost without warning. Two-hundred-yard sections of wave would fold over and break almost instantaneously, sending a wall of white water across the entire channel. I studied the waves and waited for an opening.

"You've got a set coming," Dave said quietly.

I turned and looked aft. Half a dozen cliff-sized waves rolled silently toward us, getting bigger as they came. I turned the boat 180 degrees, headed seaward, and gunned the engine. The Zodiac went nearly vertical as we made it up the face of the first wave. It was a monster. I put the tiller to port and headed for the low shoulder of the next wave as the breaker exploded on the bar like a depth charge.

Holy shit. I looked at Bubba. For a kid from Tennessee, he didn't seem too impressed. I wasn't comforted to think that maybe he didn't know any better.

I stood up again and looked out into the blackness. The set had passed, I hoped. I would have to cross the bar in the relative calm between sets. But which sets? And how would I know when it was safe to go?

The rain stopped as though someone had turned off a tap. The moon came out and lit the channel and the Laguna beyond the bar. Suddenly, the way before us was clear. The sea behind us was also lit.

"Jesus tap-dancing Christ," Bubba said.

This time he *was* impressed. Behind us, a massive set of waves crested up on the outermost part of the bar. Here was the Big Kahuna and his buddies. We were now a hundred yards from the mouth of the channel. These waves were the biggest we'd seen tonight. There would be no turning to seaward and getting away over them. Like it or not, we would have to run the channel. Now.

"Okay, let's do it," I said. As if we had a choice. I pointed the Zodiac toward the shore.

As we moved into the impact zone, I gunned the engine, trying to keep the boat in the low spot between the last wave of the first set and the first wave of the new. A foot-thick layer of sea foam danced on the water around the boat. Behind us, a gigantic wall of water felt bottom and loomed up.

In slow motion, the wave pitched out. The lip was two feet thick and fell trailing a white plume of spray. As it slammed the bar, the rumble was something we could feel in our chests. Another wave broke behind it. Then another. These waves were breaking 250 yards to seaward and rolling toward us in ten-foot walls of white water. The broken waves rushed at us, closing the distance between sets faster than I thought possible.

I gave the engine a squirt and overtook the white water in front of us, the remnant of the first set. The Zodiac bumped up, then dropped down five feet as we overhauled the broken section. We were now surfing, only we weren't riding a surfboard; we were in an inflatable boat loaded with a thousand pounds of men and equipment, and it handled like a dump truck with four flat tires.

The good news was we were slotted right down the middle of the channel. The bad news was the Big Kahuna was still closing. Fast. We streaked along, and I kept the tiller as steady as I could. Any turn right or left could broach us, and the boat would flip and be run ashore. I steered and gritted my teeth.

The wave behind kept coming. Even broken, it was bigger and faster than the wave we rode. I knew from thousands of hours of surfing that one breaking wave does not usually overtake another. I also knew that sometimes they do. When it does happen, the doubled wave is bigger and even more unpredictable. I didn't want to do the math. We were inside the channel mouth, and I could see beach, forest, and mangrove on either side of us. I knew the wave would have to peter out. Soon. The wall of white water behind us started to subside, gradually lessening until it faded out completely under us.

To my right was a rude jumble of fishing shacks, maybe five. This place was called Barra de Caratasca. It wasn't a town, just a group of huts. They showed no light, but I didn't want to be seen. I aimed the Zodiac at the left side of the channel and reduced speed. We puttered out of the impact zone and toward the darkness of the mangroves.

We were in.

I looked around the boat. Grinning like a monkey, Bubba

had his hat folded back like Gabby Hayes. Dave knew exactly how close we had cut it. He rolled his eyes. "Cowabunga," he said.

Nobody laughed. Everybody knew we would have to cross the bar again to get home.

I told Dave to contact *Fairfax County* and let them know we were in. I listened as he intoned, "Long Bow, this is Garfish. Susan, over." He flashed a thumbs-up as the ship rogered our transmission.

We headed southwest, toward the middle of the bay. Three miles passed before we caught sight of the scattered lights of Puerto Lempira, another two miles due south across the water. The rain came and went, but the night remained exceedingly black. Confident we were not visible from shore, in the middle of the bay, we turned southeast toward the landing site.

As we motored slowly along, Dave heaved a lead line from the bow of our boat, testing the depth of the water. We rode a shoal contour for a while; eventually, we veered south and found deeper soundings. This was the channel our landing craft would follow to the beach site.

We dropped a buoy and a fifty-pound anchor. The buoy was a translucent plastic milk jug into which we stuffed five infrared light sticks. The chemlights could be seen only with night-vision goggles. In daylight the buoys would be visible to the landing craft. We marked and followed the channel southeast.

Even though we had located the channel, finding the landing site was a bitch. I had to be sure of our location by hugging the shore and counting the two cove openings to the west of our beach. Using NVGs, we finally located the small, low point of land adjacent to the beach-landing site. We dropped a second buoy.

I idled back the engine. Dave and Tim slipped over the side and swam quietly toward shore. They were swimmer scouts, and would make sure the area was unoccupied before we brought the boat or the rest of the team any closer. For reasons of security, our reconnaissance mission had not been coordinated with the detachment of Honduran infantry stationed at Puerto Lempira. The Hondurans had no radio equipment that could receive coded traffic. It was decided to conduct all of the prelanding operations "in obscura" rather than to radio the plan on an open frequency. Not a bad idea, since we were right on the Nicaraguan border.

Swimmer scouts were also a good idea. Though it was likely that the Hondurans were tucked safely in their barracks, an unexpected encounter with one of their patrols might lead to a serious misunderstanding.

Half an hour passed, and we waited, pressed down as low as possible in the boat. I scanned the shoreline with my night-vision goggles. Finally, the signal came: five flashes from an infrared strobe. I put the engine in gear and motored toward the beach.

The water inside the cove was flat calm, and we glided silently against a stand of mangrove next to a broad white crescent of beach. I killed the motor. We pulled a camouflage net over the boat and moored as close in to the mangrove as we could. I broke an infrared chemlight and placed it on the boat. If we needed to extract in a hurry, I didn't want to have to crash around in a pitch-black mangrove thicket looking for our ride.

We split into two elements. Tim, Bubba, and Stan formed a swimmer line and swam three passes up and down the beach. They used their lead lines to sound the offshore area and wrote depth readings on swimmer slates attached to their wrists. Dave and I shot a compass bearing as a baseline for the swimmer element, and when they had finished, we patrolled inland a hundred meters, sketching the terrain and beach exits and taking soil samples. We rendezvoused back at the mangrove. The entire operation took less than thirty minutes and went off without a hitch.

We radioed the brevity code Katherine, indicating that we had completed our survey. We transmitted twice but got no response from *Fairfax County*. We didn't force the communication window. We'd try again when we reached the mouth of the channel and the radio would have a better shot at reaching the ship. It was time to get out of Dodge.

The camo net was pulled back and stowed, and I started the engine. The moon was out now, and the clouds appeared to be breaking up. Going back the way we came, down the middle of the bay, was no longer an option. I headed north along the eastern side of the lagoon. The shore along this part of the Laguna was uninhabited mangrove and impassable swamp. This inhospitable terrain extended south all the way to the Coco River and the border with Nicaragua.

Even though the coast was deserted, I kept the boat two hundred yards offshore, motoring north, then turning west at the top of the bay. The return trip was longer, but it validated a fundamental precept of naval special warfare—never go out the way you came in. As we puttered quietly along the shore, we couldn't know that the route we had chosen would save our lives.

The rain started and stopped, and finally, the moon set behind the trees, no longer a factor. We'd been wet and in the wind for over nine hours; the adrenaline was wearing off, and we were getting cold. I figured we would make our exit without further adventure when Dave nudged me. He was scanning the water south of us with his NVGs.

"I don't see the buoys," he said.

"Look harder."

"They're gone."

I throttled back, letting the Zodiac drift. I looked through my NVGs, panning south and then west, every place I would logically expect to see the green glow of the chemlights. There was nothing.

I turned the NVGs off, then turned them on again, listening to the soft whine as they warmed back up. When they were functional, I looked behind us. What I saw nearly stopped my heart.

Glowing green in the night was a huge spotlight.

I peered over the top of my goggles. There was no light visible to the naked eye. I looked again. The NVGs showed it plainly: a powerful spotlight sweeping the water behind the point to our right. Someone else was out in the bay—someone with an infrared searchlight.

"You copy that light?" I asked.

"Fuckin' A. Somebody's got a goddamn IR spotlight."

But who?

"Let's get into the weeds!" I said.

I opened up the engine and headed directly north toward the shore. The Zodiac skittered over the three-hundred-yard distance quickly. I throttled back at the last second, and the boat rode up on its wake as we bumped against the half-submerged roots of a dense stand of mangrove.

"Get us in as deep as you can," I said.

We yanked at the branches and roots, pulling the Zodiac as far into the trees as we could. We quickly spread the camo net over the boat and ourselves. I killed the engine. We pointed our weapons out into the bay.

Silence.

I looked through my NVGs and saw nothing. Could I have been wrong? No. Dave had seen it, too. There was something, someone, out there, shining an IR searchlight.

Then the light came again, this time closer and brighter; still behind the point to the east, but now under 150 yards away. We could not see the vessel or person, but we plainly saw the IR beam panning out across the bay.

"Fuck," Stan said.

Then we saw it. The infrared light played down on the water and reflected up, silhouetting the source of the searchlight. It was a patrol boat, maybe sixty feet long. It was outlined perfectly as its IR light shone down close and outboard. Green on green, the outline of the vessel was plainly not American. The Hondurans didn't have anything like it, either.

Lightning flashed in the sky, and through the NVGs, I got a good look. It was a Russian-made Zhuk-class patrol craft. Nicaraguan. I could see the two domes of its 14.5-millimeter machine guns, fore and aft. There were maybe half a dozen crewmen on deck. I had no idea how they failed to see us before we saw them. Seeing their IR searchlight was probably the luckiest thing that has ever happened to me.

What was a Nicaraguan PB doing in Honduran territorial waters? They weren't just in Honduran territorial waters, they were miles *inside* Laguna de Caratasca, a nearly closed Honduran lake.

The PB turned in a broad circle away from us, moving slowly toward the beach we had just reconned. The IR light periodically swept out into the bay, but away from us. I could make out two glowing balls of infrared on the aft deck of the PB. They were our marker buoys.

We had big problems. We were no match for a sixty-foot patrol boat. They were faster than we were, had greater range, radar, IR capability, and outnumbered us. Their advantages would be magnified in daylight, when they could see us from farther away, run us down, and gun our brains out.

I looked at my watch. It was 0240, three hours until dawn and our rendezvous with *Fairfax County*.

The patrol boat couldn't compete with the three-inch guns of the LST, but that didn't help us in here. There was also the small matter of effecting an exit from the bay and crossing twenty miles of open ocean. At sea, and in the open reaches of the bay, the game was all theirs.

"Maybe we should call the ship," Stan said.

"What are they gonna do, pray for us?" snorted Bubba.

"We gotta stay off the radio," I said. Before the Sandinistas took over, Uncle Sam had pumped millions of dollars' worth of equipment into Nicaragua. The radio we carried was a PRC-77. Nothing special—the standard-issue radio for American infantry units. It was certain to have been supplied to the pre-Sandinista army. Hooking a PRC-77 to a scanner was a no-brainer. If we used our radio, chances were the patrol boat would know it. If we talked long enough, they would pinpoint our location.

The only thing we could hope to do was stay in the mangrove and try to skulk out of the Laguna. My best guess was that we were seven miles from the mouth of the bay. It was twenty miles beyond that to our rendezvous point. My orders didn't cover playing hide-and-seek with the Nicaraguan navy. Or starting a shooting war.

"Okay," I said, "here's the plan. We're going to continue west across the top of the bay, staying as close in to the mangroves as possible."

"What do you think he's gonna do?" asked Dave.

"Search for us for a while. If he knows about the landings, he knows the amphibious ships will bottle him into the bay. He'll have to try to get out of the bay before daylight."

"So will we," Tim said.

"Yeah," I acknowledged, "so will we."

We'd have to cross seventeen miles of "international waters" before we got back to the ship. Not that we'd be safe in the three miles of Honduran territorial water. I didn't want to be anywhere around this guy in daylight—we were inflatable, and he was made out of steel.

"Give me some IR chemlights," I said. I peeled the covers back, tied half a dozen together, and hung them low in the mangrove. I broke and shook each to activate it, then tore the foil covers all the way down.

I figured if this guy was constantly flashing around with his IR light, that was his primary search modality. He'd picked up our buoys, and he knew that the only things putting out IR light had to be gringo. The chemlights would be visible for a mile, at least. If he saw them, he'd be certain to investigate. And that would buy us time.

I started the engine and backed slowly out of the mangrove. Staying as close as possible to the trees, we moved west toward the mouth of the Laguna. About half the time we had sight of the PB, slashing light around maybe two miles south of us.

We had to cross a small cove backed by a stretch of beach. We'd enjoyed shadow and trees as a backdrop, and now the cover was fizzling out; the mangrove had temporarily ended. To make matters worse, the beach was light-colored, and we were black, a contrast that would be even more obvious with NVGs. The space we had to cross was about six hundred yards. It looked like the mangrove, or at least heavy tree cover, picked up on the other side.

I decided to run it wide open. We scooted past the bald spot at full speed. Though our outboard motors were "silenced"—all exhaust gases exited underwater, and the engine covers were lined with Kevlar and neoprene—they sounded loud as hell to me. We made it across, and the mangrove resumed, curving slightly into a point.

"There he is," Dave said. He had the NVGs pointed aft. I lifted my goggles and saw it, too. The PB seemed to be crossing the bay. Then the light went out. I lost him for a second, then picked him up—this time his position was given away by our buoys, still carried on his fantail.

I was beginning to have some hope. This guy was no tactical genius.

I lost sight of the PB as we rounded the second point. The next cove presented the same problem: mangrove and cover on the fringes, white beach in the center. I scanned the water in front of us. There were several small frond-topped platforms clustered about fifty yards off the beach. Fishermen used them to dry their catch. The roofs were partially caved in, and they looked abandoned. I steered toward them.

There were flashes of light behind us. At first I thought they were lightning, but within a second or two came a farting sort of sound, but much louder, and it was grouped into a couple of short bursts. The PB was firing its machine guns.

I turned as a flare whooshed up into the sky above the first cove. They'd found our chemlights and opened fire. The flare ignited and drifted down. It lit us and the cove we were in, but the PB was around the point. There was no way they could see us. Yet. I knew the ruse of the chemlights wouldn't keep them busy for long.

Behind us, the flare went out, and it was silent. No more shooting. It was dark, and seemed blacker because of the flare. We were playing a game, the Nicaraguan skipper and I. Now *he* knew that *I* knew he was after us. We needed to disappear.

I steered toward the platforms off the beach. I was going to jam the boat up under one of them and wait for the PB to pass. As we got closer, I could see hammocks hanging from the poles in one of the shacks. They were occupied. I steered toward the one with the hammocks, figuring it would be better to control anyone we met rather than have them jump into canoes and paddle away.

We came up, and I throttled back on the engine. "Buy us some time, Tim," I said.

"Buenas noches," Tim called to the shack.

"Hola," came the reply.

"¿Usted tiene gasolina que poder comprar?" Tim asked. We had plenty of gas; he was just trying to get them to talk. The reply that came back surprised us.

"No habla," the man said.

We were close enough now to see that the shack was occupied by a man of about forty and a ten-year-old boy. They were both still in their hammocks. Several dugout canoes were tied to the shack.

"They're Indians," Tim said.

I remembered a piece of trivia I'd read in a guidebook. *"Parlez-vous français, monsieur?"* I asked.

"Nous parlons français," the man in the hammock said.

The Miskito Indians had been Christianized by Belgian monks. They spoke French, another factor besides race that served to marginalize them in the eyes of Hondurans and Nicaraguans.

I steered closer. *"S'il vous plaît, monsieur, aucunes lumières,"* I said, telling him not to turn on any lights.

"Qui êtes vous?" the man asked.

"Nous sommes une equipe d'étude. Du service de la pêche." A lie, and one definitely at the edge of my high school French. I had told him we were a survey team from the Department of Fisheries.

We pulled up to their shack. "Get us under," I said to Tim. "We're gonna hang here for a while."

By now the man could see that we were armed and our faces were painted green. His son said something to him in Miskito.

I said evenly, *"Nous n'allons pas vous blesser. Nous avons besoin de l'information et de l'aide."* We wouldn't hurt him, we just needed some information and help. I asked if he had seen the big gray boat come into the lagoon. Yes, he said. It came in just after dark. It was Sandinista, he said, rather matter-of-factly. They'd come into the bay maybe two hours before us, probably at slack water, when the waves were down.

Any other boats in here? I asked.

No, he said. Just them and you.

Then the PB rounded the point behind us. Its IR light was out now; it was harder to see but still visible, maybe a mile and a half back.

We had pulled the Zodiac completely under the platform. We were difficult to see. I hoped that was good enough.

The PB kept coming. We had our guns pointed at it, for all the good that would do. We had M-16s. They had a pair of dual 14.5-millimeters in turrets, plus half a dozen crewmen on deck with AK-47s.

The man and the boy watched the PB get closer.

I don't want any trouble tonight, I said in French.

"Je comprends," the man said.

Our luck held. The patrol boat passed the shacks without stopping. We were pressed behind pilings and as low into the Zodiac as we could get. When I heard the engines fade, I peeked up over the wooden deck. I could barely make out the stern of the boat, heading toward the mouth of the bay.

I lifted my NVGs. The PB had the infrared light trained on the shoreline. They'd scanned the shack and us but failed to see anything except a man and a boy in a pair of hammocks. I watched until the PB entered the channel and disappeared from view. I hoped he was headed back to Nicaragua.

"Thank you," I said to the man in English.

He nodded. I pulled my knife and scabbard off my belt and handed them to him. *"Merci mille fois."*

We pushed the Zodiac out from under the platform and started the engine. We continued toward the mouth of the bay slowly, staying close to the mangrove. I looked at my watch.

It was now 0400; we had an hour and a half before daylight would become a factor. I had no idea if the patrol boat had made his exit, or if he was hanging around in the channel or in the offing. In either case, I did not intend to accidentally run into him.

One more finger of land lay between us and the right-hand turn into the channel. We pulled into the mangrove, and Dave and I waded ashore. We patrolled to the edge of the tree line, where we had a good view of the channel. Off the bar, the surf was still impressive.

I scanned the channel, and my heart sank.

"Son of a bitch," Dave spat.

The PB was drifting in the channel, bow pointed landward, lolling in the outgoing tide.

I just kept telling myself, He can't stay there forever. I could see men on deck, talking. Their voices came to us in snatches above the background of rolling surf.

As we watched, the boat came about, bow pointed to sea. His engines reversed as he attempted to hold position in the ebbing tide. Hatches were closed and I watched as our IR buoys were tossed into a locker. They were making ready for sea. The PB drifted for a while longer, backing slowly, and then their skipper felt he had a break. The engines roared, and the PB made its run at the bar. It plowed through a couple of waves, then disappeared into the moonless dark.

"Our turn," I said.

Dave and I hauled ass back to the Zodiac.

"They're across the bar," I told the guys. "I want to get as close to the rendezvous point as I can before the sun comes up."

That was fine with the lads. We rounded the point and entered the channel. The surf was still big. The noise made it hard to speak. I drifted and watched a couple of sets, counting waves and noting the big, the bad, and the ugly. At the end of a particularly big set, I told everyone to hang on. I twisted the throttle and pointed toward deep water.

We plowed through a couple of broken waves, and the boat

took on water. I didn't have to say a word. Hats came off and the guys shoveled water over the sides.

Dave yelled, "OUTSIDE!" It's the call surfers give to warn that big waves are coming.

That's when I saw them. A set as big as highway overpasses. But these weren't walls, they were peaks—higher in one spot than another. The tide was ebbing, and to port, I was pretty sure there was a deeper channel. The waves would break first in shallow water. I headed for the deeper water and the low spot, even though our course took us diagonally across the front of the oncoming set.

As the first wave approached, I swung the tiller around to take it perpendicular on the bow.

We went up . . . up . . . up . . . and finally over. Like a moving hillside, the wave passed under us. The next wave was the same, a long, impressive climb. We watched this one break to our starboard, a gigantic fifteen-foot tube. If we'd been under that, it would have been game over.

We came down the backside of the wave, delighted to be alive.

And there was the patrol boat.

It was maybe three hundred yards away, nose on to us. Her bow wave was wide and white. She was balls-to-the-wall and headed right for us. We had definitely been seen.

We dropped into the trough, and the PB temporarily disappeared. There wasn't time to say anything. I swung the tiller and headed up the face of the next wave. At the crest, we could actually look down onto the decks of the patrol boat—now two waves inboard of us, maybe two hundred yards away. Her windshield wipers were on.

I ran onto another wave face, this time cutting it as near as I dared to the breaking section. We were now pointed directly out to sea. Behind us, the PB put her helm over and followed.

The Zodiac was climbing a near-vertical wave face. I thought, calmly, that this wave was bigger than any I had ever surfed. We were halfway up the face. The top of the wave was throwing off spray. To our right, a ten-foot wall of water was starting to go concave as it felt bottom and slowed.

Five more feet to the top. The engine growled, maxed out. As we popped over the crest, we went airborne. The propeller came out of the water, and the engine screamed. The sound was lost in the thunder of the breaking wave. We fell back to the surface, tubes vertical. We landed on our transom, then slammed down like a pancake.

Hail Mary, full of grace. We made it.

I turned around. The bow of the patrol boat exploded through the back of the wave, then seemed to slow. White water swallowed her prow, then swept in, covering her wheelhouse. Her decks were covered as she stopped, listed to starboard, and was sucked backward in the wave. I watched her mast nearly disappear as she was knocked on her beam's end and dragged back into the impact zone.

We all screamed. Yelled. Cheered. She had broached!

We rolled up onto another swell. Three more huge waves pounded the PB as we watched, pushing her back into the channel mouth. Her engines were belching white smoke as she struggled to keep off the shoals and away from the breaking waves. The PB was driven, wave after wave, back into the bay. It was a miracle, or the result of excellent seamanship, that she did not capsize or get driven onto the beach. When we last saw her, she was afloat with her engines working, but she'd had her ass handed to her. For the foreseeable future, she'd be busy trying to bail out and stay alive.

We didn't stick around to see how it came out. I went to full throttle, steered out of the impact zone, then followed the coast west and out to sea. No longer bottled up in the bay, we were again a small dot on a vast black ocean. We were as safe as we were going to be.

When we were within five miles of the rendezvous point, the lights of *Fairfax County* came into view. The first fingers of dawn were spreading over the water.

"Long Bow, this is Garfish. Katherine, Avis. We are ready for pickup."

"Nice talking to you, Garfish," came the message. "We were getting worried."

"*They* were getting worried?" Bubba said. "I almost shit my own heart."

"Stand by to be recovered," came the radio call.

"Roger, Garfish out."

I looked back toward the coast. Twenty miles out, Honduras was a low hint of green on the horizon. The sun was coming up, and the clouds were taking on a neon shade of pink. The storm had let up, and it looked like the day would be beautiful.

Once aboard *Fairfax County,* we prepared our beach chart, and I told the story of our encounter with the PB. I was told that *Fairfax County*'s radar had picked up a craft inside the Laguna during our recon. They assumed it was Honduran. Had I checked with *Fairfax County*'s Combat Information Center before I departed, they would have told me about it. Important safety tip: Check the local radar. That was a lesson I would never forget.

An hour before we made the rendezvous, *Fairfax County* had detected a small craft exiting the bay and turning east and south. Our Nicaraguan friends had finally made it out. Luckily for us, they'd had enough fun for one night.

Agas Tara went as planned. The marines landed, and the Seabees bulldozed. Across the border, the Nicaraguans fumed and accused the United States of trying to start a shooting war. An ironic turn of phrase.

Over the next couple of days, we had little to do but clean our gear and get ready to return to Little Creek. I spent some time wondering why a Sandinista patrol boat had been waiting for us. We all wondered. But there had been newspaper stories from the beginning, and the overflight by the Cuban airplane. The Nicaraguans had our amphibious ships on coastal radar. These seemed like reasons enough.

There was a better reason, but at the time none of us could know it. Chief Warrant Officer John A. Walker, Jr., and his pal, Senior Chief Radioman Jerry Whitworth, had supplied the Soviets with code keys to the U.S. Navy's KWR-37,

KW-7, KG-14, KY-8, and KL-47 cryptographic machines, as well as technical manuals that allowed the Russians to build their own copies. Ivan was reading our mail in real time.

Walker and his spy ring did much greater harm than just ratting out a few operations. Their espionage allowed the Russians to decipher almost every piece of coded traffic sent by the U.S. Navy from 1968 until 1986. At the time of Agas Tara, Mr. Walker was "working" in Norfolk, Virginia, and driving up to Washington on the weekends to make deliveries of codes to his KGB handlers. He wouldn't be arrested until 1985.

The Nicaraguans were waiting because they knew we were coming. Our reconnaissance plan, the location of the beach-landing site, the composition of our team, even Susan, Katherine, and Avis, were all in coded traffic that was open to Russian penetration. The Sandinistas knew a five-man SEAL detachment would enter after the tide change and attempt to leave before dawn. They knew there would be no Honduran naval units in the bay. They knew we would be without support. The Sandinistas knew everything—except how to corner a boatload of SEALs. And how to work their boat in the surf.

If they had succeeded in killing a detachment of "American spies," the timbre of relations between our countries might have gone from bad to bellicose. They might have started a real shooting war. But this isn't the kind of stuff you think about after an op. History is made in the dark, someone said. And sometimes, history isn't made.

Two days before Agas Tara ended, I was in Puerto Lempira's disco with Stan, Tim, Bubba, and Dave. The merengue was loud, the beer was cold, and we watched a chicken walk across the pulsing dance floor.

"I got a message from the Team today," I said between sips. "We got our orders."

Fifth Platoon was scheduled to deploy after returning to Little Creek. Rumor had it we were going someplace tropical.

"Where we going, Mr. Pfarrer?"

"Back to Hondo?"

"Panama?"

"Betty Ford?"

"Better," I said, trying to keep a straight face. "We're going to Beirut."

BOOK TWO

PEACEKEEPER

THE 'ROOT

TWO SIX-WHEELED armored cars were angled into positions that faced north and south, up and down the Beirut-Sidon highway. Around each, bulldozers had pushed up six-foot piles of debris and dirt to form barriers. The Lebanese crews straddled folding chairs in the small patches of shade afforded by ponchos strung from the main gun of each car's turret. Some of the soldiers held Belgian-made FN rifles across their laps; other weapons leaned against the tires or simply lay in the dirt at the soldiers' feet.

All day they watched the flow of traffic down to Sidon. Trucks, cars, and buses in an endless stream between the capital and Lebanon's second-largest city. Sometimes for hours on end the soldiers would do nothing but breathe back the stale dust and wave flies away from their faces.

That was sometimes. Now and again one of the soldiers would step into the road, shoulder his weapon at the windshield of an oncoming car, and wave it over to the side of the road next to the checkpoint. Sometimes they would open the vehicle's trunk, yank out the seats, and feel up the passengers.

Sometimes a little money changed hands, baksheesh, and the car would be allowed on its way without the indignity of a search. When you passed their position in an American jeep, they would bid you on your way in the dullest manner imaginable. Other times Lebanese soldiers would flash peace signs and call, "Hello! U.S.A. good." On the radio antenna of the vehicle, the Lebanese flag would hang absolutely limp in the hot afternoon. It always seemed to me the sorriest and most wrung-out flag in the whole world.

Lebanon is the most beautiful and fucked-up place I have ever been. For an idea of sample geography and climate, imagine La Jolla or maybe Capri. On much of the coast, mountains plunge directly into Homer's wine-dark sea. In winter, the mountains above the city wear a dusting of snow. The land is handsome, mountainous, and fertile. Beirut has been called the Paris of the Middle East, an epithet you can almost still believe.

The city itself is perched on a low sandstone bluff sticking like a thumb into the eastern Mediterranean. Loomed over by the Shouf Mountains, it spills away in jagged clumps to the foothills inland, and south to the camps. Beirut's much-fought-over airport lies on a sprawling level stretch south of downtown, runways arrayed in a giant X. Around the tarmac are scattered garbage dumps, refugee camps, and teeming slums.

It was not just war that gripped Lebanon but a vicious, sectarian civil war. To be honest, to this day I have no goddamn idea what the United States of America was doing in Lebanon. It was absolute folly to think for even an instant that we would somehow do any good.

More marines would die in Beirut than at Khe Sanh. By the end of my tour, what was left of the 24th Marine Amphibious Unit (MAU) would be crushed, humiliated, and hunkered in rat-infested bunkers. Snipers would fire on anyone, anywhere, within the American positions. Twenty-four MAU was sent into half a war—the wrong half—the part that involved holding a piece of flatland against enemies with high ground and artillery to spare.

This was peacekeeping, Lebanese-style.

Almost wholly ignored by the press back home, the marines, Seabees, and sailors of 24 MAU would endure almost seven months of snipers, car bombings, rockets, mortars, and artillery attacks. These marines and sailors would sustain America's most shameful military defeat since Pearl Harbor, the massive truck bomb that was to destroy the battalion landing team headquarters at Beirut International Airport. In one dreadful instant on an October morning, 243 men would be blown into very small pieces.

At the beginning of my tour in May 1983, that terrible Sunday morning was six months away. I have been warned against characterizing world affairs as they relate to my story. That warning is especially cogent when talking about Lebanon, whose politics are deadly, convoluted, and probably incomprehensible to an American mind. My own world politics were then coldly neutral. I was a commando. Naval special warfare was my profession. When ordered to accomplish a mission, I would plan, give my opinions on the merits of the tactical arrangements, then carry out my assignment. I cared for the safety of my men, my chances of success, and little else. SEALs are operators. Not policy makers.

We all knew our operations had political ramifications. War *is* politics. Our missions didn't just contribute to foreign policy; sometimes they *were* foreign policy. We were all volunteers: If I was given an operation I did not want to carry out for reasons of ethics or personal safety, I could quit. We all could.

When we first received orders to Beirut, I thought only: Well, at least we'll get some work. I could have no idea how much work we would actually get. Civil war is an almost congenital problem for Lebanon. If you were trying to design a petri dish to incubate a national self-destruction toxin, you couldn't do better than Lebanon. The country is a lot like the cartoon character Jessica Rabbit: She's not bad, really, she was just drawn that way.

After World War I the Ottoman Empire's possessions were carved up by the victorious allies. The area that now comprises Lebanon and Syria fell into the possession of France. The present-day Republic of Lebanon was cobbled together from the region's two dominant religious groups, Maronite Christians and Sunni Muslims. The Christians were concentrated in an area around Mount Lebanon, a bastion they shared with the Druze, a mysterious sect of Islam whose religious beliefs are a closely held secret. Sunni Muslims predominated in the coastal cities, Sidon, Tyre, Tripoli, and Beirut. A minority of Shiite Muslims were sprinkled in the countryside. Of the religious groups, the Christians and Sunnis tended to dominate economically.

By 1920 France had established a Greater Lebanon. Within this gerrymandered territory, Maronites comprised a little over 51 percent of the population. That was fine with France and fine with the Lebanese Christians. It is fair to say that the Shiites and Sunnis had been more or less dragooned into this artificial nation. Muslim allegiance and interest more naturally lay in a merger with Syria.

When France capitulated in World War II, Lebanon was controlled by the Vichy French government. A Free French and British force invaded unopposed in July 1941 and declared Lebanon an independent republic. As Europe burned, nobody paid much attention to Lebanon.

A series of political compromises eventually led to an agreement called the National Pact. I have read that this pact, a founding principle of the Lebanese nation, was never even written down. In purest measure, the pact was a political giveaway. In exchange for certain prerequisites, the Maronites would allow Lebanon independence from France and would acquiesce to the concept that Lebanon was an Arab country. To make sure Christians stayed on top, a 1930s census was used to draw up representative districts, resulting in a permanent Christian majority in parliament. It was further agreed that the president of the republic would always be a Maronite; the prime minister would be a Sunni; and the speaker of the parliament would be a Shiite.

This arrangement worked until 1958, when shifting census numbers made Christian dominance no longer demographically viable. In May 1958, opposition to President Camille Chamoun led to riots in Tripoli and Beirut. Chamoun appealed for Western military intervention, and U.S. Marines landed for the first time in July 1958. Chamoun left office, and a shaky peace returned. U.S. forces were withdrawn in the autumn. America's first intervention in Lebanese affairs had come cheaply. The second intervention would cost us dearly.

Lebanon sat out the 1967 Arab-Israeli war but increasingly became an unwilling haven for the Palestine Liberation Organization. Israel complained that Lebanon made no attempt to stop attacks launched from within its territory. In 1968 the Israeli defense forces (IDF) began a string of reprisals, air strikes, and incursions into Lebanon. These attacks have continued to the present day.

In 1970 and '71, the PLO was routed from Jordan after a bloody series of clashes with the Jordanian army. Large numbers of PLO members fled into Beirut and southern Lebanon. The guests quietly set about taking over. Tens of thousands of refugees filled camps around Beirut and other cities. PLO militias and splinter groups abounded. They opened offices and bought apartment buildings. PLO members manned roadblocks and shook down passing motorists. There was little the Lebanese could do.

Lebanon wisely declined participation in the second Arab-Israeli war—the Yom Kippur shindig—in 1973. During and after that conflict, the PLO operated freely from southern Lebanon. Again the Lebanese army made little effort to curtail PLO operations. In fact, the government in Beirut was less in control of its own territory. No one was in charge. Christians, Shiites, Sunnis, and Druze formed militias, and fiefdoms spread through the country. The rule of law bowed down to the Kalashnikov.

Civil war erupted again in 1975. Tragically, an estimated hundred thousand Lebanese became casualties, and hostilities ended only when a Syrian force invaded in 1976, halting Palestinian, Muslim, and Christian forces. For a while. The conflict resumed. This time think *Apocalypse Now.* The world watched in horror as a modern nation devoured itself.

Throughout 1981, Christian militias continued to battle the Syrian army. In retaliation for continued PLO attacks, the Israeli air force pummeled Beirut at will. The country was in ruin. Lebanon, as a sovereign state, had ceased to exist. Parts of Beirut began to resemble the surface of the moon.

In June 1982, in an operation called Peace for Galilee, the Israeli army invaded, ostensibly to rid the southern section of Lebanon of pesky individuals prone to lobbing mortars and Katyusha rockets at the towns and kibbutzim of northern Israel. The IDF rolled up the coast, swatting aside the Lebanese army, the PLO, and whatever Hezbollah, Syrian, or Druze forces decided to show their faces. In a matter of days, the Israelis occupied the southern suburbs of Beirut.

Yasser Arafat and what was left of the PLO cowered in the cellars of West Beirut, cornered. It is probably true that Yasser Arafat needs Israel, and Israel needs the PLO. For whatever reason, the decision was made to let Arafat and a large portion of the PLO escape. Under the supervision of a multinational force comprised of U.S. and European troops, five thousand Palestinian fighters boarded ferries and evacuated to Cyprus. The multinational force withdrew. A detachment of Navy SEALs personally saw to the security of Arafat as he passed out of Lebanon and onto Cyprus. The PLO hauled ass. The Israelis stayed and would continue to occupy parts of Lebanon until 2000.

Through this all, the Christians held on to the presidency of Lebanon. In August 1982, Bashir Gemayel was elected president. He was killed three weeks later by a car bomb that took out an entire city block.

Following his death, Christian Phalangist militiamen crossed Israeli-occupied territory in South Beirut and entered the Palestinian refugee camps of Sabra and Chatilla. More than a thousand men, women, and children were killed in an orgy of destruction. The Israelis watched the murderers come, and then they watched them go. If the Israelis were not accomplices, they were at least cheerleaders. International condemnation fell on Israel's then minister of defense, Ariel Sharon.

The condemnation faded. The martyrs of Sabra and Chatilla were mostly forgotten. The bodies were bulldozed into a dump north of the airport, and Bashir Gemayel's brother, Amin, was elected president on September 21, 1982.

Another multinational force, this one composed of U.S. Marines, British army, French legionnaires, and Italian soldiers, landed. The marines dug in at the airport and along a stretch of beach south of downtown. The British took a section in the foothills. Italian marines from the San Marco battalion and a detachment of French legionnaires occupied parts of West Beirut. In the West's eyes, this NATO force was intended to provide stability. In the Arabs' view, the infidels were obviously intended to support a continued Israeli occupation.

Then, in April 1983, the American embassy in Beirut was truck-bombed. Americans started dying. The players in this free-for-all began to choose sides relative to the presence of United States Marines at the airport.

Uncle Sam's hand was being dealt, and he didn't even know it.

The United States brokered a treaty with Gemayel and Israel in May 1983. The compact stipulated the withdrawal of all foreign troops. Having retreated to the Bekaa valley and the mountains above Beirut, Syria rejected the peace agreement. The Syrians knew the Israelis were not about to fight uphill to throw them out. So it sat: Israel eyeballing Syria, Syria eyeballing Lebanon, Lebanon at the mercy of its own militias.

In May 1983 Fifth Platoon of SEAL Team Four was delivered into this mess by U.S.S. *Portland,* a landing ship, dock—a big troop-carrying amphib. The trip across the pond was uneventful. Aboard *Portland,* it was just us, the spec-war detachment, and about three hundred marines, mostly headquarters elements of the 24th Marine Amphibious Unit.

Two days into the passage, we got a dose of real navy. *Portland*'s captain was a screamer, a martinet and petty tyrant named Zimanski. Captain Zimanski's principal hobby, besides sleeping in his chair on the bridge, seemed to be dressing down his officers at meals. The wardroom on a warship is supposed to be a place of sanctity. Manuals on etiquette specifically caution junior officers against discussing work, politics, or religion during meals. It's often said that a ship's wardroom is the officers' living room. Not so on

"Sweet Pea." Zimanski had no politics other than self-interest, and his religion was himself. That left work.

To the teeth-grinding embarrassment of the entire wardroom, Zimanski would begin by lambasting the ship's executive officer. No punches were spared, and every meal seemed to erode the man's authority and respect. The XO of a warship is next to God in the chain of command. All the poor man could do between bites was sit there and take it. Zimanski ordered his officers to be present for all meals, and he often sent the messenger of the watch to retrieve skulkers who tried to miss meals when not actually on watch. After demolishing the XO, Zimanski would switch fire onto the operations officer, the chief engineer, the first lieutenant, and so on, all around the table, until he had chewed out every single officer. This went on meal after meal. The only officers spared the ritual were the SEALs and the marines. As embarked troops and not ship's company, we fell outside the captain's ambit. That did not stop him, however, from offering opinions.

Frank Giffland and I took to flying to *Iwo Jima* whenever possible and eating as often as we could on the mess decks with our guys. Two things have to happen in a bully-victim dynamic: One person has to play the bully, and the other person has to volunteer to play the victim. We weren't Zimanski's victims, and that was going to make for an interesting cruise. Our equipment, boats, minisub, and heavy weapons were to be stored aboard *Portland,* so we would have to thrash out some sort of working relationship.

Fifth Platoon had been assigned to Mediterranean Amphibious Ready Group (MARG) 2-83. Our wire diagram connected us to the commodore of Amphibious Squadron 8. In fact, as SEALs, we were a "theater" asset. That meant we could be, and would be, called upon by the EURCOM (European Command) commander in chief to conduct special assignments.

Afloat, we were navy, working for the commodore. Ashore, operating in a USMC environment, we worked for the commander of the landing force. We did it all. Or basically, we did what we wanted. Our lines of command and accountability were nebulous, a fact all SEALs exploit to full advantage. It was our game to play the commodore off the colonel, and the general off the admiral.

Frank and I deployed with a full platoon, and we were loaded for bear. Two officers, four fully manned boat crews, a chief petty officer, and a first-class leading petty officer. In addition to our four F-470 raiding crafts, we had at our command a Seafox-class patrol boat manned by a detachment of special boat unit sailors.

The Seafox was to be our workhorse. Though it had some serious design flaws, namely sea-keeping, crew comfort, and the location and scope of its weapons suite, the Seafox was fast, had decent range, and was armed with .50-cal and M-60 machine guns. It had radar, encrypted radio capability, and an IFF, or identification friend-or-foe system. Made from carbon fiber and radar-absorbing materials, the Seafox was one of the earliest maritime applications of stealth technology. In what was a closely guarded secret at the time, the Seafox was invisible to radar.

Also attached to our unit was a detachment from Underwater Demolition Team Twenty-two. They operated an eight-man wet submarine, an SDV, or SEAL delivery vehicle. This platform gave us great options in the insertion and extraction departments. Four other ships, *Austin, El Paso, Harlan County,* and *Iwo Jima,* delivered to Lebanon the remainder of fifteen hundred grunt marines, transport and attack helicopters, amphibious personnel carriers, Seabees, bulldozers, tanks, and artillery. America was back in Lebanon, in a major way, and what we found there was enough to blow your mind.

Into a nation the size of Connecticut were jumbled together several occupying armies, a UN peacekeeping force, five mutually antagonistic Lebanese militias, and the rump section of a PLO rent by mutiny. It was the business of intelligence officers to monitor the activity of these diverse entities, and to that end captains and majors tended maps that showed troop movement and recent terrorist activity.

Snipers, car bombs, mines, and kidnappings were common fare. During the initial part of our deployment, such surprises were reserved mostly for the Israeli army. In the serenity of the headquarters area, these shenanigans were reduced to red tape on topographic maps: real-time items of intelligence to be collected, correlated, and filed.

In the early days of the multinational peacekeeping force, the U.S. occupied the airport and a string of emplacements in Hay es Salaam, the slum surrounding the north end of the runway. Fifth Platoon came ashore with the Seabees and quickly looked for a place to set up shop. Frank and I took a jeep up to the battalion landing team headquarters, a four-story cement building located 150 yards north of the airport terminal. Several factors recommended this place as our new home. For one thing, it was made of reinforced concrete.

The building had been a PLO hospital before the marines assumed it. Four levels of galleries and balconies all faced in to one another above a tiled central courtyard. It had once been a beautiful building, but it was burned and gutted by either the advancing Israelis or the retreating Palestinians, and on its vertical surfaces, inside and out, were dark streaks from fire smoke. The interior was ravaged, ceiling tiles and marble facings torn away, exposing inert electrical wire and air-conditioning vents.

The rooms were filled with field desks, radios, maps, mosquito netting, and aluminum cots. About 350 marines lived and worked here. The headquarters units slept beside their desks. The offices of operations and staff officers were marked with hand-lettered signs. A stenciled sign in front of the building said BEIRUT HILTON. Nobody called it that; the place was always called the "battalion landing team headquarters," or simply the BLT. This was the building that the world would come to know as Beirut's marine barracks.

Frank and I looked around. There were empty rooms. Plenty of space to stow our gear, hot food, latrines, and showers—occasionally even hot showers—out back. The walls were solid, and that meant we wouldn't have to dig a hole for cover.

As we checked the place out, we got the hairy eyeball from every marine who passed us. SEALs do not wear rank or tridents (the badges that identify us as SEALs) on our combat uniforms. Frank's jungle boots were not bloused into his trousers, and I wasn't even wearing boots—I was wearing high-top canvas coral shoes. Our hair was long. We both had Fu Manchu mustaches. We were carrying CAR-15s, not M-16s. We were not wearing the starched four-peaked "covers" marines and sailors are expected to wear with their battle dress uniforms. Pushed back on our heads were floppy jungle hats, and the front of mine was folded like Paddington the bear's. Marines have a great affinity for spit and polish. SEALs do not.

"I detect a potential lifestyle conflict," Frank said.

I agreed. Compared to the way our platoon dressed, Frank and I looked like recruiting posters. If we moved into the BLT, it wouldn't be long until some marine major blew a gasket.

On the drive back to the beach, Frank and I came up with a dozen sour-grape reasons why we wouldn't move into the BLT.

"Too far from the water," I said.

"Too close to the brass," he said.

"Too many jarheads."

We both knew this meant we'd have to build a place on Green Beach. "Build" meant digging a bunker and foxholes. And Green Beach, though close to the water, was far from a perfect position. It was exposed as hell. If—no, *when*—this place went to shit, we'd be open to the elements.

The American position at Green Beach occupied a strip of coastline along the Beirut-Sidon highway, maybe four hundred yards from the terminal at Beirut International Airport. The position was separated from the highway by three hundred fifty-five-gallon drums filled with tar. This barrier ran the length of Green Beach, sequestering the seventy marines, Seabees, and SEALs stationed there from the busy coastal highway. A twenty-foot watchtower stood at beach center, and the northern and southern approaches were sandbagged machine-gun nests, barbed wire, and cement tank traps.

Still, no one stationed at Green Beach took comfort in the defenses. The marines at the airport and the outposts had buildings to shelter in, and the troops north and south of the runway could take consolation in what was left of the perimeter fence. But Green Beach stood alone. It was isolated from all other American or allied positions. Green Beach was backed across the highway by a fifty-foot sandstone bluff. Although the terrain provided some cover from snipers, it also screened us from supporting fire from the other marine emplacements.

Put tactically, we were in an unsupported position. Put in grunt lingo, our shit was in the breeze.

Although the tar barrels were adequate defense against small-arms fire, any vehicle with sufficient momentum could careen off the highway, crash through the barrier, and come to rest by the flagpole. This was not just a theoretical possibility: The American embassy had been truck-bombed just a month before, and a marine trained an M-60 machine gun on every car that passed on the road. It was cold comfort to think we would probably get the truck-bomb driver who got us.

There were tents at Green Beach, but they were strictly for show. Snipers and artillery attacks were something we lived with seven days a week. Sleeping accommodations were underground. Under Frank's direction, the platoon dug an eight-by-fifty-foot hole in the sand, reinforced the sides, and roofed it over with Marston matting and two layers of sandbags. We christened our underground condo Rancho Deluxe.

We were safe six feet under, and the rancho was home. Over the coming months, our tents, left nearby as a diversion, would be gradually reduced to ribbons by snipers, ricochets, and shrapnel. By the end of our tour, Rancho Deluxe was a vermin-infested cesspool, but it held up through rocket and artillery attacks and would survive the massive truck bomb that was to destroy the marine barracks.

We settled into the somniferous beginning of our tour.

Our detachment was responsible to the commodore for the security of U.S. naval vessels within the anchorage and for the ships under way in the Beirut AO, or area of operations. We would also be available for tasking from the commander of the landing force (with the concurrence of the commodore). Those odd jobs included reconnaissance, calling in naval gunfire, air strikes and artillery support, courier runs to the embassy, liaison with allied and Lebanese forces, explosive ordnance disposal, diving services, ship-hull searches, parachute operations, direct-action missions, and underwater demolition. In short, everything that SEALs do. Our AO ran from Sidon in the south to Tripoli in the north. Hundreds of square miles of ocean and a like area of land.

Frank decided on a rotation of forces. Doc Jones and I would take boat crews Charlie and Delta. Frank and Tim, our LPO, would take boat crews Alpha and Bravo. Two boat crews equaled a SEAL squad—eight shooters. Eight guys, for us, was considered a pretty good-sized group of men.

The arrangement worked like this: One squad would do a week at Rancho Deluxe, the other a week out on the ships and in the Seafox. The squad at Rancho Deluxe would handle land ops and water security in the immediate area of Green Beach; the other squad would take blue-water ops, long-range coastal patrols, and ship security. We'd operate for a week and then switch. The platoon would combine for bigger operations, recons and direct action, countersniper ops, or deep penetrations into the hills. Later, when airplanes started getting shot at, we would establish another rotation, a detachment aboard the helicopter carrier *Iwo Jima*. This team would work directly for the battle-group staff and provide combat search and rescue (CSAR) for downed aircraft and aircrew.

Again the arrangement was pure Giffland. He generously split the command, placing great faith in me and my two boat crews. Our assignments rotated, and through them all, I enjoyed Frank's confidence and a terrific latitude for self-expression. I have heard of few other SEAL elements, anywhere, that were allowed to function in such a joint-command mode. The arrangement worked well. At the beginning of the tour, we never did the same thing long enough to get bored.

By the end of summer, boredom would not be an issue.

HOLLYWOOD PREPARES YOU in a certain way for war. The set design of the movie *Saving Private Ryan* typifies the war-demolished building as imprinted on the American psyche. It bears little resemblance to the destruction of real war. To the uninitiated, devastation not fitting the Hollywood stereotype is at first perceived as surreal, even fake. It is only after considerable exposure to real battle damage, legitimately bombed buildings, and authentic death that the vapid images of Hollywood are forsaken.

Until you look into a building hit by artillery, or see with your own eyes a house chopped open by rocket fire, you have only a film director's impressions. These are the gutted provincial buildings of World War II Europe, their raised stone walls burned on ragged edges and roof tiles broken and scattered about the street. In Lebanon I was constantly amazed by the resilience of the buildings. Almost every structure in the city had been touched by battle, and most showed an astounding stubbornness against destruction. Into the sides of single-story houses would be punched neat two-and-a-half-foot holes, the leavings of 105-millimeter tank rounds. Through these holes could be seen utterly obliterated interiors. Walking by a targeted building, I noticed that the holes appeared to have been punched with a blunt instrument, as though the ends of a telephone pole had been jammed through the walls. The damage to the exteriors would often appear slight. The real shit happened inside, where the people were. All traces of human habitation were blown to tatters by the shaped charge effect of armor-piercing shells. Often a house would stand through four or five hits. When there was no secondary fire, the edges of the entry holes looked like wet cement.

We came to learn that the Lebanese civil war was a struggle unique in modern warfare, a contest continually escalated and abated, an ongoing battle among a minimum of five sworn and ruthless enemies. Alliances in this war were brief and utilitarian, and of the several sides, none enjoyed any distinct numerical or tactical advantage.

In Lebanon considerations of terrain and technology short-circuited the fundamental precepts of maneuver warfare. There was little daily change in forces or position. With the rare exception of those times when the U.S. built a fire under the Lebanese army, there were almost no attempts by any side to capture ground. Druze, PLO, Amal, Hezbollah, and Phalangists all had a piece of the pie, and none seemed particularly disposed to take from his neighbor. So it went month after month, each of the major players controlling one part or another of the capital city, leaving the central government of the Lebanese Republic paralyzed, ineffectual, and beholden to seventeen-year-old kids working roadblocks at city street corners.

Each of the antagonists maintained a bastion of terrain, either mountainous or urban, unassailable citadels that were the respective power bases. These areas remained undisputed, defended chiefly by spectacular canyons or the raw human arithmetic of attack and defense in urban terrain. Such considerations made it inopportune to bring ground forces to bear. Without infantry to seize and control territory, the players remained static, dug in and unwilling to make the sacrifice of an assault.

This stalemate engendered a wholly original form of warfare, a kind of megasniping in which mobile long-range weapons were key. From deep within the sanctity of home turf, rockets, artillery, and mortars were used to drop high explosive on troop concentrations and area targets. When legitimate military targets were not available, opposing gunners were content to hammer a rival's "hostile" civilian centers. Neighborhoods, schools, and markets were hit, requiring retaliation in kind. Other neighborhoods would be hit, leading to an escalation of targeting, the second tier more outrageous than the last. Inevitably mosques, churches, and hospitals came under the gun, leading to more vigorous retaliation, more civilian casualties, etc. The cycle was arrested by cease-fires that came and went like daydreams. Breaks in the fighting frequently lasted less than an hour.

In the media the daily passage of shells from place to place was called an "artillery duel," a careless and inappropriate metaphor that somehow conjured the image of two noble adversaries aiming at each other's guns. As though it were good guy against bad guy, not lunatic militiamen hammering the living shit out of women and children huddled in the basement shelters of their homes.

At the start of the tour, there were plenty of opportunities to observe the interface of architecture and artillery. Foot and jeep patrols through the slums around the airport were especially educational. Spreading to the east and north of the runways was an area the marines soon named Hooterville, after the ramshackle heap of buildings in the cartoon of the same name. A warren of dirt streets and tumbledown cinderblock structures, Hooterville was probably the most frequently shelled urban area on the planet.

In the time before the Israeli withdrawal, marines made daily excursions from the airport, north, east, and, infrequently, south. SEAL squads occasionally accompanied these daylight patrols to learn the arrangement of the streets, visit the outlying marine outposts, and generally get the lay of the land.

The other units within the multinational forces also walked the beat. North of the airport, in West Beirut, the French Foreign Legion patrolled aggressively. East of the runways, in the foothills of the Shouf, a British reconnaissance company was stationed. A no-nonsense outfit straight from a deployment in Northern Ireland, the Brits used armored cars called Ferrets to conduct daily sweeps. Immediately north of the airport was a wild no-man's-land, untroubled by the Italian San Marco battalion who rarely, if ever, stepped from their walled compound. The Italians let the locals party hard. The Italian sector came to be known as Khomeiniville, and patrolling through it, or just flying over it, would become more and more of a thrill as the summer ground on.

Since the bombing of the U.S. embassy in April, the American and British legations were doubled up in a well-guarded and heavily fortified compound along the corniche in West Beirut. Hostile activity in Khomeiniville frequently closed the coast highway and prevented vehicular and foot traffic from moving north. The embassies were often cut off from the troops that were supposed to protect them.

In the beginning of the tour, the admixture of French, Italian, British, and American sectors was made livelier by the presence of the Israeli Defense Forces. Dug in to positions south of downtown, IDF armor and infantry units manned pillboxes, roadblocks, and fighting holes scattered through the Italian, American, and British sectors. These emplacements signaled the high-water mark of Israeli conquest during the Lebanese-Israeli war. In the time before the multinational force became the prime target, the IDF was sniped at constantly, which kept a constant volume of steel in the air. It was the prudent peacekeeper who knew where the IDF was, and where might be their enemies, lest one become embroiled in an argument not of one's making.

Before the lid came off, the marines patrolled twice daily, ostensibly keeping order in the sector around the airport. Peace in the city was a dream that would sour into a lurid nightmare. Walking patrol in broad daylight with half a company of marines was a trip. A gaggle of forty men is a *parade* for SEALs, not an operational force. Besides working in much smaller units, SEALs almost never operate in daylight and would never do so by choice. But this was peacekeeping, and the rules were different. Sometimes the patrols were as unreal as moonwalks. We usually moved parallel to the main body of troops, or sometimes parallel and trailing, so we might be able to react and envelop any opposing force. We were in our spec-ops battle kit: flop hats, combat vests, and individual radios, the eight-man squad packing two M-60 machine guns. Each M-60 gunner carried six hundred rounds, and the squad deployed at least two M-203 grenade launchers, as well as a pair of AT-4 antitank rockets and M-14 sniper rifles. The firepower carried by the eight SEALs nearly matched that of the marine platoon.

It was not merely a question of armament. Marine tactics were to muster up, line up, and walk the route. Period. Their patrols were not arrayed or prepared for combat. If there was danger, the marines would be the last dumb fuckers on the face of the planet to know it. In flak jackets and rucksacks, with their weapons slung and unloaded, they couldn't react. Accompanying the marines into Hooterville, I always had the feeling that the patrols were the bait and we were the hammer.

Much of the way, we hugged walls, walked backward, and leapfrogged boat crew upon boat crew, covering intersections and rooftops as the patrol lumbered on its way. Covering and moving, we'd jog five steps to every one taken by the marines. In close alleyways, there would be not a breath of wind, and the air would lay so thick that just breathing was a dull labor to which you applied the greater part of your thoughts. The heat burrowed into your skull, numbed your senses, and made simply walking an effort.

Checking doorways and alleys, we'd trot through grimy neighborhoods where shell-smashed buildings hunkered beside half-constructed ones. Above us on walls and balconies poked hand-lettered signs in Arabic saying God knew what.

In some parts of town, children clamored by us, saying in English, "Hello! What's your name? Give me cocoa!" To the delight of the kids, we'd hand over packages of hot-chocolate powder from our MREs. They would swarm around, touching us, laughing, doing weird dances. There were toy pistols, cap guns, everywhere. They poked at you, in the hands of children, from around corners and behind walls. At first they would stop your heart, and then you'd seen a million of them, and in the hot afternoons, you got numb. Some marines didn't even look. They just walked.

In Khomeiniville the hostility of the people was another kind of heat. Predominantly Shiite Muslim, the people there did not dig the multinational force. They held a separate, religiously mandated hatred for Americans. It was here that we really walked patrol. Each face was a blade. People spat at us, made contemptuous gestures, and pushed their kids indoors. As we approached blocks of houses, the women would ululate to one another in the high, trilling *lu-lu-lu-lu* that was a signal of both warning and contempt. The sound would echo off the buildings, a bizarre, stuttering howl. It made your skin crawl, and mercifully, American incursions into this part of town were short. But sometimes we were in longer than we wanted to be.

In the narrow, serpentine streets, it was not difficult to become disoriented. In the labyrinth of buildings and blind alleys, you could believe that your compass was screwed, then, trusting your sense of location, press on in some inane direction until you were hopelessly and completely lost. Wandering patrols might emerge in places Americans were definitely not supposed to be. When patrols stumbled through market squares that had never in history been profaned by the boots of Christian infidels, the eyes of the locals were like saucers. Whatever was going on would stop outright. If fruit vendors were in the process of making change, they would freeze, clutching money and merchandise like statues until we left. Whole streets would halt, and the people would stand and gawk as though the patrol were from Uranus. Other times people would only laugh, smile, and point; it depended.

But there were spookier things that happened when you were on patrol. Much spookier. Like empty streets—totally empty: abandoned bicycles, stores with their doors open and no one behind the counter, empty baby carriages. The streets would be deserted, as though the people had been lifted in midheartbeat off the face of the planet. The only sound would be the trickle of the thin ocher stream of sewage that ran down the middle of the dirt street.

It didn't take a tactical genius to figure out what had made the population take cover, and in these situations, lost or not, you kept moving. In places where portraits of Ayatollah Khomeini covered every square inch of wall space, and Ira-

nian flags hung from empty balconies, you kept moving. And
children were what you really looked for. They had grown up
in this place, weaned on the sound of artillery and ambush,
and they knew when the shit was coming like kids in Cleve-
land know how many days until Christmas. These kids lived
in the streets, played in the streets, and saw everything. On a
daylight patrol or on a jeep run, you watched the children.
Where there were no children, there was always danger.

As abruptly as the buildings had risen around us, the alley-
wide streets would open to dirt roads cutting hot green fields,
heading south back to the airport. As we trudged down the
road, an endless stream of trucks, cars, and buses would
pass, dragging behind them a jetsam of plastic bags and long
gritty plumes of dust. The scraggly fields spread east to the
foothills, low plots of vegetables worked over by squatters.
The patrols would stagger file on the rutted roads, and the
SEALs would walk behind to cover the withdrawal, scanning
rooftops as the patrol crossed the wire perimeter and reentered the airport. A three-hour walk would often leave me
trembling with adrenaline and exhaustion.

In this manner, through the months of May and June, we
learned the city. The modus operandi became foot patrols
through Hooterville and vehicle sweeps into Khomeiniville
and West Beirut. We sometimes attached ourselves to marine
jeep patrols but more often worked on our own, either on
embassy runs or liaison trips to meet up with the Foreign Legion companies stationed in West Beirut. Our jaunts were
balls-to-the-wall: two jeeps and eight men howling down the
boulevards as fast as we could drive, pulling onto medians
to pass stopped traffic. A rifleman stood in the front seat,
swinging his weapon over the windscreen to halt opposing
traffic at intersections. We didn't stop for lights, traffic jams,
or the khaki-clad traffic police. Automatic weapons were the
right-of-way. We pointed the muzzles into the windows of
stopped cars on our right and left with serious "Get back"
looks on our faces.

In the rear seats of the jeep, you tried to watch everything,
the cars and street corners, the rooftops and windows, the

million balconies. The wind against your skin was heaven; it was cool, and it meant that you were moving, and in movement there was at least the illusion of safety. Cooking down the roads too fast, you hoped, for snipers to track. In our hearts, we knew better. There wasn't one of us who couldn't ding a driver in a moving car at a hundred yards. Knowing the art of the possible, we keenly watched the roofs.

On my first run to the embassy, Bubba darted our jeep through third-world traffic as though it were nothing. Cars screeched to within a coat of paint of our fenders, their drivers shaking two fingers at us in an Arab gesture that I am certain does not mean "Peace be with you." Through it all, Bubba would grin his insane hillbilly driving smile and press the accelerator to the floor.

Jeep patrols played out in an incredible montage of poverty, wealth, people, vegetable markets, ruin, billboards, and grazing goats. Closed rues would open at a turn to grand boulevards, and the dense mass of belle epoque buildings would tumble to rubble-strewn urban canyons. From Casablanca to Armageddon in the space of a city block.

There were parts of the city where the obliteration was symmetrical and complete. In these places, the roads were dirt and cement dust, fine as talcum powder; the streets were smooth and white, the wreckage almost blinding when the sun was high. Shattered concrete and rebar lay on either side, sometimes two and three stories high. Roads were bulldozed through square blocks in a perfect grid pattern, like newsreel footage of the ruins of Nagasaki. Plastic bags and tatters of clothing fluttered from cracks in the smashed buildings and blew down the street, the city of death littered with the possessions of its victims.

Driving past the flattened buildings, the reek of putrefying flesh would drift over the jeep like a shadow, beyond abominable or nauseating or any other word you could use to qualify a smell. It was an odor that was positively evil. In a vague way, you sensed it constantly in the city. It was a lurid fetor that worked its way into your clothes, burned into your senses, and made your stomach twitch. Twisting up from the filthy streets, dust devils roiled into the heat, coming at us like ghosts, like evil genies. We would pull bandanas up to cover our faces, but the stink would follow, clutching at us until, hours later, we could jump into the sea with all our gear on, hoping mother ocean would make the smell go away. But it didn't, and I never got used to it.

Pockets of civilization bloomed amid mayhem. Parts of Beirut, affluent and self-consciously cosmopolitan, defiantly continued business as usual. The contrasts could be mind-boggling. On a street loomed over by shattered, desolate sky-scrapers, I shot a dog gnawing on a human skull. Ten blocks away, a Jaguar sedan was parked in front of a store window filled with Chanel, Gucci, and Levi's. Standing in front of the window was a woman shrouded in a burqa, a garment covering her from head to ankle. Her view of the world was a net-like rectangle covering her eyes. As we drove past, I got a glance at her feet. Under the tent, she was wearing a pair of four-inch red stiletto pumps.

At the end of each patrol, an intel guy would ask where you were and what you saw, and once, being debriefed by a gunnery sergeant who looked like my old man, I told him it was like Mr. Toad's Wild Ride. Later, when things got bad, we would sit in amazement to think of the places we had naively walked or driven during the first months.

While we were learning our way around, the population was being militarized. Unknown to us, in May, commencements were being celebrated in the Bekaa valley. Through the month of June, the first graduates of Hezbollah training camps were being infiltrated back into the city. They set about surrounding the American and French positions, quietly surveying targets, timing patrol runs, and doing their homework.

The joyrides and walks in the park would soon be over. Our tour was about to take a turn for the violent.

THAT OLD-TIME RELIGION

HE WAS CALLED "the mad mortar man." He had no other name, no face. He may have been one man or a dozen. He prowled through Hooterville in a pickup truck in which he had installed a Soviet 82-millimeter mortar. He would drive to spots where he had predetermined the fire solutions, then let fly at the compounds. Sometimes he would reach all the way over the airport and hit Green Beach; sometimes he would hit the BLT and the MSSG buildings. It was up to him.

The worst thing about mortar fire is that it gives no warning. The report of the weapon is so distant, so muffled by surrounding buildings, that you never hear it. The round travels slowly up, up, up, and then straight down on top of you. You never knew about it until it was in your shorts.

The mad mortar man was special, and his work was as unique and identifiable as his signature. He always fired just a few rounds, maybe four, in rapid succession. Then he would shift fire, driving his truck to some other spot and hitting a different part of the airport. That would be a day's work, nothing colossal; most of the time he wounded no one, but it was always enough to cancel the movie and the rounds of the chow truck. He really was an annoying son of a bitch.

It was a hot afternoon a few weeks before the Israeli withdrawal, and the hills above the city had been quiet since sunrise. Carrying my rifle and body armor, I walked from Rancho Deluxe down the berm toward the causeways. I was preparing our Zodiac for a patrol of the anchorage, a daily occurrence we called "hassling fishermen."

The causeways were a floating set of piers anchored to the beach sand, and they were Green Beach's raison d'être. Daily, landing craft disgorged trucks, jeeps, and trailers onto the piers, supplying the troops with bullets, beans, and butt wipe. Green Beach was the main link to the American, British, French, and Italian warships offshore. The causeways were the logistical nexus of the operation and would become a favorite artillery target of the Druze, PLO, and Syrian troops who occupied the high ground around us.

It was a little before noon, and I was walking along the second section of causeway, nearly to my boat when I heard it. The slightest sound, but definitely the sound of a mortar round—incoming. When they are fired from a long way off, and if the wind is just so, sometimes you can hear them. As they fall, mortar rounds make a sound like a child whispering *"woof-woof-woof."* It is the sound of the tail fins cutting the air. If you hear it, the round is right on top of you, and there's not an instant to do anything but pucker and die.

I closed my eyes and thought: I'm dead.

The round slammed into the water next to the causeway section I was standing on. I don't recall the explosion. I don't remember hearing anything except the small sound of the round dropping in on me. But the causeway section was blown into the air, and so was I.

The explosion ripped my shirt off my body. A huge geyser of sand and water shot into the sky, and the seawater that rained down on me was the temperature of blood. I made a perfect two-point landing—on my head and shoulders. Remarkably, I'd turned a somersault with my CAR-15 held tight in my hand. I got to my feet, reeled two steps, and fell. I was soaking wet. I thought it was with my own blood.

Under me, the pontoon section was punctured and sinking but was still connected to the rest of the causeway. As I staggered off it, dull thuds echoed from the hills above the airport. More rounds were on the way, and I had to find cover.

As I crawled off the causeway, I saw a Seabee lying face-down in the sand in front of me, and I grabbed him by the elbow and started to drag and pull and finally run with him back to the bunkers.

Then it came again: *woof-woof-woof.* The beach exploded as half a dozen more rounds straddled our position. As we scrambled across thirty yards of beach, rounds hit all around us. Ass over teakettle, we fell into the bunker. I was covered with sand and soot, and my hair was singed on the left side of my head. I looked like Wile E. Coyote on a bad day. As I patted myself down, checking to make sure my parts were still connected, the Seabee yelled for a corpsman.

I stood trembling in the bunker and did the math. The burst radius of an 82-millimeter round is nearly fifteen meters. In plain English, any person within a thirty-meter circle may reasonably be expected to be vaporized, killed, or crippled by the explosion. The round had detonated under five feet from me. I should have been turned inside out. But there wasn't a scratch on my body. To have survived was astounding. The chances of surviving a near-direct hit without a nick were infinitesimal.

This was the moment that I abandoned atheism.

My conversion was not an epiphany; it was more an exercise in the scientific method. Until this moment, for me, God had been an unlikely hypothesis. That hypothesis had now been supported by an experiment. A mortar round had knocked me on my ass and spit me out alive and unharmed.

In Beirut my call sign was Bad Karma. Although I was not cosmic-enabled at the time, I accepted my nom de guerre with an eye to the universal consequences of being a combat soldier. The game was life and death. I ran my operations and was as available to destruction as any person in the city. I knew that the sword of karma swung both ways.

OUR TACTICS EVOLVED as the summer progressed. As militias coalesced in Hooterville, marine combat posts outside the perimeter came under increasingly frequent attack, and the slums surrounding the Beirut airport became deadly with concealed shooting positions and ambush sites prepared by an ever expanding coterie of bad guys: Druze, PLO, Hezbollah, and Amal. The marine CPs (combat posts) offered fixed targets the militias could fire on when their mood suited. By the end of August these attacks happened several times a week.

A sign was posted at the main entrance to the airport, a blue-and-gold-stenciled piece of plywood autographed by the cast of the television show *Hill Street Blues*. It said: HEY, BE CAREFUL OUT THERE. It was right next to the checkpoint where a marine sentry made sure your weapons were *unloaded* before you left the American sector. When we passed the sentries, holding back the charging handles of our weapons to show we were in compliance, they would pass us a look like "You guys are unloaded, right?" I always smiled back as vapidly as I could. I was not about to write a letter to the mother of one of my SEALs, explaining that I was the officer who got her son killed riding around West Beirut with an unloaded rifle. Multinational force regulations to the contrary, our standing orders were for SEALs to show empty at the checkpoints, drive around the first corner, and put one in the chamber. Locked and cocked, fuckin' A.

Intelligence reports indicated that Hezbollah surveillance posts and bunkers were being built inside houses, making them both difficult to detect and harder to attack. Snipers often engaged marine targets from the windows of occupied buildings, trusting that American peacekeepers would be reluctant to fire back at an apartment block filled with women and children. As the attacks on the CPs picked up, foot patrols were very often curtailed or canceled, and vehicle patrols became the norm. Our routes through town varied; and in unpredictability there was safety.

One of the principal tenets of naval special warfare is that SEALs pick the time and place of combat. We engage the enemy on our terms and in the place of our choosing, or not at all. But this was peacekeeping, and we found ourselves increasingly the hunted, not the hunters. Adhering to the rules of engagement meant we were not free to ply our trade as we wanted, so we maximized what tools we had: surprise, deception, and firepower.

We varied our routes and the time of patrols, daylight and predawn, and moved in convoys of two or three jeeps (not Humvees). Jeeps were everywhere, and heaped with equipment. A dirty American jeep looked pretty much like a dirty Druze jeep.

SEALs are given wide latitude in the selection of weapons and equipment. In short, we use what works, no matter who made it. American weapons, particularly the M-16, have a distinctive outline. When Russian-made AK-47s and RPGs, or rocket-propelled grenades, came into our possession, we carried them on patrol. Packing the weapons of the bad guys was one way to lower our profile in town. Our woodland-pattern cammies were also distinctively Yankee. Instead of out-of-the-bag American uniforms, we often wore a mixture of desert and woodland patterns, blue jeans, and camouflage smocks from Czechoslovakia and East Germany. Our Mad Max outfits were less obvious for being eclectic, and made us look like generic Beiruti militiamen; American flags Velcroed to our shoulders kept us within the Geneva rules governing combatants and uniforms. Arab headdresses rounded out our attire. We wore the black and white Palestinian *kufiyah,* or the red and white Arab *shumagg,* depending on the neighborhood. Most often we wore the cloths tied around our necks or tucked into the collars of our cammie blouses. Occasionally, we wore them in high style, snugged down on our heads with black ropelike Ogal, very T. E. Lawrence. The purpose of the costumes was to buy us time. To anyone bumping into us, we'd look, at least at a distance, like an indigenous patrol. Even a ten-second delay by our enemies was sufficient time for us to react. Sometimes the props and costumes worked, sometimes they did not.

We had flexibility in our selection of weapons, and we generally carried heavy. The ability to lay down a withering counterbarrage, what we called a "base of fire," was the only tactic that would allow us to extract from an ambush. Each four-man boat crew deployed at least one M-60 machine gun or a Russian-made RPK-squad automatic rifle. We each carried a minimum of ten thirty-round magazines for our

M-16s. In addition, my CAR-15 was fitted with an M-203 40-millimeter grenade launcher. The 203 was capable of lobbing HE/DP grenades (high-explosive/dual-purpose fragmentation and antiarmor projectiles) to a range of four hundred yards. I patrolled with a round of "beehive" chambered in my grenade launcher, a specially designed round that turned the 203 into an extremely large shotgun. Instead of buckshot, the beehive round was filled with two hundred finned nails called "fléchettes." At the press of the trigger, the beehive would deliver a cloud of nails traveling at five hundred feet per second. It could be extremely persuasive at close range.

To designate targets for helicopter gunships, I also carried a magazine containing thirty rounds of red tracer, the color used by NATO forces. It is the wise operator who remembers that tracers work both ways. Thirty red fireballs would clearly indicate what I wanted the gunships to shoot at, and just as plainly the location from which I was shooting. I carried a second magazine filled with green tracer, the preferred color of our enemies. More than once, booger eaters stopped firing when they thought the green tracer flying back at them meant they'd opened up on friends. In addition to our combat loads, we carried radios, aircraft ID panels, smoke, frag and stun grenades, water, and first-aid kits. The weight, all told, amounted to about forty pounds per man.

As ambush attacks and vehicle bombings became more frequent, we relied increasingly on the Seafox and helicopters to insert into and extract from the city. By the last weeks in August, we stopped jeep patrols entirely but continued to visit allied positions, particularly the French.

In the French sector, a battalion of *Légion Étrangère* (foreign legionnaires) kept the hammer down. The Legion battalion was comprised mostly of Eastern Europeans, Cambodians, and Vietnamese. There were some Germans, principally escaped East Germans, and at least one American, who translated for us. Their officers were, to a man, Saint Cyr–educated. The discipline of the outfit was strict; the troopers were professional and squared away. The French forces were augmented by a detachment of Commando Hubert, French naval commandos, and we were often the recipients of their gracious hospitality.

At Green Beach we subsisted on a fairly steady diet of MREs. Only when the chow truck was able to negotiate the perimeter road did we eat hot food. Dining with the French was an enchantment. One afternoon, after conducting a harbor sweep with the Commando Hubert, we were treated to rabbit, haricots verts, green salad, fresh-baked bread, and strawberry crepes. After dinner the corporal chef apologized to me, saying they would have had something better if they'd known we were coming. American MREs consisted of squeeze packets of chicken à la king and worse. French rations looked like they'd been put together by Martha Stewart—one I ate contained canned pâté, potted mushrooms, preserved pears, and a flavor-locked package of Gruyère cheese. In each French ration box were small bottles of red and white wine and a fortifying shot-bottle of cognac. Vive la France.

One afternoon boat crews Alpha and Charlie combined with members of the Commando Hubert to run an antisniper room-clearance operation against the demolished Holiday Inn downtown. Together with the Legion's Night Movement Company, we conducted a floor-by-floor search of fifteen stories of smoke-blackened, gutted rooms. We had no contact, but the event was a nail-biter not made any easier by the copious amounts of wine the French had served with lunch.

EACH NIGHT THE THUD of artillery fire would tumble down from the hills and drift across the outposts by the perimeter road. "Stray rounds," we were told. Rounds "unintentionally" fired in our direction crashed into the fields around us on a regular basis. Occasionally they fell on Green Beach itself. These were reportedly accidents, the gratuitous leavings of someone else's fight. It was a common bitch that this didn't get us hostile-fire pay. Across polished tables in Washington it had been decided that this was not hostile fire; it was somehow more benign, gentle, unintentional. Half a world away, premeditation was figured into the Druze firing solutions.

Cease-fires came and went, and rounds fell with increasing frequency onto the American positions. Apparently, what occurred beyond the wire was not our concern, and that which fell into our sector was taken in the magnanimous spirit of peacekeeping.

In a hole along the perimeter, "stray rounds" were perceived in an entirely less forbearing way. There would be a red, silent flash in the hills, a small blink sometimes among many others, but it was a sight that the wise and the living learned quickly to recognize. It meant that a rocket-propelled grenade had been fired, and you watched for the telltale red glow of the traveling round. When the RPG was fired across your field of vision, intended for someone else, it seemed to move slowly, a red dot crawling across the sky, limping like an incredibly deadly fat man toward its target. Even when it was fired directly at you, it was sometimes possible to see it coming. When it was about halfway between the fuckers who shot it and you, the sound of the launch, a kind of *bumpfff,* would drift down from the hills. If you had seen it fired, there would be time to get down. If you hadn't seen or heard, there would be only the consuming red blast of its detonation.

While you're waiting, sweating the incoming round in the bottom of your emplacement, time seems to dilate. The sound rolls away, and the night twists silence into the beating of your heart and the dry sounds of breathing. Sometimes there was no explosion; sometimes the RPGs hit cement taxiways and skipped off. Sometimes they thumped into dirt embankments and failed to detonate. Then there would be nothing, like a switch had been thrown. Slowly, you would open your eyes. Your senses would assemble themselves in a stammering swirl, and you would realize that you were alive. The hills would then be still, and the dust would drift away into a single thought that seeped into cognition from the lower centers of your brain: *stray rounds.*

Before we knew the names of the players, the bad guys

were a faceless lot, any of the nearly half-dozen militia organizations fighting against the Lebanese armed forces. When we were fired on, the joke was that the perps were Jake and Abdul, the Druze Brothers. But now, the summer half over, things were different. We knew somebody up there in the hills, a name, and "Wally" was always watching. The head of the Druze militia was Walid Jumblat, and it wasn't hard to imagine his hypothalamic eyes constantly watching, round like an owl's, noting our movements, shelling us, shifting fire, hitting us again. It was his game, and we were made to play it.

The Police song "Every Breath You Take" became something of an anthem for us. When it was played on the local stations or broadcast from the navy mobile detachment station at the airport, people would sing along, changing the words just slightly to fit this very peculiar summer affair:

> *Every move you make*
> *Every shit you take*
> *The bunkers you create*
> *Wally's watching you.*
> *Oh, can't you see*
> *He's got the RPGs*
> *And when you hear that sound*
> *Here comes another round*
> *Wally's watching you . . .*

The little white jets of envoys came and went from the airport and, in the Shouf artillery, beat out a tempo. I bought a book of stamps, intending to write anonymous letters to my congressman, but for no reason at all I changed my mind. It became difficult to write at all. My letters from this place were a study in the descent of consciousness into sunstroke. I had written often this summer to Margot, and less often to my parents. To them all, I wrote only about the weather and the bad food, idiotic travelogue. I never mentioned the shellings, our missions, or how fucked up the place was becoming.

I am certain the inanity of my letters was a tip-off. My dad sent me long missives telling me to be careful, take care of my feet, and not to be afraid to call bullshit on stupid orders. Sage advice that served me well. My mother sent tin cylinders of Danish butter cookies and gift boxes from Hickory Farm: wax-wrapped lumps of cheddar, saltine crackers, and gelatinous canned hams. Normally, these were Christmas gifts you sent to people you didn't like. In Beirut they were delicacies devoured at once. Margot sent a picture of herself in a blue string bikini, sitting on a towel in Virginia Beach. "Hurry home," she scribbled on the back. "I have a surprise for you."

I had a surprise for her, too, believe me.

BY MID-AUGUST THE IDF had nearly completed the readjustment of their line. Forces were redeployed from the Shouf, south to the city of Sidon into a long oblique that was to form a new buffer between the borders of Lebanon and Israel. On the promontories above Green Beach, columns of smoke loomed over their burning supply dumps as IDF convoys rolled south. In the city their barracks and depots had all been abandoned. Only armor and a rear guard of infantry remained to cover the withdrawal and to work the checkpoint on the coastal highway.

The last remaining IDF position occupied a slight hillock two hundred meters south of the Lebanese university in the Shuafat. The Star of David fluttered from a staff atop a two-story building that was surrounded by bunkers, foxholes, tanks, and armored personnel carriers. The marines referred to the Israeli position as "Fort Apache," and it looked like the sandbag capital of the world.

During the ponderous course of the IDF pullback, this position became increasingly exposed and removed from the bulk of the contingent. In microcosm it played out the course of things to come: daily snipings, rocket and mortar attacks, car bombs. But the Israeli response to these attacks differed qualitatively from our own—the Israelis got even, right away. When IDF positions took fire, their reaction was always the same: a twenty-five-minute full-on barrage into the neighborhood from which the rounds had come. A chilling tactic had come to replace response in the Israeli military vocabulary: collective punishment. They would hose down the three-square-block area from which the fire had originated. The IDF fire was so intense, so instantaneous and well aimed, that even across the Shouf you seemed to sense the anger in it. These tactics did not engender any sort of community feeling, and as the IDF pulled back from Fort Apache, there was an escalation in exposure to the marine company occupying the grounds of the Lebanese university. The marines would soon inherit the annoyance felt for the previous landlords.

The folks back home might have thought that America and Israel were fast allies. Certainly the impression of the Lebanese was that America had intervened to shore up the IDF's occupation of Beirut. The fact that the marines did nothing to restrain Israeli excess bolstered this impression. In actuality, relations between the marines and the IDF on the ground remained touchy.

There were several instances of deliberate IDF provocation, of armored vehicles being driven into American-held positions, and more than one marine had pulled a weapon on an Israeli tank commander. We'd had a few run-ins ourselves. For us, it was mostly trouble at vehicle checkpoints, where IDF armor blocked the street and would deign it inconvenient to allow us to pass. Doubling back over roads we had just driven was more than a hassle. It was dangerous. We took to calling the IDF "God's army" and other things much less complimentary.

Once, aboard the Seafox, we'd been ordered south to intercept a high-speed contact. The blip turned out to be an Israeli navy patrol boat heading hell-for-leather north into the American AO. We were ordered to deflect him. Provided with courses and speed by U.S.S. *John Rodgers,* our intercept brought us into contact with an IDFN Dabur-class patrol craft. We did our best to wave him off, but we were soon engaged in a game of bumper boats, the Israeli refusing to slow or fall off until finally, weapons were pointed at each other and we both went to all-stop.

The Israeli patrol boat was a sixty-footer, bigger than us by half and armed with 20-millimeter cannon. If he opened fire, we'd be shot to pieces in a matter of seconds. I stood on the middle deck of the Seafox with my rifle hanging around my neck. For a moment we bobbed there, guns manned, waiting for someone to blink. Then, from the bridge of the Dabur, the Israeli officer in charge swung a megaphone at us. In clipped English he informed me that if I continued to block his way, he would sink us. I answered that if he proceeded any farther north, he'd be on a very short trip. I gestured over my shoulder. U.S.S. *John Rodgers,* all three hundred feet of her, was bearing down on us, bow wave brilliant against the blue water. *John Rodgers*'s five-inch .50-caliber gun was swung to port. She meant business, and so did we.

"I advise you to withdraw, Captain," I said.

The Dabur turned slowly back the way she came. As the Israeli PB motored insolently south, I took some smug comfort in thinking that at least around here, we were still God's navy.

Back on the beach, the assignments were varied, but a creeping monotony was digging in. The only antidote to boredom was not giving a shit. I had secreted a surfboard in one of our load-out boxes before we left Virginia. Of my quiver of surfboards it was my primary weapon, a six-ten cherry-red Lopez Lightning Bolt, a rounded pintail shaped by Gerry Lopez himself. I got it ashore in a body bag. I had Bubba, Cheese, and Dave help me carry it off the helicopter on LZ Brown. In a combat zone there is one thing people look at but don't see, and that is four SEALs carrying a body bag. The "body" was driven down to Green Beach in the back of a deuce-and-a-half truck, and I stashed it in one of our connex boxes outside Rancho Deluxe. The surf is not epic in Lebanon, but sometimes it comes up. Mostly knee-high mush, but I would ride the right-hand break on the south side of the causeway sections. Two of our counterparts in the Commando Hubert were also surfers, and they came down to ride occasionally. The conditions were not always pleasant. To the fundamentalist Islamic mind, there must be something inherently offensive about surfing. One afternoon the waves were up, and I paddled out. Twenty minutes after I got in the water, three Katyusha rockets straddled the beach and the coast highway. I unassed my board and ran back to the bunkers in a crouch. SEALs, Seabees, and beachmasters all cheered me. Two weeks later, it happened again. I was working a short section by the causeways when the shrieking howl came out of the sky. This time the rounds hit the beach close and south, by the Seabees' tents. As I ran to the bunkers, no one was cheering. I dove into Rancho Deluxe and a close round fell, compressing and rarifying the air around me. As the dirt came down on top of us, I heard one of the Seabees saying, "That shit ain't funny no more, man."

The implication was plain. Surfing provoked Wally. When Wally got pissed, he lobbed rockets. Rockets put holes in the water tankers, shrapnel through tent flaps, and shut off the rounds of the chow truck. I stopped surfing after that.

Over the summer we provided security for a variety of junketing VIPs. There seemed always to be one or two of them about, undersecretaries of something or another, one-star generals, or, most offensive of all, congressmen. We walked with them, Vuarnet sunglasses covering our eyes and weapons hung around our necks. Sometimes we deployed sniper teams on rooftops overlooking vainglorious press conferences. Most often it was one or two, and on occasion it was a package deal, half a dozen of them in a gaggle, their staff-officer escort herding them through the positions. It was customary to give them cammies while they toured the sector. Ostensibly, it was to reduce their signature, though I doubt a plutocrat in a three-piece suit looked any more appealing in a sniper's sights than a fat man in camouflaged utilities. They were ludicrous in their immaculate out-of-the-bag BDUs, but they wore them, always. Wore them to be photographed at the outposts, shamelessly posing with men who wore the uniform for a living, marines who often had been ordered to make themselves available.

When the hand of one congressman was put out, I took it, hot and damp, into my own. Our eyes never met, and as I prepared to say something, the hand was taken from mine and put into Frank's. The eyes passed over Frank in a like manner, quickly, emptily, and as the politician walked away, I looked down. His new camouflaged trousers had been drawn up and bloused like a trooper's, but they were tucked into black nylon support stockings and shiny black loafers.

We provided security for the visit of then vice president George Bush. After he was heloed back out to the flagship, I was in the MSSG building and saw on a public-affairs office bulletin board a freshly developed photograph of the vice president shaking hands with the president of Lebanon, Amin Gemayel. It was a standard propaganda shot, but a cartoon thought bubble had been drawn above the smiling face of President Gemayel. Just like the kids in Hooterville, Gemayel's thoughts were on American goodies: "Hello," the thought bubble read, "What's your name? Give me cocoa."

IF THE DAILY HAPPENINGS of the Lebanese civil war could be known up to the second, the precise mission of the multinational peacekeeping force was less well defined. It was written somewhere in a pamphlet entitled "Lebanon," printed and distributed by the MAU, but the mission statement was vague, buried in page after page of nonsense about the local climate, geography, and agricultural history. A very nebulous line like "to establish a climate in which the Lebanese armed forces may carry out their responsibilities." Potentially heavy stuff.

There were maps in the handbook as well, fairy-tale renditions of the positions occupied by the major players. The Druze were shown to occupy a circle five miles in radius that did not even touch Beirut. Other potential hostiles were shown in similarly sterilized posits, and the Lebanese armed forces, the LAF, was gallantly depicted as controlling the capital. The maps offered up a Lebanon that America wanted to force into being, and had precious little to do with the reality of the war.

Becoming the mentor of the struggling Lebanese Republic may have been a noble ambition, but it proved eminently shortsighted. This was a multilateral civil war, and although the several protagonists clearly enjoyed fighting one another, they each had separate axes to grind with the existing government. Increasingly, our peacekeeping efforts involved separating everyone and allowing the LAF to attack whomever they wanted. We had undertaken nation building as a half-assed collateral task. America's pretense of neutrality was slipping away fast. That fig leaf would soon be abandoned outright.

After weeks of burning supply dumps, the Israelis evacuated their last positions in Beirut on the night of August 28. The Israeli withdrawal created a dangerous vacuum that drew together the major players in a bloody land grab that reverberated through the Shouf. Everyone involved, Druze, Amal, LAF, everybody, seemed to fire at the marines. The shelling raged for days. As the sun lifted over the Shouf, Beirut sweltered under the bleak haze of cordite. In endless gray afternoons, the hills shuddered with the thumping blasts of barrage and counterbarrage.

The pretense of near-misses was abandoned for the outright bombardment of the airport. Days passed in the brief intervals between shellings. We moved uneasily in the compounds. Standing more than four steps from hard cover became something of a reckless thrill.

In the bunkers, men sat soaked with sweat, eyes round like the eyes of children in a thunderstorm. They sat for hours, grinding their teeth at the shriek of wind through the tail fins of careening rockets. Close impacts would lift sleeping men six inches off the damp floor, dropping them roughly into the rudest of all possible wake-ups. In the middle of the most accurate barrages, it was impossible not to find this all a horrendously poor joke. Perception changes under fire: Senses become keen; sight, sound, and smell are made infinitely more acute by megalevels of adrenaline and simple fear.

I had ways of passing the time then, filling my imagination with the names of dogs I might own, plans I had, the cruel

things that might be said of old lovers. In these days the sunlight seemed to take on a faint, almost apologetic quality.
Light cowered through the doorways and vent holes, a pasty,
almost palpable something that reminded me more of luminous mud than sunlight. The shellings seemed an incredibly
violent meteorological phenomenon, a kind of killer weather.
And when it broke, what spilled down upon us was this
vaguely repentant sunlight. These are thoughts best comprehended by a mind four days without sleep.

There was frustration, furious madness, looming in the
eyes of the men in September's bunkers. Watching shells sur-
round the positions my friends occupied, feeling the shock
waves, pressed to the floor of my own ditch, I felt it, too. Mi-
croseconds of homicidal anger flashed across my consciousness, the kind of indescribable hatred you can feel only for
treacherous motherfuckers who daily rain metallic death
upon you. Nothing could be made of this rage. It had no out-
let, no constructive or destructive end. The madness of the
bunkers dissipated itself in nothing. It was spent in the Zen
of sitting with a sandbag between you and oblivion, with
your thoughts streaming down your face in huge, dirty beads
of sweat.

For days the Phalangists battled the Druze for Bhamdoun,
in the hills above East Beirut. There was much fighting, day
and night, and American positions on the north perimeter
took rounds incidentally and deliberately. From the fields of
the Ash Shuafat, LAF artillery pummeled the Shouf and the
north-facing hills beyond in an endless symphony of thuds.

Eventually, Druze forces managed to overrun the Phalangist position in Bhamdoun. In retaliation, the LAF 8th
Brigade, a mixed Christian and Muslim unit, was ordered
forward. Not much was expected of this attack, but to the
shock of all—and the chagrin of the Druze, PLA, Hezbollah,
and Syrian army—8th Brigade managed to penetrate as far
as Suq al Gharb. It was at this point that the Syrian-led resistance stiffened and the LAF called for American naval
gunfire support. As I am led to understand, the politicos, led
by Special Ambassador Bud McFarlane, were in enthusiastic

agreement. Closer to the ground, the marine commander, Colonel Tim Geraghty, was not so hot on the idea. There were more than a thousand artillery pieces in the Shouf overlooking the Beirut airport, all of them owned by people unhappy with the United States. Actively siding with the LAF would put the marines squarely in the sights of those guns. For as long as he was able, Colonel Geraghty prudently declined to call for naval gunfire support of the LAF.

Frank and boat crews Alpha and Bravo operated in the vicinity of Suq al Gharb during these weeks, conducting reconnaissance and locating targets, principally hostile artillery positions and command bunkers. On September 16, several shells were fired at the American embassy in West Beirut. In response, Alpha and Bravo, assisting ANGLICO units, directed naval gunfire against Druze artillery positions in the Shouf. On the nineteenth, Frank's squad helped direct fire as U.S.S. *Virginia, Bowen,* and *John Rodgers* lobbed in an additional 350 shells, this time in support of LAF units around Suq al Gharb.

The fight was on, and the United States had picked sides.

There were now French, British, and American aircraft carriers off the coast. Occasionally, they would come in, looming like great gray beasts on the horizon. Their war planes, Etendards, Buccaneers, and Tomcats, daily roared over the Shouf, always in twos. Low and very nearly at the speed of sound, they would come in off the water, banking over the airport, roaring through the foothills too low, too fast, for the AA guns to track.

It was a show put on for the grunts. The governments of England, France, and the United States all threatened air strikes if the shellings continued. The overflights were a warning to the guilty and a belated show of resolve to the men in the bunkers. The airplanes spent probably thirty-five seconds in the same air that daily rained rounds on our heads. Bank, thunder, and blast off. As quickly as they had come, they would disappear back over the sea to the carriers. In the vernacular of the marines, they were "weasel dicks," escape artists.

But in the last part of summer it didn't matter. Nothing really mattered. The hills that had once seemed so like San Diego were now familiar, malevolent, and distinctly Lebanese. In the compounds marines had developed a sensitivity to sound so acute that they could detect incoming rounds almost as soon as they were fired. Walking was done with an eye to the nearest bunker. Into every man's spinal cord was programmed a leaping dive for cover, a reflex triggered by the sound of falling shells. It was something that you did not think about. It was a response housed in the low centers of your brain, with the same dark processes that made you breathe or sweat.

When it was explained in print, laid plain in ink and photographs between the covers of some slick news magazine, Lebanon was a distant outland that could not be heard or touched or smelled. In such descriptions it remained a distant, incomprehensible struggle, a war among a dozen distinct enemies, less a civil war than a well-equipped free-for-all. Before I came to this place, I stared into the black ink against the white page, the photographs of shocking destruction, and none of it could make me sense one instant of what the place would be like. In words and white space, there was not a breath of the country, of its people, or of the simple tragedy of this war.

It is not the purpose of newspapers to print ephemeral bullshit like ambience, and the facts were sensational enough for the folks back home. In the Shouf, the war was printed in the blackness of the Lebanese nights. From a position on the perimeter, the white crashings in the hills were nearly as meaningless as the pictures in the magazines, but to marines inside the wire, this meaninglessness differed from the meaninglessness of the war at home. Here, *violence* was the overwhelming reality. It was what you lived, breathed, and ate. Here, only the abstraction of the play-by-play was missing. Tracers are tracers, rocket fire is rocket fire, and the grunts normally had no idea who was shelling the airport or why. Sometimes, weeks later, they might read it in a magazine. It might even be explained in a letter from home. In

Beirut there was no program, no scorecard. In the long months of the deployment, marines would come to know some of the players, the ones with grudges, but that was all. The vagaries of Lebanese politics would remain to them as fleeting as sunspots.

The fighting filled your senses, made you sweat, made you dig bunkers and fill sandbags. The Lebanese civil war was not a thing elegantly laid out for you to comprehend. It was something only half understood, and every marine fully comprehended the part that would kill. The rest didn't need explaining.

HAULING THE MAIL

SOUTH OF BEIRUT INTERNATIONAL AIRPORT, fighting for the suburb of Khalda had gone on for two days. Like a ripple spreading across a pond, the violence had widened, thrust and repulse, attack and counterattack, until it engulfed the entire city. It started up again sometime around noon, dull pops in the mountains of the Shouf. A vague commotion in the hills. By evening the thud of rocket and artillery fire was incessant. At eight o'clock rounds began to fall into the Shiite neighborhoods outside the airport. Long arcs of tracer passed from hilltop to valley and back again. Before midnight Druze batteries above the city opened fire, and two Katyusha rockets slammed into Saint George's Hospital. Soon everybody, Phalangists, PLO, LAF, Hezbollah, Druze, and Amal, had all opened up and weighed in.

By dawn of the third day, it was pretty much everybody versus everyone else. To the south of downtown, the Beirut-Sidon highway was cut, and the American and British embassies were no longer connected to the Anglo-American forces near the airport. As the fighting dragged on, it was decided that SEALs could deliver the diplomatic pouches. Given the fluidity of the tactical situation, it was also thought prudent for the SEAL Team to get eyes on the embassy, should an evacuation be necessary.

After receiving our tasking, we took the Seafox from Green Beach to *Iwo Jima*. After briefing the battle-group staff, boat crews Alpha and Bravo loaded aboard a pair of Hueys. Our escort was a brace of AH-1 Cobra gunships.

The Hueys came in low over the coast, directly from

northward, at eighty knots. I sat in the portside door of the lead Huey, my feet on the skids, weapon between my knees and aimed below. Scott Speroni sat at my side, knees also in the breeze, M-16 pointed forward. We flew over bands of green, then brown, then rust-colored water as the helos crested the breakwater and crossed the harbor.

"Feet dry," the pilot's voice crackled in my headset as we passed over a burning warehouse in the port. The door gunners jacked the bolts on M-60 machine guns, slamming them back then forward and pointing muzzles at the jumbled houses streaking below us. We were now over West Beirut. The morning was clear, bright, and deadly.

I stuck my head from the helicopter. Looking behind, I could see the second Huey and the bristling shapes of our escorts, the gunships above and trailing. On the deck between Speroni and me sat the reason for our mission: two yellow nylon bags containing the U.S. and British diplomatic pouches. The bags were stuffed into two Alice packs and cinched tight.

Agreeing to fly into this shit was not the smartest thing I've ever done. Now and again, from the buildings below, a green tracer would wobble up after us. The helicopter flight may have been exhilarating, but a jeep trip from Green Beach would have been suicide. Now we depended as much on audacity as airmanship.

Even though it was broad daylight, our four-bird formation flew directly into the city, popping over the tops of buildings, swooping down where broad avenues made canyon flying possible, then up again, skimming the tops of offices, stores, and the gutted hulks of destroyed buildings. We sucked laundry off clotheslines and pedal-turned right angles at intersections. More than once, as we flew over a narrow rue, astonished faces would jerk up at us. Armed men would lift their weapons as we passed above, simply too fast to track.

We doglegged west and set up on the LZ, a median strip on the coast road three hundred meters west of the American embassy. It was an LZ the French called *Ingénue* and we called Boardwalk. The Cobras banked left, breaking in narrow silhouettes south and east as the first of the Hueys touched down on the empty street of the corniche. The second Huey hovered over a three-story building directly to the south, and Steve's assault element fast-roped from it onto the roof of the building. The guys on the roof covered our insertion and spotted for the Cobras.

Humping the Alice packs, Dale Hickman and I jogged from the helicopter and into the wreckage of a café. Hickman was a card, a wiseguy from Manitowoc, Wisconsin. His call sign was Cheese, and the Cheese was fearless. He carried a single-action .44 Magnum Ruger Blackhawk pistol in his shoulder holster. Operators were allowed some discretion in their weapon selection, and Cheese's secondary weapon was a hand cannon with a ten-inch barrel. If you asked him about it, he'd say, "Hey, size does matter."

Rudi, a tough Cubano from South Miami, and Bubba trotted after us, covering the approaches as we waited to link up with the boat crew from the second helicopter. The Hueys lifted off and, trailed by their escorts, turned north, back over the harbor and its shipwrecks, and directly out to sea. In a few moments Steve's assault element had worked their way down through the building and joined us in the smashed restaurant. Behind us, in the street, a dead man was sprawled next to an overturned moped. Obviously, there were snipers about. But none of that was as disconcerting as the quiet.

We set security, and I pointed binoculars west toward the Duraford Building, the structure that housed the American and British legations. The corniche was empty, not a person or vehicle in sight, and from the south and east, the rattle of small arms and the thud of artillery were unremitting. On many of our other visits to West Beirut, the corniche had been crowded and traffic-choked, even when there was fighting at the Green Line. Today no one was out. The shops along the promenade were boarded and still.

"Where the hell is everybody?" Rudi asked.

"Shit, man, if I lived here, I'd be gone, too," Bubba said. Suddenly, he seemed to me to be one of the blinding intellectual lights of the century. The guy was a philosopher, I thought, a hillbilly Voltaire.

But his crack didn't quite answer the question. The fighting was mostly to the south, and only an occasional artillery round was being lobbed in on West Beirut. This part of town was Sunni Muslim, prosperous and relatively untouched. Life had a tendency to go on here, no matter what was going on in the Shouf.

I decided not to give it much thought. We were inserted, there was no trouble, and I was happy enough. Between us and the American embassy were about five blocks. The embassy's marine guard detachment used the call sign Devil Dog. The Dogs had reported that the LZ on the embassy roof was taking sniper fire, so we'd followed their recommendation and put down at the secondary LZ on the median strip. The corniche turned slightly, and although we did not have a line of sight to the building, snipers around it did not have a straight shot back at us.

"Patrol order, by boat crews," I said to Steve. "Cover and move, I want to keep a fifty-yard interval."

The two boat crews would be mutually supporting but would not present a single target to anyone intent on ambush. We moved west on the litter-strewn sidewalks, hugging the buildings. We scanned the street and rooftops, checking out the few abandoned vehicles parked on the sidewalks.

We passed the embassy of the German Democratic Republic, buttoned up tight with rolling metal shutters. The quiet was unnerving. The two boat crews leapfrogged west, covering and moving until we came to a place along the road where we had a visual on the embassy. Facing our direction was a sandbagged pillbox. Covering the western approach to the embassy compound, the barrel of a marine .50-caliber machine gun jutted from a loophole. I halted the boat crews, and we took cover. Walking up and ringing the doorbell was not an option.

We were arrayed in a variety of camouflage styles, German, Czech, and desert cammie smocks. Half of us carried American weapons, half carried AK-47s. I was toting my

M-4 carbine, a half-sized M-16 variant we called a "poodle shooter." Over my assault vest I wore a set of communist Chinese magazine pouches. None of us looked particularly American. This was a good thing on patrol, but not necessarily a good thing when linking up with straight-leg American units. I did not wish to have a tiff as we approached a machine-gun nest of jacked-up leathernecks.

I called Devil Dog on the PRC-77 and told them we were approaching from the west. I used my call sign, Bad Karma, gave our number as "less than company-sized," and told them we were "in costume." There was some delay on the marine end; finally, we were cleared to approach. As an afterthought, I asked what the sniper situation was. On that I got an answer straightaway: "Haul ass."

We moved as close as possible under the protection of buildings. Then I had Steve's boat crew set up to cover us as we prepared to cross the last open space into the compound. I gave one of the Alice packs to Steve and kept the other. As Steve's boat crew sighted in on the rooftops and windows, Bubba, Cheese, Rudi, and I sprinted across the last open intersection, tumbled over the sandbagged emplacement and into the embassy compound. We were aboard without incident. We set up covering fields of fire and signaled Steve to cross.

Steve's boat crew followed, also without adventure. We were in, the nylon bags were delivered up to the embassy, we bummed some water from the marines, and we were free to go.

To the south of us, the airport, like everywhere else in town, had come under fire. There had been marine casualties. Our helo package, the Hueys and the pair of Cobras, were presently medevacking wounded from LZ Brown behind the main hangars at Beirut International. We'd have to make other plans to get out. Not having helos to ride in didn't bother us much. The embassy roof was still taking sniper fire, and none of us wanted to hang out in the middle of the median strip waiting for a ride.

I called the Seafox and requested an extraction from the

Log PT, Hell Week.
U.S. Navy

The O-course.
U.S. Navy

The only easy day was yesterday. Boat Crew Four, Hell Week, Class 114, May 1981. The author is under the middle of the boat, face in shadow. *Author's collection*

Bulletproof and invisible. Class 114's graduation picture, September 1981. The author is in the last row, second from the right. Class 114 was one of the few classes to complete Hell Week without losing a single man. Twelve operators from this class would later go on to serve at SEAL Team Six. *U.S. Navy*

A SEAL operator prepares for a water landing using an MT-1-X parachute. His descent is going a lot smoother than my last jump.
U.S. Navy

MH-53J Pave
Low special
operations
helicopter.
U.S. Air Force

Trident C-4 missile
is launched off the
coast of Florida.
U.S. Navy

Combat rubber raiding craft insertion off Vieques Island, Puerto
Rico. Dwight Light (in billed cap) and author (in jungle hat).
U.S. Navy

Fifth Platoon, SEAL Team Four conducts live fire exercises, Fort A. P. Hill, Virginia, November 1982. Point man lays down fire as his squad deploys. The smoke is from the detonation of a booby trap. *U.S. Navy*

Combat-swimmer training, Isla Peros, Puerto Rico. Author (standing, carrying fins) and Frank Giffland (mask on head). *U.S. Navy*

Woodland operations, predeployment training, Fort A. P. Hill, Virginia. Operator in foreground carries an M-4 carbine, aka a "poodle shooter." Rigged under the barrel is an M-203 grenade launcher. Operator in background carries an M-60 machine gun. *U.S. Navy*

Counterambush training, Isla Peros, Puerto Rico. Bubba at left, Surfer Dave, right (crouching). *U.S. Navy*

Dog tired after a week of night ops. Fifth Platoon's operational readiness exam, Isla Peros, Puerto Rico. Left to right: Frank Giffland, Operator 570, Cheese, Scott. *U.S. Navy*

Green Beach, with Beirut International Airport in the background. *U.S. Navy*

Green Beach, from seaward. Note the causeway sections and the fortifications on the hill. *U.S. Navy*

The author and Doc Jones at Green Beach, August 1983. Our world was about to get violent. *Scott Speroni*

The Radical Riviera. West Beirut, the Italian sector. A wild no-man's-land we called Khomeiniville.
U.S. Marine Corps

It's a wonderful day in the neighborhood. Marine patrol enters the slum of Hay es Salam, north of Beirut International Airport. This part of town we called Hooterville.
U.S. Marine Corps

Martyr's Square. The Green Line, downtown Beirut.
U.S. Marine Corps

French Foreign Legion barracks, Beirut. This building (at left) would be truck bombed on October 23.
U.S. Marine Corps

Inside the watchtower, Green Beach. In a matter of weeks, snipers would make the tower too dangerous to use.
U.S. Marine Corps

Explosion tears at right flank of Green Beach.
Scott Speroni

Fifth Platoon of SEAL Team Four and elements of the French Foreign Legion conduct parachute insertion into Beirut, July 1983. That's Hooterville below. *Claude Salhani*

Bad Karma. The author, aboard an LCU of Assault Craft Unit 2, following a foot patrol of West Beirut. *Author's collection*

A 155-millimeter howitzer of Charlie Battery, 24 MAU, fires against Shiite gun positions in the Shouf Mountains. *Claude Salhani*

Seafox SWSC (Special Warfare Support Craft) off Beirut. Frequent repainting of the shark's mouth led both Israelis and Lebanese to conclude that the U.S. had as many as four boats patrolling off the city. In actuality, the white enamel we used for the teeth kept flaking off the Seafox's carbon fiber hull. Every time we repainted the teeth, the mouth came out differently. *Frank Giffland*

The corniche, Beirut, 1983. Looking east from the Duraford building. *U.S. Marine Corps*

The author in militia costume. *Author's collection*

A marine CH-46 helicopter departs the pattern from LZ Brown at Beirut International. This low-level flying was made necessary by the amount of RPG and small arms fire coming out of Hooterville. *U.S. Marine Corps*

The battalion landing team headquarters, Beirut International Airport. The truck bomb that would destroy the building smashed through a security gate and drove straight up the main drive and into the building. *U.S. Marine Corps*

On October 23, 1983, at 0623 hours, one of the largest non-nuclear explosions in the history of warfare destroyed the battalion landing team headquarters at Beirut International Airport. To gauge the size of the explosion, note the airport's control tower and a pair of Boeing 707 jetliners in the foreground. This photograph was taken seconds after the blast, from the marine positions at the north end of the runway. The photographer was nearly a mile from ground zero. *U.S. Marine Corps*

Moments after the blast, marines begin the search for survivors. For the next two days, snipers from Hooterville would pour fire on rescuers and victims alike. *U.S. Marine Corps*

Firefight in the Ash Shuafat. In the foreground is the wreckage of the battalion landing team headquarters. *U.S. Navy*

Leaving Beirut.
U.S. Marine Corps

SEAL Team Four rigger straddles the deck of an underway nuclear submarine. *U.S. Navy*

SEAL swim pair approaches a surface target. Note absence of bubbles. Diving rigs are Draeger LAR-V oxygen rebreathers. *U.S. Navy*

Gearing up for a water drop off the coast of Honduras. Rudi (right) and Uncle Chuck trying to look fierce. *Scott Speroni*

The author exits an aircraft 30,000 feet above the Sonoran desert. That's Interstate 10 way down there. *Author's collection*

SEALs conduct VBSS (visit, board, search, and seize) exercise against the U.S.S. *Austin*. Their equipment is typical kit for shipboard CQB. Helicopters are from HCS-2 Redwolf Squadron. *U.S. Navy*

The cruise ship *Achille Lauro*. *Associated Press*

Night-vision equipment photographs a SEAL operator conducting shipboard CQB. Note the MP-5 and the night-vision monocle attached to his helmet. *U.S. Navy*

SEALs arrive aboard M/V *Cape Mohican* during a ship takedown exercise. *U.S. Navy*

seawall of the corniche. They answered right away and gave an ETA of thirty minutes. Content to be under cover, we sat in the shade of the pillbox and power-napped as a few rounds dropped to the south of us, distant thuds that echoed through the streets and alleyways.

The marines stared at our uniforms and haircuts. We didn't stare back. Cheese's hog leg of a pistol got noticed. He grinned at a marine. "It fires .44 Magnum rounds, just like Dirty Harry's."

"They let you carry that thing?" a corporal asked.

"Son, they *make* me carry this thing," Cheese answered.

Fifteen minutes passed, and the echoing gunfire from the south actually seemed to die down. The day was getting on, and it was hot. This was the midafternoon lull, another unique feature of war, Lebanese-style. We decided to take advantage of the intermission.

I called the Seafox again, confirmed their ETA, and our two boat crews moved to the western end of the embassy compound. The extraction site was a break in the seawall two hundred yards west of the embassy. The terrain was identical to the approach: We had to cross a wide intersection before we could resume the relative cover of the buildings along the coast. Along this section of the corniche, five-story buildings faced over the broad multilane coast road. Beyond the road was a ten-to-fifteen-foot seawall dropping straight into the Med. Approximately every quarter mile, stone steps were recessed into the seawall, leading to small stone boat landings. We planned to extract from the closest one.

The problem was, from the buildings seaward, there was zero cover until the seawall, and then the cover was not perfect. The seawall offered protection only in its defile and the straight drop to the sea. Once into concealment like this, we'd be bottled up until our ride arrived.

Steve's crew crossed the intersection first, jogging the twenty or so yards by shooting pairs. No sweat. They found hiding places on the other side and set up to cover Rudi, Bubba, and me. We tumbled over the sandbagged wall and sprinted across the intersection. Oddly, I noticed as we ran across the street that the streetlights were on. A red hand was blinking "don't walk" as I chugged toward Steve and his guys.

When I was halfway across the intersection, an earsplitting noise poured out of the sky—the wail of incoming Katyushas. There was nothing to do but keep running. I didn't have to tell Rudi or Bubba to hurry; they were hauling ass. My Swiss and Irish genes do not lend themselves to great bursts of sprinting speed. Truth be told, I don't dance that well, either. Legs pumping, Rudi and Bubba accelerated across the pavement. Even carrying his M-60 and six hundred rounds, Rudi was faster than I was.

I had been the last guy out over the embassy wall, and it would take me ten seconds to cover the distance. Ten seconds, when Katyushas are falling, is an eternity. I had time to consider several factors. First, the incoming rockets were almost certainly being aimed at the embassy. Second, I was probably safer because I was presently running away from the target. Third and most distressing, the Lebanese gunners very seldom hit what they were aiming at. The safest place to be, statistically, was exactly where they were aiming. I was no longer exactly where they were aiming, but somewhere *around* where they were aiming, and that was dangerous.

As the first of the Katyushas detonated, I threw myself across the sidewalk and against the wall of a building. The rocket slammed into a rooftop fifty yards away. Broken glass and roof gravel rained down into the street. The concussion shook the dust from the pavement and echoed crazily in the crowded city block. The next round smashed into the median strip in front of the embassy. The third round made a majestic screech all the way to earth but failed to detonate. Off in the blocks behind us came a crashing noise, like the sound of a car accident, but no explosion. A dud.

Rudi ran out to where I'd curled up, but I was on my feet before he reached me.

"Jesus, you're slow," he said.

I jogged to where the boat crews had gathered, the commodious doorway of a large boarded-up shop. We were grouped together, under halfway-decent cover. Instinct dictates that when under artillery fire, one should get where one is going in a hurry, but I didn't want to rush. I had no idea what group had fired on the embassy: It could have been any of half a dozen factions, and who was yanking the lanyard didn't matter. What mattered was whether they would lob another salvo. Usually, when artillery is fired, someone close to the target—not the actual gunners—spots the rounds and supplies updated targeting information. The three rockets had missed the embassy. We were in pretty good cover, and I wanted to see if they would fire again. That would confirm two things: that the embassy was the target—a virtual no-shitter—and, more important, whether there was a spotter watching the corniche. The embassy wasn't going anywhere, but we were, and we would have to pass that hundred yards of open space to get to our extraction point. If there was a forward observer, he'd certainly report us. I didn't want to become the next target.

We waited. Nothing happened. We could see the white bow wave of the Seafox rounding Pigeon Rocks and emerging onto our side of the Beirut peninsula about a mile out to sea. We worked west, clinging to the buildings. A narrow series of alleyways joined the main drag, and we traversed these, covering and moving. Two street crossings remained between the extract point and us. We repeated the sprints, and when we came to the last intersection, I peeked around the wall. A long blast of heavy machine-gun fire ripped down the middle of the street.

One block down was a white Datsun pickup truck; mounted in the cargo bed was a Russian-made DShK, a .51-caliber antiaircraft gun. In Somalia these rigs would come to be called "technicals." In Lebanon we used the term the locals had coined—machine guns in the back of pickups were called "water-skiers," for the manner in which the gunners held on when the trucks roared around town.

This water-skier didn't have us ranged yet. He fired another burst straight down the middle of the street. I ducked back behind cover, and in a matter of seconds he'd shifted fire and started pummeling the corner of the building. As I pressed against the wall, bullets knocked off big chunks of concrete and tracers skipped across the pavement and wobbled out over the corniche. Cement dust powdered my hair and worked down the collar of my cammie blouse. My head rang with the concussion of the bullets.

Remarkably, I wasn't scared. I think I might have even laughed. Our cover was solid, and though the firepower was an impressive display, we weren't going to be done in by this guy. Cutting the corner, we had a clear field of fire through the broken windows; I popped up behind one of the smashed frames, pointed the M-203, and pulled the trigger. The grenade launcher went off with a loud *pop*. As I ducked down, I heard a sharp ripping sound, a noise like tearing paper, then a cacophony of pings. It was the fléchettes tearing into the truck.

The machine gun stopped, and I heard the pickup crunch into reverse. I peered out again, this time around the corner; the water-skier was sinking back into the truck bed with a stupefied look on his face. His fist still clutched the handhold on the DShK, and the gun was now pointed up into the air, its muzzle lifting skyward as the gunner's legs buckled under him. There were a dozen spots of blood expanding across his shirt and pant legs. I watched him fold like a cut puppet as the pickup backed around the corner and out of sight.

I reloaded, and we set up on the window, waiting for the DShK to pull back into range. It was a trap they easily ignored. They'd figured out that we could cut the corner, and they were in no hurry to close up with us. A few AK-47 rounds were sprayed from their end of the block, most of them missing our building. We'd gotten the truck off our back, at least for now. But we had to cross the street to get to extract.

The appearance of the water-skier also answered the question of the spotter. We'd obviously been seen, and someone had directed the truck to jam us at the corner. I presumed that someone was still watching. As long as he hung back up the block, the DShK was not an immediate problem. What I had to worry about was additional bad guys closing in and cutting us off from both the embassy and the extract point. I called the Seafox on the PRC-77.

"Seafox, Bad Karma; be advised we are in contact at this time. We have a water-skier one block in. We are still go for primary extract."

"Seafox copies."

We still had our ride. The choices for us were to beat feet back to the embassy or to dart across the street and make the extract. It was two hundred yards back to the embassy, and several large boulevards entered the corniche through the intersections we'd have to recross. Besides opening us from cover, these streets were the threat axis, the direction from which we could expect the water-skier's friends to converge. I didn't want to run into them.

I made a tactical call. I had the Seafox in sight, we were across the street from the extract point, and my major goal was to call it a day. I told the lads, "Let's get across the street and get out of here." I got no arguments.

This would turn out to be the most dangerous part of our little junket. The buildings overlooking the corniche made our movement the tactical equivalent of showing our asses. The spotter was still out there, reporting our progress. It was logical to expect that he was on a rooftop. As soon as we moved, he'd report us and probably take a few shots. The sooner we got out of there, the better.

I ordered Steve across to the landing. Rudi and I set up a covering position, and Steve led the remainder of the two boat crews across the coast road, to the stairs, and down the breakwater. It was quiet as they sprinted to the seawall. Steve and Doug set cover for us and signaled Rudi and me to cross. As we fell back, I could hear Arabic shouts coming from down the block. The water-skier had been joined by some buddies. Rudi and I sprinted to the seawall. I still wasn't sweating it. We would be out of here well before anyone could envelop us.

I thought.

As we crossed the street, several shots rang out above us.

A handful of rounds spanged off the asphalt as we ran to the breakwater. They were wide, fifteen or twenty feet away from us, and I remember thinking, either these guys really suck, or they're a couple hundred yards away. Steve and Doug were covering us but had no idea where to concentrate fire. The sounds of gunfire echoed around the buildings, making it impossible to pinpoint the shooters.

We all piled down the stairs to the landing. I was beginning to think we would come out all right. We'd made it to the landing, and I had the Seafox in sight. I got on the radio and told them we were still in contact and ready for immediate extraction. No one answered. I called again. Nothing.

At the top of the stairs, another bullet bashed off the sandstone. There was more yelling in the street. The water-skier's dance partners were getting closer. A mile or more offshore, the Seafox was just sitting there. What the hell was going on? I was getting pissed. For the first time on this tour, I felt a lump in my stomach, and my mouth was dry.

We were cornered, and it was my fault. I'd put the squad into a bullshit spot. Another long burst of fire spattered the breakwater above us. Rock chips and grit skittered down onto the landing.

"Shit, Mr. Pfarrer. Let's shoot back at these assholes!" Bubba said.

"Stay put," I said.

In order to shoot back, we'd have to break the cover of the seawall, a move that would be instantly fatal. The volume of fire directed at us was growing. We were under good cover but we were virtually defenseless. The squad was clustered together on the landing, grouped up perfectly and waiting for some enterprising militiaman to stroll across the street and drop a hand grenade into our laps. I'd put the Team in a box.

My heart was pounding, and I was as scared as I have ever been. Not afraid of contact, but of having made a lethal tactical error. I'd fucked up, and it was the lads who would have to pay for it.

None of this would be a factor, I thought, if we could get

the Seafox in here. I could see it maybe two thousand yards off. Still sitting dead in the water. Jesus, what was wrong?

Doug was our smallest guy. He was positioned halfway up the stone steps, covered from the street but able, I hoped, to drop any bad guy smart enough to try to frag us all together on the boat landing.

I keyed the handset again. I was yelling now. "GODDAMMIT, SEAFOX, WE NEED IMMEDIATE EXTRACT!"

This time there was a reply, but it wasn't the Seafox's coxswain, Kelly, who answered the radio call. Dave Church's voice came over the earphone: "Roger, Bad Karma, Seafox is inbound. Hang tight."

Dave had been at the BLT getting his M-16 repaired when we were called up to make the embassy run. I'd left a note for him at the bunker, expecting him to wait for us. Dave was a regular go-getter and had obviously called the Seafox back to the beach to pick him up. Now he was on the boat, and I was going to kick his ass when they finally got here.

More bullets hit the sandstone above us, snapping chunks of red rock and flinging them into the water around the landing. The Seafox was coming at us, zigzagging toward shore but keeping course on. I could see that her forward M-60s were manned, not that they were going to do a lot of good. The street level was twenty feet above us, and the bad guy's vantage several stories higher than that. The M-60s could not elevate enough to shoot over our heads.

The Seafox roared up to the landing and backed her engines. Her nose kissed the seawall as the wake caught up and surged under. We all scrambled across her bow over the conn and into the back compartment. Doug and I were the last to jump from the landing.

The Seafox backed up, twisted to starboard, and roared directly out to sea. It would have been better to go east or west, staying under the protection of the breakwater, but there was no time to correct the coxswain, and as soon as we were away from the wall, bullets splattered the water around us, long thin splashes to our right and left. The water-skier and his buddies, all taking their best shots.

Again the Seafox's design faults were on display. We were in a hot extract, and none of the boat's guns could fire astern. Although she was armed with two .50-cals in her aft compartment, they were mounted port and starboard. Neither could be trained to cover our retreat.

On the corniche, our pursuers broke cover, trotting across the median and onto the seawall. Standing in the tailgate, Rudi aimed the M-60 at them and cranked off a few tightly grouped bursts. I fired as well. The men, about twenty, scattered and flattened. We could only hope to keep their heads down until we were out of range. We didn't do too great a job of suppressing their fire. A dozen more bullets zipped into our wake as we made the run offshore.

If the Seafox was a piece of shit, at least it was a fast piece of shit. In a few moments we were two miles off. I made my weapon safe and scrambled from the back compartment onto the middle deck. I was in full Irish when I got to Dave.

"What the hell took you so goddamn long?" I shouted. "We were fucking pinned in there!"

I was locked on Dave, but I noticed the two Seafox crewmen manning the M-60s. One of them dropped his helmet to the deck. The other one sat on the roof of the conn, looking like he was about to cry. Then I noticed that Dave had his pistol drawn. His expression was grim.

In the conn Kelly killed the engines and threw down his headset. He came boiling on deck. Veins were standing out on his neck. He looked as pissed as I was.

"That motherfucker assaulted me! I want him arrested!" he bellowed.

"What the hell are you talking about?" I said.

Dave's eyes narrowed at Kelly.

"He put a fucking gun to my head!" Kelly screamed, pointing a finger at Dave.

"What happened?"

"He assaulted me." Kelly continued to yammer, but I cut him off.

"I'm talking to Church," I said.

Dave's voice was tight, but he answered quietly, "This son of a bitch refused to go in."

"Refused to go in where?"

"To get you. We could see you were getting shot at. We could see the water-skier. When Kelly heard you were in contact, he said, 'They're SEALs, they can get their own damn selves off the beach.' "

I looked at Kelly, then at the crewmen, still slouched by the guns. "Is that true?"

"He pulled a gun—"

"Answer my goddamn question."

Kelly didn't say anything. It was obviously true. The rest of the SEAL squad was now standing on the middle deck, murder in their eyes.

The Seafox crewmen were special boat unit sailors. Not SEALs. This wasn't sitting too well with the Team guys who'd almost gotten hosed on the landing. I was seeing red, too. Dave still held his pistol, and he was staring at Kelly, but he continued evenly.

"I heard you calling, and shit bag here wouldn't answer. I told him to man the guns and go in, and he told me to get fucked. It was his boat, he said."

"So you drew down on him?"

"Yeah."

"He put the gun in my face!" Kelly shrieked.

"Clamp your fucking cake hole," I said.

There was a bond between special boat unit sailors and SEALs, or there was supposed to be. SBU crewmen were volunteers; they knew they'd be operating with the SEALs, in harm's way, and this was the first and only time I'd ever heard of an SBU crew shirking their duty. Special boat unit crew members have distinguished themselves in every theater in which SEALs have operated. This was a frigging disgrace, and I was pissed. I got in Kelly's face.

"Did you refuse to go in?"

"Look, man, it was hot in there. Our guns couldn't elevate—"

"I'm not your man, fuck stick. You left us in the breeze."

"And he assaulted me. I'm bringing charges!"

I exploded. And for the first and only time in my naval career, I grabbed an enlisted man and shoved him. I slammed Kelly against the radar mast. The platoon was shocked. They knew that I had an Irish temper, but they'd never seen me get physical with anybody.

I was at nose-biting distance from Kelly. "Listen to me, you fucking pansy." My teeth were clenched. "You want to press charges against Church, go ahead. I'm going to press charges against you and this crew. I'm going to arrest you right here, right now, and write you up for cowardice under fire. The penalty for that is death. You got me?" I shoved Kelly to the deck. He didn't get up. "You want to play sea lawyer, bitch, be my guest."

Kelly was silent and furious. He was wearing a pistol and looked mad enough to use it. Mad enough, maybe; stupid enough, no.

I continued to lay in to him. "For the record, dick weed, if I'd come out onto this boat and found a bullet in your brain, I'd swear under oath that it came from the beach. You pull chickenshit on us again, and I'll shoot you myself."

The lads looked at me with barely concealed smirks.

"Now get us back to the goddamn bunker."

Kelly went back into the conn and got the boat under way. The remaining crew members slunk below. The lads drifted into the back compartment, leaving me alone. I guess I still looked dangerously pissed.

The Seafox started south. I stood on the deck behind the radar mast. The wind blowing across the deck was cool heaven. I calmed down a little.

My hands were shaking as I peeled off my magazine pouches and my assault vest. My cammie blouse was plastered to my skin with sweat. I reached for my canteen. It was gone. The pouch was empty, ripped open by a bullet or a piece of shrapnel.

The juice was off, and I suddenly felt weak. Dizzy, even.

Dave walked over and handed me his canteen. "Hey, Mr. Pfarrer, I'm sorry."

"About what?"

Dave nodded down into the conn. "That shit."

"You did the right thing, Dave."

His eyes narrowed and I watched him think. The right thing would have been to shoot Kelly's sorry ass.

"You think he's gonna press charges?" Dave asked.

"If he does, I'll take him for a swim." The implication was a one-way swim. Dave smiled and walked back to the troop compartment.

I poured the water over my head, washing the cement dust and rock chips from my face, neck, and ears. We rounded the peninsula and headed south. I stood alone, holding on to the mast and rolling against the swells until we arrived back at Green Beach.

Later that afternoon Frank's squad joined us on the beach. I asked to speak to Frank alone, explained the situation, and once again he backed me up. Not just backed me up but made his own points. After we talked, I watched as Frank stormed down the causeway, boarded the Seafox, and jabbed a finger into Kelly for a while. I didn't hear much. Occasionally words like "duty," "relieved for cause," and "court-martial" came up the beach. It was the only time I ever heard Frank raise his voice.

The matter was dropped. The Seafox crew would never again disappoint, and Kelly wound up getting a medal for an op we would run in the last weeks of our tour.

The sun dipped into the sea, and we sat on the bunker drinking warm Heinekens in steel cans and watched as the battle for Khalda continued. The LAF operated from the south end of the airport, spraying everything they had against the hillside town but making no effort to move infantry forward. It was a demonstration of classic Lebanese military technique, risking little and gaining nothing, and I wondered again what the fuck we were doing here.

"Hey, Mr. Pfarrer, you want some chow?" It was Doug, holding a paper plate.

"I'll take another beer," I said.

Doug flipped me a warm green can. I pulled the top and drank deeply. The afternoon's fun was still clinging to me like road buzz. I thought I would feel some sort of elation, but I did not. I didn't know what I felt. Strangely, maybe even guiltily, I felt nothing.

Everybody in the profession of arms worries about how he'll do under fire. I'd managed to extract my force from a superior and well-positioned enemy. I hadn't lost a man, but I had nearly lost everyone. If Dave hadn't hijacked the Seafox, it all might have come out very differently.

I would never again leave myself and my men a single avenue of escape. My feelings pinballed around: guilt, then nothing, then anger at myself. The rush left me. Then I was afraid that I had screwed up. In contact, still thinking myself invincible, I had been almost giddy. That jacked-up, euphoric adrenaline feeling would continue almost until the end of my tour. Later, it would be replaced by a deadly, self-destructive cynicism. But all of that was months away. Now I was tired. Bone, dead, roadkill dog-tired.

I walked back through the Seabee encampment to Rancho Deluxe. It was a Sunday evening, and there had been a barbecue, hot dogs and hamburgers cooked in halves of fifty-five-gallon oil drums converted to grills, and just as the tables began to empty, the first round came down north of our position. Single explosions were so common that at first no one even paid attention. Five minutes later, another round fell, then another. Small arms and RPGs suddenly erupted to the south, and the show was back on.

Two rounds hit the water off the beach. One at a distance and the other close, fifty meters off beach center. It was clear that these rounds were being walked in on us, so we moved for the bunkers, pulling on flak jackets over bare chests.

By eight in the evening nothing else had fallen, though the sounds of small arms continued to drift down from Khalda. Over the radio we heard that there was heavy fighting outside the perimeter in Hooterville. At midnight Boeing 707s of Middle East Airlines began to scream off the runways. The evacuation of MEA equipment always foreshadowed bombardment and closure of the airport.

I drank another beer, realizing suddenly that I was sunburned and buzzing. We sat atop the bunker, waiting for the inevitable barrage, taking bets on the hour when it would start.

LOSING THE BUBBLE

IN WAR, BIGGER IS BETTER, and the battleship *New Jersey* was both. By the end of September she had completed a transatlantic voyage and joined the squadron of warships stationed off the coast. Sixteen-inch guns, armor plate, cruise missiles—she was the big stick in a language that everybody could understand. In a chow line, someone had said to me that bringing *New Jersey* to Lebanon was like taking a bazooka to a bullfight. It was definitely a weapon that could win, but it wasn't the *right* weapon. Looming on the horizon, the ship was an impressive sight—long, lean battle wagon— but it didn't fool anyone.

New Jersey's sixteen-inch guns fired projectiles the size of Volkswagens, two thousand pounds of high explosive at ranges in excess of twenty miles. One such shell could vaporize a city block. Clearly, the devices that turned Pacific islands into lunar landscape were not the weapons of choice in a densely populated city. Firepower and brimstone had brought down the Axis, but were not applicable to the chores of hard-core peacekeeping. Bad guys here did not congregate large bodies of troops, nor did they shell us from static massed-weapon positions. They offered no targets for such a heavy hitter.

It was not merely a coincidence that when the *New Jersey* arrived, the tactics of our antagonists underwent a dramatic change. Previously, Druze and Syrian gunners set up on isolated promontories and whaled away when they felt the urge. Now the stakes were higher, and the consequences of establishing a battery in the open were 100 percent lethal. Offshore was a ship that could alter the geography of this country. Overnight, promontory shooting ended and "shoot and scoot" began. In the civilian centers there was safety, there was cover, and in the first part of October, fire came almost exclusively from the most densely populated areas of the city. Indirect fire weapons, mortars and Katyusha rockets, were brought to bear from vacant lots and roofless buildings in the heart of Hooterville. Sixteen-inch shells would take out the mortars, but they would also get everyone else in the neighborhood. Not exactly a transaction in the spirit of peacekeeping. So it went, round after round, in the early autumn.

Offshore the ships coasted silently, indifferently turning north and south into the fire-support areas and out to sea in unending circles. No one pretended to take comfort in their presence. The ships would never be used the way the grunts wanted—guns fired furiously until their magazines were exhausted, until the Shouf was ablaze and sand was all that was left of this fucking place.

Ah, fire superiority.

It was a dream, only a dream, and in hot afternoons the low shapes of the warships trundled about, sometimes close, sometimes hull down on the hazy horizon. It was not possible to look at them without tasting the bitter frustration that was starting to poison our every breath.

It could eat you up. A kind of cabin fever that arose from confinement in the compounds. Routine became an enemy, and there was nothing, nothing, except the exact same things you did every day at the exact same time. It took possession of will and reason. But we were lucky. We frequently ran operations, recons mostly, and we counted ourselves blessed. Walking patrol at night in the Shouf, even surrounded by six varieties of bad guys, was better than sweating it inside the perimeter.

It was the shellings that imparted another sensation, a very real, very opposite perception. It was the feeling that welled in your guts when you ran for cover. Ran for your fucking life in this same dusty, well-known, and now boring place. Ran in the endless shriek of falling rounds. Boredom and fear tangled themselves together in the heat of autumn, and in the end, it was boredom that was the most dangerous. A crushing tedium that removed any other emotive state, any other possible feeling. It was boredom that made you forget to close up your body armor. Boredom that made you *want* to drive the perimeter road. Now almost nothing mattered except having enough insect repellent. The heat continued, endless and maddening.

Each afternoon Lebanese armor transiting south on the coastal highway drew fire from Khalda. These attacks became so routine that the LAF simply returned fire from the road, stopping on the median strip to allow civilian traffic to pass as they let loose with .50-caliber guns. Showers of red tracers passed up the highway, exploding fiercely into the concrete sidewalls of the town. One-hundred-round bursts were aimed by the white flashes of impact and hit nothing but buildings that had been hit a million times. In this manner, fire was traded over the course of weeks.

The return fire could shift without warning onto Green Beach. Sometimes the distances were great enough to give us a few seconds' warning. From the pillbox on left flank, binoculars brought close the damage, low-rise buildings pocked like plague victims, black streaks up their sides from smoldering fires. It ran like this for days on end.

One afternoon was memorable. There had been pitched firefights all day, and at about five o'clock, the Lebanese APCs withdrew. It was Miller time. Return fire sputtered off and finally stopped. From Hooterville in the northeast, the sounds of other, more distant firefights drifted to us on gusts of favorable wind. Our show seemed to be over.

We were not fed dinner because the perimeter remained on Condition One until 1900. On Green Beach the quiet led many to break cover, and tables in the leeside of bunkers filled with men tearing open MREs for dinner. Quite suddenly, dinner ended. A burst of 7.62 machine-gun fire spat from Khomeiniville and traveled the length of the beach. It impacted a tableful of Seabees at the north end. There were wood splinters and ricochets, MRE packets shot out of people's hands, but incredibly, no one was hit. In the time it took to breathe, small-arms fire redoubled. Discernible were the quick bursts of M-16s and FNs, the staccato bleating of Kalashnikovs.

I took cover in the rifle pits attached to Rancho Deluxe. Doc was sitting in the bottom of the hole, leisurely shaking Tabasco onto a dehydrated pork patty. He was eating it dry, without water, crunching on it like a candy bar.

"Getting a little hot out there?" he asked, continuing to munch the freeze-dried pig rectangle. Doc was utterly unruffled, like he always was. As though it were perfectly appropriate to be ducking machine-gun fire at dinner.

"I'm gonna see if I can get a shot at the snipers," I said.

"Waste of time," Doc answered. We'd been shot at so much recently that tonight's shenanigans hardly rated a response. "The marines aren't gonna want you to start a war," Doc said.

"It's already a war, Doc," I answered.

"It's just fucking Wallys. They'll mellow out when the sun goes down."

He was right, but I was no longer in a peacekeeping mood.

"I'm bored. I'm gonna try," I said.

Doc continued to chew. "Nothing too heroic, *Diawi,*" he said.

I ducked into the bunker to get my CAR-15. The rest of Delta and Charlie were sprawled on their cots, reading or sleeping. Another burst of fire skipped over the top of the bunker and banged into the vehicle barricade with the crisp sound of hammer strikes. No one even looked up. In the bunker, the guys were as blasé as if this were a thunderstorm.

Cheese peered at me from over the top of a comic book about naked vampire chicks. "You want some help, Uncle Chuck?" he asked casually, as if I were carrying two bags of groceries.

Since the extraction on the corniche, the platoon had taken to calling me "Uncle": Frank was the old man; I was the old man's kid brother. With the exception of Doc, Stan, and Tim, none of the platoon was older than twenty-two. I was twenty-six, and I was an uncle.

"You want to see if we can shut that guy up?" I asked.

"Sure," Cheese said, "I'm game."

He got his rifle and combat vest as I took down a pair of binoculars hanging from a nail over my rack. I grabbed the poodle shooter, a clip-on plastic bipod, and my shooting vest.

We waited for a lull and ran to the machine-gun position at left flank. Crouching against the side of the emplacement were the marine shore party OIC, a nice guy named Leo, and an army warrant officer who was trying to get to some other position, Charlie battery, I think. He was forced to remain here when the position went to Condition One. There were others about, sprawled against low cover, strangely inhuman shapes in helmets and Kevlar armor.

Cheese and I took cover, shifting our legs awkwardly, lazily trying to keep our weapons from touching the dirt.

"What the hell's going on?" Leo asked.

"I thought you knew," I said.

Leo spit a wad of tobacco. "It looks like Wally's between the runway and Khomeiniville." He pushed back his helmet with a thumb. "I told Battalion we were taking direct fire. We have permission to engage."

That was mighty nice of them, I thought.

Two marines sprawled behind the M-60 in the pillbox, and maybe half a dozen more marines were aiming across the open stretch of beach toward Khomeiniville. No one was firing.

"Why haven't you gone hot?" I asked.

"I can't see the shooters. I've been calling 'no joy,' and Battalion said the LAF is going to send somebody to handle it."

"Who are they gonna send," Cheese sneered, "Batman and Robin?"

I lifted my binoculars and peered through the rifle slit. I saw only a jumble of houses. Leo told his radio operator to find out if Alpha Company was shooting. Some of the weapons we heard were American-made, M-60s and 40-millimeter grenade launchers, but these were also used by the bad guys, so it wasn't possible to really tell. Long bursts of machine-gun fire passed over our heads and spattered the pavement behind us. We all tried to look cool as we kept down.

After about five minutes there had been no answer from Alpha Company, and Leo peered for a brief second over the top of the bunker. "Not enough fire for Alpha Company." He spit again. "They've been taking a lot of shit lately. If they were under orders to return fire, they'd be raising hell."

I agreed, but I didn't feel like looking over the top of the bunker to prove it to myself.

"Somebody's raising hell," the warrant officer said.

There came the sudden whistling of falling artillery, then nothing. We had time only to screw up our faces in anticipation of the impact.

"They miss?" the warrant officer asked.

"They suck," Cheese answered.

"I hate that sound," I said.

In an earnest and perturbed way, Leo said, "Fuck these people."

The sun was slipping down. We were losing the light. I put my binoculars on the jumble of houses, scanning carefully. I saw nothing. Leo got on a field telephone to Battalion and told them he was still taking sporadic fire but was unable to pinpoint the source. We spoke about guard rotation, placing additional men, his and mine, on the perimeter that night.

A runner came panting up and dived into the bunker. "Sir, there's a whole mess of troops on the highway south of right flank," he puffed.

"Bad guys?"

"We don't know who they are."

Fucking brilliant, I thought. We're being surrounded.

"Well, that's it," Leo said, brushing the dirt off his shirt-front. "I'll go take a look." He crouched to his feet and prepared to leave.

"I'm going to stay here," I said. "You mind if we take a crack at the machine gun?"

"Your guys?" he asked.

"Yeah."

"How many?" Leo looked concerned.

I smiled. "Afraid we're gonna wake the neighbors?"

"Fuck the neighbors," he said. "Do me a favor. Let me know if you're gonna fire any antiarmor stuff."

"Nothing nuclear, I promise. Just me and Cheese," I said. I didn't need his permission to engage, but we were neighbors, and seeking a consensus was considered polite.

"Knock yourself out," Leo said. He waited for a lull, then ran back to the pillbox at right flank. His marines followed.

Cheese and I snuggled down into the bunker. I handed him the bipod. He clipped it to the gas tube of his M-14 and steadied it against the sandbagged rampart. I laid my CAR-15 next to it and scanned with the binoculars as Cheese settled in behind his rifle. Small arms and artillery continued to pass overhead. In the still evening, the bullets and shells sounded exactly like the war movies I had seen as a kid. The sun was almost completely submerged in the Med. The sky at zenith was becoming a deep shade of cobalt, the horizon powder blue and dappled with clouds turning orange.

Half a dozen bullets and a couple of tracers hit the side of our pillbox. Half a second later came the sound of the weapon, a rattling echo out of Khomeiniville. It was probably an RPK machine gun.

"I can't see shit," Cheese said, sighting down his rifle.

I couldn't see anything, either. The snipers were getting better. When we first arrived, Khomeini cowboys would hang out of windows or shoot from backlit rooms. These operational procedures did not lengthen their careers as snipers. Darwinism functioned, and soon the snipers who remained learned to stay in shadow and fire three or four feet back from the window.

Actually, it was a stretch to call these guys snipers. My friends in the British Special Air Service had told me about monthlong countersniper operations against the IRA in

Belfast. SAS marksmen would be smuggled into buildings in steamer trunks and spend a week drilling a hole out under the eaves of a building, all the while setting up on an IRA shooter doing the same thing four hundred yards away. A sniper duel. That was craftsmanship. What we had tonight was a booger eater with a machine gun.

"Watch for muzzle flashes," I said. I kept the binoculars on the row of houses. The sun was down now, but the sky continued luminous. It was nautical twilight and still too bright to use the NVGs. We had fifteen or twenty minutes until dark.

The RPK fired again, missing our sandbags and striking the pavement just short of us. Ricocheting tracers wobbled into the sky, burning out at low altitudes. I hoped the RPK's muzzle blasts would give him away as the sun slipped lower.

From the Lebanese checkpoint south of the beach, a pickup truck loaded with LAF soldiers screamed past us, heading north with its lights on. There was no way to warn them or tell them to stop. As they headed for Khomeiniville and the line of houses, I could see troopers charging their weapons in the back of the truck.

"Oh, fuck," Cheese said.

When the truck was two hundred meters north, the RPK opened fire. Taillights flared, wavered, and were extinguished. The fire reached a crescendo; the truck had driven into the teeth of an ambush, and rounds skidded down the road in weird whistles. They'd been hammered.

The RPK kept firing long bursts as the soldiers sought cover behind their vehicle. As the tracers poured out of Khomeiniville, the window of the shooting position blinked white, a perfect strobed rectangle against the line of houses.

"I got the shooter," I said. I kept the binoculars to my eyes. The RPK fired again. "Second row of buildings, middle of the block."

Cheese had him, too. Pressing his cheek against the stock, Cheese drew a breath and exhaled slowly, then fired a single round. In the bunker, the report of the weapon was a deep, chest-pounding *thud*. His ejected round bounced off the ceiling. SEALs don't often fight from underground bunkers. As my head pounded with three more shots, I made a mental note: Shooting from pillboxes can give you a migraine.

Cheese fired half a dozen more rounds on semiauto as I watched. The first two struck the building low. The last four made no sparks. They went into the window. For a few seconds there was silence. Then four or five shots rang out from the wrecked LAF truck. There was still someone alive.

The RPK opened up from a different window. He fired maybe twenty rounds in a long burst. As the light continued to fade, his muzzle flashes were plainly visible. The first rounds hit the sand in front of us, and we both ducked. The bullets thumped the bunker, then ripped into the vehicle barricade. Some pretty fair shooting.

I opened the M-203 grenade launcher slung under the foregrip of my rifle, slid out the beehive round, and dropped it into the cargo pocket on my cammies. From my vest I took out an HE/DP round. "How far do you think it is to the houses?"

"Too far for forty mike-mike," Cheese said.

The max range of the grenade launcher was approximately four hundred meters. I figured the house was almost that far. I hoped it was a little closer.

"I thought all you officers played golf," Cheese said.

"What's that got to do with anything?"

"You know, man, estimating range."

"I don't play golf," I said. Another note to self: Join a country club when I get home.

To fire the 203 to maximum range, I'd have to point my weapon up at an angle of approximately 45 degrees, something I couldn't do from inside the bunker. I locked the round into the tube. Cheese changed magazines, then scrambled out of the pillbox after me. We took cover again outside as another long burst flew over us—tracers, beautiful as they flew over our heads.

I rolled the quadrant sight on the side of my CAR-15, setting it to maximum range. In more ways than one, this was going to be a long shot. Cheese watched me as I snicked the safety forward on the M-203. "Say when," he said.

We popped over the top of the bunker, Cheese holding his rifle offhand and firing steadily in semiautomatic. I saw the window, pointed the sights, and awkwardly angled the 203 up. I pulled the trigger, and the grenade launcher fired with a hollow, loud *pop*. Cheese ducked back immediately, but I crouched above the bunker to see where the round fell. The grenade lobbed through the air, traveling, incidentally, about as fast as Tiger Woods can hit a golf ball. The light from the sunset made the grenade glow coppery as it flew. I watched the projectile slam into the roof of the sniper's building. Sparks swarmed from a dirty puff of smoke. Three quarters of a second later, the report came to us: *crack-bang*.

"Too high."

The RPK fired again, this time at the truck. It apparently didn't occur to Wally that we might be lobbing grenades, and he kept shooting the soldiers pressed low under their vehicle. Tucked behind the bunker, I ejected the spent round and pushed another of the fat 40-millimeter grenades into the launcher.

We popped over the top of the bunker again, Cheese laying down cover while I aimed and shot. The RPK was silent this time, and we watched the grenade slam into the wall to the right of the sniper's perch. The armor-piercing round blew a fist-sized hole into the cinder blocks. Cheese and I remained standing as we reloaded. I took long, careful aim and squeezed the trigger. Again a deadly copper-colored golf ball sailed through the air. When the grenade was halfway to the houses, the RPK opened up again, right at us. He was shooting fast and high.

I don't know why, but I just stood there watching as the tracers flew at me. The grenade pitched for the building, and Cheese ducked, like a rational person, but I stood there as the tracers sizzled over my head. I watched the grenade until I lost the small glint of the flying projectile and it found impact. This time it passed through the black space of the window and detonated inside the building. The explosion was muffled by the walls and came to us as a ringing *thud*. Cheese and I crouched and waited. Nothing. The silence lengthened.

Cheese grinned. "You got him."

There was no more firing. I watched the LAF soldiers from the truck emerge from cover and pull a dead body from the cab. The sun was down now, and the gathering darkness was made sinister by a translucent haze of dust and fire smoke. Set alight by tracer and grenade fire, one of the buildings was starting to burn.

As we walked back to Rancho Deluxe, a Lebanese APC clanked past us on the highway, heading for the ambushed truck. From the top hatch, one of the crew casually fired a big .50-cal machine gun, aiming at a zip code, just hosing bullets as they closed in on the ambushed vehicle. I turned around and looked north. Jagged white explosions bloomed all at once across the buildings. Explosions like raindrops tore the city block from where the sniper had fired. Half-inch bullets ripping into rooftops, windows, and stairwells—a cyclone of lead.

As the APC passed, the gunner lifted two fingers, waving his hand back and forth, grinning in his tanker's helmet, and flashing us a peace sign.

IT WASN'T DIEN BIEN PHU, but it wasn't good, either. We didn't get it every day, but often enough. Often enough so we knew what was coming and who fired it the instant we heard it. We'd learned the sounds of RPGs, mortars, and Katyushas. We knew the crack of dud artillery rounds slamming into the runway, and where to find them after the barrage, stuck into the asphalt, busted-up Russian 122-millimeter shells that dumb-ass Druze artillerymen had forgotten to screw fuses into.

Beirut was a weird goddamn place, but it wasn't half as strange as Washington, D.C. As the shells whistled in during mid-September, the commandant of the Marine Corps, General P. X. Kelly—certainly a man who should have known better—told Congress that "there was not a significant danger to our marines." He went further to convince himself, adding that there was no evidence any of the rocket or artillery fire had been specifically directed against the multinational force.

Maybe he was right. Maybe they were shooting at our vehicles.

It was becoming apparent that Lebanon was a fixed idea in Washington. Who wanted it worse was also becoming obvious. The marines and sailors in the bunkers had no love for this place, and there was no love for us in the stinking, sweltering slums outside the wire. The multinational force no longer even pretended to control what happened in the city. The combined arms of an entire marine amphibious unit had not even been able to subdue Hooterville. In the Pentagon someone, somewhere, must have known how fucked and deadly this situation was becoming. There must have been one colonel, one captain, one prescient, fast-tracked major who looked at the pie charts, view graphs, shiny white papers and asked, "What the hell are we doing?"

But we were in, and politicians don't like to pull out. Pulling out makes you look weak on communism, terrorism, fanaticism, or whatever "ism" it was that we went there to be hard on. So we stayed, and things quietly, insidiously, and inexorably got worse.

It happened very suddenly in October that the summer ended. There had been some rain before, just a little, but quite at once the days were cooler and the nights damp and cold. Dust turned in now-frequent rains to mud. And in the bunkers, rain beat into the sandbagged roofs with a comfortable, almost dreamlike sound. When the showers ended, the air was clear beneath broken clouds. The hills, which had simmered brown and distant in summer haze, were close and green, their roads shining wet, almost silver, in moments of sunlight. These were the pleasant days in which cease-fire after cease-fire deteriorated into a monotony of sniping, rocketry, and ambush. In the brilliantly fresh air, the sounds of gunfire carried with an effulgent clarity.

Like everybody else, I'd had my fill of this crazy six-sided war. The tour was telling on the lads as well. They were qui-

eter. There wasn't as much grab-assing as there had been at
the start of the tour, and often they would just sit quietly in
the bunker, eight of them, together. No one would say a word
until I came down into the cool, quiet underground and gave
a warning order for a jeep run or a recon. Then they would
mount out, collecting gear and weapons and ammo like a
platoon of mutes. It was dangerous outside the wire, but it
was as dangerous inside. They weren't fearful or disaffected,
just tired. Oddly, we looked forward to operations, thinking,
rightly, that we were safer in the bosom of the night than we
were squatting in the bunker.

I had only one problem case: the assistant leading petty officer, Stan. He had done well on our Honduran adventure,
but he'd been in a pointed decline since we landed. By the
first weeks in October, he was useless to me and alienated
from his platoon mates.

Stan had been an operator, but the whole Beirut trip had
put him in the hurt locker. Although I'll make no apologies
for his conduct, it might not have been too difficult to argue
that he was shell-shocked. In most other conflicts, SEAL
Teams operated from secure rear areas, staging and planning
missions, then penetrating enemy territory and returning to a
safe haven. In the rear with the gear and the beer. In Beirut
we operated against any of several antagonists, but our position on Green Beach was open to almost constant fire. With
the exception of the occasions we staged from the ships or
patrolled in the Seafox, we were constantly in harm's way.
We had certainly taken enough shit, but the only one who
seemed to break down in it was Stan.

He was a small man, short and skinny in a juvenile sort of
way. Although he was one of the older members of the platoon, his fair skin and black hair gave him a youthful, almost
boyish look. Wally-world was no place for a family man, he
would say. Making a show of pretended courage, he was
sullen, sometimes overwhelmingly so, depending on the
mail. He was the kind of guy who could not string together
three sentences without mentioning his wife, his dogs, or his
kids. The platoon had no interest in his family; to young

bucks out in the world, wives and children are incomprehensible entanglements, and Stan's family was simply another trait that set him apart.

During the shellings, he always took deep cover, sometimes curling up under his rack, wrapped in two flak jackets. Early in the deployment this earned him the nickname Mr. Safety. And it was only this epithet that gave him notoriety. The barb in it seemed lost on him. He cultivated the name, referring to himself as Mr. Safety again and again, until everyone was sick of it.

As the summer wore on and the sniper fire became more intense and accurate, he volunteered for nothing. Any reason to move beyond the vehicle barricade was "stupid" and the officers who gave such orders were just "looking for medals." His pouts and ass-dragging were usually sufficient to piss off everyone around him. Sometimes the act was enough to get him removed from detail. He was an E-5, an electrician's mate second class, and the platoon thought he was yellow. Sometimes his boat crew went to maneuver against snipers without him. After a while no one would even ask where he was during firefights. The squad would return to the bunker, someone would kick sand under his rack, and he would be there with one flak jacket over his chest and one over his legs.

In this way his authority gradually deteriorated until he had no effect on his men. If he even tried to give an order, Dave, Cheese, Rudi, and Doug would simply tell him to fuck off. Stan was a nonentity, and he knew it; this increased his isolation.

One October morning he ate breakfast with the boat crews, boxes of cornflakes and Parmalat milk, on the benches behind Rancho Deluxe. He spoke to Rudi and Dave, saying he'd had a dream, and in it the squad had been picked apart by a sniper and only he was left unwounded. He said that in the dream he had moved forward under fire, single-handedly taken down the sniper, and captured the weapon. As he spoke, I noticed quick glances between Rudi and Dave: Oh, Jesus, quit pissing on my shoes and telling me it's raining.

I listened without speaking, and when his story was over, no one said a word. The only sounds were those of plastic spoons shoveling cornflakes. There had been heavy fighting the night before, the Druze and LAF in double overtime, and although only the usual shit had hit us on the beach, Stan had stayed buttoned down in the bunker while everyone else deployed to right flank in an attempt to spot artillery.

There wasn't a person in the platoon who thought Stan could have such a dream. Cowards do not dream brave deeds. They dream of staying alive. Fear is the blood in their veins, and courage does not very often lie in weak hearts. His dream was a lie, and to the members of his squad, eating cornflakes on this blustery morning, it was only a lie like any other they had been told.

It was now mid-October. The French had launched air strikes against the Shouf, and U.S.S. *Dwight D. Eisenhower*'s aircraft, Tomcats and A-6 Intruders, roared overhead daily on recons. It was little more than an air show. As the overflights picked up, it was decided that the SEAL rotation should now include a boat crew staged aboard *Iwo Jima* as a combat search and rescue team. Frank took the first shift. Boat crew Alfa went aboard, staging parachutes, ammunition, arranging messing and berthing, and working with the CTF61 staff to prepare E&E (escape and evasion) plans in the event that we were deployed after downed aircrew. Every day a long-range CH-53E helicopter was designated as the CSAR contingency bird. Aboard *Iwo Jima,* the CSAR job was like being a fireman. The on-duty boat crew slept late, polished gear, and waited for an alarm. After months in the bunker, clean sheets, hot water, and good food aboard *Iwo* were a blessing. We came to look at the CSAR billet as our R&R. *Iwo*'s call sign was Crosswalk. When the CSAR billet was established, we started to call her Cakewalk. Doc led Bravo aboard the next week, got the drill, and settled in. We were next, and I promised myself that once aboard, I would embrace the philosophy of Epicurus and eat seven grilled-cheese sandwiches. The day before we were to rotate, Stan asked to speak to me. He asked if he could go aboard *Iwo* permanently as the CSAR petty officer.

"What do you mean, 'permanently'?" I asked.

"I want to get off the beach," he said, "until the end of the tour."

"Everybody wants off the beach, Stan." I started to walk away, but he followed me.

"I used to work in air ops," he kept on. "I'm the best-qualified guy to check and maintain the parachutes." He did his best to appear enthusiastic. "I could be the permanent CSAR team leader."

"Steve's got more experience in air ops," I said. "I want you to stay with your boat crew."

"Why?" he asked.

I wasn't used to people answering my orders with an inter-rogative. Stan was passing from annoying to pathetic. I was blunt. "I don't think I can count on you to lead a mission."

"I could do it."

"Then start acting like it," I said.

That was that until a few weeks later. The shit continued, and one afternoon we assisted in the medevac of a badly wounded marine. We covered the LZ, a task made dodgy by the snap, crackle, and pop of incoming rounds. Dodgy and absurd, because during the dust off we did not receive per-mission to shoot back.

We popped smoke, and a Cobra gunship hovered nearby as the Huey put down, and from the BLT came a pair of marines carrying a stretcher. A navy corpsman in battle dress ran with them, crouching at a trot beside the dark litter. We jogged to the helo as the wounded man was shoved aboard. The marines ran back to the BLT across the cratered parking lot, and boat crew Delta jumped in through the Huey's slid-ing doors. I was the last to board, giving the crew chief a thumbs-up as the engine howled, lifting.

Then, in the helicopter, the corpsman put his fingers on the bloody stretcher, turning the wounded man's face so he could see it. My eyes were on Stan, pale, shaking, his gaze locked on the blood oozing across the deck. He gripped his rifle with both hands and closed his eyes. As the helo banked, I looked through the doors, out of the cabin at the beach, which flashed beneath us, the white surf, then water, green fading to cobalt. In the swirling wind of the cabin, the stretcher was now pooling with blood, an astounding amount of fluid, and I looked down at the wounded man's hand. On it there was a gold wedding band.

The medevac touched down aboard *Iwo Jima* and then took us to *Portland,* where I was to meet Frank. Our uniforms were spattered, so I had the guys go below, change into new BDUs, get showers, and grab a hot meal. I was in my stateroom, having wadded up my blood-soaked uniform, showered, and changed. There was a knock on the door.

"Come," I said.

It was Stan. He was still dressed in the cammies he'd worn during the medevac. "I need to talk to you," he said. His voice was quavering. The knees of his trousers were still black with blood.

"Why don't you get changed? Get some chow and come back." I wasn't trying to put him off; I knew that clean clothes and a meal would help him.

Stan stood there shaking. "No. I have been trying to get a chance to talk to you. I don't think I can handle this anymore," he said quietly.

I nodded at a chair, and he fell into it. He suddenly seemed lost in the folds of his cammies. A child pretending in the uniform of a soldier.

I didn't know what else to say, so I asked, "What's going on?"

"It's everything. It's being ashore." His voice trailed off. "You don't understand," he murmured. "I don't belong here. I have a family."

"We all have families."

"I mean kids."

I wasn't in the mood for a counseling session. I didn't have any gung ho left in me, either. I wasn't going to tell Stan to buck up and be a frogman: No one should have to put up with the kind of shit we were going through. We were targets. In two hours, when we left *Portland,* we would be targets again.

For a long time Stan sat looking at the deck. A tear rolled off his nose. "I want off the beach. I want to stay on the ship. I've had it."

For a split second I was disgusted—pissed that one of my operators was sitting here begging to be placed into safety. But the anger went away in an instant, and it was not sympathy, kindness, or pity that settled me. Stan was nothing to me; over the last few weeks Stan's fear and weakness had made me totally indifferent to him. I was calmed because I recognized what had made me angry. It was not the weeping, broken young man slouched in front of me. I will claim no supremacy of valor—I was reacting against my own fear.

Cowardice disgusted me because I feared it in myself. I did not hate weakness; I feared it. I feared that I would not be brave enough to lead my men. I was afraid that I would not be gallant enough, or wise enough, or proficient enough to safeguard the lives entrusted to me. My feelings for Stan had to be put aside, and I will tell you honestly that I cared nothing for him. His failings endangered men who daily did their best and better. My feelings for Stan were without even a leaven of pity, but his life had been entrusted to me as well.

There was no reason to woodshed him—Stan was right, Lebanon was no place for a family man. He was of no value to me, our mission, or his mates. The wrong man in the wrong place. We both knew he was simply meat, cannon food, a walking bull's-eye.

But we all were. All of us equal, all of us dancing on the drumhead together, and he deserved no special treatment because he was afraid.

"Look," I said. "I'm scared, too. I wake up every day in the bunker same as you. I wonder every day if this is the day I'm gonna get it."

"I can't take it anymore," he said.

"Neither can I." If Stan expected a pep talk, he wasn't going to get one. "Fuck the mission," I said. "Fuck Lebanon and fuck the multinational force. But we've got a job to do—just Fifth Platoon. That job is to get through the tour and keep one another alive. We're gonna do it—together."

"I've done my best," he said.

"You haven't done shit," I said flatly. Stan looked up, and I lowered my voice. "What matters to me is the effect you have on the platoon."

"I know what they think about me."

"They pull your weight. They do the things you won't do or can't do. And it isn't right. You want some downtime?" I continued. "Get out from under your rack once in a while. I'm not gonna reward you, take you off the line, because you're scared."

Stan blinked at me. "The SDV guys don't go ashore," he said. "Why can't we stage off the ship? Why can't we just move the platoon back onto the boat?"

He was right. The SDV detachment we'd deployed with was a bunch of athletes. They'd been ashore only twice since we'd been here. They spent their days lifting weights, tinkering with their minisub, and watching movies in their connex box. They lived in air-conditioned comfort ten thousand miles from the eye of the shit storm.

"I'm not in charge of the SDV detachment," I said.

"I want to talk to Mr. Giffland." Stan wiped his nose.

"Go ahead." Then I heard the sound of my own voice, low, quiet, utterly without feeling. Like it was playing somewhere on a transistor radio. "I don't expect you to lead, Stan. You don't have it in you. But I expect you to haul your weight. As long as you're in my squad, you will. You're going to pitch in, you're going to quit bitching, you're going to quit second-guessing my orders and start hauling your load, or I'll make sure you're on every patrol that leaves the wire, every antisniper detail, every hot medevac, every shitty job I can think of."

Stan stood.

"The helo will be on the flight deck in two hours," I said. "You're gonna be on it."

Stan walked out. I don't know if he ever spoke to Frank. I didn't mention our talk; I didn't have to. Frank was a good enough officer to know that Stan was losing the bubble. The problem was in my squad, and I was left to handle it myself.

Stan remained in the platoon, and he stayed in the rotation, doing his time ashore just like the rest of us. He did so quietly, ostracized, disregarded, and ignored by his mates.

I have no idea what courage is: worth through valor, duty over self-preservation—don't ask me. I don't know where it comes from, I don't know why some people have it and some do not. I do not know why it deserts people suddenly; I have never been able to figure out how some people find it when it is needed most. Stan had lost whatever small amount he brought to Lebanon, and I could understand why. This place was insane. It was criminal, a grotesque lampoon of a war in all things except cruel death, and I hated it.

I knew that I could have been more forgiving to a man who had simply been broken. But I was not because I was slowly being broken myself. There was certainly a better way for me to have handled this. I was not then the person I am now. I now think that I was callously short with Stan, peremptory in my evaluation, and smug in judgment. Inside, I was as beaten up as he was.

We feared different things, showed our fear in different ways. Had different nightmares. But we were both afraid. I was too strung out, too pissed off, and too cynical to say the right things. Maybe there was no right thing to say.

The platoon was what I cared about, more than my own life. Stan was a part of the platoon, but he was the weak part, the part that could make it all fail, make us sink, make us all get sucked into caution, foreboding, mistakes, and death. For that I despised him. Not because he was a coward, but because his weakness made it harder on us all.

I felt many times in Lebanon that I held seventeen lives in my hands. These men, their flesh and blood, became my life. Stan was a problem only because he diminished the whole. He pissed and moaned and placed doubts in hearts already near breaking. Stan was a problem because he showed us that we were all scared shitless, he showed us that we all just wanted to go home, and we all wanted just to live.

In this fucked-up, hopeless place, Stan showed us that we were still human.

BLOODY SUNDAY

I PUSHED BACK THE blackout curtain and felt my way, totally night-blind, up the sandbagged stairway. At the top of the steps I tried to walk but nearly stumbled and stood for a moment blinking back the inky darkness. Slowly, as my pupils dilated, the night became less opaque. I made out the shape of a rat running down the walkway at my feet, and I kicked at it furiously, missing. "Fucker!" I spat. The rat skittered away, a lump of shadow swallowed by greater darkness. Eyes wide, I began to walk.

Above the Shouf there were two *pop*s, and illumination rounds sputtered to life and coasted slowly beneath parachutes. In their light the hills were nebulous, cloudlike. I moved from the bunker to the barricade when the light had subsided, watching the hills, hearing the closer conversations of others who watched from covered positions.

Along the highway, Lebanese armor passed south, and from that direction came the sounds of sporadic fire. There was no one on the road now. The coast highway stretched away, north and south, four lanes empty. The moon drifted slowly over the Shouf, casting no light on the sea or earth. A small-arms round passed overhead, followed by the evil whistle of a ricochet. Pulling my flak jacket closed, I crossed an open space with my fists clenched. The darkness ebbed suddenly as another illume round coasted to earth. This was one of *theirs,* and I crouched against the low wall of the barricade, pressing myself into the shadow until the flare extinguished itself in the ground outside the wire.

The wind came from the Shouf in gentle gusts, scented

with the smells of the mountains. It was a cool night, in this moment absolutely silent. Crouching against the barricade, I put the night-vision goggles to my face and looked out into the Shouf.

To the naked eye, the hills showed signs of warfare, the flashes of muzzle blast scattered over a vast darkness. In the goggles, the night positively came alive. The Shouf glimmered with the reports of weapons and fountains of tracers. Explosions loomed, blinding in the goggles, flashing like point-blank strobe lights. In the green sky, illumination rounds fell to earth like ancient suns, lighting the dark city in feeble greens. In the goggles it was all green—green or on fire with an ungodly light, blinding, nearly white.

It was the evening of October 22, and the shelling had started after dinner, Katyusha rockets and 122-millimeter howitzers. These weapons kept up a steady harassing fire against the south portion of the airport and Green Beach. It was Saturday night, date night, and our choices were simple: We could sit in the bunker and get shelled, or we could patrol outside the wire and try to locate the shooters. When the moon went down, I told Doc Jones to get boat crews Charlie and Delta ready, and in a couple of minutes the lads were turned out, weapons and equipment checked, faces painted, ready to rock and roll. As they huddled around me, I pointed a red-lens flashlight at the map.

"We're going to run a recon south to Khalda and see if we can find the shooters," I said. That was the sum total of the briefing. We had operated so often in the last six months, I didn't need to explain in detail. Every man knew his assignment, his place in the patrol order, his fields of fire, and the procedures for leaving and reentering the perimeter. No one said a word as we mounted out and I waved the squad forward.

We patrolled east, up the narrow jeep road that wound through the dump just inland from Green Beach, then we exited the airport heading south, paralleling the Beirut-Sidon highway. After moving a click or two through scrub and abandoned orchards, we recrossed the highway and moved onto a bluff at the water's edge. The hillock was the site of an ancient Roman villa. It had been partially excavated, and the trenches, broken columns, and architectural bits made excellent cover. From a tactical standpoint, it was a great piece of real estate. The ruin was situated on a promontory maybe fifty feet high. The water was at our back, in case we needed to bail, and the elevation allowed us a 180-degree view of the airport, the mountains of the Shouf, the scrub and orchards of the Ash Shuafat, and the bombed-out high-rises of Khalda maybe a mile away. Our cover was solid, and the night was overcast and extremely dark. If they managed to drop a round on us here, it would be a freaking miracle.

The airport had come under fire from either Druze or Syrian units in the Shouf. It didn't matter to us who was pulling the trigger. Using NVGs, we scanned for muzzle flashes and attempted to get a fix on the position of the shooters. It was a game we had played with the Syrians for a long time, and they seldom fired more than three rounds before they folded up and moved to another location. As soon as we could verify their new firing position, they would take off again. The built-in delay of alerting our own artillery and requesting permission to call in fire virtually ensured that whoever was shooting at us could do it with impunity. The booger eaters knew that. What they didn't know is that we'd require only one shot at them. We carried a laser illuminator called a MULE (Multiutility laser equipment). It used a coded infrared laser beam to designate targets. Laser-guided rounds, called "copperheads," could be fired by the ships patrolling offshore. With the laser, we could put a sixteen-inch naval gunfire round right between their eyes. We could hit them, that is, if we could find them.

By 0100, we hadn't acquired any targets. I ordered the squad up, and we crossed the highway under a culvert. We turned right and patrolled quietly south, toward the hillside town of Khalda. We'd seen some truck headlights winding through the darkened streets, and we set up another observation position, this one in a wasted, crater-torn olive grove in the Ash Shuafat. I deployed the squad in an L facing the town. If anyone happened upon us, they would stumble into an ambush.

From up the hill came the snarl of engines. The night-vision goggles revealed a couple of trucks towing artillery pieces. Syrian army. Without a doubt, these were the shooters, but the rules of engagement forbade us from firing first. The rules of peacekeeping basically forbade us from firing at all. In order to "defend" ourselves, it was necessary for us to identify man, weapon, and muzzle flash. Lost on the command structure of the multinational peacekeeping force was the fact that any person observing these three phenomena, in order, would almost certainly be killed.

In order for me to engage the trucks, I would first have to report their position and report that I had observed them firing. That report would be forwarded up the chain of command, and I would then be advised if I might engage. It was a dangerous, bullshit arrangement.

Maybe I was getting burned out. But tonight I didn't even bother getting on the radio to report the Syrian position. I just waited. We watched for a while, pressed down into the grass. If they started to set up their guns, I would put some beehive on them and ask for permission later.

We waited. They screwed around, smoked cigarettes, and hung out a hundred yards in front of us. One of them stood on the hood of his truck and panned around with a pair of Russian night-vision goggles, but we were camouflaged nicely. He couldn't have seen us if he'd been standing right on top of us.

This wasn't going to be our night. The Syrians didn't unlimber their weapons, and after half an hour they piled back into their trucks, and the engines coughed over. Towing the artillery, the trucks moved up the hill and back into the Shouf.

The shelling continued. All we could do was watch in frustration as rockets and big-caliber rounds thudded onto the runway and the beach. All night the bad guys kept up the tactic of shoot and scoot, and we were never even able to turn on the laser. The night was a wash, and two hours before sunrise we turned north and patrolled back into the American sector and Green Beach. Rounds screeched overhead as we moved north, and we periodically hit the deck as shells dropped around us.

We crossed the perimeter without further adventure and did not return to our bunker until nearly 0500. The debrief was short; the guys were pissed and exhausted. Doc Jones sat on his rack across from me. He lit a Camel and took a long drag. "What do you want to do about breakfast?" he asked.

I hung my weapon and web gear on the nail over my cot. I said, "Screw breakfast."

"It's Sunday, they have pancakes up there at the BLT. Why don't I get a truck and we can roust the lads up there. A hot meal could do them good."

"You want to have a nice family meal, Doc?"

Dave was already in his rack. "Fuck breakfast," he said.

"Okay," I said. "Anyone who wants to go with Doc and feed their faces can go."

A chorus of "fuck you" trickled out of the bunker.

Doc lay down on his rack and closed his eyes. "Bunch of lazy bastards. Go hungry," he said.

We weren't lazy. We had patrolled all night through a steadily shifting artillery barrage. The shelling was over, and the postadrenaline crash was on us. There was maybe forty-five minutes of darkness left, and it was time to sleep. After cleaning my weapon, I remember only falling into my cot, rolling up the sweaty lump of my flak jacket for a pillow, and dropping immediately to sleep.

At 6:23 A.M. we heard something—an explosion, a big one, but one wholly unlike the sounds of artillery and rockets to which we had grown accustomed. The sound was a gut-wrenching THUD followed by a megadecibel sound, something like a long groan. I knew only that it was big and close. Then a shock wave pressed into the bunker, and the ground beneath my cot, the dirt in the very side walls of our hole, started to move, heaving like an earthquake.

It had been close, deafening, and for a second or two, I

thought it was a direct hit on us. I just lay in my rack, making sure I was still connected to the planet. I tried to imagine what in the hell it had been. Nothing I had ever heard anywhere had sounded that big.

Doc sat up. "What the fuck was that? A SCUD missile?"

Then a face burst into the dugout. "Jesus Christ. They got the BLT!"

I said, "Bullshit." In every artillery duel, every bombardment, any round that landed within a grid square of the headquarters would start the same flurry of rumor and false reports from the other positions. I got up, put on my pistol, and climbed out of the bunker. The position was frenzy. We had gone immediately to Condition One. Marines ran for weapons. The pillboxes on the flanks were being manned, and the antivehicle barricade was pulled across the road entrance.

It was like a dream, like I had somehow fallen back asleep. I climbed numbly up into the watchtower. A huge black cloud drifted into the sky seven hundred feet above the airport. From the French sector, another smudge of smoke loomed over the city. I raised the binoculars to my eyes. This is a dream, I told myself, a fucking nightmare.

The headquarters building was gone.

It was there, then it was not. Blasted flat into a squat chalk-gray pile of rubble and rebar, its topmost floors evaporated. The explosion shook the earth for three kilometers, its shock wave splitting oak doors in half at the MSSG building a quarter of a mile away. Two hundred yards through a grove of uprooted, mangled trees, the buildings housing the office of the Lebanese liaison had also been destroyed by the concussion of the blast.

It had happened just after six in the morning. On Sundays breakfast was always served late, and it was the privilege of the men at the battalion landing team headquarters to sleep in. While the marines dozed, a two-and-a-half-ton Mercedes truck drove down through a Lebanese army checkpoint and into the airport parking lots. It turned a circle, gathering speed, and crashed through a steel fence. It went across a hundred yards of parking lot, through tar-barrel and barbed-wire obstacles that hardly slowed its acceleration. The truck bulldozed its way through the sandbagged bunker at the entrance of the headquarters. Tires squealing on lobby tiles, it plowed on, dragging marine sentries on its bumper as it rushed into the open center courtyard of the building.

Then it detonated.

In the minutes after the blast, chaos reigned. No one had any idea if the truck bomb was a precursor to a move by the Syrian army, or if the airport would soon come under general attack. In one stroke, the 24th Marine Amphibious Unit had lost almost a quarter of its men. More than 240 marines had been killed in the blast, and 150 more were trapped in the rubble or lay wounded in the parking lot.

We didn't know it at the time, but across town, the French Foreign Legion barracks had been hit by an identical truck bomb thirty-eight seconds after the BLT was struck. The second bomb killed sixty legionnaires and destroyed their headquarters building.

The multinational peacekeeping force was in deep shit.

The messenger of the watch ran down from the beachmaster's bunker. He said I was wanted on the radio. CTF61, the commander of the amphibious task force, ordered the SEAL element to conduct an emergency sweep of the American anchorage. We were to check for mines and immediately interdict any craft or combat swimmers found in the exclusion zone.

A Huey set down on the beach. Doc Jones and the Seabees' two corpsmen jumped aboard and flew immediately to what was left of the BLT. Frank Giffland's squad was still aboard *Iwo Jima,* manning the search-and-rescue slot. I did not have direct communication with them but assumed Frank would proceed as quickly as possible to join forces with us on the beach.

Out in the anchorage, the landing ship *Harlan County* was heading toward the beach at flank speed. She was in the process of lowering her bow ramp, and it appeared that she was preparing to come alongside the causeway on Green

Beach. I thought this was in preparation to evacuate the airport.

I left boat crew Delta at Rancho Deluxe and told them to be prepared to destroy our bunker and equipment if we were ordered to withdraw. We loaded the Zodiac, and boat crew Charlie and I headed out into the anchorage.

We swept the area in the vicinity of the causeway and the water in front of *Harlan County*. Several small fishing boats drifted in the northern portions of the exclusion zone. It had long been suspected that fishing boats were used to spot the artillery attacks on the positions at Green Beach, and we had made captures aboard the boats previously. A boat-borne suicide attack was a very real possibility. On a normal Sunday we would have boarded and searched any small craft found within the exclusion zone. This morning the fishing boats were sunk with long bursts from M-60 machine guns and rounds from our M-203 grenade launchers.

We returned to Green Beach and ran the Zodiac up onto the sand. *Harlan County* had made it up to the causeway and disgorged an ambulance and heavy-lift equipment. I told Steve to notify CTF61 that I was headed for the battalion landing team, and that he had command of the squad until I returned. I jumped on the running board of the ambulance and rode it up the perimeter road toward the airport terminal and the battalion landing team headquarters.

The ambulance drove down the middle of the runway, and we took a couple of sniper rounds en route. The bullets pinged off the cement, and we drove balls-to-the-wall. The ambulance skidded past Rock Base and swung around to approach the BLT from the north. But we couldn't see the building, because it wasn't there anymore.

The ambulance stopped a hundred yards from the road junction, its way blocked by a burning Lebanese jeep. Carrying my CAR-15, I jumped off and jogged the rest of the way. I went down the road that passed the headquarters building, the building where the marine amphibious unit commander and his staff had set up, and from the end of that short street it hit me. A smell like fifty-seven kinds of dead, and in the grip of that indescribable stench I walked with my weapon into the open space where the headquarters building had once stood.

It was now eight in the morning. The sun shone unbearably on the whiteness of a three-story heap of rubble. There were bulldozers there already, forklifts and cherry pickers moving about car-sized pieces of concrete. The sun made it all blinding, the debris and the hot dust shimmering around the rubble. That dust clung to everything and everybody, living or dead.

I found Frank near the north side of the crater. He had taken a helo ashore minutes after the building went up. With several others, he had crawled into the still-burning building to remove dozens of TOW antitank missiles stored on the collapsed first floor. At great risk to themselves, they had removed the missiles and their high-explosive warheads before they could be detonated by the fire. This act of bravery saved the lives of the rescuers and many survivors.

Frank's hands now shook, and his skin was ashen from the dust. I didn't look much better. I was struck dumb by the most horrifying sight I had ever seen in my life.

Body parts, shredded clothing, sleeping bags, ponchos, and web gear hung in trees and littered the ground for hundreds of yards. The building had been utterly smashed, opening to a colossal crater in its center. At the center of the blast, there was nothing. Gray powder. Only the skeletal, gunmetal driveshaft of the truck that carried the bomb stuck upward from the hole.

Around the central crater, the building had dropped in on itself, floor upon floor. About the outside, close upon the sides, were the largest pieces of the concrete floors, thirty feet square, which had been blown out of position and cast up on their edges.

Tangles of one-inch reinforcing steel hung like nests of serpents. Close behind the building, the tents and huts of the motor pool were blasted, turned inside out, and ripped to shards. A hundred yards away, jeeps had their hoods and windshields ripped away by the pressure wave, radiators and wheels flattened or torn completely from the twisted chassis. Farther from the building, the personal articles of the victims were propelled from the explosion. Canteens, shaving kits, the broken hulks of tape players. Every imaginable piece of equipment in the Marine Corps inventory lay in the acres around the smoldering wreckage.

Weapons, rucksacks, and field gear.

Letters, thousands of letters, cast into the sky and fallen like snow.

Photographs of families.

PT gear, socks rolled into balls. The names of dead men stenciled on towels and T-shirts. Most appalling was the open space in the sky where the building had been.

The air was thick with the smell of cordite and burned flesh. Joining the other rescuers, we dug for survivors with our bare hands. We worked close together, keeping an eye on one another and watching carefully to make sure the places we dug would not collapse further. The entire building seemed to groan. I could hear the muffled sobs of buried men beneath my feet.

I crawled into the wreckage as deeply as I could and found myself in a coffin-sized space. Above me were heaped gigantic slabs of concrete. Between the slabs there was no space, not an inch, but a pair of boots stuck from a crack, jungle boots like my own, covered with the dust of vaporized concrete. Their owner, presumably, was smashed thin as a piece of paper between the slabs. Just inches from the boots, protruded hands and arms draped down from the crack, absolutely still and gray, like pieces of discarded statuary. In the hulk of the building, wreckage and corpses were twisted together inexorably, like sculpture made by Satan's own hands. I remember it was all gray, uniformly gray, with the exception of thin black trickles that I was shocked to find were blood. And immediately below, inclined toward the place where I dug, was an opening in the debris. I shoved myself through it. In the half-light, I could make out the shape of a torso, likewise covered in dust, its color exactly that of the concrete. It seemed at first to be part of the slab. I could not see a head or arms.

I only slowly recognized the form to be human. The cammie jacket had been ripped away, and the subtle lines of a bare chest were exposed.

I pressed my hand to the marine's chest. He was dead.

WE WORKED ALL DAY in the rubble as sniper rounds cracked and spattered the concrete around us. Frank and I were finally called back to the beach, and we walked to LZ Brown to catch a helo. The scene at the landing zone was somber. We met Doc in the hangar. He stood by a stretcher, covered head to toe in concrete powder and blood, a stethoscope looped over his neck. Doc would work in this place, without sleep or rest, for the next forty-eight hours. As each hour passed, fewer bodies were pulled from the rubble, each stretcher load less resembling anything human, until what were delivered were only fluid lumps in green bags. Burned, bloated, unrecognizable shapes to be classified, identified, embalmed, and shipped home.

On the runway the dead were laid out in neat lines, wrapped in nylon poncho liners and the shredded, gore-splattered sleeping bags in which they died. The casualties were piled into helicopters and flown to the ships in an endless series of lifts.

The faces of the men loading the helicopters were stiff with dust and shock. Between lifts, they sat, eyes wide, staring into nothing. In the endless drone of the helicopters there was no solace. In the hot blast of wind over rotor blades the men worked without speaking.

I could have never imagined a tear coming from Doc, not Doc the brazen, Doc the fearless, Doc the hard-dick killer of VC sombitches. The next night, when he stumbled back into the bunker, he collapsed on his rack and sobbed like a child.

I closed my eyes in the dark bunker and tried to will myself to sleep. I thought of a band concert I attended in the BLT three weeks before. I had sat against the wall on the fourth floor, looking down into the courtyard and at the faces that lined each of the four levels of interlocking balconies. It was a navy band, one of those admiral's bands, and we were told that we were damn lucky to get them to play for us.

For twenty minutes they played half-assed rock and roll, then packed up and were heloed back out to the flagship. But as I'd looked into the faces of the marines who watched that band, I could not have imagined this building flattened and each man who lived here, each man of 240, wasted. Not just dead, but shredded, hung in trees. Ripped open and tossed like roadkill.

Now they were gone. Simply fucking gone. What was left was sealed in metal boxes. It was often only the crap someone had peeled from the inside of a boot. In that magnitude of loss, men are only numbers killed, wounded, and missing, three finite categories roughly analogous to crushed, crippled, and vaporized. I really have no idea how they decided whose mother got what box. There was not enough left of some guys to put into a juice glass.

In the end, everybody got the same thing. Closed caskets with flags draped over them.

IN THE DAYS THAT followed there was only shock. It was almost impossible to feel grief. The horror was so overwhelming, so incredible, that we became frozen to it. There were so many bodies, so many twisted mangled heaps of flesh, that it was impossible to comprehend these were once people, comrades, friends.

Our shock was compounded when we listened at night to the BBC World Service and heard that the United States had invaded Grenada. At the time of the broadcast there was still heavy fighting on the island, and the airport had yet to be secured. We listened, slack-jawed. The marine amphibious ready group now fighting in Grenada had been on its way to relieve us. We were sitting here with our asses kicked, and our backup was twenty-five hundred miles away, fighting another war. Any faith I had in our war planners, any trust I would ever have again in the command structure, evaporated in that moment.

The thinnest cordon of marines now held the airport. The Shouf bristled with artillery, and by any conservative estimate of troop strength, we were outnumbered at least five to one. We could be wiped out and swept into the sea at any moment. It did not happen, and for the life of me, I do not know why. We were defeated, thumped, beaten. It was only the resolve, tenacity, and unflinching courage of individual marines that stood between us and Alamo time. The survivors clung together, every man aware that we were thousands of miles away from help or mercy.

In the days after the bombing, the rules of engagement changed. Marines received shoot-to-kill authorization. An astounding bit of news.

Now that the cows were gone, someone made damn sure that the barn doors were closed. At the south end of the parking lot, bulldozers had heaped great piles of red earth, vehicle barricades, in a series of staggered mounds that required passing vehicles to weave through a number of small openings under ten miles an hour. A deuce-and-a-half truck was placed across the road by the checkpoint, and a .50-caliber machine gun covered the approach. But there wasn't a building there anymore—just a pile of rubble.

Behind these new barricades, the wreckage of the BLT loomed, jagged and forlorn. When the wind came from the north, the abominable stench of the place would drift down onto the checkpoint. The smell of bodies blasted into atoms. The marines would pull cravats and neckerchiefs from beneath their flak jackets and place them over their faces to cut the smell. Then they looked like a mess of dusty, dumb-fuck deputies guarding a bank that had already been robbed.

The wreckage of the building became an archaeological dig. When an FBI explosives team arrived, their leisured, careful probing had an almost academic air about it. For a week a dozen marines dug through the crater, probing, poking, and sifting. Three FBI explosives experts huddled together under the blown-out girders that held aloft what remained of the second floor. Now and again a marine would come up from the pit carrying a scrap of metal. The FBI agents would look at it and either throw it away or tag it. Half a piston. Pieces of a water pump. A small portion of an engine block. Pieces of the truck that had detonated in the lobby. A remarkable amount of it was recovered from the fifteen-foot-deep hole it had blown into the earth.

Forensics, like hindsight, is all-seeing. Starting from the moment of detonation and working backward, the Central Intelligence Agency, Federal Bureau of Investigation, and National Security Agency were able to discern exactly what happened, how it happened, and who was responsible. Information that was extremely fascinating, but not one speck of it as valuable as a warning.

Blast-damage assessment revealed much about the bomb itself, a masterpiece of destructive engineering. It was first thought that so sophisticated a device could have been constructed only with Russian assistance. It is now known that the man who designed the bomb was an Iranian-trained member of Hezbollah named Imad Mugniyah. The intrepid Mugniyah would go on later to impress Osama bin Laden, who would take a page from Hezbollah's operational handbook and coordinate even more spectacular attacks against multiple targets. In decades to follow, Mugniyah would come to specialize in the demolition of U.S. military barracks, again constructing purpose-built bombs, most notably the tanker-truck weapon detonated outside the Khobar Towers in Saudi Arabia. That 1996 blast would kill 19 Americans and wound 170.

The bomb that destroyed the BLT was an elegant weapon purpose-built for its target. Loaded aboard a two-and-a-half-ton Mercedes truck, the bomb consisted of nearly six thousand pounds of C-4 plastic explosive, boosted by three hundred gallons of compressed propane gas. The cargo bed of the truck was lined in marble, and the explosives were loaded to form a shaped charge, focusing the blast up and out for maximum effect. The bomb was actuated by at least three mechanisms: a thirty-second timer initiated by the driver; a radio-controlled safe and arming mechanism actuated by an observer in the airport parking lot; and a dead-man switch on the steering wheel, which activated the bomb as soon as pressure was released by the driver.

The explosion vaporized the first two floors of the building and collapsed the remaining stories. It blasted a crater forty feet in diameter and threw off an eight-hundred-foot mushroom cloud. The explosion could be heard as far away as Sidon, thirty miles to the south. The FBI determined that the bomb produced one of the largest nonnuclear explosions in history.

The operational planning for the attack was equally impressive. The driver, a Hezbollah member, had been cultivated, vetted, and specially selected for a martyrdom operation. Seventy virgins awaited him in paradise. Photographs were taken of the BLT, and the explosive payload was measured to fit through the overhang and portico at the front of the building. The bumper of the truck was reinforced to plow through the steel-and-concrete fence that separated the BLT from the airport parking lot.

After the blast, satellite photos revealed that in the Bekaa valley, the bombers had marked out facsimiles of the BLT and the surrounding parking lots. They put together exact copies of the fences, tar barrels, and sandbag bunkers surrounding the building. Practice runs were made against a mock-up of the target, rehearsals were timed to the second, and the detonators and fusing mechanisms were rigorously tested.

Nothing was left to chance, and nothing would go wrong. All of these preparations went on under the noses of almost daily American reconnaissance flights. Two identical truck bombs were constructed at a Hezbollah installation in the city of Baalbek, one intended for the French, one for the Americans. With the complicity of Syrian military intelligence, the weapons were driven into Beirut on the evening of the twenty-second. An all-night artillery barrage, carried out by units of the Syrian army, made certain that the marines would be exhausted and that large numbers of them would still be asleep when the attacks were carried out at 6:23 A.M. Sunday morning.

The operation and its execution were flawless. The crater was testimony.

THE AIR FORCE TRANSPORTS that took the bodies of the battalion landing team returned in three days with fresh troops, another half of a marine amphibious unit that had been packed off piecemeal from Camp Lejeune, North Carolina, and dropped into our life. "We're here to bail you fuckers out," I heard one of them say.

They were integrated into our positions, their companies assuming emplacements on the perimeter and there digging bunkers, filling sandbags, starting from scratch. To me they seemed so incredibly *pink,* and young, and their uniforms were crisp with starch like they had just stepped out of recruiting posters.

With the starch and boot polish, they brought with them a massive case of attitude, like they had arrived on white horses and we were somehow damsels in distress. To an extent that may have been true. But nothing could prepare them for what they found over here, a situation more fucked up than a Norwegian bullfight. The rules of engagement alone were enough to blow their minds. And you could read it all over them, see it plainly as they moved, wide-eyed, through the positions or smelled what was left of a four-story reinforced concrete building. Even the old ones, the gunnery sergeant Khe Sanh veterans, found this place on the other side of believable. The survivors were like zombies, walking around taking close rounds and sniper fire like it was nothing: marines who had timing down to such a high art that they ducked only when the shit was right on top of them ("It just ain't cool to get down sooner").

Scariest of all was an elemental transformation of the chain of command. What mattered out on the wire wasn't rank, it was experience. The survivors were alive because they were cagey. They were here because they knew how Wally operated, and they had adapted. The newly arrived marines were discernible not only for their fresh uniforms and incredulous expressions but for their dangerous naïveté.

Our replacements were untested and therefore unreliable. Newly arriving officers and noncoms often found their orders ignored, especially when they were life-threatening. To a man, the survivors of 24 MAU supported the chain of command, often to the point of gallantry, but they obeyed their own. Soon the new guys learned to watch and learn. Some of them died anyway.

THERE WERE WORDS that became exhausted in my vocabulary; words like "anger" and "grief" and "fatigue" had been pushed beyond the finite limits of their definitions. They had been lived and felt to the outermost edge of reality, in ways I never could have imagined, so the words themselves meant nothing. Every ounce of meaning had been wrung out of them, and they remained jumbled letters totally disconnected from the numb and fucked way I felt.

My emotions were the frailest shadows. When I felt something, it was as though I was affected in only the most tangential way. Like living by long distance. It was impossible now to feel the rage I had once known, or to indulge the camaraderie of this ordeal. When the wind blew from the runways and the stench of the BLT was driven down to our position, the putrid-sweet odor would make me think: At least I am alive. But waking in the nights, in the absolute black stillness of the bunker, sometimes I couldn't tell if I was alive or dead.

We lay out nights beyond the wire, set in perfect ambush, waiting for militiamen to wander into our traps. But none came. The Wallys seemed to know the rules were changed. They knew there was no patience left and that what waited for them in the quiet night was payback. Along the perimeter, every marine who could get away with it aimed down into the streets of Hooterville. Men carrying weapons were dropped by single rounds of 5.56- or deadly 30.06-caliber calling cards left by the snipers of the STA platoon.

We continued to patrol, and survival depended on appearing where we were not expected. On one November morning we swept down on a car parked on the jetty south of Green

Beach. This breakwater, we knew, was often used as an aiming point for artillery strikes.

We drove south, past the parked car, then did a fast U-turn. Dave cranked the wheel, and the jeep bumped suddenly off the coastal highway, up the slight embankment at the foot of the jetty, and turned sideways, blocking the narrow dirt road. Rudi swung the M-60 across the hood of the jeep as we walked toward the car's owner, who'd been there since sunrise with pole and fishing tackle. The fisherman moved quickly for his car as we approached. Bubba stopped him as Cheese and Doug searched his vehicle.

"Do you speak English?" I asked.

The fisherman shrugged. "Little," he said. My weapon was slung forward, pointed with calculated indifference at the fisherman's chest. The man's smile slowly twisted itself with a different meaning.

"Parlez-vous français?" I asked. As I spoke, my thumb rested against the safety catch of my rifle, and my index finger rested just inside the trigger guard.

The fisherman lowered his eyes and stared at my hands. He said, *"Je parle un peu français. Anglais un peu aussi."*

I nodded, and Dave came forward to search the man's creel and gearbox.

"L'auto? C'est la votre?" I asked. Is this your car?

The fisherman shook his head and smiled. He didn't answer, or he didn't understand.

I changed tacks. *"Où allez-vous, monsieur?"* I asked.

The fisherman shrugged. *"Où?"*

"Where are you going?"

"Maintenant?"

"Yes, asshole. *Oui, maintenant.*" My eyes left those of the fisherman for an instant as Dave finished his search.

"He's got a pair of binoculars," Dave said.

I'd probably need more than that if I was going to shoot him. "You were in a hurry when you saw us coming," I said.

The fisherman answered at length. My French is barely idiomatic, and the fisherman's was thick with an Arab accent. We were having a serious communication problem.

"What did he say?" Rudi asked.

"Said he's going shopping, I think."

"He was watching the fucking beach," Doug spat.

He probably was. Sensing our mounting ire, the fisherman shifted on his feet.

"See if there's a radio or a topo map in the car." Either of which would provide convincing evidence of an artillery spotter. I asked the man for his papers. At this point the fisherman was about to lose it, and he said something subordinating and acutely plaintive in Arabic.

I raised my palm. "Your identity papers. *Donnez-moi votre pièces d'identités.*"

The fisherman nodded and reached with exaggerated slowness into his trousers. He produced a bundle of paper from which he took the blue plastic-coated identity papers. They were folded in half and in half again. As I took them, my weapon remained pointed at the man. I held the papers in front of my face so that I could look simultaneously at the photograph and at the face of the fisherman. The papers were printed in Arabic and might have said anything, they might have said that this guy played tight end for the Cincinnati Bengals, but I ran my eyes over the document and the man. I could not read Arabic, and I made no pretense of doing so. I knew how to ask for identity papers, and I always did. When I took them, I watched the faces of the people. I looked for signs of uneasiness, I looked for the language that was plain upon their faces. I looked for tampered photo edges and fear that was greater than that generated by the flash suppressor of a weapon aimed straight into their guts.

"Nothing in the car," Bubba said. He was disappointed.

"Regardez-vous la playa américaine?" I did not know the French word for "beach," so I used the Spanish word.

Somehow the fisherman understood. *"Non. Je pêche seulement ici."* His French faltered. "I make fish here only," he said in English.

I stood for a long moment with my weapon pointed at him, saying nothing and thinking less. I thought nothing of blowing this fuck out of his shoes. Why had he come here all the

way through West Beirut? What was so important that he had
driven through a widening artillery barrage? Why hang out
near an American position where more shells were falling?
To fish? The bullshit light was on, big-time.

My thumb rested against the safety switch of my rifle and
my finger tapped the trigger.

Tap, tap, tap.

In those seconds I hovered as close to casual murder as a
human being could possibly ever come. I could have killed
this man as casually as you would step on a cigarette. I am
ashamed to say that I *wanted* to kill him.

Maybe he was spotting artillery. Maybe he was reconnoitering the beach, and maybe he was just a dipshit, the kind of
guileless fuck who actually did drive through an artillery attack just to go catch some fish.

My thumb snicked the safety back from auto and onto
safe.

I handed back the papers. "*Écoutez, monsieur, il est très
dangereux içi, parce que vous êtes près de la position américaine . . .* We watch," I said, pointing back toward the beach.
"We see cars and people here, and we must check."

"I am a fisherman only."

"*Peut-être vous êtes,*" I said.

"Can I go?"

I nodded. The man picked up his equipment and began to
walk to his car. "Have a nice day," Rudi said.

It meant nothing. The muzzle of Rudi's M-60 was still
pointed squarely at the fisherman's belly.

LETTING GO

IT WAS COLD AT NIGHT NOW. And it seemed to rain often, long and often. In pelting downpours, our bunkers sagged; dirt soaked through and dribbled out of sandbags perforated by shot and shrapnel. Repeated requests by the marine amphibious unit for concrete, timber, and building materials were, incredibly, still being refused by Washington. No permanent defenses were to be erected at BIA. Our bunkers were a scandal, the best of them only what could be lumped together, and many were without overhead cover. Structural components—wood beams, pallets, chunks of beach matting—had to be bartered for, and the better one's ability to scrounge, the safer one slept. Now even the best of bunkers were melting away in the rain.

It was decided in November that Green Beach was no longer a safe position. I don't know what "safe" meant, exactly. The tar-barrel and barbed-wire barricade that separated the beach from the Beirut-Sidon highway was now looked on as wholly unsatisfactory. Charlie battery had been relocated to the sandstone bluff directly behind Green Beach, and it was decided to move the navy landing force components—Seabees, beachmasters, SEALs, and the marine shore party detachment—inland to the ridge. The beach would be manned during the day, but only a guard force was to remain at night.

This meant the bunkers that seven months of hard work had made deeper and sturdier would be abandoned, and the men on the beach would now be quartered on the ridge in GP tents.

It wasn't the most popular decision of the tour.

The move required that new bunkers be constructed, and now that the rains had begun it was impossible to dig into the soft ground. Any hole deeper than three feet quickly oozed in on itself and healed like living tissue. Protection was going to be sandbags, above ground: the kind of emplacements we called "delta hotels," or "direct hitters."

While new bunkers were being layered together, people built sandbag walls around their cots—the ultimate short-timer's security blanket, but they really provided insufficient cover. Mortar rounds are delicately fused; anything striking the tent roofs would detonate overhead, spraying sleeping men with molten steel. Heavier stuff, Katyushas and artillery, would blow the tent and its contents into rags. No one had to be reminded that a lot of the shit intended for the beach was sighted by impact on the very hill that we had been ordered to move to.

We learned in November that our tour had been extended. The 24th Marine Amphibious Unit had originally been due to rotate out the last week in October, but our relief had been diverted to Grenada. We wobbled on in what we came to call triple overtime. For some the extension was a punishment. There were others, officers and men, who saw the extra time as penance. The dead required an act of contrition, an atonement, an apology. That burden fell on us, the defeated. We had not been vigilant enough, valiant enough, squared away enough, and 240 had died. Guilt drifted down on us like smoke, and there were times that I felt it, too: We were still here because it was what we deserved.

I got on by telling myself that in a couple of weeks, four at the most, it would be over. For the survivors of BIA, it was a strange time, an empty time. For seven months marines had counted days, marked calendars, and dreamed of getting out, but now, with deliverance at hand, it was almost impossible to take joy in going home. It was as though we had all undergone a collective nervous collapse, fire teams, squads, platoons, and companies made into zombies, each of us with a moment seared into our brain, one second out of an entire lifetime that could never be erased. The bombing was something different to each of us. For some it was the thunderclap that heaved into the bunkers, or the shadow of an immense mushroom cloud rising behind the airport terminal. It was the first time you saw silhouettes blown into concrete—the complete stencils of human beings blasted into mist and plastered against the shattered walls of the BLT. It was the terrible minutes you watched a corpsman shoot morphine into a convulsing body, a marine impaled on rebar, trapped and hopeless of rescue.

The survivors kept to themselves; they were quiet and watched out for one another in a manner that was both forlorn and touching. If you sat down to eat, pulling open an MRE in a muddy foxhole, the marine next to you would reach into his pocket and, without a word, toss over a bottle of Tabasco. Marines you'd never met would hand you cigarettes, dips of Copenhagen, water from their canteens—precious things that were yours because you were still alive.

Twenty-four MAU hung together, and the marines who had reinforced us from Camp Lejeune were scrupulously ignored. Their fresh-issue cammies, farmers' tans, and like-new equipment marked them out from a hundred yards away as cherries, new meat, tourists. And they knew better than to ask about anything. The place freaked them, and the survivors freaked them, too. The veterans, to a man, had eyes that would scare a crow off a phone wire.

Beirut was no longer a piece of landscape but something not of this world—a twitchy mirage, a thing between geography and nightmare. It had become, even before we left it, a memory to be suppressed, jammed into a box lined in lead and buried in a desert somewhere. We knew we could try to ignore it, but the 'Root would not be forgotten. For the rest of our lives, dreams of that Sunday morning would stalk us, relentless and scary as cancer. We had become mute, staggering battle-fatigue cases, lurching on our feet, running on autopilot, too astounded or numb or stubbornly defiant to lie down, curl up, and suck our thumbs. In the last weeks of the tour, we just functioned. Walked post. Did our jobs. There was nothing else to do.

Fifth Platoon continued to run operations across the beach and sprints north of Beirut into Juniyah, where we would link up with LAF air-assault units and patrol inland to the shattered remains of a soccer stadium that we used as a helicopter landing zone. As we covered the LZ, hulking CH-53s would blow in, the aircraft nearly as big as the soccer field itself, and their crews would push off pallets of medical supplies, food, and artillery shells that would be loaded into trucks and hauled up to LAF batteries in the Shouf. In our last missions we were reduced to feeding the machine.

These were easy ops, and we rarely had contact. We took sniper rounds now and again, and we were getting good at shutting them up with forty mike-mike. Fire was returned coolly, deliberately, and we would occasionally ignore the asshole with the rifle and fire at cars parked in front of the sniper's hiding place. In their love for the automobile, the Lebanese are very much like Californians. In Beirut a man's car is a statement, and we made statements of our own. At first we'd just shoot out the tires, perforate the windshields, and aim at the door handles. But later, boredom making us vicious, we used 40-millimeter grenades and API rounds to demolish Mercedeses, Fiats, and Ladas. Our vandalism was a pointed disincentive to the people who allowed the gunmen the liberty of their rooftops and balconies. It was hilarious when we first started to do it. And then it wasn't funny anymore.

Whatever we did to them, it would never be enough.

IN THE HELICOPTER, the howl of engines and the thump of rotor blades suppressed thought. The flight was a milk run between the ships and Landing Zone Brown at the airport. The passengers were a mixed group heading to fifteen different destinations, to ships, outposts, and the beach. Men stared out the portholes into the sea, infinite gray waves on its surface—fifteen hundred feet below they seemed like scratches on an immense smoothness. Amid the passengers were heaped yellow and red bags of mail, cargo in crates, and three boxes that said THANK YOU FOR BUYING A PRODUCT MADE IN THE U.S.A.

My CAR-15 rested between my knees, muzzle down. I slumped forward, resting my head on the rifle butt, feeling the clatter of the aircraft through my fingers and temples, delighting in the vibration because it made me numb.

I was flying to U.S.S. *Fort Snelling,* a landing ship, dock that had delivered our relief, the Second Platoon of SEAL Team Four. It was eleven in the morning, and I looked forward to lunch aboard the ship.

I was greeted on *Fort Snelling*'s flight deck by Frank Giffland, who'd touched down a moment before. We went to the wardroom and met the officers who would replace us, Mikey Walsh and Don Tollson. Their platoon had been one behind us in the training pipeline. Mikey and Don were friends, and it was good to see them. They were dressed in khakis, a uniform we hadn't worn in months, and they looked healthy and tanned. The weekend war had agreed with them.

Mikey was a compact, muscular man with a sandy-brown mustache. Don was taller, had a wry sense of humor and the slightly asymmetrical face of a boxer. They were four or five years older than Giff and me, Mikey a lieutenant and Don a JG, and both were Mustangs. Both had served as SEAL platoon members in Vietnam, Mikey as a Stoner gunner for SEAL Team One, and Don, a member of SEAL Team Two. They shared stories from Grenada and were modest about their missions, though they included preinvasion operations, the recon of Pearls Airfield in the hours before the attack, and a fruitless chase to capture East Bloc advisers as they fled the island. The invasion had been dubbed Urgent Fury in the press, but it was known to Team guys as WWG—World War Grenada. Although SEAL Team Six had suffered casualties, Mikey and Don gave us the impression that SEAL Four's missions had gone well.

When they asked how it was over here, Giff and I said at once, "It sucks."

No one asked about or mentioned the bombing.

Frank arranged for a helicopter and offered to give Mikey and Don a tour of the area of operations. A storm had blown in. It was rainy, and the cloud deck was low. Don asked if we should put it off until the visibility was better.

"Today's a good day," Giff said. "The clouds will hide the helo."

"Should we bring sidearms?" Mikey asked.

Frank rolled up the chart. "You need to be in full battle kit," he said quietly.

They caught a Huey, and I was heloed back to *Iwo*, where boat crews Charlie and Delta waited as CSAR contingency. The storm had gotten worse, the sea and sky equally drab shades of gray, and it was raining hard when I jogged from the helicopter and into the island on *Iwo*'s flight deck.

I found the lads below, racked out in a borrowed berthing space, playing cards. The CSAR rotation was our last assignment; after this we would be hauled back to *Portland* and taken off the line. No one expected anything to happen. We had pizza for dinner. The movie was *Tora! Tora! Tora!*, and the evening's entertainment turned out to be prophetic.

The following morning a marine orderly knocked on my door and informed me that my presence was requested in the Flag Plot. Flag Plot was a combat information center set up for the commodore—his war room. I figured I wasn't being invited for coffee, and on my way up, I stuck my head into the compartment and told the lads to mount out, draw weapons, and get the gear ready to go.

"You're fuckin' kidding me," Bubba said.

"I hope I am," I answered.

A week before we were rotated onto *Iwo*, Frank's boat crews had mounted out to provide combat search and rescue for a large American air strike. Launched from *Dwight D. Eisenhower*, the air raid was supposed to be a multisquadron attack package, Intruders, Corsairs, and Tomcats delivering a six-pack of whoop-ass called an alpha strike. The entire complement of *Eisenhower*'s combat aircraft had been loaded with ordnance, launched, and flown toward Lebanon, ready to pummel the Shouf and Bekaa valley. But the air strike never happened. At the last minute Washington pulled the plug. The planes did a U-turn, dropped their bombs into the sea, and returned to the carrier. This aborted strike was the only retribution the Reagan administration was to attempt for the bombing of the marine barracks. The averted air strike was kept secret for years. Its effect on marine morale can probably be imagined.

When I entered the Flag Plot, the chief of staff informed me that there was going to be a second air strike, not American but French. Our gallant allies were going to cash in some chips. In retaliation for the Legion's dead, Super Etendards off the aircraft carrier *Marshal Foch* were going to destroy the Hezbollah headquarters and training facilities east of Beirut. The French did not have special operations forces to retrieve downed aircrew and had asked for a SEAL Team to provide search-and-rescue capability.

"When are they going to make the hit?" I asked.

"Two hours," came the answer.

Once again Giff's attention to detail would pay off. The CSAR team had already received a warning order and had been briefed previously on the type of mission, general organization, weapons, uniform, and chain of command. The platoon's standard operating procedures made the short-notice operation possible. As I was working out the communications plan, the boat crews were gearing up, inspecting weapons and equipment; they would be good to go when I returned to the briefing spaces to finalize the orders.

The French plan was audacious. The strike package, six Super Etendards, would launch from *Foch,* group into a tight formation, and head west, away from land and into the Mediterranean. Remaining in formation, the Etendards would drop under a hundred feet, pull a 180-degree turn, and close the coast. The target was to be approached from the north, the Etendards remaining in formation and flying "nap of the earth," or treetop level—make that *goat*-top level—flying down canyons and valleys and using terrain, whenever possible, to shield the formation from radar.

All of this in broad daylight.

I'll give them this, the French had balls, even if they did come from Yves Saint Laurent. I learned later that the strike package flew as low as fifty feet on the way to deliver their bombs.

The mission would not depend just on gutsy flying. The CSAR helicopter and the Etendards would be accompanied by a navy EA6B Prowler. The Prowler is the electronic-warfare version of the A-6 strike aircraft; it's capable of spoofing enemy SAM and AAA radars. If everything went according to plan, the Prowler would blind the bad guys during the strike and any rescue attempt.

The weather was an issue. SEALs love bad weather, but pilots generally do not, especially when they're flying low to the ground. It was still raining hard, but the French were confident they could operate under the ceiling. Better avionics would have helped; the American A-6 was born and bred for this sort of mission. We had the airplanes, but the French had the rocks. Designed in the 1970s, the Super Etendard was hardly state-of-the-art, but it was a capable aircraft. Etendards flown by the Argentineans sank H.M.S. *Sheffield* and M.V. *Atlantic Conveyor* during the Falklands War. The French were betting this one on pilot skill, navigational perfection, and Gallic chutzpah. And add the element of surprise. I am certain that no one anywhere was expecting an air strike in this weather.

It's often said in the military that no good deed goes unpunished. After we had coordinated the CSAR mission, the French came back and asked if we could insert an element to put eyes on the target. They wanted a battle-damage assessment after the bombing run. Recon and surveillance was a different mission completely and would require us to get a hell of a lot closer than I'd have liked.

I checked the maps again. There was a ridge overlooking the Hezbollah compound, and behind it, closer to the coast, was a wadi into which I thought we could insert a team by fast rope. The intelligence estimate indicated Syrian army units in the vicinity of the target. There was also a Syrian armored brigade backing up Suq al Gharb, and the territory north and east was under their control. Hell, most of Lebanon was under their control.

Inserting a team that might itself need rescue—endangering more men and aircraft—was not mission-enhancing. The R&S team would be at greatest exposure, and I was willing to take the job only if it was possible to get in and out cleanly. Judging from the map, which is often not a good idea, it appeared that the terrain on three sides of the observation point was steep and heavily vegetated. The ridge was within visual range of the Hezbollah facility.

The target buildings were set apart in a wide part of the valley, so they would be easy to identify—again, according to the map. Provided the weather did not sock us in, I felt we could get a fair appraisal of bomb hits with binoculars.

Face it, you don't stamp out the Rolling Stones by bombing their hotel rooms. This air strike had about it an element of payback, but the actual targets were not brick and mortar, they were human. The bombs were intended for Hezbollah leadership. After the hit, the R&S team would monitor the target; the National Reconnaissance Office would snap satellite photos; NSA would listen to the radio traffic; CIA would compile and analyze. These were all discrete bits of information, intel nuggets, to be factored into the puzzle.

Extracting the R&S element from the area after the strike would be the nub of the operation, what staff pukes call "a critical node." As oxymoronic as this sounds, you can usually expect people to wake up after you hit them. The bad guys would certainly be stirred up, and I selected an extraction site downhill and to the west of the surveillance perch. The primary extract and a secondary location would be screened from the target by the mountains, and if the helicopter was prevented from reaching us by enemy action or weather, we could patrol west to the coast. It would be a long haul to the water, over twenty clicks, but topography and darkness would be on our side. If the recon element had to escape and evade, or E&E, it would be moving through mountainous, broken terrain at night and would be almost impossible to track. It was a decent plan, not perfect but good, and I told the French that I would insert a recon team if the visibility held. I would make that decision when we were airborne in the AO.

That left the question of who to put on the ground. Seven months of combat had taught me that men will not do anything their leader won't do first. If the job was shitty, I generally did it myself, so I was going in on the recon, without question. Our maxim "One is none and two is one" holds for people as well as equipment. SEALs don't operate solo, and I'd need a partner.

We had a total of eight operators in the two boat crews, barely enough to cover both parts of the expanded mission. Dave was my point man, my swim buddy, and I felt he was one of our best operators. He was the logical choice to take with me, but I had a problem.

Stan.

I wish I could tell you that I decided to take Stan on the recon, and that he carried out the mission, acquitted himself gallantly, and ended the tour basking in the esteem and pleasant regard of his teammates. That's the way it works in the movies. It's not the way it works in the broken-nose world of real combat. Although Stan was the ranking petty officer of his squad, I was not willing to leave him in command of the troops in the helo. Taking him with me wasn't an option, either. I didn't trust him to lead my men or save my ass on the ground if the mission went south. Stan was out.

If I was going to put myself on the R&S detachment, I needed someone to take charge in the air and be ready if the CSAR mission was required. I knew I could count on Dave's ability and judgment. I needed someone who could not only get the CSAR mission done but also decline the job if the situation went totally to shit.

Now you know why BUD/S is so difficult. One bed wetter, one unreliable person, twists a knot in the plan.

I returned to the berthing space. The guys were jocked up and ready to go. I briefed the operation quickly, updating them on the weather, target location, enemy forces, coordinating instructions, and command and signal. I placed Dave second in command and put him in charge of the element that would insert and carry out the rescue. That left the R&S mission. I explained the location chosen for the insertion, and told them that recovery of downed aircrew was a mission priority. If there was contact, the R&S element would be on its own. If they missed pickup, or if the AO became too hot, they would be expected to escape and evade to the coast for pickup. I said I needed a volunteer to spot the target with me. Every hand went up, including Stan's.

"Okay, Bubba," I said. "You're on."

A big CH-53E was turning on spot two as we exited the greenroom and walked across the flight deck. The bird was completing fueling as we approached, purple-shirted deck apes dragging away the hose that had pumped three thousand gallons aboard the machine that would take us on this last op. We walked into the hot downwash of the rotors, the smell of JP-5 wafting over us. The Sea Stallion was a marine bird, diverted from an administrative flight around the squadron and directed by the air boss to return to *Iwo* and take on fuel. The 53's crew had no idea what was about to go down. Undertaking the happy business of ferrying passengers and mail, the pilots had forgotten that their ship was the CSAR contingency bird this afternoon. Like everyone else in the squadron, they had gotten up in the morning thinking that in two days they would be headed home. They were fat, dumb, and happy. The happy part would soon be over.

From the cockpit, the copilot looked up as the boat crews walked toward the helo. He saw the weapons, bandoleers of ammo, parachutes, fast ropes, and eight SEALs decked out in Czech and East German cammies, *kufiyahs,* and green face paint. His jaw fell. The pilot watched us come on with a look of bewilderment: Oh, shit, not now. Not today. We're short.

The lads climbed aboard and into the aft compartment. They quickly set about attaching the parachute static line and rigging the fast rope. I ducked onto the flight deck, slipped on a headset, and leaned forward to talk to the pilots. They were both Annapolis classmates of Frank's, good sticks who'd gotten us into and out of a couple of hot places.

"Shit, Chuck," the pilot said as he turned around in his seat. "What's going on?"

"CSAR," I answered. "The French are launching an air strike in forty-five minutes."

"The *French*?"

"Are we shutting down for a briefing?" the copilot asked.

Neither of them looked ecstatic when I said, "I'm going to brief you now."

I laid out the plan. I will never forget the crew chief's expression when I unfolded the map to show them where the R&S element was to be inserted. Unfolded it, and unfolded it, and unfolded it. I pointed to a ridge and to the Hezbollah compound, deep, deep, deep in booger-eater country.

"In there?"

"In there."

We were wheels up in three minutes and on our way. It was still raining, but the cloud ceiling had lifted. We flew directly to the R&S insert point. On the radio, *Iwo* reported that the Etendards had launched from *Foch,* starting their roundabout approach to the target. The Prowler was in position and jamming the Syrians on all frequencies. We were a go.

For only the second time in the tour, I had butterflies in my stomach. Not butterflies, fucking bats. We had briefed the op as well as possible in the time allowed, but we had not rehearsed. There were a lot of moving parts, a lashed-up communications plan, shitty weather, and worst of all, it was daylight. This was a short-fused op, and a lot of things could go wrong. Small oversights would be compounded by the enemy, the weather, and Mr. Murphy. This whole thing swung on standard operating procedures and the experience and discernment of the lads. If anything, the speed of the op served to calm me. What was winding me up was that this would be our last one. Everyone sweats the last op of a tour. I had finally come to grips with the idea that I might actually live through seven months in Lebanon, and I was edgy. Not edgy, exactly—let's just say I was safety-oriented.

As we flew toward the coast, I reminded Dave to play it conservatively, to put men on the ground only if he could be reasonably sure of grabbing the pilot and getting away. Don't needlessly jeopardize the men and the helo, I told him. He understood. We conducted a radio check, I reviewed the primary and secondary extract points and gave a drop-dead time of four hours for each. If we hadn't made the secondary extraction point in eight hours, we would be expected to make it to the coast.

I looked around the cabin. I may have been sweating the load, but the lads were not. They were kicked back, dozing in their seats, or tapping their feet as their personality types dictated. Stan was staring at the deck and looked off the back ramp of the helo as my eyes passed over him.

The crew chief leaned in to us and told me we were three minutes out from the R&S insert. Bubba and I stood up, and the crew chief lifted the hatch in the center of the cargo compartment, the "hell hole." Bubba and I walked over to the fast rope attached directly above it. One hundred and twenty feet of fast rope was coiled like a thick green python at our feet. We pulled on our gloves, and the pitch of the rotors changed, the big helicopter shuddering and the blades thumping as it pitched nose-high and came to a hover over the insert point.

I pushed my AK-47 behind my back, checking that the safety was up against the charging handle and that the shoulder strap was fastened tight. The deck of the helicopter settled, and Bubba and I held the rope, stacking our hands one above another like kids playing "who's up" on a baseball bat. Through the open hell hole I could see the ground below; I kicked the pile of rope out the hatch, and it uncoiled as it fell a hundred feet. I made sure the end of the rope was on the ground. It was—just barely—and I nodded to Bubba. "GO!" He slid down the rope.

Dave patted me on the leg as I straddled the hatch. "Remember," he said, "safety is paramount." It was a standard SEAL Team jab, a bullshit nugget of staff-puke phraseology, one used in every briefing when we were preparing to do something dangerous. It made me smile.

I dropped through the hatch and slid down the rope, feeling the thick green hawser hot on my hands through a pair of leather and Nomex gloves. As I cleared the bottom of the helicopter, the rotor wash swept raindrops up and into me. Ninety-mile-an-hour gusts slammed water drops against my legs like tossed gravel and spun me in a helix around the rope as I slid down. The gusts swirled, and I squinted.

Ten stories below me, Bubba was already on the ground. The rope had come down short of the promontory. Bubba had landed on a steep slope and fallen to the left onto his knees. Still clutching the end of the rope for balance, he looked up at me descending. As I got closer to the ground, I tightened my grip on the fast rope, slowing my descent and increasing the burn factor on my gloves. In the last twenty feet of the run, I could smell burning leather. I landed next to Bubba, somehow managing to keep my balance on the muddy slope. I flashed a thumbs-up at Dave. The rope was quickly hauled back aboard through the hell hole, and the big helicopter nosed down, gathered speed, and flew off toward the safety of the coast.

We were in.

As the helicopter flew away, the sound of the rotors reverberated and faded down the canyon. There had not been time to do a series of false insertions, standard procedure for depositing a recon element, and I hoped the echoing noise would confuse anyone who might try to figure out where we'd landed.

The slope beneath our feet was muddy and much steeper than it had looked from the air. It was still raining—misting, actually—and we pulled ourselves up on hands and knees toward the ridge. Our fists closed over bushes and roots as we crawled the 45-degree slope, kicking into the steep pitch with the toes of our boots, chunking out steps like glacier climbers. The ridge above us was shrouded in wet gray cloud. We made for the top of the wadi, climbing fifty or sixty feet to the ridgeline in about five minutes. At the top the clouds blew onto us, misty, cold, and bleak. I pulled the *ku-fiyah* up around my neck, and Bubba followed me down the other side. The terrain on the reverse side of the ridge was less steep, and the concealment of the cloud was comforting, but we needed to get below the clouds if we were to get eyes on the Hezbollah compound.

I looked at my watch. Fifteen minutes remained until the Etendards would be on target. We scuffed downslope through waist-high brush. Finally, the cloud lifted around us. The sun peeked through, encircled by a rainbow, as the bank of rain was swirled up and over the back of the mountain.

Just below the clouds, we emerged onto a dirt road. It was a washed-out track, really, scratched into the slope and hardly passable. It did not appear on my map, and a twang of worry gripped me. I was fairly certain we'd inserted in the right place, only slightly below where I had planned. We'd climbed up and over, the terrain matching expectations, and I could see the valley spread out under the cloudy sky. But there wasn't supposed to be a road.

All navigation is theory. You follow rules, take fixes, and make guesses. You never know exactly where you are until you get to a place you know. Navigation is the art of reconciling maps to reality, and I was pretty sure we were in the right place. We had to be. It was the goddamn road that was in the wrong place.

The road that wasn't supposed to be here meandered down to our right and hairpinned away into the valley. We crossed the dirt track in a place where several small boulders had tumbled across it, careful to wipe out our boot prints with a piece of brush. We settled into a large clump of juniper between the hairpins. We tucked into cover, Bubba pulling the boughs over us.

We'd made it into position with a little over five minutes to spare. I laid the AK-47 across my arm, and Bubba crouched, watching the road, as I fished the binoculars out of my pack. I pointed them down into the valley and scanned. There were several structures strewn below: low mud-brick hovels and a few flat-roofed two-story cement-and-cinder-block structures, typical Lebanese architecture. I pulled out my map and tried to puzzle out the location of the target. I wasn't at this task very long.

From behind us came a clanking noise, something like a cowbell struck out of tune and with no semblance of rhythm. I snapped my head around. Next to me, Bubba silently tapped two fingers under his eyes, the hand signal for "enemy." As quietly as I could, I snapped down the safety on my AK-47. We scooted lower into our juniper bush. From the washed-out road came the clanking again; it was the rattle of tack and harness on a forlorn-looking donkey pulling a small farm cart. The cart was of local manufacture, the transaxle of a demolished truck mounted under a rough-hewn wooden platform. Bald automobile tires wobbled as the donkey came out of the gloom, and through the branches I caught sight of an old man in a tattered *shumagg* clutching dully at the reins.

We held our breath. The cart would pass within twenty feet of us as the driver and donkey negotiated the hairpin. Pressed into cover, I lowered my head, chin almost in the dirt. The old man wore a tattered gray suit jacket over a grimy *dishdasha*. The old fellaheen was leaning back against a two- or three-foot plywood partition separating the front of the cart from the platform. On his feet he wore a pair of Reebok tennis shoes. The counters were broken down, so he wore them with his naked heels out, as though they were a pair of bedroom slippers. As the cart approached, I glimpsed something behind the partition in the back of the cart. The driver was not alone.

Two men in Syrian army uniforms sat facing backward, their muddy boots dangling off the back of the cart. The hoods of their camouflaged field jackets were pulled up, and their rifles, an AK-47 and an RPK machine gun, were laid across their laps. They were sodden from their trip through the fog, and both just sat hunched as the cart rolled down the rutted track.

Head down, the long-suffering donkey shuffled through the turn. We could plainly smell the sharp odor of the old man's Galloise cigarette as he exhaled. My eyes flicked to Bubba. He watched them, sighting across the top of his

CAR-15, his expression completely impassive. His finger was on the trigger, weapon aligned flawlessly with the back aperture and the hood of a field jacket placed square over the front sight post. It was my prerogative to initiate the ambush. If I fired, Bubba would fire; if I did not, he would let them pass.

I weighed our options. We were far up into the mountains, and the sound of gunfire, never an uncommon thing in this country, would probably pass unnoticed. Wherever these guys were going, they would definitely not be expected soon. They were traveling by donkey cart, and we were miles from anywhere. We could kill them easily. There was the question of the old man, obviously an innocent, but it would be no great species of marksmanship to head-shoot the soldiers and not kill him.

Each second brought them closer to the muzzles of our guns. It was not mercy that saved their lives. The decision was purely tactical. This road wasn't even on my map; I had no idea where it led or how frequently it was traveled. There was no way of knowing who might be traveling with them or coming up the mountain unseen. We might kill the soldiers only to alert some larger patrol behind us in the fog. Our job here was to watch, not kill, and everything that did not further the mission was merely sport. If they did not see us, I would let them live.

It is a queer, affecting thing to hold someone's life in so fine a balance. There's power in it, a weird juice that it's best not to ever get used to. The soldiers and the old man passed almost close enough to touch, and they had no idea that crouched beside them was a pair of bogeymen, emissaries of the Great Satan, slack pulled out of triggers, weapons set on rock and roll. I have done this several times, waited unseen and ready to kill if I was discovered, and it has always struck me as lunacy that the people I am ready to destroy never have the vaguest idea that their lives hang by a thread.

The cart passed, and we watched as the donkey ambled down the road and at last passed from sight. The drama had unfolded in what seemed like weeks. Bubba's thumb rocked back the safety on his rifle, and I let out a long breath. We had avoided contact by the barest of margins. There was no telling who might come down the road next, and we both pressed as far down into the brush as we could.

We sat, waiting, and rain sprinkled us. I pulled out my map again and looked into the valley. I found the buildings, printed squares and rectangles, neat, straddling wide contour lines, and I imagined taking a pencil eraser and scrubbing them out. Then Bubba tapped me on the shoulder and nodded at the valley. "Showtime," he whispered. Those were to be the only words spoken between us in nearly nine hours.

I looked over his shoulder. The Etendards were here.

From our left the first plane materialized, moving so low in the distance it seemed at first to be a truck. The faint sun briefly glinted off its canopy, and the fighter flew close on the valley floor, preposterously fast, and utterly without sound. As it banked, setting up on a group of low buildings, we could see its wide swept-back wings, mottled in stripes of gray and green-gray. The plane's black-tipped nose pointed up, it gained altitude slightly, and then the sound of its screaming engine came up the ridge to us, sharp and angry, the noise of the banking turn it had made a full ten seconds before. As the Etendard passed over a cluster of cinder-block buildings, two dun-colored cylinders dropped away from its underwing pylons. Small white parachutes bloomed behind each bomb, and the weapons pitched down as they fell behind the speeding fighter. The bombs seemed to trail the jet, traveling horizontally as it banked precipitously. The Etendard was traveling at transonic speed, nearly the same velocity as its sound waves, and as it went wings-vertical, the fuselage was engulfed in a cloud of vapor.

In the same instant the Etendard was swallowed by mist, the buildings were torn by fire. Twin hemispheric shock waves blinked up, and at the center of the concussion, a pair of dirty-orange fireballs engulfed the structures. The clouds roiled and swept up into the sky. Another explosion, a secondary from inside the buildings, threw up a column of smoke and fire. Explosives or ammunition stored in one of the buildings had detonated, and the crashing of the three distinct blasts echoed from the valley floor and rolled up to us, sounding perfectly like the sound of a thunderstorm.

The remaining aircraft made their runs. Two came in a pair, close together, and the last arrived in a group of three. All dropped drogue-retarded munitions, and the weapons struck around the shattered remains of the buildings hit by the first plane. Each time the Etendards attacked, it was like watching a Godzilla movie with the sound out of sync. Explosions gushed from the earth without a whisper, and many seconds later, the scream of jet engines and the thudding of bomb hits echoed against the hills.

As quickly as the Etendards had come, they were gone. Clouds from the explosions drifted away after several minutes, pillars of smoke that held together and lifted vertically from the earth. On the valley floor no noise came from the gutted buildings; the day was again silent. We watched, and the only sound was the murmur of wind blowing downslope.

I scanned with the binoculars. Around the rubble, people ran without purpose; vehicles came up the roads, ambulances and trucks full of men, converging on the craters and rubble and dust. Syrian armored vehicles moved in with the rescue parties, ridiculously forming a cordon around the destroyed places. My binoculars brought close gaping holes gouged into the two- and three-story buildings in the Hezbollah compound; great damage had touched each of the dozen or so structures in the complex. As the dust rolled away, I could see ZSU-23 antiaircraft guns rolled out from bunkers, and in the dirt streets swarmed armed men the precise size of ants. They scrambled atop the flat piles of rubble, removing debris with their bare hands. I knew the rescuers would be calling out the names of dead men. I knew the things they would find in the wreckage, things that did not look like human beings, and I knew how it would change them.

I wondered what it had been like for the men who planned the BLT bombing. I wondered if they, too, had watched from

the hills while the calamity of an enemy played out in minia-
ture.

It was our turn to watch now. A surfer and a hillbilly, hiding in a juniper bush, struck dumb by the baleful splendor of
an air strike.

HOME AGAIN

BACK ABOARD *PORTLAND,* I took a shower and scrubbed the camouflage paint from behind my ears. From my locker I broke out a clean set of cammies, amazed at the fragrances of starch and detergent. I found my jump boots and brushed them, then bloused my trousers. For the first time in months I'd put myself in a presentable uniform. It was nearly midnight when I walked into the empty wardroom. I drank a cup of bug juice, and the steward came in silently to bring me a cheese sandwich. I ate it slowly.

I walked through the ship to the platoon's berthing space. It was the middle of the night; everyone not on watch was tucked into his rack, and the red-lit passageways were deserted. I took several ladders below, into the troop spaces, wandering through deck after deck of empty bunks. On the way over, these same compartments had been thronged with hundreds of marines. They were now empty, the names of dead men and annihilated units still visible on masking tape stuck to lockers and bunks. *Portland* was a ghost ship.

I was glad when I came at last to the platoon's berthing space. I pushed open the hatch, and the lights inside were burning brightly. The guys were in their racks, fast asleep, and demonstrating the remarkable ability of the American sailor to sleep oblivious to dazzling light. The only sound was the small whir of a pair of electric fans.

Doc Jones sat at the table between the bunk rows. He was smoking a cigarette, looking at nothing. "I wondered when you were going to get up," he said as I entered.

"What are you doing down here, Doc? I thought you'd be in the chief's quarters."

"Fuckin' goat locker," he said. Doc stubbed out one smoke and lit another. I looked around the compartment. No one had even an eye open. Twitching in his rack, Bubba began snoring like a gut-shot bear.

Doc looked at me. "Just checking on the guys?"

"Yeah," I said, "just checking."

" 'Although slothful and ignorant, the enlisted men are cunning and devious and bear watching at all times,' " Doc said. It was an oft-repeated quote in the navy, supposedly taken from a World War I naval officer's handbook. Although I'd heard it a hundred times, I still smiled.

Doc sat and smoked, listening to the guys sleep. It finally occurred to me that he was watching over them—like a hen brooding her chicks.

"We made it, Chuck," he said at last. It was the first time he'd ever called me by my first name: not *"Diawi,"* not "cock breath," not "Mr. Pfarrer," but "Chuck."

I said, "Yeah, Doc. We made it."

Our platoon had conducted more than a hundred combat patrols and reconnaissance operations during a seven-month tour. Some were successful, some were not, but Doc, Frank, and I had taken sixteen SEALs into combat and were bringing sixteen home. I did not consider this testimony of my prowess as a commando or my leadership as an officer. I saw it as the reckoning of karma.

"You did okay," Doc said to me. No praise I have ever received in my life has moved me more. I could only nod my thanks. I felt oddly like I wanted to bawl. A moment passed with just the smoke from Doc's Marlboro hanging in the air.

"I heard you volunteered to cross-deck," Doc said.

"Where'd you hear that?"

Doc narrowed an eye at me, like there was some way a jive-ass LTJG could ever do anything that a chief petty officer would not discover. To cross-deck meant to leave the homebound ships and join the arriving troops. It was called that because the volunteer's person, equipment, goods, and chattel were shuttled from the deck of one ship across to another.

"Are you nuts?" Doc asked.

I shrugged. "I don't know." I probably was.

After I had returned from the air strike, Frank and I were pulled aside by the task force operations officer. He told us the incoming MAU was worried that their turnover was short and that the new marine infantry companies were inexperienced in urban warfare. The commander of the landing force had asked for volunteers to join the incoming units and serve a second tour. The request made sense. Only crazy people could help sane people make sense out of insanity. Peacetime cross-decks were not unusual, but I had never heard of anyone, anyone, who did not have a plate in his head asking for back-to-back combat tours.

The operations officer was a lieutenant commander, a nice guy, and he looked embarrassed even to be asking us. He apologized before I heard my own voice saying, "I'll stay." In the same breath, Frank said he'd stay.

I remember the shock on the man's face. We were both certifiable. I considered myself lucky to have lived through one tour, and now, casually, I was saying I would stay in Lebanon for another six months. I had not just said it, I had said it in front of witnesses, and I stood scratching as the commander spelled out our names on his clipboard. P as in Peter, F as in fox, A, double R, E, R. Charles, middle name Patrick. LTJG, USN. O-positive. Catholic. Suicide victim.

I was doing the unthinkable; Doc had found out, and he was busting my chops.

"What are you?" he was saying. "Some kind of retard?"

"How many tours did you do in Vietnam?"

"I don't see what—"

I cut him off. "How many, Doc?"

"Too goddamn many."

"Did you volunteer, or did they send you back?" I asked, knowing that like almost every Viet-era SEAL I knew, he'd asked for a second tour.

"You know what," Doc said, "Vietnam wasn't like the shit

we just went through. You're stupider than the average cake-eater if you asked to stay back in Wally-world."

He was right. I was insane. So was Frank.

"Why don't you go up on deck," Doc said quietly. "You look like you could use a little air."

On deck late at night, the marines at the rail had no faces. In the clear, moonless night, darkness was an almost opaque pigment that made their features uniformly dark and form-less. It was a night in which you could not have recognized your own brother. The shadowy forms were made vague by both the mottled colors of their camouflage BDUs and the wind, which pulled and inflated the uniforms so that their shapes were changeable, hardly recognizable as human.

The red glow of cigarettes would rise and fall from the rail, burning bright, then fading. This night was unseasonably mild and perfectly, eerily still. The wind across the deck was only that caused by the ship's forward movement, and around *Portland,* the sea spread away, mirrorlike and flat. The water was black, and the wake seemed afire with the unearthly light of bioluminescence.

Standing in the wind, I thought of the long lines of bodies we had laid on the tarmac. I was haunted by the letters and envelopes that had blown down the street after the bombing. Pictures of families, of children and wives, seven thousand miles away, made suddenly into widows and orphans.

I was scared now, fucking terrified, and standing alone in the darkness, I cursed myself for offering to stay. But I knew why I'd volunteered. This was not over, I told myself. It was not over, and I wanted to stay until it was.

Escaping the silence of the empty troop spaces, I stayed up on deck all night, staring into the glow of the wake until the sun rose, and then I stood with my face red from the wind and looking, in the moment of dawn, as though quite sud-denly the sun had ambushed me.

The following evening Frank heloed over from *Iwo Jima.* It had been decided that our services would not be required by the incoming troops, and we were spared a second tour in Lebanon. Somewhere up the chain of command, a small decision made by a faceless staff officer had certainly saved my life.

I can't remember if I was relieved or not. I remember only that my offer to stay had been serious, and that I was fully aware how ridiculous and self-destructive I had become.

PORTLAND CONTINUED to steam slowly west. The platoon spent days cleaning and repairing gear and weapons, making ready for homecoming and the scrutiny of the bean counters back at the Team. Our trip across the Med was unremarkable. *Portland* was still an unhappy ship, and when Frank and I could no longer abide Captain Zimanski's tantrums in the wardroom, we took meals in the connex boxes, liberating sandwiches from the crew's mess or happily accepting Doc Jones's invitation to dine in the chief's quarters.

Along with the rest of the squadron, *Portland* passed through the Straits of Gibraltar, and two days later we were in the teeth of an Atlantic gale. "Sweet Pea" was no beauty, but she was built to last, and the storm tested her. For two days hurricane-force winds and monstrous seas beat upon the squadron. From the bridge, we watched green water surge over the bow of *Iwo Jima* and roll across her flight deck. The bow of an aircraft carrier swept over by the sea was a majestic, fearsome sight.

Portland rolled and plunged, and we subsisted on coffee and sandwiches until it was calm enough for the cooks to prepare hot food. Watch on watch, day and night, the 1-MC would crackle and from the loudspeakers would come a strangely indifferent voice intoning, "Stand by for heavy rolls."

The ship, all 553 feet of her, would shudder and slow as fifty-foot waves heaved on our bow. Thumped by Atlantic rollers, the entire vessel seemed to ring, a deep, groaning clang like that from a gigantic, lopsided bell. Finally, the gale blew itself out, vomit was swabbed from the decks, and on a bright, chilly morning, the coast of North Carolina hove into view.

As we cleared the sea buoy, the lads loaded kit bags and

made a clean sweep of their berthing spaces. Frank and I went and found our friends in the wardroom, wishing them the best and thanking them for favors big and small during the cruise.

Although other units in 24 MAU came ashore to military bands and parades, *Portland* docked at an isolated pier at the port of Jacksonville, North Carolina, far from press, relatives, or hoopla. In truth, there were not that many men nor much equipment to be unloaded. "Sweet Pea's" embarked troops had been mostly headquarters elements, staff, and battalion-level support units. Almost to a man they had been killed in the bombing. Maybe two platoons of marines and a half-dozen jeeps were put off the ship. Like the empty passageways on the way home, the offload was quiet and forlorn.

The day was clear and cold, promising to be colder that night. In the general hubbub, I made sure the ship's cranes hooked up our connex boxes, the Seafox, and the SDV. Flatbeds from SPECWARGRU-2 appeared under the appropriate loads, strapped them down, and drove off. Lugging my kit bag, I went down the gangplank and tried not to look back as I trotted for our ride.

As I plopped down into a seat on the bus, I slowly began to realize that it was over. I swung my feet up on a parachute bag and tossed my hat across the aisle at Dave. "Tell me I'm dreaming," I said.

"You're dreaming, *Diawi*," said Doc. "You'll wake up and it'll be the first day of the trip all over."

"Then shoot me," I said.

Frank climbed aboard and collapsed into the seat beside me. *"Vamos,"* he said.

As we drove away from *Portland*, Cheese pressed his naked ass against the rear windows. He got a rousing ovation from the men in the bus and on the pier. *"Adios,* motherfuckers," he yelled.

Adios indeed.

As soon as we were off the base, Frank told the driver to pull over at a 7-Eleven. It had been months since the lads spent a paycheck or had any cash, but together, Frank and I had a couple hundred bucks in our pockets, wrinkled and soft from months in the safe of our stateroom. Two hundred dollars was a fortune in the backwoods of North Carolina, and the pleasures of the state were ours.

The bus doors hissed open and the lads piled out. I peeled off a hundred bucks and handed it to Doc. "Get all the beer this will buy," I said.

Doc blew into the store, strode back into the cooler, and started to stack cases of beer on a handcart. The clerk gaped at us—we looked like a gang of slow-motion robbers.

"Get what you want for the ride home," Frank said. The lads loaded up on potato chips, pig rinds, fruit pies, beef jerky, jalapeño-pickled sausages, red licorice, and even a loaf of white Sunbeam bread—delicacies only dreamed about in the Levant.

Doc wheeled the beer in front of the counter, and Frank counted out a pile of wrinkled dollars, twenties, and fives. Bubba came up to me holding an extra-large cherry Slurpee. "Can I have one of these, Mr. Pfarrer?" He looked exactly like a kid.

"Knock yourself out, Bubba," I said.

The beer and the frogmen were loaded back into the bus, and we started north. It was now just about sundown, and as we passed through the crisp evening, the little town of Jacksonville, North Carolina, was somber. Though it was the first week of December, we saw no Christmas lights. Normally, the place would have been a carnival. A returning marine battalion could be counted on to spend money, buy beer, and propose marriage to half the women in the county. The problem was, a lot fewer marines came home than had left.

We drank beer and did our best to make merry, but the gloom of our homecoming was hard to shake. We hadn't been met by bands or crowds on the pier side, but the little town had not forgotten the men she had lost. There were flags and homemade banners stuck up in front yards and windows. Under the neon lights of pawnshops and tattoo parlors, messages were cobbled together out of sliding plas-

tic letters: GOD BLESS THE MARINES and WELCOME HOME
24 MAU.

In the back of the bus, I sat with a beer and watched the
night come on. As we headed north, shops and houses gave
way to pine trees and lopsided double-wides. About halfway
out of town, the bus stopped at an intersection, two lanes
meeting two lanes under a single streetlight. As we turned
north, I looked beyond a row of battered mailboxes. In the
window of a mobile home was an American flag hung like a
curtain. In front of the flag, leaning against the glass, was a
color portrait—a photograph on brush-textured cardboard,
the kind you sit for at Kmart. It was a picture of a marine
sergeant in his dress blues. Beside him was a woman with
dishwater-blond hair. In the sergeant's arms was a kid of
about six. The corners of the garish wooden frame were hung
with black tape. Next to the picture was a hand-lettered sign,
crayon on construction paper: GOD BLESS MY DADDY.

At last we drove out of town, and the pine woods loomed
over us, our two-lane meandering 150 miles through swamp
and little redneck towns back to Virginia Beach. The night
was clear, without even a small part of moon, and I was glad
when the light left the windows, because my eyes were wet.

I STOOD IN THE PARKING LOT of the SEAL Team Four building, pulling up the collar of my field jacket, waiting. Our arrival, half drunk, at 2230 hours was noted by the watch, and
the trucks were parked in the secure area behind the compound. The lads had been driven singing and reeling to the
transit barracks, while a tide of beer cans washed around
the back of the bus. The OOD told us we were to report to the
commanding officer at 1300 hours the next day. We had a
sleep-in pass.

I'd offered to give Frank a ride to the BOQ, but my car,
parked where I'd left it in March and half an inch deep in
dust, would not start. Buzzed and smiling, Frank thanked me
and caught a cab ride to the BOQ. Carrying my kit bag, I
walked across the base, hoping the wind would sober me up.

I wound up in front of a pay phone next to the base chapel, where I called Margot.

"It's Chuck," I said. "I'm back."

Margot's voice sounded odd on the phone, distant and formal. My last letter to her had arrived five days before. Written from *Iwo Jima,* it said I had volunteered to remain in Lebanon. A postcard I sent from Spain telling her I was coming home had not yet arrived. She was surprised and happy to hear from me.

"I'm on the base," I said. "My car wouldn't start." I told her how to get a pass at the front gate and where to meet me.

The wind blew colder, and I stood with my parachute bag in the small white light put out by the pay phone. I was trembling from the cold, or something else. Above, the stars were bitter against black, and all at once none of this seemed real to me. It was as though I was sleepwalking when I saw a set of headlights coming at me. An aching sort of dread seized me, as though I'd found myself in the worst kind of dream, a dream of getting out of Lebanon, and I did not want to wake up before the car came to me. I had the terrible feeling that none of this was real, that I might come to back in the bunker, pressed into the sweaty nylon of my cot, with months to go until rotation.

Margot's car stopped next to me, and for a long moment she just stared. Her mouth opened slightly, and she told me later that she was shocked by how thin I was. The wind pulled at me, and I stood there like some kind of sunburned scarecrow, the gaunt doppelgänger of the buff jock who'd left nine months ago.

I finally said, "Hi."

She got out of the car and held me, and I was amazed by how warm and whole she felt in my arms. She was real. This was real, and I was alive.

"I have presents for you," we both said at once.

We laughed, and she kissed me, and when she pulled away, I could see something like worry in her eyes. I wasn't the only one who felt this wasn't real. I was viscerally different from the man who'd gone away in May. My eyes burned through her, like they burned through everything else.

We checked in to a hotel on the beach, drank champagne, and made love, and then I held her as she slept, and through the windows I could hear the surf pounding as a whole gale blew from the immaculately clear sky. I slept and woke and woke again.

I pulled my arm from under Margot's shoulders and walked to the windows. The first purple light of dawn was spreading across the Atlantic. The sea was rough, heaving upon itself and shimmering like a sheet of hammered silver. The coming day wavered on the horizon in a mirage brought on by the bitter cold. It was maybe twenty minutes before sunrise, and across the sea it was noon.

In Sidon and Tripoli, in Sabra, Chatilla, and along the corniche of Beirut, the sun would now be high, and I knew the muezzin's call was drifting from the minarets. It was something I had heard many times in Lebanon, in city and countryside, from minarets pocked with tank fire, from tiny loudspeakers attached to mud-brick country mosques. In a trilling cry would come the *Thuhur,* the noon call and warning to the faithful.

In the name of God,
the infinitely compassionate and merciful.
Praise be to God, Lord of all the worlds . . .

Before me was the ocean, and beyond it, a different world revolved. In the mosques and on the streets, in the hovels of wrecked buildings, on prayer mats, knelt the faithful, all facing Mecca. Their prayer was now my own.

Guide us on the straight path,
the path of those who have received your grace;
not the path of those who have brought down wrath,
nor of those who wander astray. Amen.

BOOK THREE

A
RAKE'S
PROGRESS

SOME TIME IN THE SUN

I'M NOT SURE THEY KNEW what to do with us when we came back. I am certain we did not know what to do with ourselves. It was odd enough to return from a war; it was stranger still to realize that almost no one in the United States seemed to have the vaguest concern about what had happened in Lebanon. There were no flag burners, no flag wavers; there was nothing.

The lotus-eating had apparently spread even to our own command. On my first day back, I had the amusing experience of trying to convince a Filipino disbursing clerk that I was still alive. I came home to discover that my pay and allowances had been suspended for seven weeks. Unbeknownst to me, and mercifully never discovered by my family, the navy had listed me as dead on October 23.

Although we'd sent a situation report within minutes of the bombing requesting that SEAL Team Four notify our relatives that we were all right, the Team did nothing. As a result, the entire platoon was carried as "missing" for thirteen days. During this terrible time for our families, no one at SEAL Team Four bothered to pick up a phone or lick a stamp.

Distraught, my father managed to pull navy connections to send me a message, but it didn't reach me until a week after the bombing. By then my family had endured a daily parade of television crews camped on the front lawn, hoping to catch the delivery of bad news. My mother bravely told the assembled vultures that her son was a marine lieutenant assigned to the multinational peacekeeping force, and she hoped that they would be kind enough to respect our privacy.

She did not mention that I was a SEAL, or that the navy had told her nothing.

It had been just as bad for Margot. Perhaps it had been worse. As news of the bombing splashed across the world, her phone stopped ringing. Friends and acquaintances avoided her, and even my own friends at the Team had no news to give. In this time before e-mail and long-distance phone service from the battlefield, Margot found out I'd survived only when she got a letter from me—two weeks after the blast. Until then she had floated in a half-gray limbo of grief.

The fiasco was a symptom of the command climate to which we returned. There had been a regime change at SEAL Team Four; our former CO had been kicked upstairs to the Pentagon. We also had a new XO. The new proprietors were bean counters, and Fifth Platoon was called to task for the amount of equipment we had lost, destroyed, or traded during the tour. Frank was on leave when the new XO, a guy I'll call Skip, called me in to apply a dose of real navy. He started in and I put up my hand, an extremely rude gesture for a junior officer.

"Did you read our after-action report?" I asked.

"I haven't gotten around to it," he said.

Our AAR, a folder almost three inches thick, sat on the corner of his desk. It detailed hundreds of patrols, dozens of countersniper operations, and half a dozen recons up and down the coast, against Syrian and Israeli targets.

"Why don't you read it, sir?" I asked.

The next day a chief from supply presented me with an MSLR, a materiel lost or stolen report. It listed nearly a hundred items large and small, platoon equipment valued at considerably more than I made in a year. The chief wanted me to sign the form and assume financial responsibility for the lost equipment.

I looked at the list. There was a PRC-77 radio, handset, and antenna that had been blown out of the Zodiac by a mortar round. There was an M-16 rifle dropped while its operator was being extracted by helicopter. In the classic definition of a hot extract, the weapon was lost because the red-hot gun barrel had burned through the weapon's nylon sling. A pair of night-vision goggles was listed as "returned, destroyed." No excuse there. They'd been smashed by a .51-caliber bullet after being negligently left atop a bunker while I ducked to consult a map. Uniform items, swim fins, boots, MK-13 signal flares, magazines, ammo cans, empty ammo cans. Batteries for our diving rigs. Web belts and dive socks. Office supplies and the antique Blue-Ray machine we used to print beach charts. The Blue-Ray bit the dust when it broke out of its locker during our passage through the gale.

The supply chief clicked a ballpoint and held it out to me. "Right on the dotted line, sir."

"I'll get back to you, Chief," I said.

I took the half-inch-thick stack of single-spaced pages into the platoon office. The MSLR was crap, and this was a classic case of shit rolling downhill. Our losses had been combat-related, and we had documented each piece of equipment. For supply to make good on replacement gear would require even more paperwork. The easiest thing for them to do was try to hang it on us. I didn't want to disturb Frank at home on leave, and it turned out I wouldn't have to.

The enemy's weakness is always our strength. Skip was a bean counter, and all I had to do was give him the kind of beans that he didn't want to count. The kind of beans that would give him nightmares for the rest of his life.

We had returned with a connex box full of East Bloc weapons, war booty from our peacekeeping mission. Some of the weapons we had captured, some we had traded for, some we had acquired through a back-channel equipment swap brokered by Beirut's CIA station chief. In short, this stuff was spooky, it was hot, and it stank, bad. Parked behind my office in a ten-foot-by-ten-foot fiberglass cube was two tons of career killer. Whoever possessed this stuff was immediately open to charges of weapons smuggling. Open to charges, indeed, because we had gotten the weapons back into the U.S., listing the locked, sealed, and inventoried container as "classified communications equipment."

I prepared an 1149, another form, the kind officers fill out when they take receipt of government equipment. With Doc's help, I relisted all the items we'd brought home. AK-47 assault rifles subcategorized by state of manufacture, Russian, Chinese, Romanian. Machine guns of similar provenance; Dragunov sniper rifles; snappy little AK-74s; Marakov pistols; Mosin Nagant sniper rifles (with scopes); Russian, East German, and Czech uniforms; RPG-7, RPG-16, and RPG-18 antiarmor weapons. Rocket grenades and motors. Syrian army uniforms (stained), *kufiyahs* and *shumaggs,* and Symtex plastic explosive traded for MRE battle rations. My favorites I saved for last; a pair of nasty little Skorpion machine pistols, the favorite weapon of the Red Brigades and the Bader-Mienhof gang. I recorded the serial numbers of each weapon, noting with an asterisk those we'd acquired during the CIA trade. You know, the ones with the serial numbers ground off.

I also prepared a memorandum for the record stating that we had been verbally tasked to acquire foreign weapons during our tour to augment the training armory of the Team. This statement was true, and I named names, dates, and times. I further indicated that I no longer wished to be responsible for this equipment, as I was fully aware of the regulations applying to spoils taken in battle. The entire document I classified SECRET, SPECAT, NOFORN, meaning "secret, special category, not for foreign dissemination." I knew that the yeoman of the watch would have to log the document, so my list and letter would not go astray. I dropped the file on top of Skip's in basket and went home for the weekend.

By Monday afternoon a flatbed truck from SPECWARGRU-2 had picked up the connex box and taken it away. No one at SEAL Team Four had signed for the weapons, and the armorer chief at the group had declined to sign the copy of the inventory I'd prepared. He said he'd send me a copy after he made his own count of the weapons. That never happened. I never heard about or saw the inventory again.

I'd won the first round, but I would go on very quickly to lose the war. This was a staff game, a war of memos, modified orders, and paper fortifications. It was a battlefield where inaction held the keys to victory, as sure as fire superiority did in the real world. Foolishly, I thought I'd put one over on Skip as the platoon scattered for Christmas leave.

I had toddled into an ambush.

When we returned from Christmas, we were squarely in the sights of the head shed. Indolence would be their initial weapon. I was supposed to assume command of the Fifth, and Frank was to transfer. Frank was kept on, seemingly indefinitely. When he asked, there seemed to be some inexplicable delay in his orders. That delay was essentially that the Team would not let him go. Frank was to join the MILGRU, the military advisory group, in El Salvador, another plum combat assignment. His orders stated that he was to proceed no later than January 15, and Skip made sure he stayed put until January 14 at 2355 hours. This bit of discourtesy denied Frank the traditional week's leave and proceed time, and allowed him twelve hours to pack, change continents, and jump into another war. But at least Frank got out. He was grinning like a monkey when I dropped him at NAS Norfolk.

"See you in Malibu," he said, lobbing a mock salute back at the terminal.

I shook his hand and then gave him a hug. *"Via con huevos,"* I said.

"You're a dope," he said. "Get out of there as soon as you can."

Escape proved impossible. The head shed got even, pronto. Instead of allowing me to assume command of the Fifth, they disbanded the platoon. We were suddenly all orphans, off the line operationally and out of the training pipeline as well. The new operations officer, Mad Dog Walker, took pity on us. The Fifth was broken up, but Mad Dog took pains to make our exile bearable. Five or six of the guys, including Dave, Doug, Cheese, and Rudi, went with me into the cadre. Doc was diverted to medical. The rest were scattered to departments, ordnance, engineering, intel, diving, and first lieutenant. It could have been worse. All of the lads except Sandy had received decorations and commendations in

Lebanon, and these had been forwarded by the Sixth Fleet staff. The medals and commendations had been awarded by COMSIXTHFLEET, Admiral Martin, and were to be presented by the commanding officer, SEAL Team Four.

You know, the guy I had just pissed off.

The medals sat in the captain's safe for six months. It wasn't just the fruit salad that the guys wanted; the lads had earned valuable advancement points for the decorations they'd received in combat service. They wouldn't get the points until they got the medals. The points made the difference in promotions, and promotions meant money. But the medals sat. The battle between Fifth Platoon and the front office might sound great in the retelling, but in truth, our bosses were fighting a lot of paper battles. They probably didn't even have it in for us, particularly. Some of what happened was the result of spite, but much of it was due to simple bureaucratic inertia.

I was pissed about what was being done to the lads, and I was pissed about what they'd done to Frank. But the bullshit at the Team, I realized, was just bullshit. I knew also that I'd brought it on by firing back with the 1149. I had opened an engagement against a superior force with no plan of continued attack and no way to retreat. I was screwed. I took it as best I could. Doc took it better. "Don't sweat the petty stuff," he'd say. "Pet the sweaty stuff!"

We took what pleasure we could in not being shelled every day. The Fifth hung together as much as we could, but the departments and our assignments kept us all going in different directions. I tried to keep an eye on the lads. They all drank harder than ever, and so did I. While we were gone, the Casino had been bulldozed, which might have been a good thing.

Sleep, for me, was an almost impossible thing to come by, and when it did come, it gave no peace. The week after Christmas I moved into Margot's bungalow on the beach. It was an amazement to me to wake in a bed, and it was a delight to feel her sleeping warm and sweet next to me. I was glad not to be alone.

In 1984 post-traumatic stress disorder had not yet widely entered the lexicon, but I was familiar with the concept of survivor's guilt from school. I was a textbook case. I asked myself often, like every marine and sailor who served in Lebanon, "Why did I live when so many good men died?" Finally, I accepted the fact that I had lived, in part, because I was merely lucky. I was lucky I was not at the BLT that morning. And lucky I hadn't been killed on the corniche, or in the Shouf, or in half a dozen sniper fights, or on the causeway. I consoled myself by thinking that I had helped keep sixteen men alive.

There were things that I struggled to put aside; oddly, others did not trouble me at all. I do not know exactly what this says about me, but I felt no grief for the people we killed. Their faces do not haunt me and never have. Some I remember as motionless lumps facedown in the street, legs crossed oddly, hands open, and weapons lying where they had fallen. I remember returning days later to one place we had contact, to find the bodies swollen and black with sun. In the street, trash blew around the corpses. I felt as little then as I feel now. I did not care that they were dead, and it seemed fitting to think that no one on earth had bothered to even drag them from the road. Others I can still see, turned in surprise, strobed as they tumbled back in muzzle blast, men who a second before had intended the same fate for me.

I was aware then, and am aware now, that I took human life. This will sound flippant, perhaps even nonchalantly cruel, but there are some people who need to go to hell and stay there. I watched a gang of PLO thugs drag a wounded Phalangist behind a truck until he was a bloody bundle of rags. I found the bodies of executed Palestinians, hands bound, left in the rubble for dogs to eat. I saw Druze gunners deliberately shell a hospital full of women and children. Whose side do you get on? Whose atrocity do you excuse, and whose do you come down on with a B-52?

After nearly seven months in that place, they all became alike to me—all of them off-the-rack assholes, all of them equal in my abiding and ice-cold loathing. I did not call them "ragheads" or any of the other nasty names I heard. For me, it was not necessary to dehumanize the enemy. I did not hate them, but I did not pity them, and I did not grant them mercy. The people who fought against us in Beirut made a sport of killing the blameless, and they hid behind the innocent. Some had done their best to kill us, but we killed them instead. Again, I told myself, I bore no guilt. I would do my best not to let Lebanon drag me into darkness.

I told myself these things. I told them to Margot, and I said them so well that I fooled everyone. Including myself. Lebanon would not defeat me, but it would stay with me forever, rattling after me like a tin can tied to a dog's tail. I spoke of it to no one, and those of us who went through it rarely spoke of it to one another. I came to think of Beirut as a burden, a thing too rotten and heartbreaking to be shared with anyone. The hurt was in the knowing. How could I really tell someone what it was like? And why in God's name would I want them to know?

The SEAL code said simply to swallow it, to get on with life. So I did my best to bury it. The journey into sunlight was going to be a long one, a complicated set of marches and retreats. I would continue to feel survivor's guilt, deep in a place I could not check or reconcile, and I would feel it for a long time. As a result, I set about pushing myself, hard. I would push myself relentlessly for years to come. Peace would find me eventually, and it would come from a struggle and a victory that were far off and unknowable for me while I served.

In the meantime, I congratulated myself on staying sane.

I WAS BACK IN OPERATIONS, this time as training officer, and I took the job very seriously. I enjoyed it. John Jaeger, perennial as poison sumac, was still the leading chief of the Training Department, and A. P. Hill and Camp Pickett became our joint domains. There was still advanced operator training to be served up to arriving BUD/S graduates, and the more complicated evolutions of predeployment training for platoons preparing to go overseas. It was a pipeline job, routine though not mundane, and it appeared that the prospect of a platoon command was evaporating before my eyes. I started looking for another place to go, someplace I could operate for real. That place was SEAL Team Six.

SEAL Team Six had been commissioned amid great secrecy in 1981. Six was the navy component of a special joint command, and its mission was the worst-kept secret in the community. SEAL Six was the navy's equivalent of Delta Force—a hand-picked counterterrorism outfit with a global AO. The mission of Six was easily guessed at, but not much else about the command was general knowledge.

Six was formed by Dick Marcinko, then the operations officer of SEAL Team Two. Dick Marcinko is nothing if not a wheeler-dealer, and in a short time he parlayed seventeen guys assigned to a maritime intercept outfit into an invisible empire. Marcinko built SEAL Team Six from the ground up, gathering the best operators, weapons, and equipment; clawing out a budget; and pulling every string he could to get his nascent command attached to the new joint command. The wire diagram was a short one. The commander of the joint special command reported directly to the chairman of the joint chiefs of staff. America's failure at Desert One had shown how unprepared the country was for the evolving terrorist threat; that threat was global, and 70 percent of the earth's surface is water. Delta's maritime capability at the time was nonexistent; Marcinko and Mob Six rushed in to fill the void.

Weakness was vulnerability, not just for Americans at home and abroad but for politicians. The debacle at Desert One had brought down the Carter presidency. Congress got the message, and the money started flowing. Two new operational units, SEAL Six and Special Forces Operational Detachment Delta, were to have nearly unlimited funding, manpower, and most important, a mandate. Dick Marcinko was positioned brilliantly.

The outbuilding in the SEAL Two backyard was soon abandoned for a brand-new million-dollar compound on a different base. The move was as symbolic as it was necessary. Marcinko succeeded in concocting a black program outside of the administrative and operational control of NAVSPECWARGRU-2. The unit, like Delta, was on constant war footing. Within a few hours the entire team could deploy and fight anywhere in the world. SEAL Team Six was, and is, on the highest alert level of any unit in the U.S. military.

Six made a point of attracting and keeping the best operators. It was separate, secretive, and clannish. People went over there and dropped out of sight. No one talked about the place, least of all the men stationed there. The silence added to the mystique.

In creating his kingdom, Marcinko had made enemies on all sides. The other teams resented Six's unlimited budget and the cherry-picking of their best operators. Not that Six did much recruitment. To get into the command, it was necessary to have a personal interview with Marcinko, and word was put out that only operators with several deployments and spotless operational records need apply. After a successful interview, a candidate's name would go into a pool, and orders would be cut to the command if and when the need was determined. Marcinko was almost as famous as Admiral Rickover for his antics during interviews. Front-running candidates were often rejected and shit birds taken. To the "regular" teams, there seemed no rhyme or reason as to who would be inducted and who would not. As with every other decision at SEAL Six, Marcinko was the guy making the calls. Six had become his personal fiefdom.

For a while. The knives were out for Marcinko, and by early 1983 he was overwhelmed. With no friends in the community, he was relieved of command and replaced by Captain Bob Gormly, an experienced, capable officer. Gormly inherited a can of worms. Marcinko fought his transfer in every possible way, calling in what favors he had with the joint command, admirals, and generals, and stirring up a pile of shit. In an act that endeared him to no one, Marcinko split for Europe on the day Bob Gormly assumed command, a slap in the face that made Gormly's taking over all the more difficult. Six had a growing reputation as a wild-card, shoot-from-the-hip outfit. Bob Gormly single-handedly set out to make the unit live up to its operational mandate.

To interview for Six, I had to submit a special-request chit through the chain of command, and I knew it was likely to be denied by the head shed just on general principle. Spending most of my days at A. P. Hill or Camp Pickett, I was hardly the golden boy of SEAL Team Four. One afternoon I grabbed a helo back to Little Creek. I was lucky to find the skipper and XO out of the area. I took my opportunity and struck. Mad Dog Walker approved my request to interview over at Six, and I was scheduled the next day.

I put on a clean uniform and drove to a naval station in southeastern Virginia. When I was confirmed for my interview, I was given directions from the front gate of the base: right turns, left turns, and mileage. I was not given a building number or an address. I drove to a remote corner of the base, rounded a curve, and was confronted by a serious razor-wire fence. A trim-looking guard stepped from a booth. Hanging around his neck was an MP-5 machine pistol. He checked my ID against a list, the gate rolled open, and I was admitted.

In the admin office I was fingerprinted and photographed, and I signed several security agreements. I was then escorted to a medium-sized room off the Operations Department. Behind a desk was a man with dark hair and a full mustache. He could have passed for an older Tom Selleck. There were five or six big dudes scattered on a couch and a couple of chairs. They all had shoulder-length hair.

"Sit," the man behind the desk said. He pointed to a straight-back chair in front of the desk. There were no introductions. I assumed the guy behind the desk was Captain Gormly, but I had no idea what he looked like. I had also heard stories that he put other people behind the desk and let them play skipper during interviews. I sat.

"Do you know who I am?" The man behind the desk swung his feet up on the blotter.

"Since you have your feet on the desk, I assume you're the skipper."

The mouth under the mustache smiled a little. I was prepared to get torn into, and it started pretty much right away. The smile disappeared, and Gormly's eyes narrowed.

"You're at Four?"

"Yes sir."

"How do you get along with Skippy?" someone behind me asked. I didn't turn around and kept my eyes on Captain Gormly.

"If I wasn't getting along with him, I wouldn't mention it here," I said.

"Why are you wearing a combat-action ribbon?" Captain Gormly asked.

"Beirut."

"Who were you there with?"

"Frank Giffland."

"What did you do over there?"

I briefly mentioned a few operations. While I was in Beirut, Bob Gormly had led SEAL Team Six in Grenada. They had rescued Governor Schoone and conducted the radio-station operation, an op that was already becoming a legend within the community. I was peppered with a mess of questions and given an opportunity to ask some. As I quizzed my potential employers, I saw some looks get passed. I was expected to be assertive even though I was surrounded. Finally, Captain Gormly closed the folder on his desk.

"That's enough," he said. I stood, nodded, and turned for the door. As I opened it, one of the guys on the couch unfolded his arms.

"You drink?" he asked.

"I've been known to."

"You ever go to the Raven?" he asked.

The Raven was SEAL Team Six's bar. It wasn't off limits to the other Teams, but they'd staked it out, and it was almost like their sovereign territory.

"I haven't been lately," I answered.

Someone else leaned forward. "Why not?"

"I heard it went gay," I said.

No one said anything. The lights buzzed. I walked out, convinced I'd blown it. A few weeks passed, and then I heard that my name had been placed in the pool. A few more weeks passed, and I heard nothing else.

Don't call us, kid. We'll call you.

A SEA CRUISE

IN MARCH MARGOT AND I ELOPED. We were married in a civil ceremony in Elizabeth City, North Carolina, and the vows were witnessed by the couple in line behind us. An old justice of the peace read the words. He had a glass eye that pointed west during the entire service. We didn't have a honeymoon, and I am embarrassed now to relate how utilitarian our ceremony was. There were no bridesmaids or flowers, and no one threw rice. I'd become something of an antiromantic, not the kind of man who knew how important such observances can be, not because they are ritual but because they show mutual commitment. I am not proud to say I would prove an inconstant husband. But Margot and I made each other laugh, I protected her, and she was there for me. Ultimately, that would not prove enough, but as spring came to the Tidewater, we were happy together.

We moved into a little brick duplex off Fifty-eighth Street on Virginia Beach. It wasn't much, but it was clean and comfortable, and I could walk to the beach to surf. My post-Beirut feelings were still a bit jagged, and I am not sure I loved Margot as much as I needed her. Since returning from Lebanon, I had felt a very strong need for stability. She loved me, and I did try to give back what emotion was in me. At the time we were together, I was too stressed out and one-dimensional to see much beyond my own wants.

My sleep patterns were a constant torment to Margot. Much of the cadre's work was at night, and in the field I lived like a vampire. Back home, I was tired enough to be in bed early, ten-thirty or so on weeknights, but I would often lie awake until three or four in the morning, tossing and thrashing about in bed. I'd be out the door at six A.M. for work, and this thin bit of sleep often caught up with me. On Friday afternoons I would come home exhausted and crash hard. Instead of resting on the weekends, I partied like a rock star. I have an Irishman's capacity for drink, and it was not unusual for me to engage and defeat a fifth of rum or bourbon each on Friday and Saturday night. The word "hangover" was not in the operational manual. Early Saturday I would usually surf, trying to be in the water at dawn, and Sundays I ran fourteen miles in Seashore State Park. A machine operated like that cannot last forever, but it would be years before I'd live any differently.

I did my best to settle into a reasonable domesticity. Margot was a bit of a bohemian, and perhaps even a scandal for a sixth-grade teacher. We rounded up the accoutrements of domestic arrangement: pots, pans, utensils, dishes, and eventually furniture. The little place on Fifty-eighth Street soon became a home. Margot wanted a puppy, and soon we had a canine unit named Bob, a purebred smooth-coated English fox terrier, a willful, athletic, headstrong, and foolishly brave piece of dog flesh. Fox terriers, or "smoothies," as they're called, are the only type of dog I have ever owned. It was the breed I always had as a child, and my family's last fox terrier, Happy, perished after picking a fight with an alligator on a South Florida golf course. Fox terriers aren't for everybody. Bob was more of a furry crocodile than a house pet, but he was, in a menacing sort of way, kinda cute. Margot, as she always did, graciously adapted.

It was not long after Margot and I were married that Bubba Nederlander deserted. One Monday he was not at quarters, and when I sent Dave to check, he found a short note saying simply that Bubba had had enough and was going home. Lebanon had put the zap on him, as it had on all of us, but Bubba was too uncomplicated and plain-hearted to bear up. It had not helped that when the platoon was disbanded, Bubba was fobbed off to engineering, where he did little more than flush out outboard motors and work for a chief who was one of Skip's darlings.

What Bubba had done was perplexing to us all, and we took it badly. Like a suicide, it was a desperate, pointless thing to do. A few days after Bubba took off, a pair of FBI agents were sitting in my office. They both wore dark, narrow-lapeled suits and skinny neckties, oblivious to the fact that their clothing was retro hip. After debriefing me thoroughly on what Bubba knew, and formally revoking his security clearance, they asked where I thought he would try to go.

"Mexico?" one of them said.

"Think he'll join a militia?" the other enthused.

I said, "Look for him at home."

They did, and six months later, Bubba was arrested in his small West Tennessee hometown. His training could have allowed him to disappear, but he said he wanted to go home, and that was what he did. He was court-martialed, given a dishonorable discharge, and sentenced to five years in federal prison.

Brave, simple Bubba was our first casualty.

SEAL FOUR WAS SUDDENLY in the business of fighting drug trafficking—"combating narcoterrorism" was the term then in vogue—and it was in the interest of our betters to assemble a platoon and insert them at once into Latin America. Fifth Platoon was back in business, less Bubba, Tim, Stan, and Doc. Not that the head shed had any love for us. The requirement had come down from on high. No other platoons were available or considered deployable on short notice. At the time we were reconstituted, fully a quarter of the platoon was working in the cadre, and all were grizzled combat veterans. It had not been thought necessary to put us through a complete predeployment cycle.

To assume command of the Fifth, I had to extend at SEAL Four, signing on for an additional year. I had yet to hear from SEAL Team Six. I wanted the command, and I signed without heartburn. The Team was in a hurry to get out the door, and our workups were brief. We underwent an operational readiness examination in which we simulated a demolition raid on a nuclear-power facility, a caper we pulled off with considerable panache, and two weeks later, we parachuted off Cape Henry to rendezvous with the submarine U.S.S. *Cavala* for a ride to our new home, Roosevelt Roads, Puerto Rico.

My 2IC was Ensign Greg Benham, a wisecracking New York–born Mustang who would go on to become the only SEAL-qualified trial attorney in the navy's JAG Corps. Greg was a solid operator, and the lads took to him at once. Our new leading petty officer, Juan Morales, was a recent transfer from SEAL One. Juan was an enigma, with a master's degree in art history and a New Jersey Golden Gloves rating. He asserted his authority quietly and soon joined our coterie of native Spanish speakers, quickly getting close to Rudi and Willito. The trio came to call themselves *"los Bravos,"* a tag the rest of the platoon soon mangled into *"los Patos,"* a considerably less flattering epithet, one indicative of sexual preference. We were to deploy without a chief petty officer, a highly unusual occurrence, but there was no one on earth who could fill Doc's shoes, and the vacancy was not debilitating.

FORTY MILES SOUTH of Vieques Island, Puerto Rico, U.S.S. *Cavala* came to periscope depth, and Fifth Platoon prepared to leave the submarine. We assembled our equipment in the torpedo room and tromped up the skeletal steel ladder into the forward escape trunk. Crowded with pipes and valves, the space was spherical, perhaps eight or nine feet in diameter. At the bottom of the escape trunk was a hatch, its convex shape truncating the sphere. The lower hatch was shut and dogged. There was another hatch at the top of the chamber and it, too, slightly unbalanced what would have been a perfect sphere. The top hatch was shut and secured, and a pair of red chemlights dangled from a boot lace tied to one of the hatch dogs. Hunched into the escape trunk, I stood pressed

up against five men, an outboard engine, and a rolled-up
F-470 rubber boat. There was not an inch to move in.

When the overhead light flicked from white to red, the escape trunk became a claustrophobic's worst nightmare. Air
screamed from valves in the overhead, and seawater quickly
roiled to the level of our chests. My face was soon underwater, and a shoulder above me would keep me from getting my
head in the bubble, the open space of air in the topmost section of the trunk. I found my regulator, pushed it into my
mouth, and sucked at the sweet, desert-dry air from my
scuba rig. I cleared my mask and peered around the trunk,
now a world of swirling bubbles, legs, torsos, shoulders, and
arms. The faces of three other men were visible in the red-lit
water. As the trunk filled, the air pressure in the bubble
equalized to sea pressure. Only two men, the trunk operator
and his assistant, would have their heads dry in the bubble.
The rest of us milled around in the flooded, densely packed
space, sucking on our regulators, listening to the shriek of
valves and the high-pitched voices of the trunk supervisors
in the torpedo room below playing on underwater speakers
in the chamber.

"Equalize to sea pressure," the speakers crackled.

"Equalized to sea pressure, aye."

The valves screamed and then fell silent. I pulled my legs
and flippers under me and shoved as best I could through the
men and equipment. A hatch low on the wall of the escape
trunk popped open. It was through this middle hatch that we
would exit the sub. The submarine was at a depth of forty
feet, and the lower portal was equalized to sea pressure, the
compressed air in the bubble above steady with that of the
sea outside. In simple terms, the process was like turning a
cup upside down and submerging it in a sink full of water: A
pocket of air remains trapped in the top of the cup as it is
pushed under.

Pulling open the hatch, I entered a dark tube a bit over a
meter in diameter. This tube led to a final hatch where fresh
torpedoes and missiles were loaded into the submarine when
the ship was in port; technically, the space was the weapons

handling tube. Leaving the spherical confines of the trunk, I pulled myself onto my back and maneuvered up and into the cylindrical space. As I exhaled, bubbles from my regulator wafted above me, boiling against the top of the tube. Rolling onto my side, I inched through the perfect blackness, careful not to bang my scuba bottle or dislodge the regulator from my mouth. I found the last hatch by feel, then I broke a chemlight. In its feeble green glow, I opened the hatch and felt the swirling of the open sea.

Tonight I would be the first man to leave the submarine. I was assigned as a rigger, and it was my job to attach a series of lines to the hull and conning tower to aid in the deployment of the swimmers and the launching of our boat. The rigging of a submarine is one of the few times SEALs deploy a man alone. Outside a submarine, at night, you are very alone.

I pushed myself through the second hatch, out of the pressure hull, and onto the deck of the sub. Forty feet above, the surface of the Caribbean shimmered in moonlight. As my eyes became accustomed to the scant light, I could see that the midocean water was incredibly clear, blue above and bluer still below, and the deck of the submarine spread away vast and black underneath me.

As I emerged I could feel the submarine surge forward. Like a shark, it needed to constantly move, and I could feel its power through the water. Almost three hundred feet aft, *Cavala*'s propeller turned slowly, throbbing like a living thing. I pulled lines and snap links from a locker under the fairwater, the space between the pressure hull and the deck. The bubbles swept away from my regulator in a silver tumult.

The submarine came leisurely forward, and all I had to do was hover in the water as the convex deck rolled under me. The conning tower soon loomed above, sail planes gigantic and cruciform against the moonlit surface far above. As I rigged the line to the conning tower, I felt the water pressure change around me. Then I felt something almost like electricity. It was a force, a life energy; there is no other way to describe it. A long shadow passed over me, then another, and I looked up from my work and into the blue around me. Astounded, I watched a school of yellowfin tuna swim up and past the sail of the sub and close in all around me. The light of a full moon streamed through the water, and the sides of the huge fish showed silver. Small pulses of their three-foot tails were enough to keep them perfectly on station. I was astonished that they would come so close to me.

I pulled myself down the line that I had rigged, a tangent from the bow of the sub to the top of the conning tower. I hung on the line by my fists, and my body wavered in the current like a flag on a lanyard. As I was pulled along by the sub, the school swam close beside me. I blinked and reminded myself that if I let go of the line, I would be swept away and quite possibly lost forever. In the water, bioluminescent plankton trailed behind the fish like a cascade of stars. It was one of the most beautiful things I have ever seen in my life, and I remember that it was silver above, cobalt beneath, and this vision still recurs in my dreams.

I turned, still hanging on the line, and flashed an okay to the video camera mounted on the conning tower. Watched in main control, the message was passed to the escape trunk, and the remaining men soon emerged from the hatch. As the other divers joined me on deck, the school of yellowfin veered away, maintaining a tight formation. Soon they were lost in the blue.

The F-470 was muscled through the weapons handling tube, and likewise the motor. The boat was clipped to a line and buoy, the engine screwed onto the transom, and then a lanyard was pulled, initiating two big bottles of CO_2. In a huge storm of bubbles, the boat rocketed for the surface. Gasoline bladders were removed from the locker below the fairwater, clipped to the ascent-descent line, and allowed to float to the surface by their own buoyancy. In a short while, six men and their equipment had locked out of the submarine, swum up the line, and pulled themselves into the boat.

The last man to emerge handed me a kit bag. In it were my weapon, ammunition, and web gear. Two divers, also riggers, remained floating above the deck of the sub. I clipped the kit bag to my belt and removed the scuba bottle from my back. The closer of the riggers swam forward and took the tank. I drew a final deep breath from the regulator and tilted my chin at the surface, forty feet above. Our inflatable boat was a black archlike shape against the moonlight.

I gave the riggers a thumbs-up, removed the regulator from my mouth, and blew a stream of bubbles from my lips. I swam slowly up and toward the boat, careful to ascend only as fast as the smallest bubbles around me. I continued to exhale strongly as the air in my lungs expanded. I exhaled all the way to the surface, the volume in my lungs seemingly inexhaustible. This was a trick of physics. The amount of air filling my lungs forty feet down was nearly twice the amount my lungs could hold on the surface. If I were to stop exhaling, the air in my body cavities would expand to twice its volume, bursting my lungs, embolizing my blood vessels, and killing me in a matter of seconds. A definite pain in the ass, and a calamity that could befall me if I was incredibly stupid. I made it to the boat without turning myself inside out, and pulled myself up and in.

I joined the last boat crew to be deployed from the submarine. As I tossed my face mask into the bottom of the boat, I could hear the puttering of the outboard motor. The surface somehow seemed blacker than it had underwater. I squinted in the moonlight. The Zodiac was still attached to the buoy, and the boat was slowly being pulled along, up and over the rolling swell, still tethered to the leviathan below. Behind the Zodiac, *Cavala*'s attack periscope jutted from the water, hissing as it moved through the swells. I quickly unzipped my kit bag, readied my weapon, and slipped into my combat vest. This I did in the dark, and mostly by rote. With me was boat crew Four of Fifth Platoon. Rather, boat crew Four of Fifth Platoon, reconstituted. I could make out no faces, but I knew the men in the boat with me. Rudi was there, seeming *muy cubano* even in the dark, and Surfer Dave was at the tiller. Juan Morales was in the bow. As I zipped my combat vest up over my wet cammies, I gave Dave a nod. He turned and flashed an infrared light at the periscope. In response, the attack scope dipped twice, and in the bow of the Zodiac, Juan pulled at a quick release.

The Zodiac separated from the buoy, and Dave put the helm over. We puttered down the slope of a moonlit swell as the periscope moved past us, retracting straight down and slipping below the surface. The buoy was dragged under with a small gurgle as the submarine passed below.

The Zodiac headed west as the moon set, making a passage twenty miles over the horizon to Roosevelt Roads, Puerto Rico. It was a stunning, beautiful night. To the north, the tourist hell of Saint Thomas was a yellow smudge of light on the horizon. I filled my lungs with warm ocean air. I had been a week on the submarine, an odd, fluorescent-lit trip from wintry Norfolk, and I was delighted to again be on the open sea, and happy to be with the lads.

We settled into the special warfare compound aboard the naval station at Roosevelt Roads. Western Puerto Rico is beautiful, the surf is good, and the deployment was a slice of paradise. We were attached to Naval Special Warfare Unit Four as the Caribbean contingency platoon. Grenada had recently been chastised, the Cubans were for the most part back in their box, and the Carib was quiet.

Our original mandate was counternarcotics operations. To that end, we sent out MTTs, mobile training teams, providing military advisers to several wobbly Latin American countries. Our client list read like a who's who of the world's cocaine-producing nations. We taught the usual, operations from sea, reconnaissance and surveillance, patrolling, special ops, sabotage, and the rudiments of how to plan, compartmentalize, and coordinate an operation.

The degree to which our clients applied these lessons against narcotics traffickers depended on factors beyond our control. In the Southern Hemisphere, the devil dances with several partners: corrupt and authoritarian central governments, drug dealers, guerrillas, and vicious right-wing paramilitaries. Narco dollars bought politicians on all sides, and truth and justice were in perennially short supply. We would train elite units of a country's army or national police forces, and just as soon as they went operational, they would be compromised, sold out, or disbanded by politicians and general officers on the payroll of drug lords. We did little good. I wrote reports back to Little Creek saying we were essentially wasting our time. I may or may not have been listened to, but gradually, we were withdrawn from the counternarcotics business. There were other fish to fry.

In the mid-1980s, America's pissing contest with Nicaragua continued, and the United States was deeply into training, supplying, and motivating the Contras. These efforts were focused along the Coco River in Honduras and the emerging boomtown of Puerto Lempira. It was not long after we'd settled into Roosevelt Roads that I became a frequent flier—a commuter to the covert war in Central America.

SHARP-DRESSED MEN

MY CAREER AS military adviser was served up in slices. I remember it now as sort of a slide show. I led a number of small detachments from Puerto Rico into Central America, mostly to Honduras but occasionally to other places. We'd parachute in, spend a few weeks in the bush, operating from jungle hammocks or some flyblown little pueblo, complete a training syllabus, and then be withdrawn. Our curriculum depended on the audience. For units of the Honduran army, it was frequently the basics: drill, infantry, and squad tactics. For Contra units with number designations and CIA paramilitary chaperones, our lessons were often highly technical: maritime sabotage, stalking and tracking, and the employment of spotters and snipers.

We rarely operated over a week before getting withdrawn or moved to a different location. Our perception was that we were on a very tight leash. The host nations were keenly aware of how many Americans were in country, where they went, and how long they stayed. Our hitches were usually followed by a debrief and a drunken weekend in Tegucigalpa, Panama City, or San Salvador. Then it was back to Puerto Rico, where we'd wait again for the phone to ring.

Anyone who served in Central America in the 1980s will probably agree with me that in the field, no matter how far "south" Americans were deployed, we generally felt safe. It was in the cities, during the periods we were supposed to rest and recoup, that we were in the most danger. In the field we could depend on camouflage and stealth. In the cities the more Anglo of our number stood out like circus freaks. To be obviously a *norteamericano* was to be a target.

Paranoia, we used to say, is total awareness. That was never more true than when we were at leisure in Tegucigalpa. Vigilance was our mantra, and it extended to the smallest things. Like eating. There is an art to selecting a seat in a Central American restaurant, especially if you are six-three, have red hair and freckles, and look like a gringo *consejero militar,* or military adviser. When selecting a restaurant in a country undergoing a civil war, one must consider architecture, location, and ballistics. Cuisine and atmosphere are also factors, but they are secondary. It's best to patronize only establishments recommended by fellow military advisers or spooky types from the embassy. The object is to find joints where the owners are at least open-minded on the subject of Americans. As more operators rotate through a tour, each pushes the envelope of safety and cuisine, trying and surviving a greater number of eateries. By the time I returned to Central America, there were about two dozen of these places in each capital city.

We avoided anyplace with the word "American" in its name, a case in point being Bobby's American Bar in Athens, which has been bombed at least three times in my lifetime. Also to be avoided were fancy restaurants in swank international hotels, as they are expensive and generally patronized by members of the indigenous plutocracy, who are targets, too.

Sometimes the threat level was minuscule, sometimes it was considerable, and it varied in its source. There is always a background level of extremely violent crime in such places, and Americans are targets of opportunity. I did not take that personally. The criminals were mostly amateurs, and in their lack of sophistication there was a modicum of safety. There was also political violence to consider, which I took more seriously. The threat came primarily from the left but not infrequently from the right—acts of terrorism and provocation, respectively, but the result was the same. All of us made dining arrangements with great care.

The first issue was parking, and for that I always carried two open packs of Marlboro cigarettes. Immediately after parking the car, I'd give three cigarettes to the first kid I saw, then I'd promise him the rest of the pack for watching my car. I never had anyone say no. I'd walk half a block in the direction of dinner, select a kid at random from the throng, and make him the same deal, three cigarettes and the rest of the second pack. This kid's job was to watch the first kid. I'm pretty sure this works, because I have never been car-bombed or ambushed as I returned to my vehicle.

Safe restaurants have a number of things in common. Almost invariably, these establishments are mom-and-pop operations, and Mom and Pop usually have at least one grown child living in the United States. This you'll know because the owners will almost immediately mention it to you. There might also be American icons about: football posters featuring the Miami Dolphins, Elvis on velvet, or the occasional Budweiser clock. Skittish, surly, and hostile proprietors were to be avoided, as were locations openly associated with political parties. You might dine at a place that had a poster of Che Guevara on the wall, but it was usually a onetime deal. If you sat down and everyone else got up and left, it was time to pick another restaurant.

We all had favorite places, but it was best not to be predictable. The joints were usually small, sometimes Indian or Chinese, but mostly local. A suitable restaurant contained a dozen tables at most and had to be somewhat shielded from the street. A few thick pillars or an archway or two was sufficient front cover. The place also had to have at least two rear exits, and the exits, like the front doors, had to be visible at all times from one's seat. There were a few other things to look for—thick tables, few windows, and a number of other diners between you and the front door. Heavy tables were better than light tables for absorbing shrapnel, and other diners made it difficult to throw or roll a grenade across a restaurant. As in Lebanon, we took the presence of children to be an indication of safety.

If dining alone, I sat with my back to a corner; if I was dining with a companion, one of us was responsible for watching the front while the other watched the back. It was unwise to eat with a person you would not trust with your life. As you sat down and looked at the silverware, you applied the left-hand rule, closing your eyes briefly and gripping the seat of the chair with your left hand, then imagining yourself with your pistol held out in front of you, backing toward the rear exit, left hand extended behind. This path was loaded in memory, as were various what-ifs for drive-by shootings, grenade attacks, and car bombings.

Now on to the menu. The food in Latin America is good, often terrific, but tends to reassemble a quartet of ingredients: tortillas, chicken, rice, and beans. I ate anywhere deemed tactically sound, including from street stalls and pushcarts, but I have a few ironclad rules. I am not one of those people who goes to Bogotá and complains about the hamburgers; I am, by and large, omnivorous. My rules have allowed me to feed in some of the most down-market and ungodly places on earth with little damage to my digestive tract. The only food trouble I've ever had abroad was from a bad salad served by the U.S. Marines in Lebanon.

When I am out on the economy, I drink only liquids with bubbles: beer, soda from a bottle, and *agua con gas,* or sparkling water. Rarely fruit juice, and never fresh-squeezed juice. Rum, Mescal, or liquor neat, and never with ice. I eat my vegetables when I'm back in the States and avoid lettuce, greens, and raw onions anywhere south of Key West, as they can often be shigella vectors. I will generally eat any domestic animal and several others, including cayman, nutria, peccary, and goat, if it is barbecued and well done. As far as cheeses go, hard ones yes, soft ones no. Crispy *pupusas,* the Salvadoran cousin of an empanada, can be had throughout Central America, and they are usually nontoxic if eaten at 350 degrees Fahrenheit.

I avoid seafood, especially clams, crabs, oysters, and mussels, but have never been burned by conch. A favorite is *sopa de caracol,* conch and coconut soup, and *ticucos,* a killer Honduran tamale with beans. Hot sauce and chili peppers always, as I have this dearly held theory that no human pathogen could possibly survive in a bottle of Tabasco sauce. As you might suspect, Central America has neither the cuisine nor locale for fine wine. To wash it all down there are a number of primo beers, Nacional, Imperial, Port Royal, Salva Vida, and the ubiquitous Panama. Although I infrequently eat dessert, I am a sucker for flan, especially the Panamanian sort, cool and creamy inside and slightly caramelized on top.

I'll lay no claim to being a Latin American food expert, as most of the time I spent in country I was in the field, eating MREs, rice, bananas, plantains, conch, or other things we could scrounge or barter for. I made regular trips into the urban areas, most often to give reports or to be debriefed, and I seldom stayed more than two or three nights.

Once, when Greg, Mike Darby, and I were on an overnight to Tegucigalpa, we checked in to our rooms and agreed to meet in the lobby for dinner. An hour later, we all appeared, shaved, showered, and dressed in identical black aloha shirts. The shirts had been issued to us by a three-letter government agency and were supposed to allow us to "blend." They were cut wider under the left arm to accommodate a pistol. The wooden buttons were backed with Velcro, allowing them to be torn open rapidly to access the shoulder holster. There is something inherently preposterous about a Hawaiian shirt tailored to conceal a handgun. We stood around like idiots, each in identical togs with Bianchi side-draw shoulder holsters, packing Beretta 92 SBF automatic pistols.

Greg grinned. "You can't lose," he said, "when you dress like I do."

It was a line from ZZ Top, and from that moment on we were the Sharp-Dressed Men. The shirts were ridiculous, helmeted kahunas riding surfboards, but we always wore them on liberty and carried our pistols like a posse of sunburned gangsters. We were certain that chicks dug us.

I got to put my shirt to the test one night in the bar of the Days Inn in Tegucigalpa. The physical plant of the hotel differed little from the cigarette-burned joints scattered on the side of the interstate, but at this time in Honduras, it was probably the nicest hotel in the country. It was one of the safest, located a bit out of town, with multiple approaches and escape routes; the compound was surrounded by a six-foot cinder-block wall topped with broken glass and barbed wire. It was a safe place to meet, and we were sometimes sent there to recoup. The bar was air-conditioned to 65 degrees, and there was MTV on the satellite dish. The beer was always subzero.

I had attended a briefing at the embassy that afternoon, filling the military attaché in on the nonevents of my most recent deployment to Puerto Lempira. I was to return to Puerto Lempira in the morning, and a week later, I was due to rotate back to Puerto Rico. I was hot and tired, and the charm was rapidly going out of my tropical vacation. It was a weeknight, and the hotel was nearly empty. I ate a *plato tipico* at the bar and was proceeding to drink myself good-looking while the bartender wiped glasses and wondered why the hell I didn't go back to my room.

About ten o'clock, two women entered the bar. They were in their twenties, attractive, and I guessed from their clothing that they were either Canadian or American. They were both tanned; one had shoulder-length dark hair, and the other was blond with her hair cut short like an athlete's. I nodded as they sat down across the bar, since it was rude, as well as silly, to ignore them in an empty bar. After a few moments we'd tried to send one another a drink, and I walked over and introduced myself.

Lucky for me, they were both named Vicky. They were Peace Corps volunteers who had just finished a tour in a place called Copan, near the Guatemala border. They were outprocessing in Tegucigalpa the next day and heading back to the U.S. the day after that. They were both from New England. Blond Vicky had rowed crew back in school, and I did my best to be a charming ex-oarsman. We drank pretty steadily for about an hour, and I was able to fend off any inquiries about who I really was and what I really did by being extremely interested in the elementary school where they'd taught in Copan.

About midnight dark-haired Vicky said she was going to bed. Blond Vicky tried briefly to talk her out of it but couldn't, so she kissed her friend on the cheek. I shook dark-haired Vicky's hand when she left.

We had a shot of tequila. Blond Vicky looked at me hard. "So, what brings you to Tegucigalpa?" she asked.

The yacht-delivery line wasn't going to work. We were a hundred miles from the ocean. I answered with a question: "What are *you* doing here?"

It was a great opportunity for her to improv, but she didn't take the bait. "We're in the Peace Corps," she said.

"In school, did you row port or starboard?" I asked.

"You never said what you did for a living."

"I work for the government," I said. It was true enough, and part of what's called a "layer." When asked, I would reveal that I worked for the government; when pressed, I would say I worked for the Executive Department of the government; if pinned by an inquisitive person at an embassy party, I would say that I worked for the Department of Defense. The mundane fib of "defense contractor" was safe enough.

"What kind of government contractor are you?" she asked.

"A well-behaved one," I said.

She smiled. "What are you, some kind of spy?" Making a show of patting me down, she moved her hand to the side of my shirt. She patted down my right side and under my left arm. Then her hand fell on the Walther PPK tucked into my shoulder holster. I can tell you with only a small amount of vanity that she was instantly smitten.

Twenty minutes later, we were sprawled on the bed in my room. As we kissed, I was sober enough to remember that I had a wife at home. The pang of conscience made me flinch. "I'm married," I finally said.

She kissed me again. "So am I." We kissed more, and it started going somewhere. She sat up and straightened her blouse. "Maybe I'd better go check on Vicky."

"That might be a good idea."

She looked at me the way she had after the tequila shot. "Are you all right with this?" she asked.

I heard my voice deep and flat, as though I were listening to myself speak down a long tube. "Yeah, I'm all right."

She left and pulled the door closed behind her. I lay back on the bed, staring at the ceiling. I made myself try to think of nothing, nothing being a fine substitute for wanting to follow her. At last I peeled off my shirt, slipped my arms out of my shoulder holster, and placed my gun on the nightstand.

I was in the bathroom splashing my face when I heard a knock on the door. "Who is it?"

"It's us," one of the Vickies whispered.

I opened the door, and they were both there, the blond Vicky and the brunette Vicky. The blonde kissed me, and then the brunette kissed me. They didn't say anything as they pushed their way into the room and the door closed behind them. We made out on the bed for a while in a big pile, and then the clothing started to come off. I watched them kiss and undress each other, and whatever objections I had to being an unfaithful husband wafted away like smoke. We made love until I had to leave for the airport in the morning, and I never saw them again.

On the helicopter back down-country I sat in the door gunner's seat, letting the wind snap into me. I watched the red-dirt towns and the dusty roads pass below until the ground became low and fingers of mangrove reached inland, and then the broad water of Barra de Caratasca yawned under us. Again I tried not to think of anything.

I was back in the bush outside of Puerto Lempira, lying on a simulated ambush position with a detachment of Contras. From out of the darkness, I watched a three-foot-long fer-de-lance slither over my rifle barrel. The viper was too close for me to try to pull away, so I remained perfectly still. As it moved through a thin sliver of moonlight, its scales showed silver-gray, as if it were made of chain mail. For a long moment it remained across my weapon. Light stripes and a dark diamond pattern covered its wide back. Its eye was like a shiny onyx bead. I held my breath until it disappeared back into the gloom, its skin hissing over the plastic foregrip of my rifle.

I count myself lucky that the serpent chose not to strike me dead.

THERE WERE SEVERAL more deployments, and MTTs were dispatched to the Dominican Republic. We hosted several deputations from the Teams up north, and Greg and I ran combat-swimmer training for platoons undergoing PDT. The Caribbean was quiet, and the tour stretched out. Frank was busy in El Sal, and occasionally we'd hear of some exploit or near-miss. While Frank was kicking ass, I was getting dangerously bored. I drank like a bastard and ran barely enough to keep the fat off.

Bored or not, I'd inherited Frank's command ethic, and when a detachment was called upon to tour South America, I sent Greg and boat crews Delta and Charlie. The exercise was called UNITAS, and the tour was what we liked to call "low intensity, high per diem." Strictly peacetime, it was a series of exercises and special-warfare demonstrations for our South American allies. It was all goodwill, a four-month grip-and-grin. I would have loved to go, but Fifth Platoon's mission was to stand by for contingency operations, and that mission was my responsibility. As Frank said, platoons are commanded by platoon commanders, detachments by assistant platoon commanders. Greg and I had grown close; he was a good officer, a wild man on liberty but sane when he operated, and I had complete confidence in him. When they shoved off, our world in Puerto Rico got smaller. Alpha, Bravo, and I remained in Roosevelt Roads, poised to put out any brushfires that might erupt.

We waited. There was no trouble in paradise.

Then I received a call from the SEAL officer detailer in Washington, D.C., or rather, the detailer's secretary, a no-nonsense lady named Margrethe Foster. Margrethe is the Moneypenny of the SEAL Teams. Detailers come and go, but Margrethe remains. She is the power behind the throne, the woman who knows where all the bodies are and where all the skeletons are buried. She's put a few skeletons in the ground herself.

"Okay, Pfarrer," she said, "your orders came in."

I waited while the connection from Washington crackled and hissed.

"You're going to SEAL Team Six."

BECOMING A JEDI

THE SUPPLY CHIEF was in a hurry because it was time to go home. I'd shown up late, with an inventory half an inch thick, just as he was pulling closed the steel-and-wire mesh door that separated his office and warehouse from the passageway. He grunted as I handed over my paperwork, equipment I'd need for my course in Green Team, the training cell of SEAL Team Six. The other twenty or so members of my training class had drawn their kits over the last several weeks as they arrived and checked in to the Team.

I was late for an unsurprising reason. When I received orders to Six, the commanding officer of SEAL Team Four called me in Puerto Rico and attempted to get me to decline the transfer. He said he had a great position at the Pentagon for me, an assignment that would be better for my career. As far as I knew I had no career, and I had no desire to serve at the Pentagon. I politely but firmly refused. My orders were to report aboard SEAL Six no later than September 15, and I was looking forward to the change. But through acts of either inertia or contempt, I was ordered to remain in Puerto Rico until September 14. Like Frank Giffland, I had been given one day to check out of my old command and in to my new one.

All day on the fifteenth, I had dashed around the SEAL Team Six compound, schlepping paperwork, getting ID badges, drawing weapons, parachutes, diving rigs, and radios, much to the consternation of clerks and technicians who told me this should have been done weeks ago. I learned pretty quickly that being a Green Team member didn't cut much ice at Six. None of the support guys I dealt with were even SEALs, but they all gave me a hard time. I made no excuses and asked no favors, but I soon rounded up what I needed. Supply was my last stop and the biggest haul. There were more than two hundred items on my gear list, everything from desert cammies to arctic overwhites, ice boots to shower shoes.

The chief frowned. "When do you need this?"

"Tonight," I said. "I start training tomorrow."

He pushed open the door reluctantly, and I followed him into supply. He removed a folder from a file drawer. "We didn't think you were coming," he said.

I'm sure he would have been delighted if I'd been killed by land crabs in Puerto Rico.

"What's your operator number?" he asked.

"One-five-six," I said.

He shook his head. "We already have a One-five-six."

Before I could ask to pick a new number, like 007, the chief's eyes fell on a flat cart loaded chest-high with duffel bags. It was an individual operator's load-out, all the equipment I would need to draw. The number 205 was stenciled neatly on the bags.

"I got a full load-out right over there. You have a problem with changing your number?"

"Does it get me my gear any faster?"

"You become Two-oh-five, and you can sign right here."

We were both in a hurry. I signed, and the booty was mine. In the stroke of a pen, I was Operator 205.

"It's all there," the chief said, "all of it and then some. I just inventoried it myself."

I smiled as he locked up the supply room. Thinking I had scored, I shouldered the pile of bags on the cart and wheeled it into the passageway.

"What happened to Operator Two-oh-five?" I asked.

"His parachute didn't open," the chief said.

SEAL SIX HAD THE JACK, and it showed. The equipment I'd drawn was the best of everything. I stayed up late that night, stowing the gear in my cage, a locked wire enclosure about the size of a one-car garage. Here I would keep every piece of my operational kit racked, stacked, and ready to fly. Each operator had a cage, his own personal space, warehouse, and dominion. There was little communal equipment. We all drew our own gear and were responsible for maintaining it.

I had been issued an astonishing amount of stuff. Foul-weather gear, Gore-Tex parkas, assault vests, cammies, boots, fins. Bags and sea chests full to bursting. Climbing harnesses, carabiners, chocks, jumars, and lock picks. Nomex coveralls. Custom wet suits. Flight suits. Survival kits. Sunglasses and ski goggles. Scuba rigs, a pair of twin steel 90s for open circuit and a brand-new Draeger LAR-V rebreather. An MT-1-X parachute and an impressive number of weapons. In my personal rack in the arsenal were a CAR-15 with M-203 grenade launcher, MP5-A5 and MP-5K machine pistols, and a wicked little silenced MP5-SD. I had a personal AK-47, an H&K G3 assault rifle, an M-60 machine gun, a SAW-squad automatic weapon, a stainless-steel Smith & Wesson model 686 .357 Magnum pistol, a Beretta 92 SBF, and a blue-steel Walther PPK, just like James Bond. The armory tech was blasé as he had me sign.

"This is your basic draw," he mumbled. "If you need any other sort of weapon, or if you want modifications made, just let us know."

I reported the following morning at 0600 and met my new teammates. The twenty of us were to be the fourth Green Team processed by SEAL Team Six. Some faces I recognized and some I did not. In any case, we were surprises to one another. When we were notified of our selection, we were told to tell only those people with a need to know. Several of my new teammates were old friends. Wild Bill had been in Class 114 and was a member of my boat crew during Hell Week. Bill was an NFL-sized guy with an incredible sense of humor. He was impressively strong and born into the career of spec ops—his father was a serving colonel in the Green Berets. There were three others from 114 in my Green Team: Greg Pearlman and Chris Keller, the two hot dogs who'd swiped the jumpmaster's hat back at Fort Benning, and Vinny, a tall man built like a cross-country runner, who was quiet, intense, and dedicated. He, too, had been in my boat crew for Hell Week, and I was glad to see him. They were solid guys, good shipmates, great operators, and all would be destined to have long careers at SEAL Six.

The balance of my Green Team came from SEAL Teams One, Two, and Three, as well as the SDV Teams. Surprisingly, or perhaps not, I was the only one from SEAL Four. Everyone selected was considered top-of-the-line, the officers all former platoon commanders, and most of the enlisted former leading petty officers or boat-crew leaders. The class's sole chief petty officer was Bud Denning, a taciturn guy with a subtle and cutting sense of humor. As chiefs go, Bud Denning was one of the best.

There were three other officers in my Green Team, all of us lieutenants, and all of us would become friends for life. Sean Pikeman was our class leader, senior by a couple of years; he was fresh from SEAL Team One and a jungle deployment to the Philippines. He had been raised in Stillwater, Oklahoma; he had an Okie's level head and had played all-American lacrosse at the University of Rochester. Next was Rick Cullen, unflappable, a meticulous planner and a former platoon commander from SEAL Two. Finally, there was Moose. If the Moose didn't exist, someone would have had to invent him. Built like a linebacker, he was a high-time SDV pilot from the West Coast. Driving minisubs into Korean harbors on recons wasn't exciting enough for him, so here he was. Moose was a fascinating guy with a rigorous and accomplished upbringing. Captain and quarterback of his high school football team, he also found time to play first violin in the Seattle Youth Symphony. At Claremont College in California, he ran the 880 and majored in philosophy and religion, writing his senior thesis on the death of Eric Bonhoffer, a Lutheran theologian executed by Adolf Hitler. Moose was as impressive intellectually as he was physically. He could talk about Epictetus while he benched 350, and it was only a fool who'd try to outdrink him.

Our instructors walked in, dressed in the uniform of the day, blue jeans and polo shirts. The entire time I was at SEAL Six, I would wear a navy uniform only once. This was a civilian-clothes operation.

The training cell was led by a man with the remarkable name of Traylor Court. Court was prior enlisted, had attended OCS and gotten drafted into the command by Dick Marcinko personally. Court had a gymnast's build and was one of the operators, along with Kim Erskine, who had taken down the radio station on Grenada. Court wasn't the type to raise his voice. He commanded attention and respect.

With Court were three other instructors: Toni, a six-foot, 250-pound Hawaiian surfer; Mike Daniels, your basic triathlete sniper-cum-demolition expert; and a guy we called Bam-Bam. Bam-Bam was from Gary, Indiana, and was fond of remarking that he was the only one of his three brothers not currently in prison. Bam-Bam had been the Indiana State springboard-diving champion, and in a command where everyone was an expert marksman, he was considered one of the fastest and deadliest shots. He was also quick with his fists.

There was no welcome-aboard speech. Court made a few remarks, most notably that this was a selection course. Not only was it possible to fail; for most of us, it was likely. He predicted that half of the men assigned to this Green Team would attrite. It was a variation of my welcome to BUD/S, and I am sure everyone who heard him thought they'd be among the graduates.

Court was to prove precise in his estimate. Of the twenty of us standing in the Team room, only twelve would make it through Green Team and be assigned to assault elements on the operational team. Court went on to enumerate half a dozen transgressions for which we would be immediately canned: Accidental discharge of a weapon. Any safety violation involving diving or explosives. Use or suspected use of controlled substances. Loss or mishandling of classified material. Revealing any facts about SEAL Team Six to anyone, in or out of naval special warfare. We were specifically instructed to no longer associate with anyone back in the regular Teams. We were told bluntly: "Make new friends."

This policy was rigorously enforced and had led to the alienation of Team Six from the rest of the community. The new-friends rule was a relic of the Marcinko era, and like many other Marcinko policies we would come up against, it seemed pointless and counterproductive; but they were serious about it, so we did as we were told. There was at least a glimmer of a reason behind it: SEAL Team Six was then a black program. The existence of the Team was secret, the location of the base was secret, its budget, training, organization, and tactics were all classified. The building did not say "SEAL Team Six"—it said the name of an equipment-testing unit that did not exist. The cover was backstopped thoroughly. All of us had been processed out of the navy. At least as far as our records showed, we had all been separated from the service. Paperwork variously indicating resignation, retirement, and medical release from duty had been placed in each of our service records. We were to grow our hair long and forget that we owned uniforms. As far as the world was concerned, none of us were in the navy anymore. We were now civilians working for the phantom organization. This was what we were to tell our neighbors and new friends.

To our old teammates back at Little Creek, it would appear that we had dropped off the face of the planet. We had entered the black world. From now on the Teams would be referred to disparagingly as Vanilla SOF—plain white spec ops. As aspirant members of Team Jedi, we had crossed to the Dark Side.

There was an additional consequence of joining a black operation: compartmentalization. Green Team was firewalled totally from the operational elements of SEAL Six. We were told not to ask questions, to keep to our own cages and our own Team room, and not to fraternize with the operators, even if we had known them back in the real world. The training cell was completely segregated from the operational elements. Until we had passed out of Green Team, we were visitors. Period.

"When and *if* you graduate," Court said, "you can play with your old friends."

This culture pervaded the command. It wasn't just the support guys who gave Green Team members the short stroke. In the hallways and around campus, the members of Green Team were practically invisible. Former teammates would pass by without a nod. The no-fraternization rule went both ways. This was another Marcinko innovation. You had to earn the right to be here; until then you were nothing.

The next briefing was from the command's two counterintelligence agents, a pair of cards I'll call "Lenny" and "Dougie." It was their job to make sure the command kept a low—that is, invisible—profile. They were active-duty marines, as if you could tell. Dougie had curly hair to his shoulders and a drooping Fu Manchu. Lenny sported a goatee and an earring. They were affable enough, but their message was chilling. It was their job to discern how well our covers were working, and what the general public knew about us and the command.

"Here's the deal," Dougie said. "If I ask your next-door neighbors where you work and they tell me you're a SEAL, you're outta here."

I made a mental note: Don't chat up the neighbors.

Green Team was to be eight months long, two months longer than BUD/S. It would prove every bit as grueling. We worked six days a week, from six in the morning until five at night. We would have at least one night op a week, and we would work seven days a week when we were on the road, which would be most of the time. Individuals who attrited, were injured or deemed unsuitable would have their service records reactivated and would transfer back to the Teams. Before transfer, they would sign a security-termination agreement promising fines and imprisonment for leaking any information. Again, Lenny and Dougie would be checking.

We wore beepers and were on call to be in our cages and ready to deploy on short notice. I won't mention the time requirement, but I will say this: It was stringent enough that some people sold their houses to move closer to work.

And there was a lot of work. Traylor Court would soon dispel any notions we had about being in shape. In the woods in front of the compound, Court had erected an aerial obstacle course. Rigged through the trees were caving ladders, rope bridges, monkey bars, bits of pipe, inclined boards, and horizontal beams. Negotiating the course required a variety of rock-climbing moves: chimneying, laybacks, mantles, and countless full-body lifts. We used to say Court was trying to separate the men from the baboons, but the course had a purpose. At Six, we climbed things: the sides of buildings, oil rigs, cliff faces, and anchor chains. As I gradually gained confidence and strength, I was to fall out of Court's trees half a dozen times, but I would never fall on an operation.

We were required to swing through Court's masterpiece after our daily six-mile run, which happened after our first hour and a half of PT, which started every morning at 0600. Morning calisthenics, like the run and the aerial O-course, were led by Court in person. Not all of our cardio conditioning was roadwork or swinging through trees. We swam thousands of laps and played water rugby in the Team's indoor Olympic swimming pool. I was in shape when I got there, and I got harder. We lifted weights in a health-club-sized weight room. We did a twenty-mile cross-country run over hill and dale, forest and swamp. We swam around the island of Key West. By the end of training, I would weigh 220 pounds and be able to run ten miles in sixty-five minutes, knock out a hundred sit-ups in ninety seconds, and chin myself with one hand.

As fun as the exercise was, we were there to learn a trade, and the greater part of each day was spent absorbing the component skills required of a counterterrorist operator. We were put through an intense combat-swimmer curriculum, building on and expanding the underwater skills we'd learned in the Teams. The training required us to swim mile-long course legs underwater and affix magnetic mines to targets on time and without detection. We conducted underwater recons against port facilities and offshore oil platforms. We swam to piers, surfaced, and shot targets, disappearing back underwater and swimming a mile or two out to sea.

When I reported to Green Team, I might have been a bit jaded. I'd been in combat, I was a platoon commander, I had led numerous detachments and spent a good part of my career doing spooky stuff in Central America. I thought I'd been around the block, and I didn't expect to have the shit scared out of me. But it happened in Green Team, often. It was taken for granted that we were all experienced operators and that we would learn quickly. Some of the things we learned were just plain dangerous. In the evolutions we practiced, everything either went perfectly or people died.

"Pay attention," Bam-Bam used to say, "because if you fuck this up, it will kill you." Every day Green Team battled the combined forces of Mr. Murphy and Mr. Darwin.

We attended survival schools for desert, woodland, and arctic environments. We learned how to take over ships at pierside and under way. We attended special driving schools, learning how to do bootlegs and J-turns, how to avoid roadblocks and vehicle ambushes. We also learned how to conduct the Pitt maneuver, an offensive driving technique used to knock other cars off the road. Much to the chagrin of our instructors, we kept these skills sharp on a series of rental cars. We were taught intelligence tradecraft, studying the arcana of dead drops, load signals, and countersurveillance. We took classes on the organization and tactics of the KGB, the East German *Stasi,* and the Cuban intelligence organization, the DGI (*Dirección General de Inteligencia*).

We learned to operate and field-strip each of the weapons we'd been issued, those and about a hundred others besides. We attended shooting schools, studying combat pistol craft and police shotgun technique from national champions like Rogers and Chapman. In an exercise called an El Presidente, we would stand, hands raised, pistols holstered, with our backs turned to three man-shaped silhouettes. On command, we would about-face, draw, fire two rounds into each target, reload, and fire two more rounds into the trio. I was considered fair at this. I could fire twelve shots and reload my weapon in just over five seconds. The best operator on the team could do it in four and a half.

Combat shooting differs qualitatively from traditional marksmanship. In normal rifle and pistol craft, shooters are taught to close one eye, relax, align the target, and squeeze the trigger slowly. To rush a shot is to cheat the process. Combat shooting is, by necessity, a hasty business. When people are shooting back at you, speed is life.

We were first taught to shoot from the ready position, squared toward the target, knees slightly bent, and weight forward on the toes, a position called "the modified isosceles." Our MP-5s were secured over the shoulder and to the chest by a special assault sling. When the weapon is raised to engage the target, the sling becomes another point of stability, like a third steadying hand. On the command to fire, we would snap off safe, fire two rounds in quick succession (called a "double tap"), snap the safety back on, and return to the ready position. Initially we shot at reactive targets, armored silhouettes and dish-sized head plates. The pinging of the bullets off the metal targets and the fleeting puff of lead spatter were instant feedback, a process called "point of impact/point of aim." Eye, hand, bullet, target, brain.

Combat shooting is dynamic, not static, and we did not spend much time shooting at stationary targets. We were taught to move and shoot, shoot and move and shoot, while the targets were moving. This required a different sort of aiming, completely unlike the target-focused techniques of long-distance marksmanship. We were taught to open both eyes, keeping the scan on and avoiding target lock. There is a bit of a trick to this, especially for marksmen used to shooting at bull's-eyes printed on paper targets. Most right-handed people are right-eye dominant, and most lefties favor their left eye. The dominant eye is better exercised and slightly more acute. In traditional marksmanship, the nondominant eye is closed. We learned a technique to gray out our nondominant eye, keeping it open but using our dominant eye to process the target and align the sights. The nondominant eye maintained peripheral vision, the location of the next target and the position of obstacles. Basically, one eye scanned and the other killed.

In order to shoot accurately, we still had to acquire a correct sight picture, front and rear sights aligned, target centered over the front sight post; but in combat shooting, this process is compressed into a split second. There is no time to squeeze the trigger slowly; it is pulled rapidly and evenly. You must subtly anticipate the weapon going off, and learn by feel your own reaction to the muzzle blast and the cycling of the gun. All of this is exactly contrary to long-distance marksmanship, in which shooters are taught to relax, regulate their breathing, and squeeze the trigger so gently that they are surprised when the weapon goes off.

We often aimed on the run, or popping up from behind obstacles. Compensation for the jerk of the trigger had to be built in to the target scan, the aiming, and the firing of the weapon. Working day and night, we became masters of the fast-targeting, rapid-fire skills of combat shooting. Everything we did was timed and scored, and Green Team got smaller in the first four weeks. The class was ranked in a ratio of hits over time. Those scoring in the lowest 20 percent of our class cleaned out their cages and returned to Planet Vanilla.

Our next task was to learn the science and art of CQB, close-quarters battle. Combat shooting is an individual event; CQB is a team sport. Like everything taught in SEAL Team, we learned component skills and gradually built up to operational capability.

Sometimes called "room clearance" or "surgical shooting," CQB was developed by the British SAS and put into practice in Northern Ireland. Counterterrorism is the science of *combating* terrorism, and CQB is the reason terrorists rarely seize buildings and hold hostages these days. It is the antidote to the hostage-barricade situation, whether the venue is a building, a cave, an airliner, an offshore oil platform, or a cruise ship. In the chaotic environment of a counterterrorism rescue, the mission is to secure the hostages and neutralize the terrorists. Discipline, teamwork, target discrimination, and exceptional marksmanship make this possible.

We would learn to shoot the bad guys from among the hostages in a place called the Kill House, an indoor 360-degree shooting facility. Movable walls allowed us to configure the range into multiple compartments, and we could make floor plans to match any target. We trained first in single rooms, shooting at man-sized printed silhouettes. Some targets were depicted holding weapons, some were hostages, some held weapons and police badges. After entering the room, we had to almost instantly scan, determine the threat, and either shoot or hold fire. We entered in teams of two, four, eight, and ten, and the targets were positioned differently each time. Sometimes the lights were on, sometimes they were off. We ran the target while instructors in the control booth pumped in disco fog and flashed strobe lights. Sometimes they blared music or jet-engine noise, and always, multiple video cameras taped us so the run could be played back in slow motion and analyzed.

Each of us fired tens of thousands of rounds, running scenarios as many as fifty times a day. When we were not in the Kill House, we shot next door in an elaborate cinematic target area. Our room targets became increasingly elaborate—furniture, couches, bookcases—and hidden bad guys were added. Stapled behind the critical areas of each target was a three-by-five index card marking kill areas on the human body. For every bullet we fired that missed a card, we had to buy a case of beer.

We were soon engaging targets in multiple-room scenarios. This required an extemporaneous flow of shooters through the operational area. Room clearance requires precision, an almost Zenlike awareness of the situation, and complete mastery of the weapon. Shooting pairs grouped and split up as the Team surged through hallways and rooms. It is at this "flow through target" that SEAL Team Six is unmatched. The extreme level of training makes this possible. It is not enough to say that we practiced multiple-room clearance. In one year the operators of SEAL Six fire more bullets than the entire United States Marine Corps. We weren't just *good* at multiple-room CQ; there is no one in the world who comes close.

As our skills coalesced, the targets became more varied and elaborate. We trained on airliners, ships, and offshore oil and gas facilities. We practiced on buses and passenger trains.

Our training evolutions became full mission profiles, with the officers of Green Team each responsible for planning and briefing operations under the watchful eye of Court and his minions. In these highly realistic training evolutions, the bad guys continued to be paper silhouettes, but the hostages were real, breathing human beings. Scattered through the targets—just as hostages would be—the volunteers were service members, members of the joint command, and sometimes they were Washington VIPs, secretaries, senators, and representatives. It was our job to penetrate, neutralize the terrorists, secure the hostages, and extract. We trained to do this all using real bullets and live breeching explosives. In Green Team, like in the real world, there was no margin for error.

There was not one operational readiness exam but two dozen. Every combination of insertion and extraction method imaginable was married to differing target sets. A big-city SWAT team has the luxury of jumping on a bus and driving to the target. We were training for operations that would take place in denied areas, an enemy's backyard. We would have to sneak in and liberate the hostages, and we would have to fight our way out. The training operations reflected this. In eight months we operated in every environment and across every SEAL mission: direct action, reconnaissance and surveillance, operations against infrastructure, counterterrorism, and hostage rescue. Sean, Moose, Rick, and I each planned, briefed, and led half a dozen missions. Failure in a training op was grounds for instant dismissal. Over half of us hung on, and eight months after we'd started, we twelve graduated after a raucous celebration on an offshore oil rig we had just "captured."

The night of our last op happened to be Traylor Court's birthday and his last day at the command. In the SEALs, there is one thing you hide from your brothers at all times: the date of your birth, because SEAL Team birthday celebrations are not pleasant. One of the Green Team instructors had leaked that it was Court's birthday, and we made sure it would be a special event. As soon as the oil platform was in our hands, together with the Green Team instructors, we turned on Court, handcuffed him, and duct-taped him to a chair.

There was a brief trial of the kangaroo variety. Charges of inhumanity, cruelty to tadpoles, impersonating a baboon, and a few other capital offenses were read. Having been found instantly guilty, Court was sentenced to a shot or a shot: After each successive charge, he was allowed to choose between a shot of peppermint schnapps, injected into his mouth from a veterinary syringe, or being shot with one of the wax bullets we used for hostage training. I'm not sure which was worse; the wax bullets were propelled by a .38-caliber pistol cartridge primer, and they hurt like hell. Of course, peppermint schnapps hurts, too. After about a dozen rounds of each, Court was released from bondage, given a pardon signed by King Neptune himself, and carried to the oil platform's flight deck to be taken back to shore. The dozen shots of schnapps had taken their toll. As we waited for the helicopter, Court had to be twice prevented from demonstrating what he called his Tarzan swan dive from the flight deck. It took half a dozen guys to get him on the helo and strap him into a seat. Court was toast, but we were finished, and when we returned to Virginia, we'd be assigned to operational elements.

Green Team was over. We were Jedi at last.

Well, almost.

HIGH SPEED, LOW DRAG

THE TRIP FROM GREEN TEAM to the operational side of the house was like a trip to the moon. Although we had been aboard for eight months, we had been cloistered from the rest of the command. We had an idea what to expect operationally—Court and the Green Team cadre had seen to that—but nothing could prepare us for what we would find politically. SEAL Six was the creation of Dick Marcinko, and it still bore the strong imprint of his character. As we reported to our assault-group assignments, the spectre of Demo Dick wandered the passageways like Marley's ghost.

Under Dick Marcinko, SEAL Team Six was a rigid meritocracy married to the worst sort of personality cult. Marcinko had been a Mustang, and although he was a commander, a senior member of the community, and the captain of the Team, he had little use for officers. Under his tenure, there was a faux sort of equality. Everyone was equal, with those attached longest to Marcinko being more equal than others.

Since the days of Mob Six, Marcinko had kept alive a spirit of devotion to the leader, deliberately marginalizing and undercutting the commissioned officers. He was in the habit of replacing assault-group commanders often, and canning them instantly if they conflicted with the senior chiefs or him. All wires led to Marcinko, patriarch, commanding officer, and burning bush.

To his credit, Marcinko valued operational skill above any other attribute save loyalty, and at Six everybody operated; everybody shot, swam, and jumped, from the captain on down.

Failure was not an option, and Marcinko pushed himself as hard as he pushed his operators. Although this system would not tolerate cake-eaters like my buddy Skip, it brokered no dissent. There was one opinion, and that was Marcinko's. This sort of royal-court organization prompted genuine devotion, but it also brought out the worst portions of cronyism, backstabbing, and flattery.

After Marcinko's less than graceful departure, Bob Gormly did much to change things, gaining control of the most unruly elements, cutting out deadwood, and curbing a bit of the cowboyism that was rampant under the old regime. He had led SEAL Team Six into Grenada and through the command's baptism of fire, a turning point for naval special warfare. Six had spectacular successes, leavened by tragedy; before the opening of hostilities, four SEALs were lost conducting an at-sea rendezvous. The loss was made bitter because of its futility. On the ground in Grenada, SEAL Six more than proved its mettle. The rescue of Governor General Schoone and the operation against the transmitter site of Radio Free Grenada are epics in the annals of special warfare. Under Bob Gormly, Six had shown it was worth its salt.

Though Bob Gormly's stamp was on the command, Marcinko's legacy clung stubbornly. Following Green Team, Sean, Moose, Rick, and I were sent to different assault groups. Each unit had played a differing role in Grenada, and each had a unique character and ethos. As senior officer, Sean was given charge of an assault group. His task as a walk-on was not easy. He was a nonparticipant in Grenada, so he had an uphill struggle asserting command. But the fight would be well rewarded. Under Sean's steady leadership, his group would later play a pivotal role in capturing the hijackers of *Achille Lauro*.

Moose and Rick were assigned to an assault group that called themselves the Pirates. The skull and crossbones was proudly on display in their offices, and the Pirates were perhaps the toughest and most clannish of all the assault groups in SEAL Team Six. They had overthrown several officers but had performed valiantly in Grenada and were second to none in operational capability. The Pirates were commanded at the time by an extremely talented and dedicated officer named Bo. He was a former Army ranger and a guy who led by example. Moose and Rick were in good company.

I was detailed to the third assault group, under the command of a hard-bitten gunslinger named Johnny King. Johnny was a fellow Mississippian, but in style and temperament, we could not have been more different. Johnny was from upstate, a little town outside of Tupelo, far from the moderating breezes, French wines and cheeses of the Gulf Coast. He was opinionated, rough around the edges, and he did things his way. The term "badass redneck" might be a bit delicate. As I checked in to the Team, one of my future boat-crew members gave me a heads-up in Spanish: *"Es un hombre duro."* He's a hard man.

I was soon to learn this outfit had a talent for understatement.

Hard case or not, Johnny King was one of the bravest and best officers I ever served with. Johnny was a stickler, and his assault group was perhaps the most squared-away unit on the Team. Johnny's world was SEAL Team Six, and his purpose in life was the mission of the Team.

"Boys, we're here to kill Tangos," he used to say, "Tango" being the phonetic designator and pejorative for "terrorist." Twisted by Johnny's Mississippi drawl, "Tango" became a three-syllable word. The extra syllable seemed to go into some sort of revolving account, because just as often Johnny would cut a syllable out. Like saying "High-why" instead of "Hawaii," and "Chine-ee" instead of "Chinese." When he found out I was from Biloxi, he said, "Boy, what happened to the way you talk?"

The other officer in my assault group was Ed Summers. He was from Florida and had been a former Professional Karate Association full-contact kickboxing champion. He was a great guy, extremely direct, even crusty, and one of the best shooters and athletes on the Team. Ed was in special warfare for the long haul, having served as a SEAL platoon commander and SDV pilot before coming to Six. Like Johnny,

Ed would have a distinguished and storied career in spec war. After a lengthy stint at Six, he would go on to command my alma mater, SEAL Team Four. On his own, Ed would have been a hard-ass extraordinaire, but in the shadow of Johnny King, he seemed as affable as Mr. Rogers.

The assault group's chief petty officer was Chuck Mc-Gregor. In the olden days at Six, the chiefs were Marcinko's henchmen. Chuck McGregor was nobody's toady, and he didn't look like a chief at all. Chiefs in the navy are usually grizzled and thick about the middle. Chuck looked like a twenty-year-old California surf dude. He was possibly the sole person on the Team who did not philander, blaspheme, drink, or use tobacco. He was a devout Christian, carried a Bible in his briefcase, and often said things like "Darn it."

As you might imagine, a person like this might be subject to a bit of ribbing. In Chuck's case, you'd be wrong. Chuck was plank owner, one of the original members of Mob Six, and although his personality and lifestyle might have been anomalous, he was here, quite simply, because he was one of the best operators in naval special warfare. He was the best athlete among a command full of triathletes; he'd climbed El Capitan twice; he'd served in Grenada; and he could outrun, outswim, and outshoot every one of his potential detractors. He was like a Boy Scout among a gang of cutthroats, and he would become one of my closest friends in the command. When we operated together, we used the call sign Chuck Squared.

I settled into the place I had been detailed. "Detailed" is the word, because during my first months on the operational team, I was a boat-crew member, a spear-carrier, and nothing else. Johnny could have cared less that I'd had combat service, and he could hardly have given a shit about my tours in Central America. As in my formal probation following BUD/S, I would have to prove I was worth following before I would be assigned to lead. Johnny seemed to view me as an experimental piece of equipment shipped from some far-off navy laboratory: He decided to plug me in and wait to see if I'd catch fire before he used me for real.

For my first six weeks on-line, I had no authority and little more responsibility in the assault group than to suit up, show up, and shut up. Even as Bob Gormly put the Team back under the chain of command, the meritocracy raged in Johnny King's outfit. I bristled a bit—I was being paid by the navy to lead, not follow—but I suffered my second probation with good humor. Green Team had taught me that I had a lot to learn.

The command was on a war footing, and the operational tempo was high. In addition to standing by for real-world contingencies, we had a lot of deployments and exercises. When we weren't on the road or in the bush, we were in the Kill House, shooting. The exercises were hardly a break. The consequences of failing at even a practice mission were still dire, and each evolution was planned, briefed, and executed precisely. Gradually, I was allowed to contribute to the briefing process and then to the planning cycle. I still held no position of authority. In exercises we operated against a variety of targets—ships, airplanes, buildings, and infrastructure targets—sometimes in concert with other units and sometimes on our own. The draft from my Green Team was integrated into boat-crew assignments.

It was not until a training deployment to Puerto Rico that I would be incorporated into the command structure of the assault group. The trip was a cakewalk: three weeks in Roosevelt Roads, combat-swimmer training, and jungle work on Isla Peros. I was assigned to put the trip together, almost as busywork, and I guess I finally managed to impress somebody. I prepared a week and a half of combat-swimmer training, finding an ex-Liberty ship for us to practice maritime sabotage and ship boarding on, and I put together essentially the same jungle course we'd taught in Honduras. It was like being in the cadre of SEAL Four all over again. Following the trip, Johnny called me into his office one morning after PT. "I'm placing boat crews Four, Five, and Six under you," he said. "I'm gonna try you out as an assault-element commander. You go tell your guys."

I thanked him and walked out, not exactly feeling vindicated or even trusted. He'd made it clear that I was on a test-drive, and if he wasn't happy, I would have a short future as a lieutenant spear-carrier. I rounded up the guys and told them of the reorganization. By accident or design, I'd been put with three of the Spanish speakers, Alex, Hoser, and Luis, as well as two of the surfers. Operationally, we had some depth. Alex was a veteran of the radio-station op and a breaching and demolition expert. Hoser was a veteran of the Chuting Stars, the navy's parachute team, and was our sky god, air-operations boss. Stick and Coyote were the heavy-weapons guys; Toad was our lead climber; Mike was our engineering and boat expert; and Doc Luke was our resident wiseass-cum-hospital corpsman. Like Alex, Luke was a veteran of the radio-station op and an *hombre duro.* At our end of the compound, there were more Hawaiian shirts than polo shirts, more reggae than country-and-western, and we all had it in for fried plantains, *arroz con pollo,* and jungle work. The Rastamen were born. I would command this assault element for three years, under two different group commanders, and serve with the Rastas until the day I left the service.

Although I settled in at once with the Rastamen, it took a slow while to feel like I was part of the Team. Compartmentalization was still part of our lives. I'd see Sean and Moose daily when they were not deployed, but work was not often talked about, even at work. The assault groups had different assignments, and information was kept in separate pipelines. It might seem odd, but if you returned to snowy Virginia in the middle of February with a tropical suntan, no one would ask where you'd been. The entire place was on a need-to-know basis. When we operated together, we were briefed together; when we operated separately, the information was kept separate as well.

The secrecy sometimes approached the ridiculous. Once Ed and I briefed the captain of a ship we were to exercise against. Our orders and our in-house printed business cards said that we were civilian contractors working for the nonexistent equipment-testing unit. In the coordinating briefing, Ed and I described the conduct of our mock attack. Four pairs of swimmers using rebreathers would attach simulated magnetic mines to the hull, propellers, and shafts of the destroyer while it was anchored off Mayport, Florida. Two other swim pairs would board the ship and body-snatch (that is, kidnap) two of the ship's officers. As we described the operation, the captain kept looking at our business cards. The exercise didn't seem like equipment testing. Finally, he asked Ed, "What command are you guys with?"

Ed answered crisply, "You're not authorized to ask that question."

The exercise went off; six mines were planted on the ship while the crew maintained a constant security patrol on deck. Much to the amazement of the captain, his chief engineer and weapons officer were missing at the conclusion of the exercise. They had been grabbed out of their staterooms by our swim pairs, bound, gagged, and spirited over the side. They were returned to him the following morning, dripping wet, grinning, and sworn to secrecy. It was just another night of testing equipment.

While our activities were cloaked to the world at large, we were fairly open with family. Margot had attended an SO (significant other) briefing given by the Team. She knew I was still in the SEALs, and she was told that there were covers in place. She was also cautioned not to make known any of the details of my work, and that under no circumstances, even in the event of my injury or death, was she to speak to the press. She took the warnings in stride, like she took everything else. Margot was a trooper.

Our assault group conducted training operations all over the country, moving men and equipment surreptitiously, landing air force C-141s at civilian airports in the dead of night and off-loading our unmarked trucks and SUVs. We were issued in-state license plates for our vehicles, and our visits were always coordinated with local law-enforcement and state police agencies. Before we went out the door, we were briefed on the counterintelligence and operational security picture. Every deployment and exercise had a cover for movement, a cover for action, and a cover for status. All hands were briefed with answers to who we were, why we were there, and what we were doing. None of these answers had anything to do with SEAL Team training.

The cover stories and secrecy had an effect. We all became glib liars, able to use aliases, deflect questions, and deal out misinformation. The real world became a mirage. We avoided "regular people," or duped them outright. We seldom operated in the same area twice in a year, and if we did, we took great pains with our cover stories, so that we built up a "legend"—a plausible excuse for our repeat appearances. One of my favorite covers was that we were NFL alumni attending a billfishing tournament. Try telling that story inconspicuously in a bar full of sports fans.

We kept the cover stories sharp because we all knew that Lenny and Dougie were never far behind. During and after our excursions, they would sniff around, asking questions of desk clerks and bartenders, assessing the footprint we'd left. If a front organization or cover story was punctured— meaning if someone figured out or even guessed we were SEALs—Lenny and Dougie would make sure casual or determined questions were stonewalled. They were also there to finger the guilty. Any operator who violated security or blew a cover was immediately shown the door. Off duty, they were great guys, but it was their job to bust our chops. We kept a low profile.

Sean, Moose, and I continued to be close, and we hung out off duty whenever we could. Like the rest of the command, we became habitués of the Raven. It was then a slightly down-market bar and grill on the south end of Virginia Beach. It was orders of magnitude nicer than the Casino, and the waitresses, called Ravenettes, were all local belles. Although a constant tide of tourists washed in and out, the Raven's steady customers were members of SEAL Team Six. We all drank there, and we drank a lot. All SEAL Teams are hard-partying outfits, and Six led the way. Naval special warfare is no place for the weak of heart, limb, or liver. We worked hard and played harder. Hangovers were puked up at the side of the road following the morning run, swim, and obstacle course.

The new-friends rule and the benevolent snooping of Lenny and Dougie kept the operators at Six to themselves. The social circle included fellow Sixers and the small number of wives and girlfriends. The planet may have been our AO, but our world just got smaller and smaller.

Margot and I bought a three-bedroom house in a cookie-cutter development at the south end of Virginia Beach. It was soon furnished and somewhat decorated. Our home was comfortable, and we entertained often. Moose and Sean were frequent guests, and we often had "lost weekend" parties, drunken barbecues that went on for days. I was, I will admit, not the greatest of husbands, but Margot and I seldom argued; she continued to love me, and I continued to need her. My work was kept in separate compartments, and so was my life. On the road I frequently cheated on her, wowing the babe of the night with the sailboat story or the working cover, depending on my mood. They were one-night stands, and then I was gone. I felt guilty, but not enough to stop fooling around. Perhaps I had become one of those people who needs to be loved too badly. I lied as well at home as I did on the road. When I returned home, my adultery, like everything else, was stuffed into a compartment. The compartments, I thought, were airtight. It would be a long time before I learned how much lies cost.

I was away from home a great deal, and often called away unexpectedly. Margot and I developed a sort of silent code. If the trip was planned in advance, I would conspicuously pack my civilian clothes and leave my kit bag open on our bed. Wool sweaters for a two-week trip in August would give her at least an idea that I was heading to colder climes. Likewise, packing a dozen Hawaiian shirts in the dead of winter would tell her I was bound for someplace sunny. Some trips were unannounced, but I would try to give Margot a warning. If I called home from work and left the message "I'll pick up something on the way home for dinner," she knew not to expect me for a week. For Margot the trips were doubly hard—she did not know where I was, and I couldn't telephone her while I was deployed. She would often try to figure out where I was by watching CNN.

Most of the time she was right.

FULL MISSION PROFILE

IN A WORLD WHERE TERRORIST ACTS were all too ordinary, Mohamed Abul Abbas prided himself on innovation. Known to the world as Abu Abbas, he was a member of the executive council of the PLO, a confidant of Yasser Arafat, and the leader of the Palestine Liberation Front (PLF). Abu Abbas would go on to mastermind glider-borne assaults against Israel and pioneer the use of armed speedboats to attack swimmers and vacationers on Tel Aviv beaches. Abbas was nothing if not creative. With Arafat's go-ahead, he selected four operatives to carry out the most ambitious terrorist act of his career.

The man chosen to lead this operation was Youssef Magied al-Molqi. Al-Molqi was not bright, but he was brutal and eager. Like the glider attacks and the speedboats, this operation would bear the hallmark of Abbas's harebrained grasp of tactics. Ill-conceived and messily executed, Abbas's latest brainchild would be a dead-end operation that would end in failure. That probably didn't occur to al-Molqi, and it didn't matter to Abbas—he would direct the attack from the safety of a hotel suite.

Their target was the Italian cruise liner *Achille Lauro*. The vessel was nearly as sorry as the men who would seize her. If you were looking for a jinxed ship, *Achille Lauro* would fit the bill. Six hundred and thirty feet long, she entered service in 1947 as *Willem Ruys,* sailing for the K. R. Lloyd line. She plied the Rotterdam-Jakarta route and then the transatlantic trade, all without success. She was sold to the shipping magnate Achille Lauro in 1964 and renamed for her new owner.

It is said that to rename a ship is to invite bad luck, but somebody must have forgotten to tell Signor Lauro. Soon after she was renamed, *Achille Lauro* was rent by an explosion and fire. It would be the first of many calamities. In 1972 the ship was involved in a collision at sea that would sink the livestock carrier *Yousset*. Nor was all the trouble nautical. Lauro Lines was soon in financial straits, and in 1982 *Achille Lauro* would be seized for debt in Tenerife, Spain. By the mid-1980s the ship was a faded princess reduced to churning out cut-rate cruises in the Med.

On October 7, 1985, Youssef al-Molqi and three accomplices—Ibrahim Abdel Atif, Ahmed al-Hassani, and Bassam al-Asker—came aboard *Achille Lauro* in Alexandria, Egypt. Most of the ship's 670 passengers had debarked at Alexandria for a day trip to the pyramids. By late morning *Achille Lauro* weighed anchor and headed out into the Mediterranean, cruising off the coast of Egypt and intending to return that evening to retrieve the day-trippers. As the ship steamed out of Alexandria, al-Molqi and his buddies retired to their second-class cabins and waited.

Remaining aboard the cruise liner were approximately 90 passengers and a mostly Italian and Portuguese crew of 340. Ten of the passengers were American; among these were sixty-nine-year-old Leon Klinghoffer and his wife, Marilyn. While *Achille Lauro* dawdled off the Egyptian coast, al-Molqi's accomplices burst into the main dining salon, spraying machine-gun fire into the ceiling. The word was flashed to the bridge that armed men had seized control of the ship.

Thus began al-Molqi's short career as a pirate.

THE FIRST CLUE the world had of any trouble was a distress call received by a radio station in Gothenburg, Sweden. Before communications were lost with the ship, her captain, Gerardo de Rosa, managed to send one brief message. The news story of the hijacking was soon flashed around the world.

In the operations shop at SEAL Team Six, CNN was constantly playing on a TV angled in a corner, and it was from

CNN, instead of any official message traffic, that SEAL Team Six learned of the incident. In the hours following the hijacking, we remained at standby. There was no notice from the joint command to deploy or to move to a heightened alert status. Although we hung on every tidbit fed us by CNN, higher-ups first thought that this was an Italian ship and an Italian problem.

The prime minister of Italy at the time, socialist Bettino Craxi, refused early offers of help from the Reagan administration. While the Italian government indicated that it was prepared to use force to retake the ship, it saw negotiation as its best opportunity with the hijackers. That might have been a viable course of action; the Italian naval commandos with whom we would soon be working did not make much of an impression. Truth be told, the Italians had no forces or assets capable of retaking the ship. Their only choice was appeasement.

Sometime in the early evening, the information evolved that there were American citizens aboard the ship. They were clearly in danger. Craxi's firm refusal of help no longer mattered. Under international law, the United States is within its rights to board and seize a vessel under the control of pirates, and the decision was made to deploy SEAL Team Six.

Our load-out went flawlessly. The command had deployed on several real-world operations and frequently practiced recall drills. Within a short period of time, the entire command was staged at a naval air station close to the Team area. There we waited—interminably, it would turn out—for the air force to show up with transports. Several more precious hours passed while we sat at the end of a blacked-out runway amid piles and pallets of gear. Like everyone else at the command, I was fuming. But I wasn't as mad as Moose, who had been detailed to Rome to serve as the joint command's liaison with the American embassy. It was an important assignment—he would advise the ambassador directly—but he knew it would put him far from the action. He looked deflated as he left for his plane.

In southeast Virginia the night of Monday, October 7, was

cool and misty. There was a restrained sort of eagerness among the gaggle of shooters waiting for the plane. This was a mission the Team had been created for. It was one we knew we could accomplish. We could not know as we waited that this operation would end exactly as it had begun—sitting in confusion on a darkened runway. It would be the wee hours of Tuesday, October 8, before the first of several air force transports touched down and dropped their ramps.

As the planes carrying the Team headed east, a plan was developed to retake the ship. Briefed as the immediate-action contingency, SEAL Team Six was prepared to step from the plane and move directly against the target. This plan was sound and would have worked. But finding our target would be another matter, because *Achille Lauro* had vanished somewhere in the eastern Mediterranean.

Soon after the hijackers had shot up the dining room, they ordered the ship north. Although Captain de Rosa had bravely managed to slip out the one message, the terrorists had stationed armed men on the bridge of the ship and ordered radio silence. The captain had no choice but to obey. As *Achille Lauro* steamed north, Captain de Rosa knew his ship had become a needle in a haystack.

Sixth Fleet aircraft scoured the entire eastern Med looking for the hijacked cruise liner, to no avail. As the planes carrying SEAL Team Six neared the Mediterranean staging base, the terrorists made their presence known. Announcing that they were members of the Palestine Liberation Front, they demanded the release of fifty compatriots being held in Israeli jails. They also requested entrance to the port of Tartus, Syria, where, it was suspected, they would be reinforced.

To the shock of al-Molqi and the consternation of Abu Abbas, the ship was refused entry into Syrian waters. Syrian president Hafez Assad, never a man adverse to terrorism, had based his decision on political rather than humanitarian considerations. At the time, the Syrian leader was estranged from Yasser Arafat. When the hijackers identified themselves as members of the PLF, a faction close to Arafat, President Assad saw his chance to jab his sometime ally.

This put al-Molqi in an increasingly dangerous position. The hijackers knew that the ship could be retaken. They continued to make threats, and set a three P.M. deadline. To show their earnestness, the hijackers selected twenty passengers and sat them in a circle on one of the decks. They knew these hostages would be visible to aircraft. Three P.M. came and went.

Leon Klinghoffer had been among the passengers selected for the circle. The terrorists found it difficult to roll Mr. Klinghoffer's wheelchair up the stairs to join the others, so they left him on a lower deck. Sometime after three, al-Molqi decided it was time to send a message. He clomped down the ladder way to Klinghoffer. Point-blank, al-Molqi fired two bullets into the man in the wheelchair, one round into his chest and a second into his head. Al-Molqi then waved his gun at two crewmen and had them toss Klinghoffer's corpse into the sea. The wheelchair was tossed over after him.

Intercepted communications between the terrorists and associates in Tartus and Genoa revealed to the gathering American assault forces that the terrorists' plan was in some disarray. The Syrians still adamantly refused them entry into Tartus, and the PLO was coming to the realization that the operation was headed for a ditch. Abu Abbas ordered the terrorists to return to Port Said, Egypt, expressly commanding that no further passengers be harmed.

This was an interesting contradiction. Although the terrorists claimed that all the passengers were safe, Captain de Rosa had radioed the port authorities in Tartus that one passenger had been murdered. All these communications were monitored, and intelligence data was communicated to the assault force in real time. As night fell over the Med, *Achille Lauro* slipped to the south. She went into radio silence and again disappeared.

The Rastas, along with our three assault groups, were now staged in a hangar in the eastern Med. We'd all been here before. The Team had made several real-world deployments to this base, often to be pulled back at the last second. We called these operations Gerbil Cages because they made us feel like rodents running on a treadmill. As the politicians hemmed and hawed, many of us began to think this op, too, would be another gerbil killer.

We were shielded from much of the political wrangling, and that was just as well. Moose, however, was in the middle of it. As the American ambassador blew a gasket, Craxi's government dithered. The Italians clearly wanted to cut a deal with the PLO. But now an American citizen had been murdered; for Ronald Reagan and General Carl Stiner, the commander of the joint special operations task force, a deal was out of the question. The Team was assembled, the fist was clenched, we were ready to strike.

The only problem was, we had no idea where to hit. Incredibly, *Achille Lauro,* a six-hundred-foot floating hotel, continued to elude the entire United States Navy. She would be missing for most of the night.

Earlier in the fall, Johnny King had been replaced as my group commander, and Ed Summers was kicked upstairs into operations. Our new group leader was Archie Lane. Old Arch and I did not always see eye to eye, but our working arrangement functioned well. Archie gave a lot of attention to the higher-ups, which left me to handle the jobs he didn't want to do and the day-to-day operation of our group. The lads called Archie the Watcher, because if the mission involved getting wet, we did the op and Archie watched.

I was assisting the ops guys with paperwork when Ed Summers called me over. "What are you working on?" he asked.

"Loss-of-communication plans," I said. It was a bullshit job, one that could be done by a monkey with a box of crayons.

"Well, start on this." He handed me a piece of paper. It read: "Bridge and 0-1 level."

"The op is a go," he said. "Your assault element is going to take down the bridge." It would be the Rastas' job to attack the bridge of the ship and take back the radio rooms and communications facilities adjoining the pilothouse. It was the nexus of the entire operation. "You're a lucky fuck," he said. "We're launching at 2100 hours tonight, just after dark. You need to brief-back the skipper and General Stiner in two hours."

Ed walked away. My first task would be to coordinate the flight packages of the several helicopters, troop carriers, and sniper birds that would deliver the Rastas to the ship. A second flight of helicopters, led by Archie, was to clear the lido deck and the cabins and salons farther aft. The other assault groups would take down the engineering spaces, then search and clear the ship's crew quarters and public areas.

I had the most straightforward and simple portion of an amazingly complex and tricky mission. Though it was basic, my piece of the operation needed to be thought out. I was certain we would run into bad guys when we attacked the bridge. I was equally certain that innocent crew members would be in the pilothouse. The good and the bad would have to be sorted out by the Rastas.

At this time the terrorists claimed to have twenty men aboard *Achille Lauro*. We estimated that, including sleepers (hijackers who were deliberately blended with the hostages), they might have as many as forty. Our estimates were extremely high and reflected American cognitive dissonance. We all knew what it would take to seize a ship; our extrapolations were based on our own experience. We thought we would need a minimum of twenty men. We believed, wrongly, that no one would be so stupid as to attempt a hijacking with only four shooters.

It turns out we grossly overestimated the intelligence and tactical acumen of the PLO. Thinking they might even know what they were doing, we planned for heavy resistance. And we planned to blow their shit away.

We continued to refine and brief the assault, but we had little hard data on the target. What we lacked most were plans for or even pictures of the ship. As we thrashed about on the second iteration, the deliberate attack, no one at SEAL Six even knew what *Achille Lauro* looked like.

Using a clip videotaped from an Italian news broadcast,

we had a general idea by midafternoon. The ship's markings were white over blue, and she wore a white star on each of her two aggressively raked funnels. Her lines were lean and low, and despite the modern air put on by her smokestacks, she was old, laid down on a design put to paper in 1938.

The sum total of our initial hard copy was one threefold eight-by-ten travel brochure. With the help of a couple of the Team's more artistic shooters, I set about preparing a line drawing of the ship. The drawing was assembled by picking out details of naval architecture from the tiny photos in the brochure. There were lots of pictures of women in bathing caps and waist-high 1950s-era bikinis, but damn few shots of what we really wanted: photos of the bridge and the positions of masts, antennas, and weather decks.

For planning purposes, we had to have not just a sketch but something approaching a scale drawing. In order to fly helicopters around the ship at night, we needed estimates of the height of various masts and the size of decks. I broke out a pair of dividers and was glad I'd paid attention in seventh-grade drafting class. Scaling up from the known size of an internationally approved lifeboat, thirty feet, we were able to estimate dimensions and clearances from the photographs. We soon cobbled together a few sets of working sketches, and these were used for the initial planning briefs.

There was a moment of mirth when a contingent of Italian naval commandos arrived at the hangar. Nattily attired in flight suits and mirrored shades, they all had matching ascots. But they had arrived with a set of ship's plans. I was standing next to General Stiner when he struck a deal with the Italians. He offered to take them along on the operation and keep them out of the action. In exchange for the plans, the Americans would recover the ship, but the Italians would get the credit. The arrangement would be our little secret.

The plans quickly changed hands.

Using the diagrams, we were able to verify the dimensions of our sketches. The plans were undated, and the brochure showed several modifications not depicted in the drawings. *Achille Lauro* had been frequently modified, if for no other reason than to repair collision and fire damage. We had no way to know which was more recent, the pamphlet or the blueprints, so we amended the diagrams for worst case. All of the assault groups soon had deck and compartment drawings with which to plan their assaults.

I briefed the Rastas on the conduct of the bridge takedown, and we attended a general meeting to coordinate our actions with those of the other assault groups. The afternoon wore on, and as the sun slipped down, we inspected weapons and gear and rehearsed on floor plans marked out with tape on the hangar floor. We were ready.

And that's when they pulled the plug.

Achille Lauro had again been found. This time she was heading south in Egyptian territorial waters. Though the ship was still within our grasp, Washington made the decision not to launch the rescue. It was one thing to seize the vessel on the high seas; it was another to do it in broad daylight, under the nose of a putative and touchy ally. Apparently, Washington did not want to offend one of its few Arab friends.

The hijackers sought refuge in the anchorage outside of Port Said, a decision that saved their lives. I have no doubt that come nightfall SEAL Team Six would have reached *Achille Lauro* undetected. Once we were aboard, al-Molqi and his friends would have been as good as dead.

Even as we stood down, events in Cairo put the terrorists farther from our reach. It was announced that the hijackers had agreed to surrender to Egyptian authorities at 4:20 P.M. The surrender was "without preconditions," but a deal had been struck. Soon after the ship anchored, the Egyptian foreign ministry let loose with the first of a series of outright lies and half-truths. The foreign minister stated that all the hostages were safe and that the terrorists had left the ship and were now headed out of Egypt.

Standing around a TV in the hangar, we watched a CNN news clip showing the hijackers being taken ashore in an Egyptian navy patrol boat. It was hard not to feel defeated as we watched them mug and flash victory signs for the camera. They looked like college kids who'd pulled a prank.

In the hours after the terrorists had left the ship, international news organizations began reporting that the hijackers had murdered a hostage. The Egyptians backpedaled fast. President Hosni Mubarak told a credulous set of reporters that the hijackers had left Egypt and that he was not sure where they had gone.

They were in fact at an Egyptian air base, sitting at that moment aboard an EgyptAir 737. Arafat and Abbas were ass-deep in negotiations, trying to find a country that would accept the hijackers. They initially had no takers, but at last Tunisia agreed. Just south of Sicily and to the west of Libya, Tunisia is a moderate Arab state and home of the PLO's headquarters. It was probably with some sense of relief that Abu Abbas joined al-Molqi and the others aboard the 737. Also accompanying them were about ten members of Egypt's counterterrorism unit, Force 777, and an Egyptian intelligence officer. Their getaway was almost complete. Abbas and his thugs had every reason to believe that in a few hours they would be in Tunis, farting through silk.

Unbeknownst to Abbas, and unimagined by Hosni Mubarak, the NSA heard every word of the negotiations. They knew Mubarak had detailed a state-owned airliner to evacuate the murderers. They knew Abbas had joined the hijackers. They knew the destination was Tunisia. They even knew the tail number of the aircraft—2843.

On the evening of October 9, SEAL Team Six's aircraft departed from the forward staging base, heading west across the Med toward home. Aboard our aircraft were Captain Gormly and the operations staff of SEAL Six. The mood aboard the plane was somber. It looked to all hands like another Gerbil Cage, and no one was happy about it. The medical officers passed out sleeping pills for the long trip home. We called the capsules "doggie downers"; they were ass kickers, but I was too wound up to sleep. I was too wound up even to be put to sleep. I slipped my pill into the pocket of my flight suit and tried to read a book.

I could not concentrate. Like everyone else on the plane, I felt that we had been ready to go, and that even if we could not have prevented the murder of Leon Klinghoffer, we certainly could have retaken the ship. As if it had not occurred to me before, I weighed the fact that like the rest of the world, we danced to the tune of the politicians. Bettino Craxi had been powerless against a gang of criminals and had looked for the easiest way out. Mubarak, too, wanted no trouble with the PLO. He was not above lying to the world to allow the murderers to escape. The dance went on.

Maybe twenty minutes into our flight, we found out that we were still dancing. Word reached us that F-14 Tomcat fighters from U.S.S. *Saratoga* would soon intercept the EgyptAir 737. The plane would be forced to land at the U.S.-Italian air base at Sigonella, Sicily. We were back in the game.

Sean's C-141 was diverted to Sigonella. His assault group would be responsible for setting security on the airplane once it was down, and preventing it from taking off. Our C-141 would land directly behind the 737, take custody of the criminals, and return them to the United States. No one on our aircraft expected the terrorists to come peaceably, and we geared up to assault the 737, an operation we had rehearsed many times. As soon as we were told what was going on, about a dozen guys lined up at the plane's single toilet to vomit up their sleeping pills. It was simple luck that I had not taken mine.

As we closed in on Sigonella, we were updated constantly. We were told that aboard the 737 were all four of the suspects, along with Abu Abbas. He was to be captured as well. We were told that aboard the plane were approximately a dozen armed Egyptian "secret service" officers. There was a very brief discussion of the SEAL Six rules of engagement. They remained in effect. Once we were sent in to capture the terrorists, armed resisters, Egyptian or Palestinian, would be met with deadly force.

We were informed when the Tomcats made intercept, and fifteen minutes from touchdown, the lights in the troop compartment switched to red. The order was passed to lock and load. The clatter of dozens of charging weapons rattled in the ocher light. I threaded a magazine into my MP-5, drew back the charging handle, and knocked it loose with the heel of my hand. We sat adjusting to night vision, tense, jacked up, waiting.

When the 737 touched down on the runway, we landed seconds behind it. The Rastas were the first assault element off the airplane. As we piled onto the tarmac, I detailed two shooters to remain constantly with Captain Gormly. Not that he needed protection: The skipper was in assault gear. Bo's group quickly deployed to the left rear of the 737, and the Rastas and the rest of our group were assembled directly off the tail. We knelt on the tarmac and waited.

The 737 sat just ahead, its nose wheel blocked by a truck. Captain Gormly headed forward to link up with Sean, who'd established a command post behind the aircraft. Sean's group had surrounded the plane, and he had snipers deployed to observe and cover it.

The EgyptAir 737 blazed with light, and the noise from its ground power unit was a loud whine. Behind us, a second C-141 landed and came to a stop with its engines running. The several jet engines made hearing difficult. Although the runway was black around us, lights from hangars and taxiways quickly washed out our night vision. As we prepared to attack the 737, we were deaf and almost blind.

General Stiner alighted from the second C-141 and trotted forward to meet Captain Gormly. They contacted the 737 on the ground-control frequency and were told by the pilot that there was an Egyptian ambassador aboard who wished to speak to them. Thus would commence a terse and sometimes heated series of arguments. I did not see or hear much of the discussions. I had my hands full. As I looked out toward the hangar lights, I could see several trucks approaching at high speed. Behind the trucks came police cars, dozens of them, blue lights spinning on their roofs. We were being surrounded by a large number of Italian troops, police, and carabinieri.

I ordered the Rastas down flat on the runway, one set of boat crews facing the hangars and the other facing the taxiways. As the Italians trotted toward us, we sighted down on them, perfect silhouettes against the glare. I told my guys to hold their fire and not to shoot unless I initiated.

The situation was extremely tense, and I am certain that this is the closest NATO forces have ever come to firing on each other. We were deployed around the 737 and meant to defend it. The Italians streaming in were preparing to take the aircraft into custody. It turned out that when the 737 veered off the active runway, it had turned onto the Italian, not American, side of the base.

The hijackers were on sovereign Italian soil. So were we.

More Italian forces poured into the darkness. Bo reported on the radio that armored cars were being moved close to his position. I reported that there were at least a hundred Italians facing me on my portion of the runway, and more were on the way. If this thing went hot, it would be charming. The Italians were plainly illuminated. We would rip them to pieces. The runway was extremely dark, and I knew if they opened up, the Italians would probably make the routine mistake of shooting over our heads. This was small comfort. Both Bo's assault group and mine were laid out on a flat stretch of runway, totally without cover.

The airfield at Sigonella was beginning to look like the last reel of *Butch Cassidy and the Sundance Kid*. More and more Italians kept showing up, on foot, in the backs of trucks, and piled onto the hoods of cars. Italian command and control was always in question, and the Keystone Kops routine didn't make me feel any better about what might happen.

I knew I could count on my guys to remain buttoned down. I knew they would not fire unless fired upon. I also thought that SEAL Team Six would make a mess of anyone who moved against the 737. What I feared most was an accident. I was afraid that the Italians might not be under firm control, or that some Italian conscript would screw up. One shot, accidental or otherwise, could set off a firefight that would kill both Americans and Italians. I stood and walked the length of our position. I knew I was making myself a target, and that was my intent.

"Everybody take it easy," I said, as much to any Italians in earshot who could speak English as to the Rastas. I said a little lower, "Keep your fields of fire, but everybody be cool."

The Rastas were cool and didn't need me to remind them. I walked back toward the nose of our C-141. Archie was there with the rest of the assault group. He may have liked to watch, but he was a badass. Two Italian officers demanded to be let aboard our plane. Archie told them to eat a meatball.

An hour passed, then half of another. Tensions on the runway lessened. What we thought would be an imminent assault had petered out into a game of sitzkrieg. The troops stared at one another across cement and grass. We didn't blink, and the Italians didn't go away.

By the stairs of the 737, I could see the several Italian officers standing with Captain Gormly and General Stiner. There was still some gesticulating, but the tone had lightened. When I saw General Stiner and the ranking Italian drive off, I knew there would be a parley, and I knew it would mean more waiting. The disposition of the hijackers would be determined by diplomats, not the assault groups surrounding the 737. The real battle was being fought on Moose's end, in Rome.

I walked out on the runway, about a dozen yards closer to the Italian lines. I pulled up my body armor, slung my MP-5 behind my back, and unzipped the bottom of my flight suit. I took a long piss on the cement. Laughter snickered out of the Italian position and then from behind me, where the Rastas were laid out. I zipped up and walked back toward my men. I'd made my own political statement.

The Rastas, along with Bo's and Sean's assault groups, were soon back aboard the C-141s, part of a phased withdrawal of American and Italian forces that had been negotiated by General Stiner. The deal also placed the hijackers in Italian custody.

We all thought it was bullshit but were too pissed off and tired to say much. We'd had two near misses in two days: We missed the ship, and we missed Abbas and his hijackers. All sorts of praise would be heaped on this operation, and I may be the only person involved who thinks it was less than glorious, politically or militarily.

As we flew back to Virginia Beach, I found the sleeping pill half melted in the pocket of my flight suit. I scooped up the powdery mess and popped it in my mouth. It was bitter, and as I dropped into a twitchy, dreamless sleep, I was beginning to think that I'd had enough of being a SEAL.

BETTINO CRAXI HAD DONE his best to keep Italy out of the counterterrorism business, but when EgyptAir 2843 touched down in Sicily, the entire mess was back in his lap. With the release of the terrorists by Hosni Mubarak, Italy had almost been let off the hook. If the hijackers had made it safely to Tunisia, the Craxi government would not have to prosecute the murder of Leon Klinghoffer or face the knotty consequences of holding four Palestinian terrorists in jail. But Washington was determined to see al-Molqi and his accomplices brought to justice. We wanted Abbas as well. All Craxi wanted was to have the whole goddamn mess go away.

Eventually, Washington and Rome would split the difference.

The hijackers were led off the plane in handcuffs and delivered into Italian custody. That left Abbas and one other high-ranking PLO terrorist, an aide to Arafat who had helpd plan the attack. They claimed diplomatic status, and the Egyptians chimed in that they considered the airplane to have been on a diplomatic mission, and therefore, inviolable Egyptian territory. Abbas presented an Iraqi diplomatic passport while simultaneously identifying himself as a member of the PLO executive. For what it mattered to Craxi, the terrorists might as well have shown season tickets to EuroDisney. The Italian government had been forced to take the murderers into custody; it wanted nothing at all to do with a big fish like Abu Abbas.

The next day Abbas and the PLO officer put on Italian air force uniforms and were smuggled aboard a Yugoslavian airliner. An extradition request was forwarded to Belgrade, with predictable results. The Yugoslavians honored Abbas's "diplomatic" status, and he was allowed to depart for Yemen. Within two days Abu Abbas was safely in Baghdad.

AN ITALIAN COURT eventually sentenced al-Molqi to thirty years for the murder of Leon Klinghoffer. Ibrahim Abdel Atif, the second in command of the operation, got twenty-four years, and Ahmed al-Hassani, fifteen. Bassam al-Asker would be granted parole in 1991. Abu Abbas was convicted in absentia, and Italian and Egyptian courts both issued warrants for the arrest of General Stiner. Go figure.

Abu Abbas continued as a senior member of the PLO and lived freely in Palestine authority territory. When asked in 1996 about the murder of Leon Klinghoffer, Abbas claimed in a *Boston Globe* interview that the sixty-nine-year-old stroke victim had it coming: "He was handicapped but he was inciting and provoking other passengers. So the decision was made to kill him."

Abbas subsequently called the *Achille Lauro* operation a mistake. It is a mistake he may now have occasion to regret. On the evening of April 15, 2003, U.S. Special Operations Forces raided a villa on the outskirts of Baghdad. As Saddam's regime crumbled under Operation Iraqi Freedom, Abu Abbas was snatched from his bed by members of the U.S. Joint Special Operations Command and taken into custody. The mastermind of the *Achille Lauro* fiasco is presently undergoing questioning at a U.S. military facility.

WHILE IN ITALIAN PRISON, al-Molqi and al-Hassani would both be granted twelve-day "vacations" for good behavior. Al-Hassani was the first of the hijackers to walk free and is still at large. Al-Molqi dropped out of sight during his summer parole in 1996 but was recaptured at a Spanish resort and eventually remanded to Italian custody. I am certain he looks forward to his next vacation.

SIX WEEKS AFTER it was forced down by American F-14s, the EgyptAir 737, tail number 2843, was hijacked by members of the Abu Nidal Organization and flown to Malta. During a botched rescue attempt by members of Egypt's Force 777, the hijackers and sixty passengers were killed in a fire started by a smoke grenade. The wreckage of the aircraft was eventually purchased by a rich collector.

FOLLOWING THE HIJACKING, *Achille Lauro* labored on in some disrepute. In December 1994, on a cruise from Genoa to the Seychelles, the ship caught fire off the coast of Somalia. It was evacuated without the loss of a single life. The ship sank, a burned-out hulk, on the afternoon of December 2—Margot's birthday.

ADVENTURES IN ANTITERRORISM

THE MORNING WAS STILL and hot, and a slender wind came down from the brown hills, tripped over the jumbled-together houses, and exhausted itself just short of our position, on a narrow strip of beach facing the Arabian Sea. Wind from the village carried with it the smells of the small town: diesel fumes, cooking oil, and goat shit. Out in the harbor was a U.S. Navy amphibious ship unloading crates of ammunition into a number of landing craft and a larger boat, a 134-foot LCU.

I was in command of a ten-man SEAL detachment assigned to provide security for the Americans ashore and the ship at anchor. In the operation order, our mission was called Alpha Tango, or antiterrorism. These sorts of operations came under the rubric of force protection, and this was the sort of op we called Rent-a-SEAL. The cross-beach operation was part of a routine military-assistance package, and the exercise was carried out sullenly by all involved.

The several landing craft ferried supplies onto the beach and dropped their ramps. Four-wheel-drive forklifts operated by Navy Seabees would then unload the cargo, pallet by pallet, and place it in Volvo trucks parked along the highway. The trucks were driven by grinning Arab men in *dishdashas* and Ray Ban sunglasses.

The ship's call sign was Texas Pete, and occasionally she would radio one of the boats, chastising the tardy or inquiring of the beachmasters as to the progress of the load-out.

On the beach, the sun beat upon a pile of sandbags, three radio antennas, and a ten-man detachment of U.S. Navy beachmasters. As the sun climbed, the beachmasters strung a camouflage net over the top of their bunker. The net hid nothing; the pile of sandbags was in the wide-fucking-open and easily visible from the coast road, one hundred yards away. In plain fact, there was really nobody to hide from.

The sandbags had been filled and assembled by soldiers of the host nation, a moderate Arab state whose military was trained, equipped, and mollycoddled by the United States. Not much thought or effort had been expended on the construction. The sandbags formed a U, the open portion of which faced the village, the only direction from which harm could possibly come. This morning none of that mattered; the sandbags were a place to set the radios, and the cammo net was simply to cut the sun.

Beside the beachmasters, maybe a dozen soldiers from the home guard stood around in khaki and green uniforms. Their officers wore elaborate racks of ribbons, row upon row, remarkable for a country whose primary weapon was crude-oil prices.

The local troops were on the beach to provide security, I guessed, but they mostly sat staring at the Americans, or by turns went to lie in the back of their truck or doze beside it in the small patch of shade. What rifles they had were in a pile on the seat.

I'd placed three shooting pairs by the line of trucks. One pair watched the empty vehicles as they pulled off the road and into the loading line. The second pair covered the first and checked out oncoming traffic. A sniper and spotter scanned the rooftops of the buildings in the village.

It was a thin veneer of protection. We were open to any competent marksman concealed in the village, but we were safe, I felt, from a vehicle bomb. This was post-Beirut, and America was in awe of the truck bomb—with good reason. Besides the marine barracks, the embassy in Lebanon had been bombed twice; several other attacks had been attempted; and American legations worldwide were on alert. Even the most benthic staff wonk at U.S. Central Command had been smart enough to include vehicle bombs as a threat and to list them as a contingency in our operations order. Although the threat was largely hypothetical, it was wise to remember that truck bombs not only killed people, they ruined careers.

At any rate, we weren't sweating it. We were in an ostensibly allied country, and the line of waiting trucks effectively blocked the approach of any vehicle intent on mayhem. There were two SEAL shooting pairs between the highway and the beachmasters. Again, this was not sure proof against a crater, but our principal defense was the beach itself. The sand was soft, and it was not likely that any vehicle leaving the highway would get over fifty feet off the asphalt before it bogged down. I was more worried about snipers, but not very.

I sat with my three remaining shooters, Rudi, Dave, and Cheese, against the tubes of our F-470 Zodiacs. Our two boats were beached between the trucks and the sandbags, engines tilted up, inflatable hulls lolling in the minuscule waves. It was hot, getting hotter, and the flies were starting to bite. We were bored shitless.

The Zodiacs had made a sweep of the harbor before Texas Pete anchored, checking for obvious inconveniences like floating mines, submerged wrecks, or uncharted hazards to navigation. We'd landed an advance element and provided security while the beachmasters hooked up with their hosts.

The landing craft came and went, and I yawned. We'd been up since 0300. I was hungry and tired. I lifted my binoculars and swept the water. In the harbor were a number of fishing boats rafted together. A few scraggly-looking fishermen tended long lines. We'd checked each boat before sunrise, shining streamlights into the faces of the fishermen, checking their gear and under the planks in their bilges.

In the shallowest reaches of the anchorage, a number of lateen-rigged dhows swung lazily at anchor. We had checked these as well, boarding and searching each one, then diving under their keels to look for attached explosives before Texas Pete entered the harbor and plied her boats.

I was thinking about taking the Zodiac back out to the ship

and scoring some sandwiches for the lads when a fishing boat came away from the quay about five hundred yards to the east. I put the binoculars on it without thinking, pressing the laser range finder like a reflex.

The first thing I noticed was that the boat was in pretty good shape. The local fishing craft were about twenty feet long, a cross between an Arab dhow and a longboat. All were dilapidated. Some were rigged for sail, and nearly all had puttering, battered outboards attached to their transoms. The boat chugging away from the quay was longer, maybe thirty feet, freshly painted blue and white, and on its transom was a brand-new Yamaha outboard.

I zoomed the lenses. There were four men aboard. They were buffed out, nut brown from the sun, and two of them wore Speedo bathing suits.

I handed the binoculars to Rudi. "What's wrong with this picture?" I asked.

Rudi pointed the binoculars at the boat. "Nice underwear," he said.

It was extremely unusual for Arab men, even fishermen, to show so much flesh. Cheese took the glasses and got a load of the Speedos. He said, "Hey, Rudi, looks like these guys are from Miami Beach."

Rudi snatched the binoculars back and tossed them to me. I took another long look at the boat.

Whoever these guys were, they looked like Arnold Schwarzenegger compared to the tubercular-looking fishermen we'd searched before the landings. Even more suspicious, they were puttering into the anchorage. The locals pushed their beat-up craft as fast as they would go. These guys were creeping.

I went up the beach toward Luke, standing by the line of trucks. "Tell me I can go home now," he said as I walked up.

"We've got a boat out there that looks a little hinkey. I'm gonna take the Zodiac and check it out," I said.

Luke squinted into the anchorage and smirked. "Very efficient, sir. Carry on."

"Keep an eye on us," I said. Luke nodded and went back to staring at the trucks.

I walked back to the Zodiacs. Rudi had already locked and loaded his M-60 and slung it around his shoulders. It was a point of pride for SEAL M-60 gunners that in every other service, it took three men to handle the same weapon. The big machine gun was like a toy in Rudi's hands.

"Time for a skivvy check?" he asked.

"I'll let you check their skivvies," Cheese said.

Cheese hung his M-14 around his neck, and he and Dave started to drag the Zodiac back into the water. We pushed the bow around and splashed through the foot-high waves. I hopped into the bow, and Dave pointed us seaward and revved the engine.

Out around the point, the blue and white boat came on, now paralleling the beach. They were headed in the direction of Texas Pete, not in any hurry. One of the men was pulling at a large heap of monofilament net, again seeming perfectly normal—except none of the boats we had boarded this morning used nets. All were long-liners.

The sun is making me paranoid, I told myself. These yo-yos are probably just out for sardines. A voice in my head answered back: Paranoids are occasionally right.

I told Dave to head offshore. He put the helm over and turned away from the blue and white boat and directly out to sea. The men in the fishing boat were doing their best to seem normal, so I wanted to appear innocuous to them. If we were to catch them with anything, we'd need to gain an element of surprise. It was broad daylight. They could see us perfectly, and we could see them. Chasing them down would take longer than coming at them on an intercepting course.

I told Dave, "Let them pass the beachmasters' position, then double back and cut them off from the ship."

"When do you want to put the swerve on them?" he asked.

"After we get outside the harbor mouth. This is only gonna work if they think we're headed somewhere else."

Dave played it like a pro. We zoomed out into the anchorage, careful to keep from watching them too closely. Sitting in the bow of the Zodiac, I casually turned now and again, casting an eye on the boat.

Dave glanced over his shoulder. "They're past the beach. Looks like they're heaving to."

They were maybe five hundred yards to leeward and a hundred yards offshore. They had cut their engine and were adrift. Four hundred yards seaward from the fishing boat, Texas Pete sat at anchor.

"What are they doing?" asked Dave.

I was now lying against the thwart tube, balancing the binoculars and keeping low. "They're screwing with their nets," I said.

"Say when," Dave said.

I put the binoculars away. "Let's do it."

I checked my weapon. It was a MAC-10 machine pistol with a long black silencer. My usual equipment, a CAR-15, was in the armory with a broken trigger assembly. I'd taken the MAC-10 this morning only because it was small, and the silencer, which was the size of two beer cans laid end to end, usually impressed the natives. It had definitely made an impression this morning. When we came ashore, one of the allied officers had pointed to my weapon and said, "Look, a gun like *Scarface*." Gangsters loved the MAC-10. Granted, it was small and deadly, but it was a triumph of style over substance. If you discounted looking cool, MAC-10s were essentially useless. They were cheaply made of pressed steel, and worse, they fired from a bolt-open position. This meant that you walked around with the bolt back and the chamber of the weapon wide open—a perfect place for sand, dirt, mud, and cosmic debris to accumulate. MAC-10s were extremely short, more pistol than machine gun, and without the added length of the silencer, nearly impossible to aim. That the silencer weighed more than the gun was not considered a feature.

The weapon was designed, essentially, to spray bullets, another factor that made the MAC a nonfavorite. The weapon could fire better than eleven hundred rounds a minute, meaning it would tear through its thirty-round magazine in about a second and a half. That makes for a pretty short gunfight.

Lastly, the MAC-10 fired a .45-caliber bullet, great for knocking people over but not too good on range. The silencer, besides cutting down on bang-bang, slowed the bullet to subsonic speed, further reducing range and accuracy. In short, the MAC-10 was great for drive-by shootings and killing people in closets but not too good for anything else.

Today it was all I had. Crouching in the bow of the Zodiac, I folded out the wire shoulder stock and made sure the silencer was screwed on tight. Keeping their weapons low, the other guys made ready, locking and loading. Dave put the tiller over, and the Zodiac swung in a wide arc. We were now on an intercepting course with the fishing boat, and I felt like a dumb shit for bringing a MAC-10 out here.

As the Zodiac came about, I had eyes on the fishing boat. The men on deck were grouped amidships, standing around the pile of net. One man sat in the stern, next to the outboard. They were still drifting; they seemed not to have noticed that we had turned.

As we watched, one of them lifted a pair of binoculars and took a long look at the ship. Binoculars, definitely a fashion accessory beyond the reach of most fishermen in the Arabian Sea. I didn't have to say anything. Everybody in the Zodiac knew that this was no ordinary fishing boat.

Dave opened the throttle. Our course kept us between the ship and the fishing boat. I prayed these guys were not suicide bombers preparing to ram the ship. If they suddenly came about and went to full throttle, I doubted that we would be able to intercept them.

We continued on. Closer, closer. Finally, at about two hundred yards, the man at the stern snapped his head around. He saw we were on him, and he caught sight of Rudi standing in our bow, holding the bowline in one hand and his M-60 in the other. It was obvious we were coming for them.

The man in the stern of the fishing boat yanked the starter, and their engine roared to life. He pushed the tiller over, and they pulled a tight circle away from us and back toward the point.

Dave adjusted course to run them down. "Put some muzzles on their boat!" I yelled over our screaming engine.

Cheese leveled his M-14 at the fishing boat. I watched his trigger finger switch his weapon from safe to fire. We were under seventy yards from the boat and closing fast.

They saw us, and saw that we had guns pointed. Most legit fishermen would have heaved to and raised their hands. These guys were making a run for it, and we all puckered a little.

"Halt!" I shouted in Arabic. It was one of the only Arabic words I knew. "HALT!" I yelled again. The man in the stern glanced at me, then looked away. His hand seemed to twist harder on the throttle. They were balls-to-the-wall. So were we. But our bearing held constant, and our range decreased. Dave had us on a perfect collision course.

"Don't fire unless I initiate," I said to the guys. This was going to be a confrontation, and we were all starting to get jacked up, but I didn't want any innocents shot. That included Mrs. Pfarrer's little son Chucky.

The Zodiac was closing rapidly. Dave kept us expertly pointed at the fishing boat. Foam was spraying from our bow as it cut the water. Fifty yards. Twenty yards. Things were happening fast, but for me, everything seemed to slow. It was adrenaline time again.

My vision was crystal clear, and each second felt like a minute. The sunlight and sky looked perfectly white. The water was emerald green, and the fishing boat became the bluest thing I had ever seen in my life.

I heard myself yelling "Halt" again. The strange Arabic word, guttural and low, rang in my ears like someone else's voice.

The man at the engine was wearing a tan shirt unbuttoned to the waist. As we closed, my eyes clicked to the three other men, now crouched in the middle of their boat and bracing for impact. One of them was crawling toward a canvas-covered lump next to the fishing nets.

The Zodiac hit them amidships. The fishing boat lurched, and our rubber boat bounced off. Dave turned hard to starboard, laying the Zodiac perfectly alongside the boat. We were close enough to spit into their faces.

They were a little higher than us in the water, so I stood in the bow, balancing on my toes and pointing the MAC-10 at the man holding the tiller.

I heard Dave yelling from the stern, "Heave to, motherfucker!" It struck me as funny that the word "motherfucker" may have been the only English these guys understood.

They may have heard us, but they didn't stop their boat. White water splashed up between us as we slammed together. For a few seconds we zoomed along, parallel. I had eye contact with the man at their engine, and I was aiming down the length of the boat, past and through the men by the nets.

"Stop your boat!" I yelled in English.

Incredibly, the man at their tiller flipped me the finger. Straight up, middle finger from a fist, he flashed the bird. A very cosmopolitan gesture for an Arabic fisherman.

I obviously wasn't getting any respect. Shooting these guys was still a bit extreme; this was, after all, a country friendly to the United States. We were in their harbor, and I wasn't even a game warden. But I intended to search their boat, and to do that, I was goddamn well sure going to make them stop.

I decided to fire across their bow. I swung the MAC-10 forward and aimed it at the wooden forepeak of their boat. I pushed the safety off and pulled the trigger. The bolt snapped forward, and the first bullet in the magazine fed sideways. The bolt smashed down on the bullet, jamming it halfway out of the ejection port. The unfired shell jutted from the chamber as the bolt slammed forward with an audible *clack*.

My MAC-10 had jammed.

Not just jammed but jammed visibly. A textbook malfunction called a "stovepipe." Everyone, SEAL and Arab, could see the unfired bullet sticking from the ejection port of my weapon.

I thought: Oh, fuck.

Then several things happened very quickly. One of the men in the middle of the boat yanked back at the canvas. I saw the red crescent-shaped magazine of an AK-47 rifle. He clutched at the weapon and jerked it upward.

Rudi saw it, too. He yelled, "GUN!"

I wasn't thinking now. I was just acting. Pure physicality, deed without cognition or plan, a state in Zen Buddhism called "satori." Right now "satori" might have translated into "shit sandwich." In the fishing boat, they were going for their guns, and my weapon was jammed solid.

I did an amazingly stupid thing—and it probably saved my life. I jumped from the Zodiac into the fishing boat. Cheese, who was probably the second craziest bastard I ever met, jumped right in after me. My weapon was useless, and now I was dick to dick with one of the Speedo boys. He was turning toward me, trying to get the AK-47 above the gunwale and pointed at me. I smashed the MAC-10's silencer forward and down, a neat, clean thrust straight at him, as though the silencer were a bayonet. My machine pistol was useful only as a club.

The muzzle of the silencer caught him right between the eyes. I smashed the bridge of his nose as hard as I could. There was a crunching sound, and his face split open. The man sprawled back, dropping the rifle and taking one of the other men down with him. They fell into the bottom of the boat, and Cheese was on them like a terrier. He clipped the second man under the chin with the butt of his M-14. Blood spattered and a tooth flew. I recocked my MAC-10 and shook the jammed cartridge from the chamber.

Rudi had leaped aboard. He had the M-60 stuck in the eyeball socket of the man at the tiller. He yelled, "THE MAN SAID 'PARE SU BARCO,' BUNDEJO!" Pure Miami Spanglish. And it worked.

The guy in the stern killed the engine. He raised his hands. There was general yelling in Arabic and English. The others put their hands up. Rudi covered the man in the stern, and Cheese and I herded the others into the bow.

"Who speaks English?" I shouted.

"I do," sputtered the man with the smashed mouth.

"Stay in the bow. Don't move," I said.

My heart was pounding. Miraculously, no one had fired a shot. I could see two AK-47s lying in the bottom of the boat. I picked them up and tossed them into the Zodiac. "Check under the nets," I said.

Cheese moved to the middle of the boat. He pulled up the nets, and we saw two sets of scuba tanks. Swim fins. Face masks. Next he lifted the canvas cover. There, in the sparkling sunlight, were two taped-together piles of Yugoslavian-made TNT. The explosives had been assembled into concave-shaped charges, each containing maybe ten pounds of TNT assembled around a two-pound chunk of Symtex. They were improvised limpet mines, and they had been improvised by someone who knew what he was doing. The TNT had been formed into an explosive "lens" capable of shaping the blast in a concentrated area. Fixed to the bottom of a ship, these charges were designed to punch three-foot holes into a steel hull. Both mines had fuses screwed into them. They were ready to go. These guys were combat swimmers, and Texas Pete had been their target.

The realization hit us like a bucket of ice water.

Cheese pointed his M-14 into the bow. "If you move," he said, "I'll kill you all."

Luke and Stick roared up in the second Zodiac. True to his word, Luke had kept an eye on us. They'd seen us make the bust, and when they saw the rifles come up, they'd headed over to give us a hand. They crossed the bow of the fishing boat, thwart to bow, and stood with weapons pointed. Their guns now commanded the length of the fishing boat.

We quickly tied the prisoners' hands with zip ties and blindfolded them with their shirts. Two of them were bleeding, one from the mouth and one from the face. Their blood soon soaked through the shirts and dripped into the bilges.

Each man was searched thoroughly. They had no additional weapons. Nor did they have wallets, ID papers, money, or pocket change. As Cheese covered the prisoners, we searched the boat inch by inch. By the outboard engine we found a folded nautical chart of the harbor with the position of the beachmasters and the anchorage of Texas Pete marked in pencil. Stuffed into the folded chart was an additional sheet of paper scrawled over in Arabic. The only Arabic I can read is numerals, in order to get the license plates of cars. The numbers are written right to left. The paper listed four-digit numbers: our radio frequencies. Also on the paper were the VHF frequencies used by the landing craft and the beachmasters. We searched for a radio but found nothing.

I bent down and studied the limpet mines. It didn't appear that the timers had been set, though I couldn't be sure. It wasn't likely that these guys would arm the mines until they were placed against the hull of the ship. That was standard operational procedure for a maritime sabotage attack. But it was also standard operational procedure to make swimmer attacks at night. These guys had made their go in broad goddamn daylight. This was a wild-card operation, so dumb and ballsy that it might have worked. Just as the U.S.S. *Cole* bombing would prove a few years in the future, you couldn't count on the bad guys to do things our way.

"What do you want to do about the mines?" Rudi asked.

"Nothing right now. We'll have Steve make these things safe when we get ashore." Our explosives ordnance disposal tech, Steve, was ashore with the trucks. What these things didn't need was an amateur trying to take them apart. I recognized the clock detonators as Yugoslavian, and beyond that, I didn't know squat. I knew that the safe and arming devices we used on our mines were automatically booby-trapped after the delay times were set. Any attempt to dislodge the mines or to remove the fuse would detonate the explosive.

We ran the fishing boat onto the sand in front of the beachmasters' position. The prisoners were muscled over the side, and we sat them on the beach ten yards apart. The beachmasters and the allied troops had seen the punch-out on the fishing boat, and their radios were crackling. One of the allied officers waded into the water and pulled himself up on the gunwales of the fishing boat. His eyes got big when he saw the mines. He splashed back to his jeep and got on his radio. He sent his traffic in high-speed Arabic.

Standing with the beachmasters was a Pakistani-American marine lieutenant, a member of the shore party. I nodded to the Arab officer on the radio. "What's he saying?" I asked.

"He's calling his unit. He's asking for a team from the security service to get down here."

This would quickly turn into a pissing contest. I didn't know who was going to wind up with custody of the prisoners, but I wanted local American input. I told the bosun in charge of the beachmaster detachment to call the ship. I got on the radio and talked to Texas Pete, actual. The "actual" postscript meant I was talking to the commanding officer in person. I told him we had four prisoners, mines, and weapons. I asked him to contact the embassy and have them send someone knowledgeable down here. "Someone knowledgeable" was a CIA officer. I was deferential to the captain but firm about what I wanted. SEALs may be assigned to do a job for someone, but we pull up short of working for anyone. We'd made a legit capture, and this was a SEAL gig now. Texas Pete's commanding officer outranked me, but he did what I wanted done. The landing crafts were immediately recovered. The LCU was bigger, and recovering it would require Texas Pete to flood her well deck, an operation that took time. It was time to get the ship away from the beach.

In the real world, things don't always happen like they happen in the movies. We'd wrapped up these jokers, but I didn't know if they had backup or if they'd been merely a diversion. I thought there might well be more bad guys in play. I didn't know if there was another boat packed with explosives waiting to ram the ship. I sent a Zodiac and four shooters to do a hull search of Texas Pete and the LCU to make sure nobody had managed to put a mine on them. Both were clean.

Texas Pete weighed anchor. I advised him to stay offshore and under way; we'd ferry the beachmasters out to the ship by Zodiac. The LCU would also stay under way, but closer to the beach. After we figured out who the players were, the LCU could land and pick up the four-wheel-drive forklifts.

We pulled everyone back from the fishing boat. Steve climbed in and rendered the mines safe. He handed the unfused explosives over, and I put the two charges on top of the Zodiacs.

In about an hour, a Mercedes sedan pulled up to the trucks. It was followed by a jeep driven by an Arab in a khaki uniform and a black beret. Close behind came a white Chevy Suburban with tinted windows, definitely an embassy ride. Out of the Mercedes came two Arabic men in suits. Out of the Suburban came a sandy-haired man and a thickset, red-haired marine gunnery sergeant. The sandy-haired man was wearing a safari jacket, a fashion statement usually tendered only by network journalists and CIA gumbies. All smiles, Mr. Safari Jacket shook hands with one of the suits. They walked down the beach toward us, the Arab's shoes filling with sand.

One of the suits broke off and started talking to the senior allied officer, a major with a dark mustache. There was a lot of gesturing.

The guy in the safari jacket walked my way, his eyes on the explosives piled atop the Zodiac.

"From the embassy?" I asked.

"You must be Lieutenant Pfarrer." He smiled. That the man knew my name was surprising. That he pronounced it correctly meant that he'd been on the radio, or that he spoke German. "This is Gunnery Sergeant Foster. He's an Arabic speaker," he went on.

"Lieutenant Malik speaks Arabic as well," I said.

"Has he interrogated them?"

"Nobody's talked to them."

The sandy-haired man looked at the prisoners. "Why are they bleeding?"

"We had a little punch-up on the boat," I said.

"Nobody shot?"

"No shots were fired," I answered.

That seemed to make him happy. The gunnery sergeant

and the lieutenant went around talking to the blindfolded men on the beach. Nobody answered. They sat in the sand and bled.

"Was there anything else in the boat?" the sandy-haired man asked.

"Two AKs and this." I handed over the nautical chart and the frequencies. The man's expression didn't change. I didn't know what to make of this guy. I wasn't into asking questions he probably wouldn't answer, so I said nothing.

We stood together silently as one of the suits walked over and said something to the man who had been on the tiller. From under his blindfold, the man spat something back in Arabic, and the guy in the suit kicked him hard in the mouth. I suspected this was going to get a lot uglier in private.

"Are you assuming responsibility for the prisoners?" I asked.

"No," Mr. Safari Jacket answered.

I was about to say something, but one of the suits called to the major in English, "Put these men into our jeep."

"Is that all right with you?" I asked Mr. Safari Jacket.

"Fine with me," he said. "I'm going to need to take the explosives."

I was getting over this whole thing. "Be my guest," I said.

He walked over and lifted one of the TNT piles onto his shoulder, then hefted the second one onto his other shoulder, balancing them like two sacks of potatoes. It occurred to me that he either knew exactly what he was doing or had no goddamn idea. There was enough explosive stacked on his head to blow him into the rarest gas in the universe: Safari Jacket 225.

The prisoners were led up the beach, still blindfolded. Two were put into a jeep, one into the Mercedes, and one into another jeep. Everybody drove off.

Mr. Safari Jacket and the gunnery sergeant tossed the explosives into the back of their Suburban, slammed the doors, and started the engine. The allied officers and troops piled into their vehicles and followed the Mercedes and jeep away.

The Suburban pulled onto the coast road, did a U-turn, and followed the convoy.

They were gone and it was over, just like that.

We stood there like idiots. The beachmasters looked at us. We looked at them.

"Is that it?" Rudi asked.

"That's it." I hadn't expected a ticker-tape parade, exactly, but maybe something. The man hadn't even asked why we went out to search the boat.

"What are we gonna do with the boat?" Luke asked.

"Fuck, I don't know. Sink it."

"What about the AKs?" Cheese asked.

I could see the wheels turning in his square Norwegian head: He expected to keep them as war booty. For a brief moment I imagined Cheese, home on liberty, deer-hunting with a Chinese-made assault rifle. No Bambi in the state of Wisconsin would be safe.

His face fell when I said, "Field-strip the rifles and toss them into the boat."

The LCU came ashore and recovered the forklifts. The beachmasters and Lieutenant Malik decided to go on the LCU when they discovered that there was a hot lunch aboard. The LCU drew up its ramp, backed off the beach, and headed for Texas Pete, now hull down on the hazy horizon.

We towed the fishing boat a half mile offshore and tossed in a hand grenade, and the bottom ripped out of her with a *thump*. The boat went down by the stern and disappeared in an oily swirl of wood splinters and fish scales. Cheese's AK-47s went down with it.

To this day I have no idea what happened to the men we captured. The choices run from summary execution to imprisonment and torture. If they were locals, it's more likely that they were ransomed back to their families. Anyone of value wouldn't go unexploited in this country. They were either terrorists or members of a hostile military. If they were terrorists, as far as I know, this was the first and only time a combat-swimmer operation had been attempted. Combat swimming is a craft that takes a lot of practice. Practice costs money. Governments train combat swimmers, not raggedy-ass Tangos.

Why they thought they could run an op in broad daylight, I still can't figure out. Maybe they didn't dare run it at night. Maybe they thought we'd buy the local-fisherman charade. A lot of maybes and a lot of never-gonna-knows.

Anyway, they weren't my problem—they were gone, probably to a bad place at the end of a piece of piano wire. Although they were turned over to the local leg breakers, I did not feel any responsibility for their fate. They were breathing when I last saw them. Texas Pete and the landing craft were safe, and I wasn't going to lose any sleep over what happened to four hostiles. If you want to step up and play frogman, you take the chances.

When we returned to Texas Pete, I got on the secure voice back to the flagship. I recounted the story of the capture and the turnover of the prisoners. I added that we had sunk the boat because we didn't know what the hell else to do with it. The amphibious group liaison officer wrote up the incident for the admiral. I never saw the report or the message traffic about the incident. I wrote citations for Cheese, Rudi, and Dave, but nothing ever came of them. They received no official recognition. Like everything else about this event, their commendations were swept under a rug.

Five months later, I received a navy achievement medal. The accompanying citation said essentially that I was an earnest and diligent young officer and was conscientious in providing security for the task force. It mentioned nothing about the men we had captured, the boat, or the explosives.

The medal came in a blue leatherette box, complete with a lapel pin to wear on my civilian attire. I wondered if it had been sent to the right guy.

WANDERING

I WAS IN THE DITCH for a couple of minutes, and the rain pattered into my face. The last thing I remembered distinctly was standing on the tail ramp of the 727, the other jumpers around me, the screaming engines, and the voice in my headphones shouting, "GO! GO! GO!"

Then it came back to me—a plunge from the airliner and the rough tumble through the sky. I remembered falling headfirst and watching Virginia Beach spin below me. The streetlights were white and ocher and the roads slick with rain. My parachute malfunction was a blur. Strangely, when I thought back on it, I *saw* myself falling, flailing at the risers, and spinning wildly as half the parachute deployed. It was as though I'd viewed it from a fixed point outside my body. It was like a movie, scenes from someone else's life. I'd watched myself falling down and away, through a turmoil of gray cloud, down and down toward the drop zone. The memory of my fall shimmered like a mirage in my brain.

Sprawled in the gully, I tried to sit up, and my ribs shot pain. My right leg was angled back, calf and foot twisted under my left thigh, and the weight of my backpack pressed down, pinning me to the ground. Pulling the quick-release, I dropped the rucksack from its hook points on my parachute harness and pushed it off my legs. I rolled over and slowly came to my hands and knees. I took a few deep breaths. My ribs were killing me, but everything else seemed to work.

Now I felt the wet grass and the mud under my hands. My fingers pounded, and I flinched when a raindrop struck me directly on one of my ripped-up fingernails. I flicked the black blood from my fingertips. None of the pain mattered. I was on the ground, and I was alive.

I gathered up my parachute and limped out onto the road. Thunder rumbled somewhere behind me. I could not help but look into the sky. The clouds were low and heavy and rushing past. I looked to the place where I had been just above the gray, swirling mist, and I felt as though I had fallen off a ladder.

Headlights loomed out of the rain and swept over me. It was one of the white Suburbans from the drop zone. The truck's tires hissed on the wet road as it jerked to a stop. The window was down. Behind the wheel was Hoser, still in his jumpsuit. His dreadlocks were wet, and he looked frantic.

"Jesus Christ, Chuck." I was standing in the road, almost half a mile from the place I was supposed to land. "Get in," he huffed. "Somebody had a total and burned into the cove."

I grinned as I walked to the back of the truck. "Relax," I said. "That was me."

The rest of the jumpers had watched me fall past the formation. They'd seen that I had a bag lock and that my parachute had not come free from the deployment container. They'd shouted to one another as I fell down and into the cloud deck. No one saw my canopy open, and no one saw my downwind slam into the beach or my wild drag across the road. They had taken a muster on the drop zone, and Coyote and I were the only ones missing. Coyote would be located, perfectly happy and intact, on the way back to the DZ. He had overshot the landing spot and come down behind the picnic area adjoining one of the soccer fields. That left me, and here I was, banged up but happy to be alive.

Hoser looked at my parachute rig as I lumped it into the back of the truck. The twinkie dangled free of its Velcro sheath, mute testimony to my close call.

"You throw away your rip cord?" Hoser asked.

I had. It was the first step in the emergency process. If my jump had gone right, I would have wrapped the cord around the handle after deploying my main canopy and tucked it into my flight suit as I descended. My rip cord was somewhere at the bottom of Little Creek Cove, the only one I ever lost in more than three hundred jumps. Every time a team member tossed a rip cord, the penalty was a case of beer. That night at the Raven, I would gladly pay the price.

After a rowdy good-bye party—the navy calls it a "hail and farewell"—I was out-processed the next day. I cleaned out my cage and my desk. As I walked around the buildings, I said good-bye to many friends. The wishes were cordial, but people looked at me sideways. I was no longer a shooter; I was no longer a member of the tribe. I was out. I had done the one thing that no SEAL is ever permitted to do: I had quit. And now, even with the handshakes, the jokes, and the backslapping, I was already a memory. I had set myself apart.

Lenny and Dougie came to debrief me, a bit more seriously this time, because I was going into the real world. Going out and staying out. I surrendered my military ID cards and my several passports. I was allowed to keep one, a plain civilian model, "clean" papers that I had not used to travel. I watched as a CANCELED stamp was thumped across my other documents. Finally, I walked into the captain's office. I read and signed my fitness report, my report card as an officer. It would be the final entry into my service record. Even though I had resigned my commission, Bob Gormly had recommended me for early promotion. It was the best and most complimentary evaluation I'd ever received. I thanked him, and he thanked me. He wished me luck on the outside, and I was gone.

As I drove toward the front gate of the base, a marine sentry leaned out from the guard shack. He raised a white-gloved palm at my car as he stepped into the road. I stopped. As I rolled down my window to ask why, he took a paint scraper to my windshield and quickly removed the base sticker from the glass. Lenny and Dougie had called ahead and told the sentry to stop my car. There would be no more driving onto the base. Balling up my sticker in his hand, the marine walked away without a word. The last thing that connected me to the Team had been peeled off and tossed into a trash can.

I sat behind the wheel of my car and felt numb. The weight of everything seemed to cave in on me. I felt like a man who had lived a hundred lives and died a hundred times. The realization that I was now a civilian was crushing.

I drove home as tears ran down my face.

Incredibly, the radio in my car played Bob Dylan's "Knockin' on Heaven's Door."

MARGOT AND I SEPARATED that fall. The time apart was my idea, and it hurt Margot very much. I had intended to enroll in the University of Virginia for a summer term. I'd planned to take organic chemistry, calculus, and a few other science courses I would need to round out my psych degree. When I got out of the Teams, I'd planned to sit the MCAT exams and try to get into medical school. I never enrolled. A dull sort of ennui clung to me. I didn't know what I wanted to do, so I did nothing.

I started to have nightmares that I was sinking through deep ocean water. The dreams were always without sound. Blue, infinite blue above and beneath, and nothing beyond the suffocating sensation of plummeting into emptiness. I would wake shouting.

Margot had wanted me to stay in the navy. She used to say that there were two kinds of Navy SEAL: the kind who could do anything, and the kind who couldn't do anything else. Maybe she thought I was the latter. Maybe she knew I would not be happy doing anything else.

I did my best to move on. I had missed the start of the summer semesters. Med school was a delusion, and I would have to start making money somehow. I thought blithely that I would become a writer. Margot told me that I had lost my mind. She was probably right. My making a living as a writer would be a struggle for more than the usual reasons. Like my father and my brother, I am dyslexic.

Back in college, I had written a screenplay with a friend, Richard Murphy, whom I'd met during my internship. It was the story of a man who escapes from prison and hides out as a counselor in a summer camp for retarded adults. We'd written it with high hopes. No one wanted to buy it, and I went off and joined the navy. Murph is a good and constant friend and managed to track me down at SEAL Team Four.

"Hey," he had said on the telephone, "I've got some news for you. You remember that crummy screenplay we wrote back in L.A.?"

"Yeah."

"Well, it got nominated for a Focus Award. I got in the master-of-fine-arts program for screenwriting at NYU, and we're going to be signed by the William Morris Agency."

I became the only naval officer in America to have a William Morris agent. Murph and I wrote another screenplay, this one about Ernest Hemingway in Cuba at the start of World War II. It was cobbled together from pages we sent to each other, Murph in New York and me in Honduras, Lebanon, and the Dominican Republic. I wasn't sure this stuff would go anywhere, but I enjoyed the research, I enjoyed writing, and I liked working with Murph. We sent in the script, and it sold in a week, optioned by Bob Nixon, a former ABC producer who'd just taken Jimmy Buffett into Cuba to visit Hemingway's farm outside of Havana. Bob said that as he read the screenplay, he'd been sure we had visited Hemingway's finca. We'd read about it in a book.

That summer, working in the spare bedroom in our house, I wrote a screenplay on my own. It was the story of three officers and their trials through BUD/S. I pecked it out on a manual typewriter and finished it on a 512K Macintosh computer. I sent it to my agent. It was optioned by Orion Pictures.

If anything, this small success seemed to drive Margot and me further apart. We started to have arguments. They were not loud, but they settled nothing and made everything worse. I was in another wild spiral, but this time it wasn't the result of a parachute malfunction. Margot's patience never ran out; she never gave up on us, but I gave up on her and on myself. I moved to Manhattan. A very strange thing to do, because I am not a person who likes cities.

I fell in love, suddenly and completely, with a Cuban actress. I was separated from Margot, though we were still married; I was messing around, as usual. My new love put into me a melancholy, contradictory feeling: a dull shame like fog and a thrill like bright sunshine. Magda Esteffan and I moved into an apartment on Seventy-eighth Street and Second Avenue, not far from the Carlisle Hotel. Magda worked as a cabaret singer and got bit parts, mostly commercials. I would meet her late at night, after she'd sung her sets, and we would go out to dinner at three A.M. We slept during the day, and when she'd go off to work, I would stay in the apartment and rewrite the script for Orion. It was as much of a bohemian lifestyle as I have ever led. The city was overwhelming for me, and I never did quite get used to it. Magda and I were in love, and time went by very quickly.

We lived in Manhattan about a year, then moved to Los Angeles. I had three thousand dollars to my name, but I was determined to write for a living. We moved into a small apartment in Marina del Rey. I was lucky enough to find another writing assignment, and then another. Orion Pictures made my first movie, *Navy SEALs,* and Universal Studios hired me to write *Darkman.* Several more screenwriting deals followed. Margot and I were divorced, an extremely civil affair conducted by mail, and Magda and I broke up. I made a lot of money and spent all of it. I wrote more screenplays.

I married again, because I am persistent and because I do not like to be alone. Julia Craig was beautiful, athletic, and intelligent. She had rowed crew at Princeton, and her father, like mine, was career military. We seemed well matched, but love had somehow bloomed between two very incompatible people. Our marriage was a disaster, and our divorce was long and unpleasant. I went broke again, made more money, and lost that, too. I was getting very good at barely getting by.

IN LOS ANGELES I would often be asked if I missed it, "it" being, I guess, the SEAL Teams. The question would often be posed with a glance to my expanding midsection, and I will admit that since I got out, my age in years and the waist of my trousers in inches seemed to be on a merge plot. I would usually answer that I missed the guys. The teamwork. Sometimes I would answer that I did it as long as I thought I could, and that I got out at the top of my game. Both of these statements were true as far as they went, but they meant nothing. What, honestly, do you say to someone who has not been there? What do you say to someone who's never jumped out of a commercial airliner, or sunk a ship by affixing a limpet mine, or killed a sniper: what do you say to someone who couldn't have the wildest fucking idea, not one clue in the world, what it was like?

Sometimes the questioners were more direct. Sometimes I was asked how many people I killed. I became adept at turning away the question with a question of my own: "What do you feel guilty about?"

BY 1996 I WAS twice divorced, and I felt like damaged goods. A woman I knew told me that I should have come with a warning label.

I was set up for a blind date, a dinner in Omaha, Nebraska. I was researching a film script that involved an attempt on the life of the first lady, and I had decided to set it in the Midwest. I somehow convinced the studio to send me there. My friend Lee Shepard had an even harder time convincing my date to go out with me. I had little to recommend me: I was divorced, divorcing again, and worked in Hollywood. That doesn't play too well in Omaha. But my date relented, and I was given her office number at a law firm downtown. She told me that she had to prepare for trial all afternoon, but I could come up to her office at six. I stepped off the elevator precisely on time. I was met in the lobby by the most beautiful woman I have ever laid eyes on. Stacey looked like Catherine Deneuve. I was flummoxed and stammered a hello. She had me wait in her office for an hour while her meeting went into overtime.

When she came back, I was still in awe. Stacey suggested that we go for a drink at the Omaha Press Club, on the top floor of her building. I learned later that she had prearranged a fake "back to the office" phone message so she could bail if our drinks went badly.

They almost did. I'd run into a formidable woman. Stacey had been a debutante, a valedictorian, and was a fine horse-woman. She also knew how to buck hay, fix a cattle fence, and drive a backhoe. Before returning home to Omaha, she'd practiced law in Virginia, D.C., and Maryland. Nothing about the SEALs or Hollywood impressed her at all. She had a gravelly laugh and a nose that was perfect.

"I got the nose in New Orleans," she said. "You should have seen my old one."

I laughed. She was scaring me like a sky dive scares me. I quickly downed a pair of martinis. Stacey sipped a glass of wine, then ordered another.

"Why don't you look at me?" she asked.

"What do you mean?"

"I mean you don't look at me when you speak to me. That's considered rude around here."

"I'm sorry," I said. "I wasn't trying to be evasive." I looked into her huge green eyes. Then I looked away.

"There, you're doing it again. Why don't you look at me when we talk?" she asked.

I said, "Because you're too beautiful."

Stacey took a long drag on her cigarette. She let the smoke out slowly. She said, "Nice line. Does it work in L.A.?"

Stacey and I were married in Omaha eighteen months later. In December 1998 she bore us a son, Paddy. In the three days of her labor, she did not complain, cry, or curse me once.

I learned a lot about valor from her.

FAREWELL TO ARMS

THE DOCTOR SNAPPED the curtain open, then fluffed it closed behind him. It gave an illusion of privacy. The recovery room was full, and there were patients behind curtains to the right and left of me.

"How are you doing?" He smiled. He was handsome and nattily dressed, like the doctors on TV.

"You tell me," I said. There was drool crusted on my chin, and I was still groggy from being put under. I had just undergone a colonoscopy.

The doctor placed the clipboard on my bed and opened it briefly before he spoke.

"You have cancer," he said.

I felt like the world had stopped and I had been thrown off.

"Colon cancer," he continued. "We found a malignancy about the size of a golf ball. We're admitting you into the hospital immediately. I've scheduled surgery for tonight."

"How bad is this?" I stammered.

"I'm going to be honest with you. A tumor this size has been growing for a while. Maybe for as long as five or six years. The problem is that it puts out cancer cells. Metastasizes them. There's a good possibility it has spread."

I closed my eyes. The first thing I thought was that this news would make Stacey cry.

"I've already told your wife," the doctor said.

Just like the doctors on TV.

I CAN'T SAY that cancer struck me without warning. Hindsight is brilliant, but I had ignored a mound of important signals: nagging fatigue, a cough that wouldn't go away, and an endless series of aches and pains that I chalked up to approaching middle age. There was also colon cancer in my family, and it fell upon the men. I should have had warning enough.

Stacey took the news gallantly and was at my side throughout. I underwent surgery that evening. Following the removal of the tumor, lymph nodes, and twelve inches of my large intestine, I suffered a secondary infection of the surgical wound and spent the next three weeks in the hospital with a tube down my nose.

The official verdict was Stage Three colorectal cancer. Although the surgeons had removed the tumor, they had not lessened the threat. By the time I was diagnosed, the tumor had spread cancer into my lymphatic system. Millions of cancer cells had metastasized throughout my body.

Four weeks after I came home from the hospital, I started chemotherapy, six weeks on, two weeks off, for six months. The chemo drug, 5-Fluorouracil, had some nasty side effects: skin lesions, chronic nausea, mental confusion, fatigue, and ulcerating mouth sores. The treatment was every bit as virulent as the disease it was supposed to cure. It even caused leukemia in some patients, a by-product far beyond what I would consider collateral damage.

I took my chemotherapy on the eighth floor of the Saint Vincent's Medical Center in Jacksonville, Florida. The oncology unit looks out over the Saint John's River, and patients are seated in Naugahyde recliners facing the river. Every Thursday afternoon I would have lab work done, then I would kick back and get stuck by needles. I'd lay motionless while an IV machine pumped me full of Leucovorin, steroids, and 5-FU. Sometimes the treatments took two hours, sometimes four. Orderlies brought trays with orange juice and ice chips—the ice for the painful hard-edged sores that bloomed under my tongue. Sipping an iced drink, I looked over the beautiful stretch of river alongside thirty or forty other patients. All of us either bloated, emaciated, hairless, or all three. Ours was a very exclusive resort.

I began to call the chemo unit Club Dead.

The steroids made me blow up like a toad, and the 5-FU made me confused and forgetful, a phenomenon, the nurses told me, called "chemo brain." One morning I couldn't remember my own phone number. I thought I might be losing my mind. The skin on my hands and feet blistered and peeled off in sheets. My sense of smell became extremely acute, and I swore I could detect the chemo drugs on my skin, a sharp, piercing tang like the odor of steel. The smell nauseated me. I doused myself with cologne and stank of it, perfume and cancer and drugs. My abdomen swelled, and my eyes became puffy slits. People I knew well passed me on the street without recognizing me. I was always exhausted, and I whined like a child.

Weeks passed, spring became summer. In the afternoons I would sleep curled in a ball on the couch with a bucket beside me. There were times I felt that the chemo was killing me at only a slightly slower rate than it killed the cancer. I had dreams in which I thought my soul had slipped out of my body. In those dreams, my soul-self stood for hours and watched a bloated, red-faced man snore loudly under a comforter.

The steroids did not help my temper; the smallest frustrations would throw me into a rage. As soon as my anger had blown itself out, I would become tearful and contrite. Through it all, madness, fear, and regret, Stacey kept me in line. As I mentioned, she is a formidable woman.

Six months passed, and I finished chemo. I was the graduate of another hard school.

In the SEAL Teams, we say a survivor is a victim with an attitude. I am well now, and getting better. I refused to believe, and still refuse to believe, after all I have been through, that cancer is the thing that will kill me.

I will not be a victim of anything. I am a fighter.

I have a bit of advice to offer. Hold on to the people you are close to, and love them fiercely. Get up every morning and live like there is no tomorrow. Because one day you'll find it's true.

ACKNOWLEDGMENTS

I HAD MUCH HELP and encouragement early in this project and during the most difficult parts of it. There is nothing in this book that did not benefit from suggestions and help. I would first like to thank Joel Millner of Larchmont Literary in Los Angeles, and Julia Lord of Julia Lord Literary in New York. I have worked with Joel for over a decade, and Julia is a friend who steered me through the rocks and shoals of a trade that was strange to me. Their support helped take a scattered idea and turn it into a book. I would also like to thank several friends whose early help was vital: first off, friend, author, war correspondent, and screenwriter David Freed, for his kindness and for his example of clean, sparkling writing. My friend Peter Gaele, adventurer, screenwriter, and raconteur, graciously showed me what a book proposal looked like; and my colleague and friend Lee Johnson gave me the examples of a writer's life and of her fine, steady prose.

It is axiomatic to thank Mom and Dad, but I wish to thank mine especially, for literally keeping the lights on as I wrote. Particular thanks to my father, who researched, verified, fact-checked, and located most of the official photos in the book. He is a formidable researcher, one hell of a naval officer, and a great dad. Many, many thanks also to my friend and teammate Scott Speroni, my comrade in Lebanon, who provided numerous hard-to-find photos and was a steady hand when we shared danger.

For preparation of the manuscript and copyediting, I wish to thank Patrick Miller and especially Lisa Essenberg, who not only rode herd on an ever expanding gaggle of pages but also provided mission-critical research. For framing my narrative in a factual context, I would like to thank my friend, historian Eric Hammel, whose book, *The Root: Marines in Beirut, August 1982–February 1984,* is the definitive history of America's misadventure in Lebanon. Thanks to the staff of the UDT/SEAL Museum, who managed to dig up a photograph of Class 114. And thank you to Vic Duppenthaler of Uniflight, Inc., for photos and information on the venerable and stealthy Seafox.

I'd like to thank my old friend Richard T. "Murph" Murphy, the man who got me into the writing game, and the person who, more than any other, taught me how to write plainly. Thanks to my comrades F.G.S. and L.L., who served with me in Beirut, read the manuscript, and contributed their recollections. Thanks also to my dear friends Jerri Hente, Lisa Paul, Colonel Marvin "Ski" Krupinsky, his wife, Jackie, Benham and Robert Howard, Dr. "Mac Daddy" Evans, Liz Grenamyer, Matt Wolfe and Tripp Newsome, Cap'n Gary Blohm, Blair and Bobby Woolverton, Bruce Truesdell, Bob and Pam Currey, Dorothy Alstrin, my teammates Kim Erskine and Ian Conway, Matt and Lynn Keller, and Beau St. Clair, all of whom read chapters and told me where to get off.

An early reader was my friend Sue Schuler, whose love for life was an inspiration. Her battle with cancer is now over, but the world is richer for the example of her grace, courage, humor, and dignity. We miss you.

Thanks to everyone who was a part of these stories, to teammates and comrades, friends and acquaintances. To my betters whom I have praised, my apologies for being impertinent; to commanders and teammates I have suddenly found wanting, I apologize for not having had the courage to speak up sooner.

Kind and sincere thanks to my editor, Bob Loomis at Random House, who took the chance that a screenwriter could write a book. He is the bravest man I've met lately.

My undying gratitude and love to my wife, Stacey, and my son, Paddy, for their patience and understanding. Stacey's love sustained me through the darkest part of my illness, and I am sorry that they often made do without the help of a father and husband. Thank you for loving me.

My thanks to the marines and sailors of the 24th Marine Amphibious Unit, and the men of SEAL Team Four and SEAL Team Six. My profound and humble gratitude to the many families, wives and mothers, fathers, sons and daughters, who placed the ultimate sacrifice upon the altar of liberty. My thanks, however heartfelt and respectful, are trivial compared to the tragedy of your loss. Please know there is not a day that passes when I do not ask why your sons were taken but I was not.

Finally, I wish to thank the men of naval special warfare, the *operators,* who daily place themselves before our enemies—and at the mercy of the sea.

GLOSSARY OF SEAL TERMS

1-MC The public-address system aboard a naval vessel.

1130 A naval special warfare officer. 1130 is the career designator assigned by the Bureau of Naval Personnel to qualified SEAL officers.

1180 U.S. Navy officer designator for a probationary special warfare officer.

5326 Naval education code (NEC) for a combat swimmer, the Bureau of Naval Personnel's designation for an enlisted SEAL operator.

5.56 The caliber of an M-16 rifle in millimeters. NATO ammunition for the M-16 and M-4 carbine.

7.62 The caliber of an M-60 machine gun in millimeters. NATO ammunition for the M-60, G-3, and M-14 rifles. These weapons fire the NATO standard 7.62 × 51 cartridge. Russian-made weapons, like the AK-47, fire the same caliber bullet using a shorter cartridge, 7.62 × 39. Russian ammunition is referred to as "7.62 Intermediate."

A2 Barret .50-caliber long-range sniper rifle. Used by SEAL Teams against high-value targets and as a counter-sniper weapon.

AAA Antiaircraft artillery.

Across the Beach A SEAL operation originating from sea. SEALs may insert or extract using a combination of swimming, boat, submarine, parachute, and helicopter.

Alice Pack   Sometimes called a "jungle ruck." A small backpack used for combat operations.

Amal   Meaning "action," Amal is an anti-Western Shiite militia in Lebanon.

ANGLICO   Air/Naval Gunfire Liaison Company. A unit assigned to the marines, specializing in the coordination of air strikes, artillery, and naval gunfire.

Antiterrorism   Defensive measures used to reduce the vulnerability of personnel and facilities to terrorist acts. Such measures include guard patrols, vehicle barricades, and hardening targets, as well as the immediate actions taken by military and security forces following a terrorist attack. Also called "AT."

AO   Area of operations. Bailiwick.

AOT   Advanced operator training. Post-BUD/S training to prepare SEAL platoon members for deployments.

API   Armor piercing, incendiary. Ammunition designed to pass through armored vehicles and start fires inside.

Assault Element   A SEAL unit varying in size from four to twenty-five operators. Elements are tailored to fit specific mission requirements.

AT   Antiterrorism.

AT-4   An 84-millimeter (3.36-inch) recoilless antitank rocket, used in antiarmor and bunker busting.

Attack Board   A grouping of depth gauge, watch, compass, and underwater GPS used by SEALs for navigation during underwater attacks.

AWACS (E-3 Sentry)   The AWACS E-3 is an airborne warning and control aircraft that provides all-weather surveillance, command, control, and communications. The E-3 Sentry is a modified Boeing 707/320 commercial airframe with a rotating radar dome.

Banana   A SEAL trainee, or anyone not qualified as a SEAL operator. They're called "bananas" because they're yellow on the outside and squishy on the inside.

BDU   Battle dress, utility. The three-color camouflage uniforms worn by marines and soldiers.

Beachmaster   Navy personnel assigned in an amphibious operation to coordinate the movement of supplies and personnel across the beach. Their marine counterparts are called the "Shore Party."

Beehive   A 40-millimeter round fired from the M-203 grenade launcher. Instead of explosives, Beehive rounds contain hundreds of finned nails, called "fléchettes," that shotgun the target.

Berthing Space   Compartments aboard a ship, used as sleeping quarters.

BIA   Beirut International Airport. The collective positions of the main body of 24 MAU.

Black Hawk (see also MH-60)   The MH-60 helicopter, the workhorse of special operations. Its navy equivalent is the SH-60, the SeaHawk.

Black Shoe   A surface warfare officer, a ship driver, so named because SWOs wear black shoes with their khaki uniforms. Pilots wear brown shoes.

Boat Crew   A variably sized SEAL element; literally, the number of SEALs inserted by one boat or helicopter. Usually no smaller than four operators, a boat crew can be as large as twenty.

Body Snatch   Also called "personnel interdiction," the kidnapping of high-value enemy personnel. Also an operation or ambush designed specifically to capture prisoners.

Booger Eater   Generic term for bad guys.

Bounce   To hit the ground following a parachute malfunction.

BUD/S   Basic underwater demolition/SEAL training. A twenty-six-week ordeal conducted at the Naval Amphibious Base, Coronado, California. All SEAL operators attend this course. BUD/S is the only school in the U.S. military where officers and enlisted men attend together and take the same coursework.

Budweiser   The badge awarded to qualified naval special warfare operators. Called a "trident" by the navy, it is the emblem and insignia of the SEAL Teams. The device features a pistol, an anchor, a trident, and a screaming eagle that is vaguely reminiscent of the logo on a can of Budweiser beer. In the naval service, enlisted warfare badges are silver, and the officers' are gold. The Budweiser is the only gold navy warfare device worn by both officers and enlisted.

C-4   Composition 4. Plastic explosive.

Cadre   The hard-core operational and training elements of a terrorist organization. Also the training cell within a SEAL Team.

Cake-Eater   Naval officer. Any commissioned officer.

Call Sign   Radio shorthand for a particular unit or individual. When followed by the word "actual" (as in Texas Pete, *actual*) it denotes that one is speaking to the unit's commanding officer.

CAR-15 (see also M-4; Poodle Shooter)   A short-barreled version of the M-16. SEALs favor the CAR for its compactness and accuracy.

Caustic Cocktail   A toxic vapor of barilime and seawater, inhaled after the malfunction of a scuba rebreather rig. Not very tasty, and can be downright lethal.

CCT Combat control teams. Air force special operations forces specializing in air-traffic control and communications.

Chemlight A chemical light stick used to mark objects. Chemlights are made in various colors as well as infrared.

Chu Hoi Vietnamese, meaning "surrender." A defected Viet Cong who agreed to help U.S. forces. *Chu Hois* were sometimes used by the SEALs to guide search-and-destroy missions. The term is still used to tag a defector agreeing to serve as a scout or guide. Also called "Kit Carson scouts."

Cleared Hot Granted permission to open fire. Cleared for action.

Click Kilometer. One click equals one kilometer in range or distance.

Combat-Action Ribbon Navy and marine award for participation in combat. The navy's equivalent of the army's Combat Infantryman Badge.

Commando Hubert French naval commando.

Commodore A naval officer, usually a senior captain, who is in charge of a squadron of ships. The title also applies to the captain in administrative control of a NavSpecWarGru, a group of SEAL Teams.

Coronado Island suburb of San Diego, home to West Coast SEAL Teams and the naval special warfare training unit.

Corporal Chef The senior enlisted rank in the French Foreign Legion, equivalent to sergeant major.

Counterterrorism Offensive measures taken to deter, prevent, and respond to terrorism. These active measures include assaulting hostage barricade sites; retaking hijacked vehicles, vessels, or aircraft; and direct action against terrorist personnel, support, and infrastructure. Also called "CT."

CP Combat post. A marine position, usually platoon-sized, such as the one located outside the perimeter wire of Beirut International Airport.

CQB Close-quarters battle. The precision shooting used by SEALs to clear ship spaces and rooms. CQB is the epitome of surgical shooting. SEALs frequently practice dynamic target shooting in which terrorist targets are mixed with real "hostages."

CRRC Combat rubber raiding craft. Inflatable boats used by the SEALs. Although modern boats are made of bulletproof Kevlar, the "rubber" has stuck from World War II days, when the boats were made of rubberized nylon.

CSAR Combat search and rescue. Operations mounted to retrieve downed aircrew from enemy territory.

CTF Commander, task force.

Delta Special Forces Operational Detachment Delta, aka Delta Force. It is a frequent SEAL joke that the high-profile Delta Force is SEAL Team's best cover.

Dhow A lateen-rigged Arab sailing vessel. Ubiquitous in the Middle East as a coastwise trader and fishing vessel.

Diawi Vietnamese. Captain (in the army), lieutenant (navy).

Dien Bien Phu Valley "citadel" occupied by the French in North Vietnam. Surrounded by the Viet Minh, Dien Bien Phu was overwhelmed on May 7, 1954, after a 169-day battle. This epic defeat marked the end of French hegemony in Indochina.

Ding To hit with a bullet. To kill.

Direct Action Combat actions undertaken against enemy targets.

Dirt Poisoning   The cause of death when your parachute doesn't open.

Dog-Face   A member of the United States Army.

Draeger LAR-V   German-made rebreathing scuba. Rebreathers emit no bubbles and are used for sneak attacks and maritime sabotage operations.

Druze (see also PSP)   A secretive Islamic sect endemic to the mountains of Lebanon. The political arm of the Druze community is the Progressive Socialist Party (PSP). Founded in 1948, the PSP is nationalist and anti-Western in orientation. The PSP and the Druze militias are led by Walid Jumblat.

Dust Off   Evacuation of wounded by helicopter.

E & E   Escape and evasion. Individual efforts made to retreat and extract from hostile territory. A last-ditch effort to retreat.

F-470   CRRC made by Zodiac Industries. Used for coastwise operations and insertions and extractions.

Fast Rope   A spongy, hawserlike rope used to deploy troops rapidly from helicopters. Also called a "zip line," fast ropes are manufactured in 30-, 60-, and 120-foot lengths.

FAV   Fast-attack vehicle. An armed dune buggy organic to SEAL Teams.

FLIR   Forward-looking infrared.

FN   Fabrique Nationale, a Belgian-made 7.62-millimeter assault rifle.

Forty Mike-Mike   Forty-millimeter grenades fired from an M-203 grenade launcher.

Frap   A parachute malfunction. Used as both a noun and a verb.

Frog Hog   A female SEAL groupie.

Fuerzas Especiales   Colombian special forces.

Full Mission Profile   A SEAL mission cycle from planning, rehearsal, deployment, insertion, infiltration, actions at the objective, exfiltration, extraction, recovery, and debriefing.

GP   General Purpose. As in GP tent. Sometimes, General Principles. For example, "I punched him out just for GP."

Goon Squad   The slow and the stupid. In BUD/S, the slowest 20 percent of any run or evolution. Instructors single out these class members for extra physical instruction.

GPS   Global positioning system. Navigational aid utilizing a series of military satellites to exactly pinpoint any location on earth.

Grab-assing   Horseplay. Goofing off.

Greenroom   The compartment on an aircraft carrier where personnel are held before being released onto the flight deck.

Gun-deck   In the navy, to "gun-deck" means to retroactively fill in a logbook or to fake a document. Derives from the practice of quarterdeck watches retreating to the gun deck to make log entries.

HAHO   High-altitude, high-opening parachute jump.

HALO   High-altitude, low-opening parachute jump.

HE/DP   High explosive/dual purpose. A round fired by the M-203 grenade launcher designed as both an antiarmor and an antipersonnel weapon.

Helmet-fire   To panic. Also, to be absentminded or to make a mistake.

Hezbollah "Party of God." Hezbollah is an umbrella group of Shiite Muslim militants in Lebanon. Formed about 1983, Hezbollah is a social as well as a military force, establishing schools, clinics, and welfare organizations for the Shiite minority. From 1983 to 2000 Hezbollah waged a guerrilla war against Israeli occupying forces and the towns and villages of northern Israel. Subsidized and trained by Iran, Hezbollah operates in the southern slums of Beirut and the Bekaa valley.

Hooterville The slum of Hay es Salaam, surrounding marine positions at the north end of the Beirut airport.

Hop and Pop A low-altitude, low-opening parachute drop.

HSAC High-speed assault craft. High-speed, highly capable open-ocean assault boat. Armed with a variety of 7.62-millimeter and .50-caliber machine guns. HSACs are capable of over-the-horizon operations against land and sea targets.

Hydrographic Recon A clandestine beach survey. Also called a "sneak-and-peek."

IDF, IDFN Israeli defense forces, the Israeli army. "N" indicates a naval unit.

Indige Indigenous. Of or belonging to a certain locale. A local indigenous personnel or local vessel (indigenous craft).

IR Infrared. Invisible light frequencies below red, used passively in night-vision goggles, and actively as an infrared spotlight.

IR Strobe A blinking signal light using infrared light.

Jake and Abdul Bad guys. From a tour in Beirut where the bad guys were referred to as "Jake and Abdul, the Druze Brothers."

JP-5 Jet propulsion (grade) 5. Jet fuel.

Kalashnikov Any of a variety of Russian-made assault rifles designed by Mikhail Timofeevich Kalashnikov. Kalashnikov weapons include the AK-47, the AK-74, RPK and RPD machine guns, as well as the Dragunov sniper's rifle.

Katyusha 122-millimeter Russian-made artillery rockets.

K-Bar SEAL Team fighting knife.

Kufiyah An Arab headdress.

LAAW Rocket (Light Antiarmor Weapon) M-72 light armor antitank rocket. Replaced by the larger, more capable AT-4.

LAF The Lebanese armed forces (pronounced "laugh"). The army of President Amin Gemayel.

LALO Low-altitude, low-opening parachute drop.

LCU Landing craft, utility. The LCU is a tank-carrying landing craft, 134 feet in length. Also called a "U-boat."

Lead Wings Army "silver" jump wings. Issued to BUD/S graduates after parachute training at Fort Benning, Georgia. Naval special warfare operators on probation are forced to wear these army wings before they make ten navy jumps and earn the navy's "wings of gold."

Leg An army term (usually "nasty leg") designating any soldier who is not airborne-qualified. A nonparatrooper, i.e., a member of a nasty-leg infantry unit.

Limpet Mine A magnetic mine used by SEALs in underwater attacks against enemy shipping, and in maritime sabotage operations. If you don't like it, limpet.

Little Creek Naval amphibious base located in Norfolk, Virginia. Home of the East Coast SEAL Teams.

Lock Out Procedures used to leave and enter a submerged submarine.

Low Intensity, High Per Diem   A boondoggle, or a cake-walk operation.

LT   Lieutenant. Navy officer's rank (0-3), comparable to a captain in the marines, army, and air force.

LTJG   Lieutenant, junior grade, navy officer's rank (0-2), comparable to a first lieutenant in the marines, army, and air force.

M-203   Rifle-mounted 40-millimeter grenade launcher.

M-4 (see also CAR-15)   Carbine version of the M-16.

M-60   Standard-issue infantry machine gun. The M-60 fires the 7.62-millimeter NATO round.

MARG   Mediterranean amphibious ready group.

Maronite   Maronites are the largest Christian sect in Lebanon. Maronite areas include East Beirut and the mountains of northern Lebanon. Traditionally a class of merchants, traders, and businessmen, Maronites tend to dominate the Lebanese economy. By custom, the president of the Lebanese republic is a Maronite.

MAU   Marine amphibious unit.

MH-53 (see also Pave Low)   Long-range heavy-lift special operations helicopter. The navy and marine version, the CH-53, is called the "Sea Stallion."

MH-60 (SeaHawk)   Black Hawk helicopter. Workhorse of special operations forces.

Mk-5   Patrol boat replacing the Seafox.

MK-13   Day-night smoke and illumination flare carried by SEALs.

MK-15   Computerized semiclosed diving rig known for its unreliability. Also called the "black death."

MP-5   German-made machine pistol used by SEALs for ship takedowns, room clearance, and close-quarters battle.

MRE   Meal, ready to eat. Standard military battle rations. Not long on taste, also known as "meal, rarely enjoyed."

MSC   Miltary Sealift Command. Service and support ships manned by civilian crews.

Muezzin   The official attached to a mosque who chants the *azan,* a call to the faithful to come to prayer. The *azan* is performed five times a day, at dawn, noon, midafternoon, dusk, and evening.

MULE   Multiutility laser equipment. A laser target designator.

Mustang   A commissioned officer with prior enlisted service.

Naval Special Warfare   Navy SEAL Teams, SEAL delivery teams, and special boat units.

NCDU   Naval combat demolition units, World War II forerunners of the navy's famed underwater demolition teams.

NOD   Night observation device.

No Joy   Radio-speak for "I do not see the target."

Nonqual   A nonoperator. A person outside of the SEAL community.

NRO   National Reconnaissance Office.

NSA   National Security Agency.

NVGs   Night-vision goggles.

O$_2$ Hit   Convulsion resulting from oxygen toxicity. Principal danger involved in rebreathing diving apparatus. Under pressures greater than two atmospheres, pure oxygen becomes toxic.

Operator Number   Three-digit number given to SEAL operators to identify them within an operational unit.

Organic In military argot, equipment or personnel assigned and controlled by a specific unit. The fast-attack vehicles were organic to SEAL Team Six.

Pave Low (see also MH-53) MH-53 air force special operations helicopter. Descendants of the famed Jolly Green Giants of Vietnam, Pave Lows are equipped with miniguns, an advanced navigation suite, and FLIR, and are capable of in-flight refueling. Used to support combat search and rescue operations as well as to insert and extract special operations forces.

PDF Panamanian Defense Forces. Manuel Noriega's army.

Phalange A Lebanese Christian militia originally formed in 1936 as a Maronite paramilitary youth organization by Pierre Jumayyil. Militant and violent, the Phalange bore responsibility for the 1983 massacres at Sabra and Chatilla, where upward of eight hundred Palestinian men, women, and children were massacred.

PJ Air force pararescueman. Comes from the abbreviation for "parajumpers." Air force personnel specially trained to conduct combat search and rescue operations.

PLA Palestine Liberation Army. A Syrian-backed Palestinian group.

Platoon Traditional SEAL operational unit comprised of two officers and twelve enlisted men.

PLO Palestine Liberation Organization.

Poodle Shooter (see also CAR-15) CAR-15 rifle. So called because it is small and light.

PSP (see also Druze) Lebanese Progressive Socialist Party.

PT Boat Patrol/torpedo boat.

Qur'an Koran, literally "the recitation." The Muslim holy book, revelations made to Mohammed by the angel Gabriel.

R&S Reconnaissance and surveillance mission.

Raven, The Onetime SEAL Team hangout in Virginia Beach. Now a tourist attraction.

Red Wolf Navy helicopter combat support squadron (HCS) helicopters. Specially equipped SH-60s that operate with SEAL Teams.

Ring Out To quit. From the three-rings-and-you're-out quitting method at BUD/S.

ROE Rules of engagement. Orders dictating the circumstances and limitations under which U.S. forces may initiate combat.

Rope-a-Dope A static-line parachute drop, so called because the jumper's parachute is opened by a static line (rope) attached to the aircraft.

RPG (Rocket-Propelled Grenade) Russian-made recoilless antiarmor weapon. Prized by SEALs for range and penetration.

Rubber Duck At-sea parachute drop of a CRRC.

SAM Surface-to-air missile.

SBU Special boat unit.

SDV SEAL delivery vehicle. A wet minisub used to deliver SEALs into target areas and also to attack enemy ships and facilities.

SDV Team SEAL delivery vehicle team. A SEAL unit specializing in maritime sabotage and operation of SEAL submersibles.

Seafox A stealth patrol boat used by SEALs. Armed with twin .50-caliber machine guns and a pair of M-60s, the

Seafox was made of low-observable carbon fiber and plastic. Like a Stealthfighter, the Seafox was invisible to search radar. It was replaced by the more heavily armed and faster MK-5 patrol boat.

Sea-keeping   The capability of a ship or boat to accomplish its intended mission, including performance in a seaway, crew comfort, and equipment operability.

SEAL Team   SEAL Teams are comprised of a number of platoons or detachments, as well as support personnel. Usually captained by a commander (0-5), platoons and detachments are commanded mostly by lieutenants or lieutenant commanders. Although SEAL Teams are geographically specialized, all are trained to operate in any environment. Geographical areas of focus are as follows: SEAL Team One, Southeast Asia; SEAL Team Two, Northern Europe; SEAL Team Three, the Middle East; SEAL Team Four, South America; SEAL Team Five, Korea; SEAL Team Six, worldwide; and SEAL Team Eight, Africa.

Shift Fire   Coordinated movement of SEAL Team fire. Instantaneous engagement of a second target. Also used to indicate a shift in focus or a change of tasking.

Shiite   Also known as Shia. Shiites comprise the second largest Islamic sect in Lebanon. The word "Shia" comes from *"Shiat Ali,"* or party of Ali. Shiite Muslims believe that Ali, Mohammed's cousin and son-in-law, should have succeeded the Prophet. Traditional Shia territory includes East Beirut and its southern suburbs, southern Lebanon, and parts of the Bekaa valley.

Sleeve   A slick sleeve, i.e., a person without a navy rating. A useless idiot. A non–SEAL Team member, regardless of rank.

Sneak Attack   Underwater maritime sabotage operation, usually conducted at night with rebreathing scuba.

Sock A $2\frac{1}{2}$ pound ribbon of C-4 plastic explosive. Called a sock because it is sewn into a canvas tube resembling a green GI sock.

Soft Duck Insertion of a CRRC by helicopter.

SOP Standard operating procedure.

STA Platoon Scout and target acquisition platoon. Marine snipers.

Stick A group of parachute jumpers. Normally the number of jumpers who can be dropped in one pass over the drop zone.

Sunni The largest Muslim sect in Lebanon. Those who believe that Mohammed's successor should have been chosen by the community came to be known as Sunnis. Sunni territory includes West Beirut and most of the surrounding countryside. Politically pragmatic, Lebanese Sunnis are generally regarded as Islamic moderates.

Swim Pair Also called a "shooting pair." The swim pair is the basic element of the SEAL Teams. A swim buddy is responsible at all times for the life of his partner. If your swim partner is killed, you are responsible for recovery of the body.

Symtex A type of plastic explosive.

Tadpole BUD/S student. An inexperienced operator.

Tango Terrorist. A bad guy.

Target Lock Loss of situational awareness resulting from overconcentration on the target. The state of being too goal-oriented.

UDT Underwater demolition team. The original frogmen, specializing in maritime sabotage, reconnaissance, and recovering NASA space capsules.

UNODIR Navy acronym meaning "unless otherwise directed."

VBSS   Vessel board, search, or seizure. Also called an "underway," this is the operation in which SEALs board and seize a ship on the high seas.

Wadi   A canyon or watercourse.

Wally, Wallys   Lebanese bad guys. The term is derived from members of the Druze militias and their leader, Walid Jumblat.

Wally-world   Lebanon.

Wanna-be   A civilian poseur. A fake SEAL. When in the vicinity of a Vietnam memorial, also called a "Wall phony."

Water Wings (see Black Shoe)   U.S. Navy Surface Warfare Badge. The device worn by Surface Warfare Specialists.

Wish Me Dead   A .50-caliber sniper rifle.

XO   Executive Officer. The officer second in command.